NATO'S SECRET ARMIES

This book tells the story of NATO's secret anti-Communist stay-behind armies that were set up by the CIA and MI6 after the Second World War in all countries of Western Europe and in some countries became tragically linked to right-wing terrorism.

Daniele Ganser is a Senior Researcher at the Center for Security Studies at the Federal Institute of Technology (ETH) in Zurich, Switzerland.

CONTEMPORARY SECURITY STUDIES

NATO'S SECRET ARMIES

Operation Gladio and terrorism in Western Europe

Daniele Ganser

FRANK CASS
LONDON AND NEW YORK

First published 2005
by Frank Cass
2 Park Square, Milton Park, Abingdon, Oxon OX14 4RN

Simultaneously published in the USA and Canada
by Frank Cass
270 Madison Avenue, New York, NY 10016

Frank Cass is an imprint of the Taylor & Francis Group

Transferred to Digital Printing 2005

© 2005 Daniele Ganser

Typeset in Times by
Integra Software Services Pvt. Ltd, Pondicherry, India

British Library Cataloguing in Publication Data
A catalogue record for this book is available from the British Library

Library of Congress Cataloging in Publication Data
A catalog record for this book has been requested

ISBN 0–7146–5607–0 (hbk)
ISBN 0–7146–8500–3 (pbk)

TO BEA

I will always admire how you live up to the principles
that you perceive to be true, wise and enlightened.

What difference does it make to the dead, the orphans and the homeless, whether the mad destruction is wrought under the name of totalitarianism or the holy name of liberty or democracy?

Mahatma Gandhi (1869–1948)

The growth of Intelligence abuses reflects a more general failure of our basic institutions.

US Senator Frank Church (1976)

CONTENTS

CONTENTS

FOREWORD

At the height of the Cold War there was effectively a front line in Europe. Winston Churchill once called it the Iron Curtain and said it ran from Szczecin on the Baltic Sea to Trieste on the Adriatic Sea. Both sides deployed military power along this line in the expectation of a major combat. The Western European powers created the North Atlantic Treaty Organization (NATO) precisely to fight that expected war but the strength they could marshal remained limited. The Soviet Union, and after the mid-1950s the Soviet Bloc, consistently had greater numbers of troops, tanks, planes, guns, and other equipment. This is not the place to pull apart analyses of the military balance, to dissect issues of quantitative versus qualitative, or rigid versus flexible tactics. Rather the point is that for many years there was a certain expectation that greater numbers would prevail and the Soviets might be capable of taking over all of Europe.

Planning for the day the Cold War turned hot, given the expected Soviet threat, necessarily led to thoughts of how to counter a Russian military occupation of Western Europe. That immediately suggested comparison with the Second World War, when Resistance movements in many European countries had bedevilled Nazi occupiers. In 1939–1945 the anti-Nazi Resistance forces had had to be improvised. How much the better, reasoned the planners, if the entire enterprise could be prepared and equipped in advance.

The executive agents in the creation of the stay-behind networks were the Central Intelligence Agency (CIA) of the United States and the Secret Intelligence Service (SIS or MI6) of the United Kingdom. Other major actors included security services in a number of European countries. In all cases identical techniques were used. The intelligence services made an effort to establish distinct networks for spying on the occupiers, that is espionage, and for sabotage, or subverting an enemy occupation. To establish the networks the CIA and others recruited individuals willing to participate in these dangerous activities, often allowing such initial, or chief, agents to recruit additional sub-agents. Intelligence services provided some training, placed caches of arms, ammunition, radio equipment, and other items for their networks, and set up regular channels for contact. The degree of cooperation in some cases ranged up to the conduct of exercises with military units or paramilitary forces. The number of recruits for the secret armies ranged from dozens in some nations to hundreds or even thousands in others.

The Resistance example was always an obvious one. Observers of the secret Cold War assumed the existence of the networks; so there are occasional references to the stay-behind networks in spy memoirs and literature. But by and large the subject was acknowledged with a wink and a nod. Until almost the end of the Cold War. In the summer of 1990, after the collapse of Soviet-dominated regimes in Eastern Europe, but prior to the final disintegration of the Soviet Union, the Italian government made public the existence of such a network in that country. Over the years since there has been a recurrent stream of revelations regarding similar networks in many European nations, and in a number of countries there have been official investigations.

For the first time in this book, Daniele Ganser has brought together the full story of the networks the Italians came to call 'Gladio'. This is a significant and disturbing history. The notion of the project in the intelligence services undoubtedly began as an effort to create forces that would remain quiescent until war brought them into play. Instead, in country after country we find the same groups of individuals or cells originally activated for the wartime function beginning to exercise their strength in peacetime political processes. Sometimes these efforts involved violence, even terrorism, and sometimes the terrorists made use of the very equipment furnished to them for their Cold War function. Even worse, police and security services in a number of cases chose to protect the perpetrators of crimes to preserve their Cold War capabilities. These latter actions resulted in the effective suppression of knowledge of Gladio networks long after their activities became not merely counterproductive but dangerous.

Mining evidence from parliamentary inquiries, investigative accounts, documentary sources, trials, and individuals he has interviewed, Ganser tracks the revelation of Gladio in many countries and fills in the record of what these networks actually did. Many of their accomplishments were in fact antidemocratic, undermining the very fabric of the societies they were meant to protect. Moreover, by laying the records in different nations side by side, Ganser's research shows a common process at work. That is, networks created to be quiescent became activists in political causes as a rule and not as an exception.

Deep as Dr Ganser's research has been, there is a side to the Gladio story he cannot yet reveal. This relates to the purposeful actions of the CIA, MI6 and other intelligence services. Because of the secrecy of government records in the United States, for example, it is still not possible to sketch in detail the CIA's orders to its networks, which could show whether there was a deliberate effort to interfere with political processes in the countries where Gladio networks were active. There were real efforts carried out by Gladio agents but their controllers' orders remain in the shadows, so it is not yet possible to establish the extent of the US role overall in the years of the Cold War. The same is true of MI6 for Great Britain and for security services elsewhere. At a minimum Dr Ganser's record shows that capabilities created for straightforward purposes as part of the Cold War ultimately turned to more sinister ends. Freedom of Information in the United States provides an avenue to open up government documents; but that process is exceedingly slow and subject to many exemptions, one of which is intended precisely to shield records on activities of this type. The United Kingdom has a rule that releases documents after a certain number of years, but there is a longer interval required for documents of this type, and exceptions are permitted to government when documents are finally released to the public. The information superhighway is barely a macadam path when it comes to throwing light on the truth of the Gladio networks.

In this age of global concern with terrorism it is especially upsetting to discover that Western Europe and the United States collaborated in creating networks that took up terrorism. In the United States such nations are called 'state sponsors' and are the object of hostility and sanction. Can it be the United States itself, Britain, France, Italy, and others who should be on the list of state sponsors? The Gladio story needs to be told completely so as to establish the truth in this matter. Daniele Ganser has taken the critical first step down this road. This book should be read to discover the overall contours of Gladio and to begin to appreciate the importance of the final answers that are still lacking.

John Prados
Washington, DC

ACKNOWLEDGEMENTS

When looking for a PhD research topic in early 1998, I became interested in the Gladio phenomenon, of which I had not previously heard. After some research I realised that despite its great importance for the most recent political, social and military history of Western Europe and the United States, only very limited work had been carried out on the phenomenon of the secret NATO armies, with no single study on the topic available in English. As the complex structure of the network and the mysteries surrounding it increasingly caught my interest, many well-meaning friends advised me against taking it as a PhD topic. Very sensibly they argued that I would gain access neither to the archives of the secret services, nor to primary data on the topic from NATO and its Office of Security. Furthermore they predicted that the number of countries, which by the end of my research had unexpectedly risen to fourteen, as well as the time frame I intended to investigate in each of these countries, five decades, not only would wear me out, but would also necessarily leave my findings fragmented and incomplete. That in addition to these problems I would have to work with texts in more than ten different European languages, of which I personally could only read five, made matters crystal clear: Gladio was not a suitable PhD research topic.

With great fascination for the phenomenon, a certain degree of youthful stubbornness, and above all a supportive environment I nevertheless embarked upon the research project and dedicated the next four years of my life to the investigation. At the time my determination to proceed, and my ability to convince my advising professors, was based on one single original document from the Italian military secret service SIFAR, dated June 1, 1959 and entitled 'The special forces of SIFAR and Operation Gladio'. This document proved that a CIA- and NATO-linked secret army code-named Gladio had existed in Italy during the Cold War, yet further original documents were very hard to come by. In retrospect I therefore have to admit that my well-meaning friends had been right. For among the numerous obstacles that arose during the years of research many were the ones predicted.

First of all, the field of research was indeed large, both as to the number of countries, and to the time frame. I started with a focus on Italy, where operation

Gladio was exposed in 1990. Based on the Italian sources I quickly realised, however, that the so-called stay-behind armies had existed in all 16 NATO countries during the Cold War. Further research led me to conclude that of the 16 NATO countries both Iceland, with no armed forces, and Canada, far removed from the Soviet frontier, could be neglected. Yet, while I was somewhat relieved to calculate that this would leave me with the analysis of stay-behind armies in 14 countries, I found with a certain surprise that secret stay-behind armies with indirect links to NATO had also existed in the four neutral countries, Sweden, Finland, Austria and my native Switzerland, during the Cold War. In this book I am presenting the data for the NATO countries only. A forthcoming publication will deal specifically with the equally sensitive issues of secret NATO-linked stay-behind armies in the neutral countries.

Next to the challenges that arise with respect to the number of countries, gathering data for each single country too proved difficult. It was most distressing that governments, NATO and secret services withheld requested documents despite a FOIA request to the CIA, numerous letters to NATO, and official requests to European governments. Next to only a very small number of primary documents, the analysis had therefore to be based on numerous secondary sources, including parliamentary reports, testimonies of persons involved as reported by the international press, articles, books and documentaries, needless to say, such secondary sources can never be a substitute for the original primary documents, and all future research must clearly aim for access to primary documents. If, however, the data presented hereafter first of all enables researchers to gain an overview of a phenomenon which otherwise might have remained inaccessible, and in the second place enables processes which in the future will lead to access to primary documents, then the main purposes of this book will have been achieved.

That despite the mentioned numerous obstacles, the years of intensive research have led to a hopefully valuable international analysis of the stay-behind armies and the secret war in Western Europe is to a large degree attributable to the international professional help and support that I was allowed to enjoy. First of all I want to thank my two academic advisers for their truly valuable assistance, Professor Georg Kreis of Basel University, and Professor Jussi Hanhimaki of the Graduate Institute of International Studies in Geneva, formerly with the London School of Economics and Political Science where we met in a most stimulating environment. Their feedback on numerous drafts sharpened my questions when they were too vague. Their frank criticism helped me to focus on the secret armies when I was drifting away. And their experience in the field of academic research restrained my judgement, and opened the way for a balanced understanding. When I presented my Gladio research and passed my final PhD exams in September 2001, we all felt that it was a timely book, for in that month, investigations into international terrorism had become a high priority on the agenda. During the subsequent years we have in a very strange way become accustomed to living in a world that suffers from both war and terrorism, and my warm thanks therefore also go to Professor Andreas Wenger, Director of the Center for Security Studies in Zurich, for his support for future research into Gladio and terrorism here at the institute.

Furthermore my gratitude goes to Washington-based CIA author William Blum who first drew my attention to Gladio and taught me a lot on covert action and secret warfare. Very warm thanks also go to Professor Noam Chomsky in Boston who not only encouraged my research, but also provided me with valuable contacts during our meetings in the United States and in Switzerland. In Cambridge, Professor Christopher Andrew supported my research, while in Washington, Professor Christopher Simpson drew my attention to interesting contacts in the United States. In Austria, Professor Siegfried Beer provided me with valuable data and kindly encouraged my research. In London, finally, I copied numerous valuable documents at the Statewatch institute, where Trevor Hemmings proved to me how excellent work can be done with little money.

It must be stated here at the outset of the book that all quotes other than from English originals are translations by the author, who alone bears responsibility for their accuracy. At the same time it goes without saying that the numerous countries could not have been investigated without the help of my international network, which assisted me both in the initial phase of locating and getting hold of the documents, and during subsequent translation hours. In Germany I want to thank journalist and Gladio author Leo Müller, as well as Erich Schmidt Eenboom from the research institute on peace and politics. In the Netherlands, Dr Paul Koedijk and Dr Cees Wiebes, as well as Frans Kluiters, all members of the Netherlands Intelligence Studies Association, kindly shared with me valuable Gladio material and interesting days in Amsterdam, while academic Micha de Roo assisted me with the Dutch translations. In Denmark, I want to thank Professor Paul Villaume of Copenhagen University who shared interesting data with me, and Eva Ellenberger of Basel University who helped me to understand the Danish texts. In Norway, I want to thank my friend Pal Johansen for our excellent time at the London School of Economics and Political Science and his professional help in crucial times when it came to the translation of Norwegian texts. In Austria, journalist Markus Kemmerling and the Zoom political magazine supported my research. In Basel, Ali Burhan Kirmizitas helped me greatly with the translation of Turkish texts and provided me with important documents on Gladio in Turkey. Academic Ivo Cunha kindly shared with me data on Gladio in Portugal and in Spain, while my university friends Baptiste Blanch and Francisco Bouzas assisted me with the Portuguese and Spanish translations. My friend and fellow academic Martin Kamber finally had the energy to plough through an early PhD manuscript of over a thousand pages, whereupon he wisely let me know that the text had to be shortened. Thanks to Ruth Eymann I was able to retreat to a both beautiful and silent chalet in a remote valley of the Swiss mountains to carry out that task.

After the PhD thesis had been accepted insigni cum laude at the history department of Basel University in Switzerland, Frank Cass and Andrew Humphrys of

ACKNOWLEDGEMENTS

Taylor and Francis, UK, and Kalpalathika Rajan of Integra Software Services, India, helped me greatly to make my research publicly accessible on the global book market. Last but not least, complete research independence was guaranteed by the generous financial support of The Swiss National Science Foundation, the Janggen-Pöhn Stiftung in St Gallen, the Max Geldner Stiftung in Basel, and the Frewillige Akademische Gesellschaft in Basel. Special thanks go to my mother, my father and my sister, to Sherpa Hänggi, Marcel Schwendener, Tobi Poitmann, Däne Aebischer, René Ab Egg, Laurenz Bolliger, Philipp Schweighauser, Niko Bally, Yves Pierre Wirz and Andi Langlotz for numerous inspiring and controversial late-night discussions on international politics, global trends and problems, and our personal quest for happiness and meaning in life.

Daniele Ganser
Sils Maria, Switzerland

ACRONYMS

ACC	Allied Clandestine Committee
AN	Avanguardia Nazionale
AP	Aginter-Press
BCRA	Bureau Central de Renseignement et d'Action
BDJ	Bund Deutscher Jugend
BfV	Bundesamt für Verfassungsschutz
BI	Bureau Inlichtingen
BND	Bundesnachrichtendienst
BUPO	Bundespolizei
BVD	Binnenlandse Veiligheidsdienst
CAG	Centro Addestramento Guastatori
CCC	Cellules Communistes Combattantes
CCUO	Comité Clandestin Union Occidentale
CERP	Centre d'Entrainement des Reserves Parachutistes
CESID	Centro Superior de Informacion de la Defensa
CGT	Confederation Generale du Travail
CIA	Central Intelligence Agency
CIC	Counter Intelligence Corps
CIG	Central Intelligence Group
COI	Coordinator of Strategic Information
COS	CIA Chief of Station
CPC	Clandestine Planning Committee
DCI	Democrazia Christiana Italiana
DCI	Director of Central Intelligence
DDO	CIA Deputy Director of Operations
DDP	CIA Deputy Director of Plans
DGER	Direction Generale des Etudes et Recherches
DGS	Direction General De Seguridad
DGSE	Direction Generale de la Securite Exterieure
DIA	Defence Intelligence Agency
DO	CIA Directorate of Operations
DP	CIA Directorate of Plans

DST	Direction de la Surveillance du Territoire
ETA	Euskadi Ta Askatasuna
FBI	Federal Bureau of Investigation
FDP	Fronte Democratico Popolare
FHO	Fremde Heere Ost
FE	Forsvarets Efterretningstjeneste
FJ	Front de la Jeunesse
FM	Field Manual
GESTAPO	Geheime Staatspolizei
IDB	Inlichtingendienst Buitenland
ISI	Inter Services Intelligence
I&O	Intelligence en Operations
JCS	Joint Chiefs of Staff
KGB	Committee of the Security of the State
KKE	Greek Communist Party
KPD	Kommunistische Partei Deutschland
LOK	Lochos Oreinon Katadromon
MfS	Ministerium für Staatssicherheit, short Stasi
MHP	Millietici Hareket Partisi
MI5	Security Service
MI6	Secret Intelligence Service (SIS)
MIT	Milli Istihbaarat Teskilati
MRP	Mouvement Republicain Populaire
NATO	North Atlantic Treaty Organization
NIS	Norwegian Intelligence Service
NOS	NATO Office of Security
NSA	National Security Agency
NSC	National Security Council
NSDAP	Nationalsozialistische Deutsche Arbeiterpartei, short Nazi
OACI	Organisation Armee contre le Communisme International
OAS	Organisation de l'Armée Secrete
OeWSGV	Oesterreichischer Wander- Sport- und Geselligkeitsverein
OG	Organisation Gehlen
OHP	Ozel Harp Dairesi
OKK	Ozel Kuvvetler Komutanligi
OMPAM	Organizzazione Mondial del Pensiero e dell' Assistenza Massonica
ON	Ordine Nuovo
OPC	CIA Office of Policy Coordination
OSP	Office of Special Projects
OSS	Office of Strategic Services
P-26	Projekt 26
P-27	Projekt 27
P2	Propaganda Due
PCF	Parti Communiste Francais

PCI	Partito Communisto Italiano
PIDE	Policia Internacional e de Defesa do Estado
PKK	Parlamentarische Kontrollkommission
PSI	Partito Socialisto Italiano
RAF	Rote Armee Fraktion
ROC	Rocambole
RPF	Rassemblement du Peuple Francais
S/B	Stay-behind
SAC	Service d'Action Civique
SACEUR	Supreme Allied Commander Europe
SAD	Sezione Addestramento Guastatori
SAS	Special Air Service
SAZ	Sectie Allgemene Zaken
SDECE	Service de Documentation Extérieure et de Contre Espionnage
SDRA	Service De Renseignements et d'Action
SECED	Servicio Central de Documentacion de la Defensa
SEIN	Servicio Informacion Naval
SGR	Service General de Renseignement
SHAPE	Supreme Headquarters Allied Powers Europe
SID	Servizio Informazioni Difesa
SIFAR	Servizio di Informazioni delle Forze Armate
SIS	Secret Intelligence Service (MI6)
SISDE	Servizio Informazioni Sicurezza Democratica
SISMI	Servizio Informazioni Sicurezza Militare
SOE	Special Operations Executive
SPD	Sozialdemokratische Partei Deutschland
SPG	Special Procedures Group
SS	Schutzstaffel
TD	Technischer Dienst
TMBB	Tripartite Meeting Belgian/Brussels
UNA	Untergruppe Nachrichtendienst und Abwehr
UNO	United Nations Organisation
VALPO	Valtion Poliisi
WACL	World Anticommunist League
WNP	Westland New Post

INTRODUCTION

As the Cold War ended, following juridical investigations into mysterious acts of terrorism in Italy, Italian Prime Minister Giulio Andreotti was forced to confirm in August 1990 that a secret army existed in Italy and other countries across Western Europe that were part of the North Atlantic Treaty Organization (NATO). Coordinated by the unorthodox warfare section of NATO, the secret army had been set up by the US secret service Central Intelligence Agency (CIA) and the British Secret Intelligence Service (MI6 or SIS) after the end of the Second World War to fight Communism in Western Europe. The clandestine network, which after the revelations of the Italian Prime Minister was researched by judges, parliamentarians, academics and investigative journalists across Europe, is now understood to have been code-named 'Gladio' (the sword) in Italy, while in other countries the network operated under different names including 'Absalon' in Denmark, 'ROC' in Norway and 'SDRA8' in Belgium. In each country the military secret service operated the anti-Communist army within the state in close collaboration with the CIA or the MI6 unknown to parliaments and populations. In each country, leading members of the executive, including Prime Ministers, Presidents, Interior Ministers and Defence Ministers, were involved in the conspiracy, while the 'Allied Clandestine Committee' (ACC), sometimes also euphemistically called the 'Allied Co-ordination Committee' and the 'Clandestine Planning Committee' (CPC), less conspicuously at times also called 'Coordination and Planning Committee' of NATO's Supreme Headquarters Allied Powers Europe (SHAPE), coordinated the networks on the international level. The last confirmed secret meeting of ACC with representatives of European secret services took place on October 24, 1990 in Brussels.

As the details of the operation emerged, the press concluded that the 'story seems straight from the pages of a political thriller'.[1] The secret armies were equipped by the CIA and the MI6 with machine guns, explosives, munitions and high-tech communication equipment hidden in arms caches in forests, meadows and underground bunkers across Western Europe. Leading officers of the secret network trained together with the US Green Berets Special Forces in the United States of America and the British SAS Special Forces in England. Recruited among strictly anti-Communist segments of the society the secret Gladio soldiers

1

included moderate conservatives as well as right-wing extremists such as notorious right-wing terrorists Stefano delle Chiaie and Yves Guerain Serac. In its strategic design the secret army was a direct copy of the British Special Operations Executive (SOE), which during the Second World War had parachuted into enemy-held territory and fought a secret war behind enemy lines.

In case of a Soviet invasion of Western Europe the secret Gladio soldiers under NATO command would have formed a so-called stay-behind network operating behind enemy lines, strengthening and setting up local resistance movements in enemy-held territory, evacuating shot-down pilots and sabotaging the supply lines and production centres of the occupation forces with explosives. Yet the Soviet invasion never came. The real and present danger in the eyes of the secret war strategists in Washington and London were the at-times numerically strong Communist parties in the democracies of Western Europe. Hence the network in the total absence of a Soviet invasion took up arms in numerous countries and fought a secret war against the political forces of the left. The secret armies, as the secondary sources now available suggest, were involved in a whole series of terrorist operations and human rights violations that they wrongly blamed on the Communists in order to discredit the left at the polls. The operations always aimed at spreading maximum fear among the population and ranged from bomb massacres in trains and market squares (Italy), the use of systematic torture of opponents of the regime (Turkey), the support for right-wing coup d'états (Greece and Turkey), to the smashing of opposition groups (Portugal and Spain). As the secret armies were discovered, NATO as well as the governments of the United States and Great Britain refused to take a stand on what by then was alleged by the press to be 'the best-kept, and most damaging, political-military secret since World War II'.[2]

1

A TERRORIST ATTACK IN ITALY

In a forest near the Italian village Peteano a car bomb exploded on May 31, 1972. The bomb gravely wounded one and killed three members of the Carabinieri, Italy's paramilitary police force. The Carabinieri had been lured to the spot by an anonymous phone call. Inspecting the abandoned Fiat 500, one of the Carabinieri had opened the hood of the car that triggered the bomb. An anonymous call to the police two days later implicated the Red Brigades, a Communist terrorist group attempting to change the balance of power in Italy at the time through hostage-takings and cold-blooded assassinations of exponents of the state. The police immediately cracked down on the Italian left and rounded up some 200 Communists. For more than a decade the Italian population believed that the Red Brigades had committed the Peteano terrorist attack.

Then, in 1984, young Italian Judge Felice Casson reopened the long dormant case after having discovered with surprise an entire series of blunders and fabrications surrounding the Peteano atrocity. Judge Casson found that there had been no police investigation on the scene. He also discovered that the report which at the time claimed that the explosive used in Peteano had been the one traditionally used by the Red Brigades was a forgery. Marco Morin, an expert for explosives of the Italian police, had deliberately provided fake expertise. He was a member of the Italian right-wing organisation 'Ordine Nuovo' and within the Cold War context contributed his part to what he thought was a legitimate way of combating the influence of the Italian Communists. Judge Casson was able to prove that the explosive used in Peteano contrary to Morin's expertise was C4, the most powerful explosive available at the time, used also by NATO. 'I wanted that new light should be shed on these years of lies and mysteries, that's all', Casson years later told journalists in his tiny office in an eighteenth-century courthouse on the banks of Venice's lagoon. 'I wanted that Italy should for once know the truth.'[1]

On February 24, 1972, a group of Carabinieri had by chance discovered an underground arms cache near Trieste containing arms, munitions and C4 explosive identical to the one used in Peteano. The Carabinieri believed that they had unveiled the arsenal of a criminal network. Years later, the investigation of Judge Casson was able to reconstruct that they had stumbled across one of more than hundred underground arsenals of the NATO-linked stay-behind secret army that

3

in Italy was code-named Gladio, the sword. Casson found that the Italian military secret service and the government at the time had gone to great lengths in order to keep the Trieste discovery and above all its larger strategic context a secret.

As Casson continued to investigate the mysterious cases of Peteano and Trieste, he discovered with surprise that not the Italian left but Italian right-wing groups and the military secret service had been involved in the Peteano terror. Casson's investigation revealed that the right-wing organisation Ordine Nuovo had collaborated very closely with the Italian Military Secret Service, SID (Servizio Informazioni Difesa). Together they had engineered the Peteano terror and then wrongly blamed the militant extreme Italian left, the Red Brigades. Judge Casson identified Ordine Nuovo member Vincenzo Vinciguerra as the man who had planted the Peteano bomb. Being the last man in a long chain of command, Vinciguerra was arrested years after the crime. He confessed and testified that he had been covered by an entire network of sympathisers in Italy and abroad who had ensured that after the attack he could escape. 'A whole mechanism came into action', Vinciguerra recalled, 'that is, the Carabinieri, the Minister of the Interior, the customs services and the military and civilian intelligence services accepted the ideological reasoning behind the attack'.[2]

Vinciguerra was right to point out that the Peteano terror had occurred during a particularly agitated historical period. With the beginning of the flower power revolution, the mass student protests against violence in general and the war in Vietnam in particular, the ideological battle between the political left and the political right had intensified in Western Europe and the United States in the late 1960s. The vast majority of people engaged in the left-wing social movements relied on non-violent forms of protest including demonstrations, civil disobedience and above all heated debates. In the Italian parliament the strong Communist Party (Partito Communisto Italiano, PCI), and to a lesser degree the Italian Socialist Party (Partito Socialisto Italiano, PSI), sympathised with the movement. They criticised the United States, the Vietnam War and above all the distribution of power in Italy, for despite their numerical strength in parliament the PCI was not assigned ministerial positions and hence was deliberately kept outside the government. Also the Italian right knew that this was a blatant discrimination and a violation of basic democratic principles.

It was in this Cold War context and the battle for power in Western Europe that the extreme left and the extreme right resorted to terror. On the extreme left the Italian Communist Red Brigades and Germany's Rote Armee Fraktion (RAF) were the two most prominent terrorist groups in Western Europe. Founded by students of the University of Trento with little to no military training, the Red Brigades included Margherita Cagol, Alberto Franceschini and Alberto Curcio. Like the RAF, they were convinced that violence had to be employed in order to change the existing power structure that they perceived as unjust and corrupt. Like the RAF the terror of the Red Brigades did not attack mass gatherings of the population, but very selectively targeted individuals whom they thought repre-sented the 'state apparatus', such as bankers, generals and ministers whom they kidnapped and often assassinated. Operating above all in the 1970s the death toll of the Red Brigades in Italy reached 75 people. Then, due to their limited military and strategic skills and experience they were rounded up, arrested, tried and imprisoned.

On the other side of the Cold War spectrum also the extreme right resorted to violence. In Italy the network included secret Gladio soldiers, the military secret services and fascist organisations such as Ordine Nuovo. Contrary to the terror of the left, the terror of the right aimed to strike fear to the bones of the entire society and hence secretly planted its bombs among the population to kill large numbers indiscriminately in order to wrongly blame the Communists. The Peteano terror, as judge Casson found, belonged to this sort of crime and continued a sequence that had started in 1969. In that year, shortly before Christmas four bombs had exploded in public places in Rome and Milan. The bombs killed 16 and maimed and wounded 80, most of which were farmers who after a day on the market had deposited their modest earnings in the Farmer's Bank on the Piazza Fontana in Milan. According to an evil strategy the terror was wrongly blamed on the Communists and the extreme left, traces were covered up and arrests followed immediately. The population at large had little chances to find out the truth, as the military secret service went to great lengths to cover up the crime. In Milan one of the deadly bombs had not gone off due to timer failure, but in an immediate cover-up the bomb was destroyed on the scene by the secret service, while parts of a bomb were planted in the villa of well-known leftist editor Giangiacomo Feltrinelli.[3]

'The official figures say that alone in the period between January 1, 1969 and December 31, 1987, there have been in Italy 14 591 acts of violence with a political motivation', Italian Senator Giovanni Pellegrino, president of Italy's parliamentary commission investigating Gladio and the massacres, recalled the very violent period of Italy's most recent history. 'It is maybe worth remembering that these "acts" have left behind 491 dead and 1181 injured and maimed. Figures of a war, with no parallel in any other European country.'[4] Following the Piazza Fontana massacre of 1969 and the Peteano terrorist attack of 1972, prominent massacres in Italy included a bomb which on May 28, 1974 exploded in Brescia in the midst of an anti-Fascist demonstration, killing eight and injuring and maiming 102. On August 4, 1974 another bomb exploded on the Rome-to-Munich train 'Italicus Express', killing 12 and injuring and maiming 48. The atrocities culminated on a sunny afternoon during the Italian national holiday when on August 2, 1980 a massive explosion ripped through the waiting room of the second class at the Bologna railway station, killing 85 people in the blast and seriously injuring and maiming a further 200. The Bologna massacre ever since ranges amongst the largest terrorist onslaughts that Europe had seen in the twentieth century.

Contrary to the Red Brigades who ended up in jail, the terrorists of the right mysteriously escaped after each massacre because, as Vinciguerra correctly pointed out, the security apparatus of the Italian state and the military secret services protected them. As the Piazza Fontana terror was years later traced back to the Italian right, Ordine Nuovo member Franco Freda was questioned whether in retrospect he feels that powerful people higher up in the hierarchy including Generals and Ministers had manipulated him. Freda, a declared admirer of Hitler who had published 'Mein Kampf' in Italian in his own small publishing house, replied that according to his understanding nobody can escape manipulation: 'The life of every one is manipulated by those with more power', right-wing terrorist Freda declared. 'In my case I accept that I have been a puppet in the hands of ideas, but not in the hands of men from the secret services here [in Italy] or abroad. That is to say that I have voluntarily fought my own war, following the strategic design that came from my own ideas. That is all.'[5]

In March 2001 General Giandelio Maletti, former head of Italian counter-intelligence, suggested that next to the Gladio secret army, the Italian secret service and a group of Italian right-wing terrorists, the massacres which had discredited the Italian Communists had also been supported by the White House in Washington and the US secret service CIA. At a trial of right-wing extremists accused to have been involved in the Piazza Fontana massacre, Maletti testified: 'The CIA, following the directives of its government, wanted to create an Italian nationalism capable of halting what it saw as a slide to the left, and, for this purpose, it may have made use of right-wing terrorism.' 'The impression was that the Americans would do anything to stop Italy from sliding to the left', the General explained and added: 'Don't forget that Nixon was in charge and Nixon was a strange man, a very intelligent politician, but a man of rather unorthodox initiatives.' In retrospect the 79-year-old Maletti offered criticism and regret: 'Italy has been dealt with as a sort of protectorate' of the United States. 'I am ashamed to think that we are still subject to special supervision.'[6]

Already in the 1970s and 1980s the Italian parliament, within which the Communist and Socialist parties controlled a large share of the power, had become increasingly alarmed by the fact that a seemingly endless chain of mysterious massacres shocked the country without that the terrorists nor the people behind them could be identified. Although rumours among the Italian left already at the time had it that the mysterious acts of violence represented a form of undeclared secret warfare of the United States against the Italian Communists, the far-fetched theory could not be proven. Then, in 1988 the Italian Senate established a special investigative parliamentary commission presided by Senator Libero Gualtieri under the telling name of 'Parliamentary Commission of the Italian Senate for the Investigation of terrorism in Italy and the reasons why the individuals responsible for the massacres could not be identified: Terrorism, the massacres and the political-historical contest.'[7] The work of the parliamentary investigation proved to be extremely difficult. Witnesses withheld testimony. Documents were destroyed. And the commission itself, made up of the competing political parties from the Italian left and the Italian right, was split on what exactly the historical truth in Italy was, and disagreed on how many of its sensitive findings should be presented to the public.

Judge Casson, meanwhile from the testimonies of Peteano terrorist Vincenzo Vinciguerra and the documents he had discovered, started to understand the complex secret military strategy that had been employed. He gradually started to understand that he was dealing not with private, but with state terrorism, paid by tax money. Under the name 'strategy of tension' the massacres aimed to create tension among the entire population. The right-wing extremists and their supporters within NATO feared that the Italian Communists would become too powerful and hence in an attempt to 'destabilise in order to stabilise' the secret right-wing soldiers linked to the Gladio armies carried out massacres, which they blamed on the left. 'As far as the secret services are concerned the Peteano attack is part of what has been called "the strategy of tension"', Judge Casson explained the strategy to non-experts in a BBC documentation on Gladio. 'That's to say, to create tension within the country to promote conservative, reactionary social and political tendencies. While this strategy was being implemented, it was necessary to protect those behind it because evidence implicating them was being discovered. Witnesses withheld information to cover right-wing extremists.'[8] Right-wing terrorist Vinciguerra, who like others with contacts to the Gladio branch of the Italian military secret service, had been killed for his political conviction, related: 'You had to attack civilians, the people, women, children, innocent people, unknown people far removed from any political game. The reason was quite simple. They were supposed to force these people, the Italian public, to turn to the State to ask for greater security. This is the political logic that lies behind all the massacres and the bombings which remain unpunished, because the State cannot convict itself or declare itself responsible for what happened.'[9]

The monstrosity of the diabolic plan was only slowly being uncovered, and still today a great number of missing links remain and above all original documents are lacking. 'With the massacre of Peteano, and with all those that have followed', Vinciguerra explained on trial in 1984, 'the knowledge should by now be clear that there existed a real live structure, occult and hidden, with the capacity of giving a strategic direction to the outrages'. The structure, he said, 'lies within the state itself. There exists in Italy a secret force parallel to the armed forces, composed of civilians and military men, in an anti-Soviet capacity that is, to organise a resistance on Italian soil against a Russian army'. Without giving the code name this testimony revealed the NATO-linked Gladio secret stay-behind army. It is, Vinciguerra explained, 'a secret organisation, a super-organisation with a network of communications, arms and explosives, and men trained to use them'. Vinciguerra disclosed that this 'super-organisation which, lacking a Soviet military invasion which might not happen, took up the task, on NATO's behalf, of preventing a slip to the left in the political balance of the country. This they did, with the assistance of the official secret services and the political and military forces.'[10]

More than two decades have passed since right-wing terrorist Vinciguerra had offered this far-reaching testimony, which for the first time in Italy's history linked both the Gladio stay-behind and NATO directly to the terrorist massacres that the country had suffered from. Only now, years later, does a larger research public understand what Vinciguerra actually meant, as the existence of the secret stay-behind network has been confirmed and the arms and explosives had been dug up.

Is Vinciguerra thus a credible source? The events following the trial suggest that he is. The secret army was discovered in 1990. And in what amounted to an indirect confirmation that the right-wing terrorist had revealed the truth, Vinciguerra immediately lost all higher protection he had enjoyed during the previous years. In marked contrast to other right-wing terrorists that had collaborated with the Italian military secret service and walked free, Vinciguerra after his revelations was sentenced for life and imprisoned.

But Vinciguerra had not been the first to draw the link between Gladio, NATO and the massacres, he had not been the first to reveal the Gladio conspiracy in Italy. In 1974 the Italian investigating judge Giovanni Tamburino in the course of his investigation into right-wing terrorism in Italy had taken the unprecedented step of arresting General Vito Miceli, the chief of the Italian military secret service SID on the charge of 'promoting, setting up, and organising, together with others, a secret association of military and civilians aimed at provoking an armed insurrection to bring about an illegal change in the constitution of the state and the form of government'.[11]

Miceli, previously responsible for the NATO Security Office, on trial on November 17, 1974 furiously revealed the existence of the Gladio army hidden as a special branch of the military secret service SID: 'A Super SID on my orders? Of course! But I have not organised it myself to make a coup d'état. This was the United States and NATO who asked me to do it!'[12] With his excellent transatlantic contacts Miceli got off lightly. He was released on bail and spent six months in a military hospital. Forced by the investigations of Judge Casson, Prime Minister Andreotti 16 years later exposed the Gladio secret in front of the Italian parliament. This angered Miceli greatly. Shortly before his death in October 1990 he shouted: 'I have gone to prison because I did not want to reveal the existence of this super secret organisation. And now Andreotti comes along and tells it to Parliament!'[13]

In prison Peteano bomber Vinciguerra explained to judge Casson that not only Ordine Nuovo but also other prominent Italian right-wing organisations such as Avanguardia Nazionale had cooperated with the military secret service and the Gladio secret army to weaken the political left in Italy: 'The terrorist line was followed by camouflaged people, people belonging to the security apparatus, or those linked to the state apparatus through rapport or collaboration. I say that every single outrage that followed from 1969 fitted into a single organised matrix.' Right-wing terrorist and Ordine Nuovo member Vinciguerra explained that he and his fellow right-wing extremists had been recruited to cooperate with the Gladio secret army to carry out the most bloody operations: 'Avanguardia Nazionale, like Ordine Nuovo, were being mobilised into the battle as part of an anti-Communist strategy originating not with organisations deviant from the institutions of power, but from the state itself, and specifically from within the ambit of the state's relations within the Atlantic Alliance.'[14]

Judge Casson was alarmed at what he had found. In an attempt to eradicate this rotten core of the state he followed the traces of the mysterious Gladio underground army which had manipulated Italian politics during the Cold War and in

January 1990 requested permission from the highest Italian authorities to extend his research to the archives of the Italian military secret service Servizio informazioni sicurezza Militare (SISMI), until 1978 known as SID. In July 1990, Italian Prime Minister Giulio Andreotti consented and allowed Judge Casson to research in the archives of Palazzo Braschi, the headquarters of SISMI in Rome. It was inside Palazzo Braschi where Casson discovered the documents, which proved for the first time that a secret army code-named Gladio existed in Italy as a sub-branch of the military secret service with the task to carry out unorthodox warfare. Moreover Casson found documents that connected both the biggest military alliance of the world, NATO, and the world's only remaining superpower, the United States, to Gladio, subversion, and right-wing terrorists in Italy and also other countries in Western Europe. This knowledge meant that Casson for some time was in serious danger, of which he was aware, for Italian judges with too much knowledge had been shot in the streets of Italy before: 'From July until October 1990 I was the only one who knew something [about operation Gladio], this could have been unfortunate for me.'[15]

As Casson survived, the knot unravelled. Based on the documents he had discovered, Casson contacted the parliamentarian commission, which under Senator Libero Gualtieri was investigating the massacres and terrorism. Gualtieri and his fellow Senators were greatly worried by the findings which Casson had made and agreed that the investigation into the Gladio secret army had to be included in the work of the commission, for it represented the key to both the massacres and the reasons why they had remained mysterious for so many years. On August 2, 1990 the Senators ordered the head of the Italian executive, Prime Minister Giulio Andreotti, 'to inform the parliament within sixty days with respect to the existence, characteristics and purpose of a parallel and occult structure which is said to have operated within our secret service of the military with the aim to condition the political life of the country'.[16]

The next day, on August 3, 1990, Prime Minister Andreotti took a stand in front of the parliamentary commission and for the first time in Italy's post-war history confirmed as acting member of the Italian government that a NATO-linked secret security structure had existed in the country. Andreotti assured the Senators that he would present a written report to the parliamentary commission on the secret security structure within 60 days: 'I will present to the Commission a very precise report which I have asked the Defence Department to prepare. It is about the activities based on NATO planning that have been started for the eventuality of an attack and occupation of Italy or parts of Italy. As far as I have been informed by the secret services such activities have continued until 1972. After that it was decided that they were no longer necessary. I will provide the Commission with all the necessary documentation, be it on the problem in general, be it on the specific findings made by judge Casson in the context of his investigations into the Peteano massacre.'[17]

Aged 71 at the time of his Gladio testimony, Giulio Andreotti, is not a regular source by any standards. At the time of his testimony he looked back on a lifelong political career with probably no parallels in any country of Western Europe. As the leading representative of the conservative Christian Democratic Party (Democrazia Cristiana Italiana, DCI), which had functioned as a bulwark against the PCI during the entire Cold War, Andreotti had enjoyed the support of the United States. He personally knew all US presidents, and by many within and outside Italy was considered to be the most powerful politician of Italy's First Republic (1945–1993).

Although the governments in Italy's fragile First Republic had changed in short intervals Andreotti throughout the Cold War had cunningly managed to remain in power in numerous coalitions and had thus established himself as the dominant presence in the Italian government residence at Palazzo Chigi in Rome. Born in Rome in 1919, Andreotti became Minister of the Interior at the age of 35, and thereafter established an unprecedented record by holding the office of Prime Minister seven times, and serving furthermore 21 times as Minister, of which six times as Foreign Minister. His admirers compared him with Julius Cesar and called him 'divine Giulio', while his critics have accused him of being the quintessential back-room wheeler-dealer and nicknamed him 'the uncle'. Allegedly Andreotti's favourite gangster movie was 'Good fellows' for Robert De Niro's line 'never rat on your friends and always keep your mouth shut'. Most agreed that it was part of Andreotti's strategy which had allowed divine Giulio to survive a large number of Italy's intrigues and crimes, many of which he was directly involved in.[18]

By exposing Operation Gladio and the secret armies of NATO 'the uncle' had broken his silence. As the First Republic collapsed with the end of the Cold War, powerful Andreotti, then an old man, was dragged in front of numerous courts in Italy which accused him of having manipulated the political institutions, of having cooperated with the mafia and of having given secret orders according to which opponents were assassinated. 'The Justice system has gone crazy', acting Italian Prime Minister Silvio Berlusconi shouted when in November 2002 the appeals court in Perugia sentenced Andreotti for 24 years in prison. As the judges received death threats and were put under police protection, the television channels interrupted their broadcasting on the Italian football league to report that Andreotti had been found guilty for having given Mafia boss Gaetano Badalamenti the order to kill investigative journalist Mino Pecorelli in 1979 in order to cover up the truth on the assassination of Aldo Moro, the chairman of the DCI. The Catholic Church attempted to save the reputation of divine Giulio when Cardinal Fiorenzo Angelini, upon learning the shattering news, declared: 'Also Jesus Christ was crucified before his resurrection.' Yet despite all the alarm Andreotti did not end up behind prison bars as the verdicts were overruled in October 2003 and 'the uncle' walked free.

During the first Gladio revelations in front of the Italian Senators on August 3, 1990 'the uncle' had with reference to the secret stay-behind army cunningly claimed that 'such activities have continued until 1972' in order to limit the personal damage which loomed. For in 1974 as acting Defence Minister Andreotti had gone on the

10

record stating to a judicial inquiry investigating right-wing massacres: 'I can say that the head of the secret services has repeatedly and unequivocally excluded the existence of a hidden organisation of any type or size.'[19] In 1978 he made a similar testimony in front of judges investigating a right-wing bombing in Milan.

When the Italian press revealed that the secret Gladio army, far from having been closed down in 1972 was still active Andreotti's lie collapsed. Thereafter in August and September 1990, like seldom before during his time in office, Andreotti very actively transferred international messages, searched contacts and had meetings with numerous ambassadors.[20] As international support was not forthcoming, the Prime Minister, fearing for his power, went into the offensive and attempted to highlight the responsibility of the White House in the United States and numerous other governments in Western Europe who had all not only conspired in the secret war against the Communists but actively participated in it. In order to draw attention to the involvement of foreign nations, Andreotti employed an effective but somewhat awkward strategy. On October 18, 1990 he sent his messenger to walk in a great hurry the few steps from the government residence at Palazzo Chigi in Rome to Piazza San Macuto where the parliamentary commission resided. The messenger delivered Andreotti's report entitled 'The so called "Parallel SID" – The Gladio Case' to the secretary at the reception of Palazzo Chigi. A member of the parliamentary commission, Senator Roberto Ciciomessere, heard by coincidence that Andreotti's report had arrived and passed by the secretary at Palazzo Chigi. Upon looking through the text the Senator was mightily surprised, for in it Andreotti provided not only a brief description of operation Gladio, but contrary to his August 3 statement admitted also that the occult Gladio organisation was still active.

Senator Ciciomessere asked for a photocopy, yet this was denied, as according to standing procedures, first the President of the commission, Senator Gualtieri, was to read the report. Yet Gualtieri never got to read this first version of Andreotti's report on operation Gladio. For exactly when Gualtieri was about to put the sensitive document into his briefcase three days later to take it home and read it over the weekend the telephone rang, and on the phone was the Prime Minister himself who told the Senator that he immediately needed his report back 'because a few passages need reworking'. Gualtieri was annoyed but assented reluctantly and sent the document back to Andreotti's Palazzo Chigi after photocopies had been made.[21] The unusual manoeuvres of Giulio Andreotti sent a roar through Italy and heightened the attention. The newspapers headlined 'Operation Giulio' in a word play on 'Operation Gladio' and between 50,000 and 400,000 annoyed, scared and angry people organised by the PCI marched through central Rome in one of the biggest demonstrations in the capital for years chanting and carrying banners: 'We want truth.' Some marchers dressed up as Gladiators. While PCI leader Achille Occhetto told the crowd in the central Piazza del Popolo that this march will force the government to reveal the dark secrets long held back: 'We are here to obtain truth and transparency.'[22]

On October 24 Senator Gualtieri had Andreotti's report on the 'Parallel SID' back in his hands. Shortened by two pages this final version was now only ten pages long. Senator Gualtieri compared it with the photocopies made of the first version and immediately noted that sensitive parts especially on the international connection and similar secret organisations in other countries had been cut out. Furthermore the secret parallel organisation, which before had been spoken of in the present tense implying continuous existence, was now spoken of in the past tense. The awkward strategy of Andreotti to send in a document, withdraw and amend it, only to provide it anew, could thus hide nothing. Observers agreed that the manoeuvre necessarily drew attention exactly to the amended parts, hence the international dimension of the affair, in order to take away some weight from Andreotti's shoulders. But no international support was forthcoming.

In his final report Andreotti explained that Gladio had been conceived as a network of clandestine resistance within NATO countries to confront an eventual Soviet invasion. After the war the Italian military secret service Servizio di Informazioni delle Forze Armate (SIFAR) predecessor of the SID, and the CIA had signed 'an accord relative to the "organisation and activity of the post-occupation clandestine network", an accord commonly referred to as Stay Behind, in which all preceding commitments relevant to matters concerning Italy and the United States were reconfirmed'. The cooperation between the CIA and the Italian military secret service, as Andreotti explained in the document, was supervised and coordinated by secret non-orthodox warfare centres of NATO: 'Once the clandestine resistance organisation was constituted, Italy was called upon to participate...in the works of the CCP (Clandestine Planning Committee) of 1959, operating within the ambit of SHAPE [NATO's Supreme Headquarters Allied Powers Europe]...; in 1964 the Italian secret service also entered the ACC (Allied Clandestine Committee).'[23]

The secret Gladio army, as Andreotti revealed, was well armed. The equipment provided by the CIA was buried in 139 hiding spots across the country in forests, meadows and even under churches and cemeteries. According to the explanations of Andreotti the Gladio caches included 'portable arms, ammunition, explosives, hand grenades, knives and daggers, 60 mm mortars, several 57 mm recoilless rifles, sniper rifles, radio transmitters, binoculars and various tools'.[24] Andreotti's sensational testimony did not only lead to an outcry concerning the corruption of the government and the CIA among the press and the population, but also to a hunt for the secret arms caches. Padre Giuciano recalls the day when the press came to search for the hidden Gladio secrets in his church with ambiguous feelings: 'I was forewarned in the afternoon when two journalists from "Il Gazzettino" asked me if I knew anything about arms deposits here at the church. They started to dig right here and found two boxes right away. Then the text also said a thirty centimetres from the window. So they came over here and dug down. One box was kept aside by them because it contained a phosphorous bomb. They sent the Carabinieri outside whilst two experts opened this box, another had two machine guns in it. All the guns were new, in perfect shape. They had never been used.'[25]

Contrary to the testimony of right-wing terrorist Vinciguerra of the 1980s, Andreotti stressed in his 1990 report that the Italian military secret service in general as well as the Gladio members in particular had nothing to do with the terror that

Italy had suffered from. He explained that all Gladiators before their recruitment had gone through intensive testing and were chosen based on the 'rigorous application' of the Secret Service Act to ensure their 'scrupulous fidelity to the values of the anti-fascist republican constitution' and to exclude anyone who held administrative or political office. Moreover, the law required that, as Andreotti noted, 'the preselected subjects do not have a penal record, do not partake in active politics, nor participate in any sort of extremist movement'.[26] At the same time Andreotti stressed that the members of the network could not be questioned by judges and that member names and further details on the secret army were classified. The 'operation, on account of its current forms of organisation and application – as foreseen by NATO directives and integrated into its relative planning – is to be carried out and refined in a framework of absolute secrecy.'[27]

The Andreotti revelations on the 'parallel SID' shocked Italy. For many, a secret CIA NATO army in Italy and beyond seemed hardly credible. Was such a structure at all legal? The Italian daily *La Stampa* harshly commented: 'No raison d'état could be worth maintaining, covering up or defending a secret military structure composed of ideologically selected members – dependent upon, or at least under the influence of, a foreign power – that allegedly serves as an instrument of political struggle. No definition could be given to it other than high treason and an attack on the Constitution.'[28] In the Italian Senate representatives of the Green Party, the Communists and the Independent Leftist Party accused the government of having used the Gladio units for domestic surveillance and acts of terror to condition the political climate. Above all the Italian Communists Party (PCI) was convinced that not foreign armies but they themselves had been the true target of the Gladio armies during the entire post-war period. Commentators insisted that 'with this mysterious Parallel SID, conjured up to head off an impossible coup by the left, we have seriously risked making a coup d'état by the right possible . . . We cannot accept that . . . this super SID was passed off as a military instrument destined to operate "in case of enemy occupation". The true enemy is only and has always been the Italian Communist party, i.e. an internal enemy.'[29]

Unwilling to shoulder the blame alone Prime Minister Andreotti on the very same day that he presented his final Gladio report stepped in front of the Italian parliament and declared: 'Each chief of government has been informed of the existence of Gladio'.[30] This caused massive embarrassment and compromised, among others, former Socialist Prime Minister Bettino Craxi (1983–1987), former Prime Minister Giovanni Spadolini of the Republican Party (1981–1982) who at the time of Andreotti's revelations was President of the Senate, former Prime Minister Arnaldo Forlani (1980–1981) who in 1990 was serving as secretary of the ruling DCI, and above all former Prime Minister Francesco Cossiga (1978–1979) who in 1990 was the acting Italian President. The high-ranking magistrates thus drawn into the abyss by Andreotti reacted with confusion. Craxi claimed that he had not been informed, until he was confronted with a document on Gladio he had signed himself as Prime Minister. Spadolini and Forlani also suffered from general amnesia, but later had to make smaller amendments to their statements. Spadolini to the amusement of the Italian public stressed that there was a difference between what he knew as former Defence Secretary and what he knew as former Prime Minister.

Only Francesco Cossiga, Italian President since 1985, proudly confirmed his part in the conspiracy. During an official visit he paid to Scotland he pointed out that he was 'proud and happy' for his bit in setting the secret army up as junior Defence Minister of the DCI in the 1950s.[31] He declared that all Gladiators were good patriots and testified that 'I consider it a great privilege and an act of trust that...I was chosen for this delicate task...I have to say that I'm proud of the fact that we have kept the secret for 45 years.'[32] With his embracement of the compromised army linked to terrorism the President upon his return to Italy found himself in the midst of a political storm and requests across parties for his immediate resignation or for his impeachment for high treason. Judge Casson was audacious enough to ask head of state Cossiga to testify in front of the investigating Senate committee. Yet the President, no longer happy, angrily refused and threatened to close down the entire parliamentary Gladio investigation: 'I'll send the law extending its mandate back to Parliament and, should they re-approve it, I will have to examine the text anew to see if the conditions exist for the extreme recourse to an absolute [Presidential] refusal to promulgate.'[33] The attack was completely without any constitutional grounds and critics started to question the President's sanity. Cossiga stepped down from the Presidency in April 1992 three months before his term expired.[34]

In a public speech in front of the Italian Senate on November 9, 1990, Andreotti stressed once again that NATO, the United States and numerous countries in Western Europe including Germany, Greece, Denmark and Belgium had been involved in the stay-behind conspiracy. To prove this point, classified data was leaked to the press and the Italian political magazine *Panorama* published the entire document, 'The parallel SID – Operation Gladio' which Andreotti had handed to the parliamentary Commission. When France tried to deny its involvement in the international Gladio network Andreotti mercilessly declared that France as well had secretly participated in the most recent Gladio ACC meeting which had taken place in Brussels but a few weeks ago on October 23 and 24, 1990. Thereupon, somewhat embarrassed, also France confirmed that it had been involved in Gladio. The international dimension of the secret war could no longer be denied and the military scandal swept across Western Europe. Following the geographical zones of NATO membership it thereafter crossed the Atlantic and also reached the United States. An Italian parliamentary commission investigating Gladio and the Italian massacres in 2000 concluded: 'Those massacres, those bombs, those military actions had been organised or promoted or supported by men inside Italian state institutions and, as has been discovered more recently, by men linked to the structures of United States intelligence.'[35]

2

A SCANDAL SHOCKS WESTERN EUROPE

Journalists of foreign newspapers sat around in the press club in Rome in summer 1990 and lamented that their paper had absolutely no nerve for the delicate Gladio story and its international dimension. For, the revelations of Italian Prime Minister Giulio Andreotti on August 3 to the Italian Senators concerning the existence of a secret NATO-linked stay-behind army across Western Europe had come at a particularly disturbing moment. Andreotti had made his far-reaching revelation just the day after on August 2, 1990 when Iraq's dictator Saddam Hussein had invaded and occupied Kuwait. Newspaper editors and military advisers in Paris, London and Washington feared that the Gladio story might seriously damage the image of numerous Western democracies and above all destabilise the preparations for the Second Gulf War. For on August 2, in New York, the United States, Great Britain and France, 'alarmed by the invasion of Kuwait', had with the consent of China and Russia in the United Nations Security Council passed UN Security Council resolution 660, ordering 'that Iraq withdraw immediately and unconditionally all its forces to the positions in which they were located on 1 August 1990'.

Western and world media thereafter focused on the 'Gulf story' and reported how the United States under President George Bush Senior in the world's largest military operation since the Second World War led a large coalition of countries including Germany, France, Great Britain, Belgium, Italy and the Netherlands, who in Operation Desert Storm in January and February 1991 expelled Saddam Hussein from Kuwait.[1] Thus, quite by coincidence, the global media networks fed the world two bizarre stories at the same time: a clean war in the Gulf and the Gladio scandal in Europe that did not happen.[2]

Following the revelations of Italian Prime Minister Giulio Andreotti the scandal transgressed the Italian border when on October 30, former Socialist Prime Minister of Greece Andreas Papandreou confirmed to the Greek daily *Ta Nea* that in 1984 he as well had discovered a secret NATO structure in Greece very similar to the Italian Gladio which he had ordered to dissolve. Passionate calls for a parliamentary investigation of the secret army and its suspected involvement in the right-wing military coup of 1967 followed in Greece but were defeated by the acting conservative government. Defence Minister Varvitsiotis explained that a former Greek military attaché in Washington who had worked in NATO would look at the accusations while he promised: 'The government must not fear anything.'[3]

From Greece the scandal swooped over to Germany where on November 5 Green parliamentarian Manfred Such, having learned of the scandal from the German daily *TAZ*, formally requested the German government of Helmut Kohl to comment on the suspected existence of Gladio structures in Germany. While the German Defence Ministry contemplated a strategy how the request should be handled about the private television channel RTL shocked the German public by revealing in a special Gladio report that former members of Hitler's Special Forces SS had been part of Germany's Gladio network, while also in numerous other countries right-wing extremists had been recruited into the anti-Communist secret army.

Tensions heightened even more when German government spokesman Hans Klein in a confused manner thereafter publicly explained that 'the German Gladio was *not*, as has been claimed, a secret commando troop or a guerrilla unit', adding that he could not discuss details for reasons of strict secrecy.[4] Klein's statements caused an outcry among opposition Social Democrats and Green politicians who sensed a platform for the upcoming national elections. Member of Parliament Hermann Scheer, defence expert of the German Socialist Party (SPD), criticised that this mysterious right-wing network might well be some sort of a 'Ku-Klux-Klan', designed more for clandestine operations against the population and the opposition than for an unlikely Soviet invasion. Scheer insisted that 'in order to avoid that a cover up destroys the traces' an investigation of Gladio had to be carried out as soon as possible.[5] 'The affair is a case for the national public prosecutor (Generalbundesanwalt)', Scheer explained, 'because the existence of an armed military secret organisation outside all governmental or parliamentary control is incompatible with the constitutional legality, and therefore must be prosecuted according to the criminal law'.[6]

Socialist parliamentarian Wilfried Penner, a member of the parliamentary control commission (PKK) of the German secret service, emphasised that he had never heard of the secret NATO network and 'the mafiotic entanglements', stressing 'that this mess must be dealt with publicly, in front of all eyes'.[7] Also Burkhard Hirsch, the government controller of the secret service and PKK member, was 'extremely worried' because 'If something remains secret so long, then my life experience tells me, that there must be something rotten about the affair.'[8] Yet the call for a full-fledged investigation suddenly evaporated amongst the German Socialists when the acting government revealed that also Socialist Ministers, during their time in office, had covered up the secret whereupon despite the protests of the German Green party the affair was dealt with silently behind closed doors.

In Belgium in the evening of November 7, Socialist Defence Minister Guy Coeme addressed a startled public when he confirmed that a secret NATO-linked army had also existed in Belgium. With an implicit reference to the Brabant massacres in the 1980s during which people were gunned down by mysterious men in black in several supermarkets the Defence Minister added: 'Furthermore I want to know whether there exists a link between the activities of this secret network, and the wave of crime and terror which our country suffered from during the past years.'[9] Greatly disturbed, Belgian Prime Minister Wilfried Martens confronted the flashlights of the press declaring: 'I have been Prime Minister for 11 years now, but I have been completely unaware that such a secret network existed in our country.' The journalists noticed that the Prime Minister 'so self-confident in other circumstances' was 'far from being relaxed'.[10] Whereupon the Belgian parliament decided to form a special committee to investigate the Belgian stay-behind and after having closed down the network a year later presented a valuable 250 pages strong public report.[11]

Most sensitively the Belgian parliamentarians discovered that the secret NATO army was still active. They found that a secret meeting of Generals directing the secret stay-behind armies in the numerous countries in Western Europe had been held in the secret NATO-linked Gladio headquarters ACC as recently as October 23 and 24, 1990. The meeting of the ACC had taken place in Brussels under the chairmanship of General Raymond Van Calster, chief of the Belgian military secret service SGR (Service General de Renseignement). The General was furious when journalists followed the lead and his phone kept ringing all the time. He first lied to the press when on November 9 he flatly denied having chaired the international ACC meeting, claiming that Gladio was a purely Italian affair. Later he admitted that indeed a secret network had also been erected in Belgium after the Second World War 'to collect information in case of a Soviet invasion'.[12] While he angrily insisted that there was 'no direct link with NATO', he refused to reveal further details and at the same time emphasised: 'We have nothing to hide.'[13]

In France the government of Socialist President Francois Mitterand attempted to avoid further embarrassment when on November 9 a low key official claimed that in France the secret army 'had long been dissolved'.[14] In addition General Constantin Melnik, chief of the French secret services from 1959 to 1962, in the leading French daily spread the rumour that the French Gladio had 'probably already been dissolved after Stalin's death in 1953, and certainly did not exist anymore at the time when De Gaulle was President of France [thus after 1958]'.[15] The French press sided with the government who was preparing for the war in the Gulf and refrained from asking sensitive questions and hence 'an affair which made front page headlines in the other daily European newspapers only got a small note at the bottom of the page in Paris'.[16]

Italian Prime Minister Andreotti mercilessly shattered the French cover-up when on November 10, 1990 he declared with some amusement that France also had taken part in the very recent meeting of the Gladio directing body ACC in Belgium on October 23, 1990. Somewhat embarrassed, French Defence Minister Jean Pierre Chevènement thereafter attempted to limit the damage by claiming that the French secret army had been completely passive: 'As far as I am aware it never had more than a sleepers' role and a role of liaison.' Asked by the radio journalist whether France would now face similar political turmoil as Italy and Belgium, after speculations about domestic and terrorist activities of the secret Gladio army, the Defence Minister calmly replied: 'I don't think so'.[17] Journalists noted that the government was making every effort to prevent that the Gladio revelations were recognised as 'a domestic monstrosity'.[18]

In Great Britain, spokespersons at the Defence Department declared day after day to the inquisitive British press: 'I'm afraid we wouldn't discuss security matters', and 'It is a security matter. We are not speaking about it', and 'We cannot be drawn into discussing security matters.'[19] As the press continued to raise the Gladio topic day after day British Defence Secretary Tom King tried to handle the thoroughly distressing affair with a casual joke: 'I am not sure what particular hot potato you're chasing after. It sounds wonderfully exciting, but I'm afraid I'm quite ignorant about it. I'm better informed about the Gulf.'[20] In the context of the preparations for Operation Desert Storm and the war against Iraq, the British parliament did not press for a parliamentary investigation or an open parliamentary debate but backed the government of Prime Minister John Major. And still in summer 1992 there was no official British explanation on Gladio, leaving journalists as Hugh O'Shaughnessy to lament that 'The silence in Whitehall and the almost total lack of curiosity among MPs about an affair in which Britain was so centrally involved are remarkable.'[21]

In the Netherlands, Prime Minister Ruud Lubbers, in office since 1982, decided to deal with the sensitive topic by writing a letter to parliament on November 13 in which he confirmed the existence of a secret army also in the Netherlands while stressing that there 'was never any NATO supervision over this organisation'.[22] Thereafter Lubbers' and Dutch Defence Minister Relus Ter Beek briefed Parliament's Intelligence and Security Committee behind closed doors on the sensitive details of the Dutch Gladio. 'Successive Prime Ministers and Defence Ministers have always preferred not to inform other members of their cabinets or Parliament', Lubbers declared to parliament, adding that he was proud that some 30 Ministers had kept the secret. While parliamentarians criticised the inherent danger of a secret army unknown to parliament or the population at large, it was decided not to carry out a parliamentary investigation of the secret network, nor to present a public report. 'I don't particularly worry that there was, and perhaps still is, such a thing', Hans Dijkstal of the opposition Liberals said. 'What I do have problems with is that until last night Parliament was never told.'[23]

In neighbouring Luxemburg, Prime Minister Jacques Santer on November 14, 1990 took a stand in front of parliament and confirmed that a secret army linked to NATO had also existed in Luxemburg. 'The only activities of these persons, and this is the case for the entire time period in which this network has existed, have been limited to the training in preparation of their missions, including the training of how to behave individually in a hostile environment, and how to coordinate efforts with allied countries', Santer insisted.[24] The request of parliamentarian Jean Huss of the Luxemburg Green Alternative Party which asked first of all for an open debate in parliament on the issue, and in the second place for the establishment of a parliamentary commission of inquiry into the topic, was declined in a majority decision.

When the international press related that 'In Portugal, a Lisbon radio station has reported that cells of the network associated with Operation Gladio were active during the 1950s to defend the rightist dictatorship of Dr Salazar', the government in power reacted with a flat refusal.[25] Portuguese Defence Minister Fernando Nogueira on November 16, 1990 declared that he had no knowledge of the existence of any kind of Gladio branch in Portugal and claimed that there existed neither in his Defence Ministry, nor in the General Staff of the Portuguese Armed Forces 'any information whatsoever concerning the existence or activity of any "Gladio structure" in Portugal'.[26] A retired General disagreed with the claim of the government and under the condition of being allowed to remain anonymous confirmed to the press that a secret parallel army also existed in Portugal 'dependent on the Defence Ministry, the Interior Ministry, and the Ministry for Colonial Affairs'.[27] In neighbouring Spain, which similar to Portugal during most of the Cold War had been a right-wing dictatorship which fought the political opposition with terror and torture, Alberto Oliart, Defence Minister in the early 1980s, considered it to be 'childish' to ask whether also under dictator Franco a secret right-wing army had existed in the country because 'here Gladio was the government'.[28]

In Denmark, Defence Minister Knud Enggaard due to public pressure was forced to take a stand in front of the Danish parliament Folketing where on November 21 he rejected the claim that 'any kind' of NATO-supported CIA organisation had been erected in Denmark. 'Further pieces of information on a secret service operation in case of an occupation is classified material, even highly classified material', the Defence Minister emphasised, 'and I am therefore prohibited from giving any further information in the Danish parliament'. Member of Parliament Pelle Voigt, who had raised the Gladio question in parliament, noticed that 'the Defence Minister's answer was contradictory and an indirect confirmation of the fact that Denmark, too, had its secret network'.[29] Thereafter a discussion of the secret army took place behind closed doors in the committee of the Danish parliament concerned with the supervision of the secret service.

When in Norway the press started to confront the government with Gladio questions, it was provided with what arguably was the shortest comment on the continent of a government concerning the secret army. 'What Hansen said then still applies', Defence Ministry spokesman Erik Senstad explained in a reference to 1978 when after the discovery of the Norwegian stay-behind Defence Minister Rolf Hansen had admitted the existence of a secret army to the Norwegian parliament. Rear Admiral Jan Ingebristen, who in 1985 had stepped down as head of the Norwegian Supreme Defence Command intelligence service, amidst public criticism insisted that it was only logical that the armies had to remain secret: 'There is nothing suspicious about it. But these are units that would stay-behind in occupied territory and it is therefore necessary that they be kept top-secret.'[30]

19

In Turkey the ruling elite took a stand on the Gladio issue on December 3 when General Dogan Beyazit, President of the Operations Department of the Turkish military and General Kemal Yilmaz, Chief of the Turkish Special Forces confirmed to the press the existence of a secret NATO army in Turkey directed by the 'Special Warfare Department' with the task 'to organise resistance in the case of a Communist occupation'.[31] While the Generals stressed that the members of the Turkish Gladio were all good 'patriots' the press and former Prime Minister Bulent Ecevit stressed that the secret army called Counter-Guerrilla had been repeatedly involved in torture, massacres and assassination operations as well as the coup d'états the country had suffered from and was presently employed to fight the Kurdish minority in the country. Thereafter the ruling military refused to answer questions from parliament and civil Ministers, and Turkish Defence Minister Giray warned that 'Ecevit had better keep his fucking mouth shut!'[32]

As the Counter-Guerrilla continued its operations, even the US State Department in its 1995 human rights report noticed that in Turkey 'Prominent credible human rights organisations, Kurdish leaders, and local Kurd asserted that the government acquiesces in, or even carries out, the murder of civilians.' The report of the State Departement noted that 'Human rights groups reported the widespread and credible belief that a Counter-Guerrilla group associated with the security forces had carried out at least some "mystery killings"'. In the United States, journalist Lucy Komisar tried to gain more information but found that her government was hardly different from the Turkish Generals when it came to military secrets. '"As for Washington's role, Pentagon would not tell me whether it was still providing funds or other aid to the Special Warfare Department; in fact, it wouldn't answer any questions about it." Komisar was repeatedly turned away: "I was told by officials variously that they knew nothing about it, that it happened too long ago for there to be any records available, or that what I described was a CIA operation for which they could provide no information."' One Pentagon historian said, 'Oh, you mean the "stay-behind" organisation. That's classified.'[33]

The issue of the Counter-Guerrilla, however, did not go away. On November 3, 1996 a speeding black Mercedes hit a tractor and crashed on a remote highway near the Turkish village of Susurluk, some 100 miles south of Istanbul. A prominent member of the Turkish Counter-Guerrilla, a top police official and a member of parliament were killed in the crash. To many it was the physical proof of how closely the entire government was involved in the dirty war of the Counter-Guerrilla, and thousands protested against the 'Susurluk state' and demanded that the country be cleansed 'from the gangs'. In January 1998 Prime Minister Mesut Ylmaz had to inform millions of television viewers the results of a seven-month-long parliamentary investigation into the Susurluk scandal. 'It is the anatomy of a disgraceful mess', he began his statement and thereafter admitted that an 'execution squad was firmed within the state' while 'All parts of the state were aware of what was going on.'[34]

Given the far-reaching revelations across Western Europe, the Gladio scandal was also discussed by the parliament of the European Union (EU) on November 22, 1990.

At the time the EU numbered 12 countries, all of whom were affected by the scandal.[35] The 12 had greatly increased cooperation among each other and were about to establish the common European market without borders for persons, goods, services and capital, while security policy and defence matters in the new organisation still rested within the sovereign control of each EU member state. 'Mr President, ladies and gentlemen, there is one fundamental moral and political necessity, in regard to the new Europe that we are progressively building' Italian parliamentarian Falqui wisely opened the debate on that day. 'This Europe will have no future if it is not founded on truth, on the full transparency of its institutions in regard to the dark plots against democracy that have turned upside down the history, even in recent times, of many European states.' Falqui insisted that 'There will be no future, ladies and gentlemen, if we do not remove the idea of having lived in a kind of double state – one open and democratic, the other clandestine and reactionary. That is why we want to know what and how many "Gladio" networks there have been in recent years in the Member States of the European Community.'[36]

French parliamentarian Dury shared these concerns and among the united European delegates declared: 'What worried us in this Gladio affair was that these networks were able to exist out of sight and beyond control of the democratic political authorities. That, I think, is the fundamental issue which remains.' Dury concluded that the history of the Gladio armies had to be investigated: 'For our part, we believe that light has to be shed on this whole affair so that we can recognise all its implications and stop the problem lingering on or occurring with other organisations, or prevent other temptations from arising.' Also the role of NATO, according to Dury, had to be investigated, although 'as for the responsibility of NATO and SHAPE, I don't think one should talk about a conspiracy', Dury said, 'but I think we must keep up this spirit of inquiry and this concern for everything to be brought out into the open. We know very well that some people in Gladio also sit on NATO committees' and hence he concluded: 'I feel that it is part of our democratic duty to be able to shed proper light on all these kinds of problems.'[37]

'Mr. President, the Gladio system has operated for four decades under various names', Greek parliamentarian Ephremidis addressed the EU. 'It has operated clandestinely, and we are entitled to attribute to it all the destabilization, all the provocation and all the terrorism that have occurred in our countries over these four decades, and to say that, actively or passively, it must have had an involvement.' Ephremidis sharply criticised the entire stay-behind network: 'The fact that it was set up by the CIA and NATO which, while purporting to defend democracy were actually undermining it and using it for their own nefarious purposes.' With an implicit reference to the involvement of the Greek Gladio in the 1967 coup d'état he criticised that 'the democracy we are supposed to have been enjoying has been, and still is, nothing but a front', and encouraged the EU parliament to investigate the matter further: 'The fine details must be uncovered, and we ourselves must establish a special sub committee of inquiry to hold hearings and to blow the whole thing wide open so that all the necessary steps can be taken to rid our countries of such clandestine organisations.'[38]

French parliamentarian De Donnea shared a different perspective when he declared: 'Mr. President, it was perfectly legitimate at the end of the Second World War, for the majority of our states to set up services whose purpose was to prepare underground resistance networks that could be activated in the event of our countries being occupied by the forces of the Warsaw Pact.' Hence, the French parliamentarian highlighted, 'We must therefore pay tribute to all those who, while the cold war lasted, worked in these networks.' To De Donnea it was clear that the clandestine armies had to remain secret, 'For these networks to remain effective, it was obviously necessary for them to be kept secret', while at the same time he wanted to have clarity as to alleged links to terrorist activities: 'Having said that, if there are serious indications or suspicions to the effect that some or all of these networks have operated in an illegal or abnormal way in certain countries, it is in everyone's interest for matters to be brought into the open and for the guilty to be punished.'[39]

Dutch MP Vandemeulebroucke captured the feeling of many Europeans well when he summarised that 'This affair leaves a bad taste in the mouth, since it has been going on for as long as the European Community has been in existence, and we claim to be creating a new form of democracy.' Vandemeulebroucke stressed that it was above all the secrecy of the entire affair that greatly worried him as a parliamentarian, for 'the budgets for these secret organisations were also kept secret. They were not discussed in any parliament, and we wish to express our concern at the fact that ... it now emerges that there are centres for taking decisions and carrying them out which are not subject to any form of democratic control.' The Dutch parliamentarian concluded: 'I should like to protest most strongly against the fact that the American military, whether through SHAPE, NATO or the CIA, think they can interfere in what is our democratic right.' While he acknowledged that the European Parliament itself did not have the competence to deal with the affair, 'I realise that we in the European Parliament have no competence regarding peace and security matters', he explained, 'and hence the compromise resolution asks for parliamentary committees of inquiry to be set up in each of the twelve Member States so that we do get total clarification'.[40]

Following the debate the parliament of the EU decided to pass a resolution on the Gladio affair in which the parliamentarians critically reflected upon the Gladio phenomenon and in seven points, formulated as a preamble to the resolution, attempted to summarise the main features of the Gladio phenomenon:

1   'Having regard to the revelation by several European governments of the existence for 40 years of a clandestine parallel intelligence and armed operations organisation in several Member States of the Community';

2   'whereas for over 40 years this organisation has escaped all democratic controls and has been run by the secret services of the states concerned in collaboration with NATO';

3   'fearing the danger that such clandestine networks may have interfered illegally in the internal political affairs of Member States or may still do so';

4   'whereas in certain Member States military secret services (or uncontrolled branches thereof) were involved in serious cases of terrorism and crime as evidenced by various judicial inquiries';

5   'whereas these organisations operated and continue to operate completely outside the law since they are not subject to any parliamentary control and frequently those holding the highest government and constitutional posts are kept in the dark as to these matters';

6   'whereas the various "GLADIO" organisations have at their disposal independent arsenals and military resources which give them an unknown strike potential, thereby jeopardising the democratic structures of the countries in which they are operating or have been operating'; and

7   'greatly concerned at the existence of decision-making and operational bodies which are not subject to any form of democratic control and are of a completely clandestine nature at time when greater Community co-operation in the field of security is a constant subject of discussion'.

Thereafter, as a first point of criticism following the preamble, the resolution of the EU parliament 'Condemns the clandestine creation of manipulative and operational networks and calls for a full investigation into the nature, structure, aims and all other aspects of these clandestine organisations or any splinter groups, their use for illegal interference in the internal political affairs of the countries concerned, the problem of terrorism in Europe and the possible collusion of the secret services of Member States or third countries.' As a second point the EU 'Protests vigorously at the assumption by certain US military personnel at SHAPE and in NATO of the right to encourage the establishment in Europe of a clandestine intelligence and operation network.' As a third point the resolution 'Calls on the governments of the Member States to dismantle all clandestine military and paramilitary networks.' As a fourth point the EU 'Calls on the judiciaries of the countries in which the presence of such military organisations has been ascertained to elucidate fully their composition and modus operandi and to clarify any action they may have taken to destabilize the democratic structures of the Member States.' Furthermore as a fifth point the EU 'Requests all the Member States to take the necessary measures, if necessary by establishing parliamentary committees of inquiry, to draw up a complete list of organisations active in this field, and at the same time to monitor their links with the respective state intelligence services and their links, if any, with terrorist action groups and/or other illegal practices.' As a sixth point the EU parliament addresses the EU Council of Ministers, above all in its reunion as Defence Ministers, and 'Calls on the Council of Ministers to provide full information on the activities of these secret intelligence and operational services.' As a seventh point, the resolution 'Calls on its competent committee to consider holding a hearing in order to clarify the role and impact of the "GLADIO" organisation and any similar bodies.' Last but not least in its final point the resolution explicitly addresses both NATO and the United States, as the EU parliament 'Instructs its President to forward this resolution to the Commission, the Council, the Secretary-General of NATO, the governments of the Member States, and the United States Government.'[41]

The dog barked loudly, but it did not bite. Of the eight actions requested by the EU parliament not one was carried out satisfactorily. Only Belgium, Italy and Switzerland investigated their secret armies with a parliamentary commission, producing a lengthy and detailed public report. And although the resolution was forwarded to the respective branches of the EU, NATO and to United States, NATO Secretary-General Manfred Wörner and senior US President George Bush neither supported a detailed investigation nor offered a public explanation.

3

THE SILENCE OF NATO, CIA AND MI6

At the time of the Gladio discoveries in 1990, NATO, the world's largest military alliance, was made up of 16 nations: Belgium, Denmark, Germany, France, Greece, the United Kingdom, Iceland, Italy, Canada, Luxemburg, Norway, Portugal, Spain, the Netherlands, Turkey and the United States, with the latter commanding a dominant position within the alliance. NATO reacted with confusion to the revelations of Italian Prime Minister Andreotti and feared for its image when the secret stay-behind armies were linked to massacres, torture, coup d'états and other terrorist operations in several countries of Western Europe.

After almost a month of silence on Monday November 5, 1990, NATO categorically denied Andreotti's allegation concerning NATO's involvement in operation Gladio and the secret armies. Senior NATO spokesman Jean Marcotta said at SHAPE headquarters in Mons, Belgium that 'NATO has never contemplated guerrilla war or clandestine operations; it has always concerned itself with military affairs and the defence of Allied frontiers.'[1] Then, on Tuesday November 6, a NATO spokesman explained that NATO's denial of the previous day had been false. The spokesman left journalists only with a short communiqué which said that NATO never commented on matters of military secrecy and that Marcotta should not have said anything at all.[2] The international press protested against the ill-advised public relations policy of the military alliance when it related with bitterness: 'As shock followed shock across the Continent, a NATO spokesman issued a denial: nothing was known of Gladio or stay-behind. Then a seven word communiqué announced that the denial was "incorrect" and nothing more.'[3]

As trust in NATO diminished, the headlines ran 'Undercover NATO group "may have had terrorist links"'.[4] 'Secret NATO network branded subversive: Commission finds that Gladio, the alliance's underground arm in Italy, became a focal point for fascist elements bent on combating the Communists by instigating terrorist attacks to justify repressive laws.'[5] 'Bomb used at Bologna came from NATO Unit.'[6] A NATO diplomat, who insisted on remaining anonymous, reasoned in front of the press: 'Since this is a secret organisation, I wouldn't expect too many questions to be answered, even though the Cold War is over. If there were any links to terrorist organisations, that sort of information would be buried very deep indeed.

If not, then what is wrong with taking precautions to organise resistance if you think the Soviets might attack?'[7]

According to the Spanish press, NATO Secretary-General Manfred Wörner immediately after the public relations debacle of November 5 and 6 held a Gladio information meeting behind closed doors on the level of NATO ambassadors on November 7. 'The Supreme Headquarters Allied Powers Europe (SHAPE), directing organ of NATO's military apparatus, coordinated the actions of Gladio, according to the revelations of Gladio Secretary-General Manfred Wörner during a reunion with the NATO ambassadors of the 16 allied nations', the Spanish press related. 'Wörner allegedly had asked for time, in order to carry out an investigation with respect to the "no knowledge at all' statement" which NATO had issued the previous day. 'These precisions were presented in front of the Atlantic Council meeting on the level of ambassadors, which, according to some sources, was held on November 7.' The highest-ranking military officer of NATO in Europe, US General John Galvin, had confirmed that what the press was reporting was to a large degree correct but had to remain secret. 'During this meeting behind closed doors, the NATO Secretary General related that the questioned military gentlemen – precisely General John Galvin, supreme commander of the Allied forces in Europe – had indicated that SHAPE co-ordinated the Gladio operations. From then on the official position of NATO was that they would not comment on official secrets.'[8]

According to sources that wished to remain anonymous, NATO's Office of Security allegedly was involved with operation Gladio.[9] Located at NATO headquarters in Brussels, the secretive Office of Security has been an integral part of NATO ever since the creation of the Alliance in 1949. The NATO Office of Security coordinates, monitors and implements NATO security policy. The Director of Security is the Secretary-General's principal adviser on security issues and directs the NATO Headquarters Security Service and is responsible for the overall coordination of security within NATO. Most importantly the Director of Security is also the Chairman of the NATO's Security Committee in which the Heads of Security Services of member countries meet regularly to discuss matters of espionage, terrorism, subversion and other threats including Communism in Western Europe that might affect the Alliance.

In Germany, researcher Erich Schmidt Eenboom reported that in order to design a counter-information strategy against the spreading Gladio revelations the chiefs of several Western European secret services, including those of Spain, France, Belgium, Italy, Norway, Luxemburg and Great Britain, had met several times in late 1990.[10] Most plausibly these meetings took place within the secretive NATO Office of Security. 'The fact that the secret Gladio structures were coordinated by an international committee only made up of members of the different secret services', the Portuguese daily *Expresso* reflected, 'leads to another problem concerning the national sovereignty of each state'. Above all the military secret services during the Cold War had in several countries been largely outside any democratic control. 'Obviously various European governments have not controlled their secret services', while NATO cultivated most intimate ties with the military secret services of all member states. 'The implication is that obviously NATO follows a doctrine of limited trust. Such a doctrine claims that certain governments would not act sufficiently against Communists, and were thus not worth being informed on the activities of NATO's secret army.'[11]

Under the headline 'Manfred Wörner explains Gladio', the Portuguese press related further details of the NATO meeting of November 7. 'German NATO Secretary General Manfred Wörner explained the function of the secret network – which had been created in the 1950s to organise the resistance in case of a Soviet invasion – to ambassadors of the 16 Allied NATO countries'. Behind closed doors 'Wörner confirmed that the military command of the allied forces – Supreme Headquarters Allied Powers Europe (SHAPE) – coordinated the activities of the "Gladio Network", which had been erected by the secret services in various countries of NATO, through a committee created in 1952, which presently is being chaired by General Raymond Van Calster, Chief of the Belgium military secret service', later revealed to be the ACC. 'The structure was erected first in Italy before 1947, and thereafter spread to France, Belgium, United Kingdom, Holland, Luxemburg, Denmark, Norway, Greece', the newspaper reported. 'The Secretary General also said that SHAPE had issued "false information" when it had denied the existence of such a secret network, but he refused to explain the numerous contradictions into which the various governments had fallen, by confirming or denying the existence of Gladio networks within their respective country.'[12]

The press in the midst of the scandal repeatedly asked the highest civilian official of NATO, Secretary-General Manfred Wörner, for an explanation or at least a comment. But Wörner was unavailable for interviews as the alliance never made statements about military secrets.[13] The term 'military secrets' became a focal point of further discussions among journalists who started to search for retired NATO officials who might be more willing to comment on the whole affair. Joseph Luns, 79-year-old retired diplomat, who from 1971 to 1984 had served as NATO Secretary-General, in a telephone interview from his Brussels apartment, told reporters that he had been unaware about the secret network until he read about it in the papers recently: 'I never heard anything about it even though I had a pretty senior post in NATO.' Luns conceded however that he had been briefed 'occasionally' on covert action operations, claiming that 'it's improbable but it is possible' that Gladio could have been set up behind his back without his knowledge.[14]

'The only collective body that ever worked was NATO, and that was because it was a military alliance and we were in charge', US President Richard Nixon once tellingly observed.[15] He was correct to point out that although NATO had a European headquarters in Belgium, its main headquarters was located in the Pentagon in Washington. During its entire history NATO's highest military commander for the European territory, the SACEUR (Supreme Allied Commander Europe), operating from his headquarters SHAPE in the Belgian town Casteau, had always been a US General. Europeans were allowed to represent NATO with the highest civilian official, the Secretary-General. But ever since US General Eisenhower was nominated as first SACEUR, the highest military office in Europe was always given to US Generals.[16]

Retired CIA officer Thomas Polgar confirmed after the discovery of the secret armies in Western Europe that they were coordinated by 'a sort of unconventional warfare planning group' linked to NATO.[17] This was also confirmed by the German press, which highlighted that this secretive department of NATO had during the entire Cold War remained under the dominance of the United States. 'The missions of the secret armies are co-ordinated by the "Special Forces Section" in a strictly secured wing of NATO headquarters in Casteau', the German press related. 'A grey steel door, which opens as a bank vault only through a specific number combination, prohibits trespassing to the unauthorised. Officers of other departments, who are invited, are checked right after the door at a dark counter. The Special Forces Section is directed by British or American officers exclusively and most papers in circulation carry the stamp "American Eyes Only."'[18]

Given the strength of the Communist parties in several countries of Western Europe, NATO had engaged in secret non-orthodox warfare ever since its creation in the years following the Second World War. According to the findings of the Belgian parliamentary investigation into Gladio, secret non-orthodox warfare even preceded the foundation of the alliance. As of 1948, non-orthodox warfare was coordinated by the so-called 'Clandestine Committee of the Western Union' (CCWU). According to the press all Gladio 'nations were members of the "Clandestine Committee of the Western Union" (CCWU) and participated regularly in its reunions through a representative of their respective secret service. The secret services are generally in direct contact with the S/B structures.'[19]

When in 1949 the North Atlantic Treaty was signed, CCWU was secretly integrated into the new international military apparatus and as of 1951 operated under the new label CPC. At that time European NATO headquarters were in France and also the CPC was located in Paris. Like the CCWU before it the CPC was concerned with the planning, preparation and direction of non-orthodox warfare carried out by the stay-behind armies and Special Forces. Only officers with the highest NATO security clearances were allowed to enter CPC headquarters were under the guidance of CIA and MI6 experts the chiefs of the Western European Secret Services met at regular intervals during the year in order to coordinate measures of non-orthodox warfare in Western Europe.

When in 1966 French President Charles de Gaulle expelled NATO from France, the European headquarters of the military alliance, to the great anger of the Pentagon and US President Lyndon Johnson, had to move from Paris to Brussels. Secretly, the CPC also moved to Belgium, as the Belgian Gladio investigation found.[20] The historical expulsion of NATO from France offered what until then seemed to be the most far-reaching insights into the darker secrets of the military alliance. 'The existence of secret NATO protocols committing the secret services of the signatory countries to work to prevent Communist parties from coming to power first emerged in 1966', covert action scholar Philip Willan relates, 'when President de Gaulle decided to pull France out of NATO's combined command structure, denouncing the protocols as an infringement of national sovereignty.'[21]

While original copies of the secret anti-Communist NATO protocols remain classified, speculations concerning their content have continued to increase after the discoveries of the secret anti-Communist stay-behind armies. US journalist Arthur Rowse in his Gladio article claims that 'A secret clause in the initial NATO agreement in 1949 required that before a nation could join, it must have already established a national security authority to fight Communism through clandestine citizen cadres.'[22] Italian expert on secret services and covert action, Giuseppe de Lutiis, found that when becoming a NATO member in 1949, Italy signed not only the Atlantic Pact, but also secret protocols which provided for the creation of an unofficial organisation 'charged with guaranteeing Italy's internal alignment with the Western Block by any means, even if the electorate were to show a different inclination'.[23] Also Italian Gladio researcher Mario Coglitore has confirmed the existence of secret NATO protocols.[24] A former NATO intelligence official, who insisted on remaining unnamed, after the Gladio discoveries in 1990 went as far as to claim that the secret NATO protocols explicitly protected right-wing extremists who were deemed useful in the fight against Communists. US President Truman and German Chancellor Adenauer allegedly had 'signed a secret protocol with the US on West Germany's entry into NATO in May 1955 in which it was agreed that the West German authorities would refrain from active legal pursuit of known right-wing extremists'.[25]

Italian General Paolo Inzerilli, who commanded the Italian Gladio from 1974 to 1986, stressed that the 'omnipresent United States' dominated the secret CPC that directed the secret war. CPC according to Inzerilli had been founded 'by order of the Supreme Commander of NATO Europe. It was the interface between NATO's Supreme Headquarters Allied Powers Europe (SHAPE) and the Secret Services of the member states as far as the problems of non-orthodox warfare were concerned.'[26] The United States, together with their allied junior partner Great Britain and France, dominated the CPC and within the committee formed a so-called Executive Group. 'The meetings were on the average once or twice a year in Brussels at CPC headquarters and the various problems on the agenda were discussed with the 'Executive Group' and the Military', Inzerilli related.[27]

'Our stay-behind was co-ordinated together with the other analogous secret European structures by the CPC, Co-ordination and Planning Committee of SHAPE, the Supreme Headquarters of the Allied Powers in Europe', Italian General Gerardo Serravalle revealed. The predecessor of General Inzerilli, General Serravalle commanded the Italian Gladio from 1971 to 1974 and related that 'in the 1970s the members of the CPC were the officers responsible for the secret structures of Great Britain, France, Germany, Belgium, Luxemburg, the Netherlands and Italy. These representatives of the secret structures met every year in one of the capitals.'[28] Each time high-ranking officers of the CIA were present during the meetings. 'At the stay-behind meetings representatives of the CIA were always present', Serravalle remembered. 'They had no voting right and were from the CIA headquarters of the capital in which the meeting took place.' Furthermore, 'members of the US Forces Europe Command were present, also without voting right'.[29] 'The "Directive SHAPE" was the official reference, if not even the proper Allied Stay-Behind doctrine', Serravalle explains in his book on Gladio and stresses that the recordings of the CPC, which he had read but which remain classified, above all 'relate to the training of Gladiators in Europe, how to activate them from the secret headquarters in case of complete occupation of the national territory and other technical questions as, to quote the most important one, the unification of the different communication systems between the stay-behind bases'.[30]

Next to the CPC a second secret command post functioning as a stay-behind headquarters was erected within NATO in the early 1950s, called ACC. Like the CPC, ACC also was directly linked to the US-controlled SACEUR. According to the findings of the Belgian investigation into Gladio the ACC was allegedly created in 1957 'responsible for co-ordinating the "Stay-Behind" networks in Belgium, Denmark, France, Germany, Italy, Luxemburg, Holland, Norway, United Kingdom and the United States'. During peacetime the duties of ACC according to the Belgian Gladio report 'included elaborating the directives for the network, developing its clandestine capability and organising bases in Britain and the United States. In wartime, it was to plan stay-behind operations in conjunction with SHAPE; organisers were to activate clandestine bases and organise operations from there.'[31]

Italian Gladio General Inzerilli claims that 'the relations in the ACC were completely different' from those in the CPC. 'The atmosphere was clearly more relaxed and friendly compared to the one in the CPC.' ACC, founded by ' a specific order from SACEUR to CPC' allegedly 'became a sub branch' of the CPC'.[32] Allegedly the body served above all as a forum in which Gladio know-how was exchanged between the numerous secret services chiefs: 'The ACC was an essentially technical Committee, a forum where information on the experiences made were exchanged, where one spoke of the means available or the means studied, where one exchanged information on the networks etc.' Italian Gladio commander Inzerilli recalls, 'It was of reciprocal interest. Everybody knew that if for an operation he lacked an expert in explosives or in telecommunications or in repression, he could without problems address another country because the agents had been trained in the same techniques and used the same materials.'[33]

Most prominently the so-called Harpoon radio transmitters featured among the material used by all ACC members. They were developed and produced in the 1980s on the orders of NATO's Gladio centre ACC by the German firm AEG Telefunken for a total of 130 million German Marks and replaced an older communication system which had become obsolete. The Harpoon system was able to send and receive encrypted radio messages over a distance of 6,000 km, and thus connected the different stay-behinds also across the Atlantic. 'The only material element which all stay-behind members of the ACC shared is the famous Harpoon radio transmitter', Belgian Gladio agent Van Ussel, who himself operated Harpoon stations during his active time in the 1980s, revealed in the 1990s. As he understood it, 'this system was regularly used for the transmission of messages between the radio bases and the agents (above all during radio exercises), but was above all destined to play a central role for the transmission of intelligence in case of occupation'.[34] There was an ACC basis in the European States and one in the United Kingdom from where the units in the occupied countries could be activated and commanded. ACC manuals allegedly instructed Gladiators on common covert action procedures, encryption and frequency-hopping communication techniques, as well as air droppings and landings.

The presidency of ACC rotated every two years among the member nations and in 1990 was held by Belgium. The ACC meeting of October 23 and 24 was presided by Major General Raymond Van Calster, chief of the Belgium military secret service SGR. General Inzerilli recalled that 'in contrast to the CPC there was no fixed and predetermined Directorate [in the ACC]. The presidency in the Committee was held for two years by a member rotating between all the member states in alphabetical order', hence the ACC did not feature 'the same predominance of the Great Powers'. Inzerilli preferred the work in the ACC to the work in the more strongly US-dominated CPC and testified: 'I must say, also after having personally had the experience of being President of the ACC for two years, in its total it was really a non-discriminatory committee.'[35]

Future research into operation Gladio and the stay-behind network of NATO must beyond any doubt focus on the transcripts and recordings of ACC and CPC. But still years after the discovery of the top-secret network, the official response, much like in 1990, is characterised by silence and denials. When the author during his research in summer 2000 contacted NATO archives with the request for more information on Gladio and specifically on ACC and CPC the military alliance replied: 'We have checked our Archives and cannot find any trace of the Committees you have mentioned.' When the author insisted, NATO's archive section replied: 'I wish to confirm once more that the Committees you refer to have never existed within NATO. Furthermore the organisation you refer to as "Gladio" has never been part of the NATO military structure.'[36] Thereafter the author called NATO's Office of Security but was not allowed to either speak to the Director, nor know his name, for that was classified. Mrs Isabelle Jacobs at the Office of Security informed the author that it was unlikely that he would get any answers concerning sensitive Gladio questions and advised the author to hand in Gladio questions in writing via the embassy of his home country.

Thus the Observation Swiss Mission at NATO in Brussels forwarded the Gladio questions of the author to NATO, with Swiss Ambassador Anton Thalmann regretting that: 'Neither to me, nor to my staff the existence of secret NATO committees, as mentioned in your letter, is known.'[37] 'What is the connection of NATO to the Clandestine Planning Committee (CPC) and to the Allied Clandestine Committee (ACC)? What is the role of the CPC and ACC? What is the connection of CPC and ACC with NATO's Office of Security?', the author had inquired in writing and on May 2, 2001 received a reply from Lee McClenny, head of NATO press and media service. McClenny in his letter claimed that 'Neither the Allied Clandestine Committee nor the Clandestine Planning Committee appear in any literature, classified or unclassified, about NATO that I have seen.' He added that 'Further, I have been unable to find anyone working here who has any knowledge of these two committees. I do not know whether such a committee or committees may have once existed at NATO, but neither exists at present.'[38] The author insisted and asked 'Why has NATO senior spokesman Jean Marcotta on Monday November 5, 1990 categorically denied any connections between NATO and Gladio, whereupon on November 7 another NATO spokesman had to declare Marcotta's statement of two days before had been false?' to which Lee McClenny replied: 'I am not aware of any link between NATO and "Operation Gladio". Further, I can find no record that anyone named Jean Marcotta was ever a spokesman for NATO.'[39] And there the matter rested.

The CIA, the most powerful secret service of the world, was not more cooperative than the world's largest military alliance when it came to the sensitive issue of Gladio and stay-behind questions. Founded in 1947, two years before the establishment of NATO, the main task of the CIA during the Cold War was to combat Communism globally in covert action operations and promote the influence of the United States. 'By covert action operations', US President Richard Nixon once defined the tactic, 'I mean those activities which, although designed to further official US programs and policies abroad, are so planned and executed that the hand of the US Government is not apparent to unauthorised persons.'[40] Historians and political analysts have ever since described in detail how the CIA together with US Special Forces in silent and undeclared wars in Latin America had influenced political and military developments in numerous countries, including most prominently the overthrow of Guatemala's President Jakobo Arbenz in 1954, the failed attempt to overthrow Cuba's Fidel Castro in the 1961 Pay of Pigs invasion, the assassination of Ernesto Che Guevara in Bolivia in 1967, the overthrow of Chile's President Salvador Allende and the installation of dictator Augusto Pinochet in 1973, and the sponsoring of the Contras in Nicaragua after the revolution of the Sandinistas in 1979.[41]

Beyond the Americans the CIA also carried out numerous covert action operations in Asia and Africa, among which the most prominent were the overthrow of the Mossadegh government in Iran in 1953, the support to the white South African Police which in 1962 led to the imprisonment of Nelson Mandela, the support for Osama Bin Laden's Al Qaida in Afghanistan after the Soviet invasion of 1979, and the support to Communist Khmer Rouge leader Pol Pot from bases inside Cambodia following the defeat of the US in Vietnam in 1975. From a systematic scientific perspective the covert action departement of the CIA according to the definition of the FBI is therefore a terrorist organisation. Beacuse 'Terrorism', according to the FBI, 'is the unlawful use of force or violence against persons or property to intimidate or coerce a government, the civilian population, or any segment thereof, in furtherance of political or social objectives'.[42]

When in the mid-1970s the parliament of the United States realised that the CIA as well as the Pentagon had increased their power almost beyond control and had also abused it on numerous occasions, US Senator Frank Church wisely observed that 'The growth of Intelligence abuses reflects a more general failure of our basic institutions'. Senator Church at the time presided over one of three critical investigations of the US parliament into the US secret services which in the second half of the 1970s presented their final reports that until today remain among the most authoritative documents on US secret warfare.[43] The overall impact of the investigation of the US Congress was however marginal and the secret services supported by the White House continued to abuse their power as the Iran Contra scandal in 1986 highlighted. This led historian Kathryn Olmsted at the University of California to 'the central question': 'After starting the investigations, why did most members of the press and Congress back away from challenging the secret government?'[44]

While the debate concerning the existence or non-existence of a 'secret government' in the United States continues, the Gladio evidence shows that the CIA and the Pentagon have repeatedly operated outside democratic control during the Cold War, and also after the end of the Cold War remained unaccountable for their actions. Admiral Stansfield Turner, Director of the CIA from 1977 to 1981, strictly refused to answer questions about Gladio in a television interview in Italy in December 1990. When the journalists insisted with respect for the victims of the numerous massacres in Italy, the former CIA Director angrily ripped off his microphone and shouted: 'I said, no questions about Gladio!' whereupon the interview was over.[45]

Retired middle ranking CIA officers were more outspoken about the secrets of the Cold War and illegal operations of the CIA. Among them Thomas Polgar, who had retired in 1981 after a 30-year-long career in the CIA and in 1991 had testified against the nomination of Robert Gates as Director of the CIA because the later had covered up the Iran Contra scandal. When questioned about the secret Gladio armies in Europe, Polgar explained with an implicit reference to CPC and ACC that the stay-behind programs were coordinated by 'a sort of unconventional warfare planning group linked to NATO'. In the secret headquarters the chiefs of the national secret armies 'would meet every couple of months in different capitals'. Polgar insisted that 'each national service did it with varying degrees of intensity' while admitting that 'in Italy in the 1970s some of the people went a little bit beyond the charter that NATO had put down'.[46] Journalist Arthur Rowse, formerly on the staff of the *Washington Post*, thereafter in an essay on Gladio in Italy drew 'The lessons of Gladio': 'As long as the US public remains ignorant of this dark chapter in US foreign relations, the agencies responsible for it will face little pressure to correct their ways. The end of the Cold War', Rowse observed, 'changed little in Washington. The US...still awaits a real national debate on the means and ends and costs of our national security policies.'[47]

Specialising in the research on CIA covert action and the secret Cold War, the academics of the independent non-governmental 'National Security Archive' research institute at George Washington University in Washington filed a Freedom of Information Act (FOIA) request with the CIA on April 15, 1991. According to the FOIA law all branches of the government must be accountable to public questions concerning the legality of their actions. Malcolm Byrne, Deputy Director of Research at the National Security Archive, asked the CIA for 'all agency records related to . . . The United State Government's original decision(s), probably taken during the 1951–55 period, to sponsor, support, or collaborate with, any covert armies, networks, or other units, established to resist a possible invasion of Western Europe by Communist-dominated countries, or to conduct guerrilla activities in Western European countries should they become dominated by Communist, leftist, or Soviet-sponsored parties or regimes.' Furthermore Byrne highlighted: 'With reference to the above, please include in your search any records relating to the activities known as "Operation Gladio", particularly in France, Germany, or Italy.'[48]

Byrne correctly pointed out that 'any records obtained as a result of the request will contribute significantly to public understanding of United States foreign policy in the post World War II era, as well as the role of intelligence information, analyses, and operations in United States policy-making at the time'. Yet the CIA refused to cooperate and on June 18, 1991 replied: 'The CIA can neither confirm nor deny the existence or non-existence of records responsive to your request.' When Byrne appealed this refusal of the CIA to provide any Gladio information the appeal was turned down. The CIA based its refusal to cooperate on two catch-all exemptions to the FOIA law, which protect documents: that is, either 'properly classified pursuant to an Executive order in the interest of national defence or foreign policy' (exemption B1), or 'the Director's statutory obligations to protect from disclosure intelligence sources and methods, as well as the organisation, functions, names, official titles, salaries or the number of personnel employed by the Agency, in accord with the National Security Act of 1947 and the CIA Act of 1949, respectively' (Exemption B3).

When European officials attempted to challenge the secret government they were hardly more successful. In March 1995 the Italian Senate commission headed by Senator Giovanni Pellegrino after having investigated Gladio and the massacres in Italy placed a FOIA request with the CIA. The Italian Senators asked the CIA for all records relating to the Red Brigades and the Moro affair in order to find out whether the CIA according to the Gladio domestic control task had indeed infiltrated the Red Brigades before they killed former Italian Prime Minister and leader of the DCI Aldo Moro in 1978. Refusing to cooperate, the CIA raised FOIA exemptions B1 and B3 and in May 1995 declined all data and responded that it 'can neither confirm nor deny the existence of CIA documentation concerning your inquiry'. The Italian press stressed how 'embarrassing' this was and headlined: 'The CIA has rejected the request to collaborate with the Parliamentary Commission on the mysteries of the kidnapping. Moro, a state secret for the USA.'[49]

The second Gladio inquiry to the CIA by European government officials came from Austria in January 1996 after top-secret CIA Gladio arms caches had been discovered in the mountain meadows and forests of the neutral Alpine state. US government officials declared that the United States would cover the costs arising from the digging up and recovery of the CIA networks.[50] The Austrian investigation of the scandal under Michael Sika of the Interior Ministry on November 28, 1997 presented its final report on the CIA arms caches and declared 'that there can be no absolute certainty about the arms caches and their intended use'. Hence 'In order to reach a rigorous clarification access to the relevant documents, especially in the United States, would be desirable.'[51] Member of the commission Oliver Rathkolb of Vienna University thus placed a FOIA request in order to gain access to the relevant CIA documents. Yet in 1997 the CIA Chairman Agency Release Panel declined also Rathkolb's information request under FOIA exemptions B1 and B3, leaving the Austrians to lament that the CIA was unaccountable for its actions.

As FOIA requests are the only method available to get hold of any CIA Gladio documents, the author on December 14, 2000 placed a FOIA request with the CIA, whereupon two weeks later the CIA replied to the author's request 'pertaining to "Operation Gladio"' in an evasive manner by stating that 'The CIA can neither confirm nor deny the existence or non-existence of records responsive to your request.' By raising FOIA exemptions B1 and B3 the CIA Information and Privacy Coordinator, Kathryn I. Dyer, with her letter declined all information on operation Gladio.[52] The author appealed this decision of the CIA and argued that 'The documents that were withheld must be disclosed under the FOIA, because the secrecy exemptions (b)(1) and (b)(3) can only reasonably refer to CIA operations which are still secret today.' With data of his research the author proved that this was no longer the case, and concluded: 'If you, Mrs. Dyer, raise FOIA secrecy exemptions (b)(1) and (b)(3) in this context, you unwisely deprive the CIA from its voice and the possibility to take a stand in a Gladio disclosure discourse, which will take place regardless whether the CIA decides to participate or not.'[53]

In February 2001 the CIA replied that 'Your appeal has been accepted and arrangements will be made for its consideration by the appropriate members of the Agency Release Panel. You will be advised of the determinations made.' At the same time the CIA stressed that the Agency Release Panel deals with appeals 'on a first-received, first-out basis', and that at 'the present time, our workload consists of approximately 315 appeals'.[54] The author's Gladio request was thus shelved and put off. At the time of writing, almost four years later, the CIA Agency Release Panel had still not answered the author's request for information.

The British secret service MI6 was the third organisation – after NATO and the CIA – to have been central to the stay-behind operation. MI6 did not take a stand on the Gladio affair in 1990 because with a legendary obsession for secrecy its very existence was only officially confirmed in 1994 with the passing of the Intelligence Services Act that specified that MI6 collected foreign intelligence and engaged in covert action operations abroad.

While the British executives and MI6 refused all comment, Conservative Party member Rupert Allason, editor of the *Intelligence Quarterly Magazine* under the penname Nigel West and author of several books on Britain's security services, at the height of the Gladio scandal in November 1990 confirmed to Associated Press in a telephone interview that 'We were heavily involved and still are...in these networks.' West explained that the British 'certainly helped finance and run, with the Americans' several networks and through the MI6 together with the CIA were directly involved: 'The people who inspired it were the British and American intelligence agencies.' West said after 1949 the stay-behind armies were coordinated by the Command and Control Structure For Special Forces of NATO within which also Britain's Special Air Service (SAS) Special Forces played a strategic role.[55]

'Britain's role in setting up stay-behinds throughout Europe was absolutely fundamental', the British BBC reported in its Newsnight edition with some delay on April 4, 1991. Newsnight reader John Simpson criticised that MI6 and the British Defence Ministry were withholding all information on the subject while 'on the back of revelations that Gladio existed it has emerged that other European countries had their own stay-behind armies – Belgium, France, Holland, Spain, Greece, Turkey. Even in neutral Sweden and Switzerland there has been public debate. And in some cases enquiries have been set up. Yet in Britain, there is nothing. Save the customary comment of the ministry of defence that they don't discuss matters of national security.'[56] Simpson related that ever since the fall of the Berlin Wall, the British with fascination and horror had learned of the conspiracies and terror operations of the Stasi, the Securitate and other secret services in Eastern Europe. 'Could our side have ever done anything comparable? Surely not' he noted with ironical intonation and then turned the spotlight on the Western security services: 'Yet now information has started to emerge of the alleged misdeeds of NATO's most secret services. In Italy a parliamentary commission is investigating the activities of a secret army set up by the state to resist a possible Soviet invasion. The inquiry has led to the disclosure of similar secret forces across Europe. But the Italian group, known as Gladio, is under suspicion of being involved in a series of terrorist bombings.'[57]

The BBC was unable to get government officials to take a stand on the Gladio affair, and the official confirmation that MI6 had been involved came only years later and through a rather unusual channel: a museum. The London-based Imperial War Museum in July 1995 opened a new permanent exhibition called 'Secret Wars'. 'What you are about to see in the exhibition has for years been part of the country's most closely guarded secrets', the visitors were greeted at the entrance. 'It has been made available to the public for the first time here. And most important of all, it's the truth...Fact is more incredible and exciting than fiction.' An inconspicuous comment in one of the windows dedicated to MI6 confirmed that 'Among MI6's preparation for a Third World War were the creation of "stay-behind" parties ready to operate behind enemy lines in the event of a Soviet advance into Western Europe.' In the same window a big box full of explosives carried the commentary: 'Explosives pack developed by MI6 to be hidden in potentially hostile territory. It could remain buried for years without any deterioration of its contents.' And next to a booklet on sabotage techniques for 'stay-behind' parties a text read: 'In the British Zone of occupation in Austria, junior Royal Marine officers were detached from normal duties to prepare supply caches in the mountains and liaise with locally recruited agents.'[58]

Former MI6 officers rightly took the exhibition as a sign that they could now speak out about the top-secret Gladio operation. A few months after the exhibition had opened, former Royal Marine officers Giles and Preston, the only MI6 agents to be named in the Gladio exhibition next to a photo 'in Austrian Alps 1953–1954', confirmed to author Michael Smith that throughout the late 1940s and early 1950s the British and Americans had set up stay-behind units in Western Europe in preparation for an expected Soviet invasion. Giles and Preston at the time were sent to Fort Monckton near Portsmouth in England where the MI6 trained the Gladiators together with the SAS. They were given instruction in codes, the use of a pistol and covert operations. 'We were made to do exercises, going out in the dead of night and pretending to blow up trains in the railway stations without the stationmaster or the porters seeing you', Preston recalled his own training. 'We crept about and pretended to lay charges on the right part of the railway engine with a view to blowing it up.'[59]

Giles remembered that they also took part in sabotage operations on British trains that were in public service, as for instance during the exercise at the Eastleigh Marshalling Yards: 'We laid bricks inside railway engines to simulate plastic explosives. I remember rows and rows of steam engines all under thick snow, standing there in clouds of vapour', Giles recalled. 'There were troops out with dogs. The guards came past and I was actually hiding among the cylinder blocks of these engines as they went past. We were also opening up the lubricating tops of the axle boxes and pouring in sand. What happens is that after about fifty miles the sand in the axle box starts to turn them red hot and they all overheat.'[60] The agents were hardly bothered that the locomotives were in public use: 'That wasn't my problem. We were playing for real', Giles explained. 'I had to do a ten-day course in Greenwich, learning about following people in the street and shaking off people following me', Preston recalled, 'the practicalities of being in the intelligence world'. Then they were flown to Austria in order to recruit and train agents, and oversaw the 'underground bunkers, filled with weapons, clothing and supplies' of the Austrian Gladio which had been set up by 'MI6 and the CIA'.[61] When the author visited MI6 headquarters on the banks of the Thames in London in 1999 he was not too surprised to be told that MI6 does not comment on military secrets.

4

THE SECRET WAR IN GREAT BRITAIN

The final and definite account of the Cold War will never be written, as history evolves together with the societies that produce and consume history. But a consensus has emerged among scientists in numerous countries that the most prominent feature of the Cold War, as seen from the West, was the fight against Communism on a global scale. In this struggle that characterised the history of the twentieth century like few other features the former superpower of the world, Great Britain, lost its leading position to the United States. The latter used its struggle against Communism to increase its power decade after decade. And after the fall of the Soviet Union in 1991 and the end of the Cold War, the Empire of the United States dominated the world like no other Empire before in history.

The conservative establishment in Great Britain was greatly worried when for the first time in the history of mankind in 1917 a Communist system was installed in a remote but large agricultural country. After the revolution in Russia the Communists seized entire factories and explained that from now on the means of production belonged to the people. The investors, in many cases, lost everything. In his 'Origins of the Cold War', historian Denna Frank Fleming observed that many of the social changes brought about by the Russian revolution, including the radical abolition of both the Church and the landed nobility, 'might have been accepted by the world's conservatives in time, but the nationalisation of industry, business and the land – never'. The example of the Russian revolution was not to be repeated anywhere ever. 'J. B. Priestly once said that the minds of England's conservatives snapped shut at the height of the Russian Revolution and had never opened again.'[1]

Largely unknown in the West, the secret war against Communism hence started right after the Russian revolution when Great Britain and the United States sent secret armies against the newly founded Soviet Union toddler nation. Between 1918 and 1920, London and Washington sided with the Russian right and financed ten military interventions against the USSR on Soviet soil, all of which failed to overthrow the new rulers but created considerable suspicion among the Communist elite and dictator Stalin concerning the motives of the capitalist West.[2] In subsequent years the Soviet Union strengthened its security apparatus and eventually became a totalitarian state and routinely arrested foreigners on its soil blaming them to be secret agents of the West. As the difficulties of overthrowing Communism in Russia became apparent, Great Britain and its allies concentrated on a strategy of preventing Communism from spreading to other countries.

In July 1936 fascist dictator Franco staged a coup d'état against the Spanish left-wing government and in the subsequent civil war defeated the opposition and the Spanish Communists while enjoying the silent support of the governments in London, Washington and Paris. Among the reasons why Adolf Hitler was not stopped very early ranged this one he essentially had the right enemy: Soviet Communism. During the Spanish Civil War Hitler and Mussolini were allowed to bomb the Spanish opposition. After having started the Second World War, Hitler launched three massive offensives against Russia in 1941, 1942 and 1943, which almost dealt a death blow to Russian Communism. With more victims than any other country during the Second World War the Soviet Union lost over 15 million civilians and 7 million soldiers, while another 14 million were injured.[3] Russian historians have later argued that despite Moscow's urgent request the United States, which lost 300,000 soldiers during the Second World War, when liberating Europe and Asia, had together with Great Britain deliberately refrained from establishing a second front against Hitler in the West, which naturally would have diverted Nazi troops and thus eased the onslaught on the USSR. Only after Stalingrad the tides turned and the Red Army defeated the Germans and marched west, so Russian historians argued the Allies, who feared losing ground, quickly established a second front and after the 1944 Normandy invasion met the Soviet army in Berlin.[4]

British historians confirmed the history of intrigues that had both shaped their country and others. 'England in modern times has always been a centre of subversion – known as such to others, but not to itself', British historian Mackenzie observed after the Second World War. 'Hence the strange two-sided picture: England to the outer world was the model of intrigue, subtlety and perfect secrecy, to itself it seemed above all bluff, simple and well-meaning.'[5] Mackenzie argues that the legendary secret warfare of the British goes back 'into the history of the "small wars" which made the British Empire'.[6] As the Second World War was about to begin, the British strategists in the Defence Department concluded that their covert action 'must be based on the experience which we have had in India, Iraq, Ireland and Russia, i.e. the development of a combination of guerrilla with IRA tactics'.[7]

In March 1938, shortly after Hitler's annexation of Austria, a new department was created in MI6, labelled Section D, with the task to develop subversive operations in Europe. Section D began to establish 'stay-behind' sabotage parties in countries threatened by German invasion.[8] When in 1940 the German invasion of southern England seemed imminent 'Section D set about getting up a store of arms and recruiting agents all over Britain, without informing anyone else. The British domestic secret service MI5 became quite alarmed when it started receiving reports of Section D's activities and several of their agents were arrested as spies before the truth was discovered.'[9] The recruitment and organisation of stay-behind agents by members of Section D looked highly secretive to any observer: 'The appearance of these strangers [Section D agents] in their city clothes, sinister black limousines and general air of mystery caused alarm among the local inhabitants', former SOE operative Peter Wilkinson remembers. The secret agents also 'infuriated subordinate military commanders since they refused to explain their presence or discuss their business except to say that it was "most secret"'.[10] Half a century later the 'Secret Wars' exhibition of the Imperial War Museum in London revealed to the public how 'MI6 Section D, following the stay-behind doctrine, also set up resistance armies in England called "The Auxiliary Units" equipped with guns and explosives'. These first British Gladio units 'received special training and were instructed to "stay-behind" enemy lines in case of a German invasion of the island. Operating from secret hideouts and arms caches, they would be able to carry out sabotage and guerrilla warfare against the German invaders.'[11] Whether the plan would have worked out in practice was never known in the absence of the German invasion. But by August 1940 'a rather ramshackle organization' covering the most vulnerable invasion beaches had been established along the North Sea coasts of England and Scotland.[12]

Section D of MI6 was secret warfare restricted to Great Britain. This changed when in July 1940 British Prime Minister Winston Churchill ordered the creation of a secret army under the label SOE to 'set Europe ablaze by assisting resistance movements and carrying out subversive operations in enemy held territory'.[13] The Prime Minister's War Cabinet Memorandum of July 19, 1940 records that 'The Prime Minister has further decided, after consultation with the Ministers concerned, that a new organisation shall be established forthwith to co-ordinate all action, by way of subversion and sabotage, against the enemy overseas.' SOE was placed under the command of the Labour Ministry of Economic Warfare under Hugh Dalton. After German forces had occupied France and seemed unstoppable, Minister Dalton insisted that a secret war had to be fought against the German forces in occupied territories: 'We have to organise movements in enemy-occupied territory comparable to the Sinn Fein movement in Ireland, to the Chinese Guerrillas now operating against Japan, to the Spanish Irregulars who played a notable part in Wellington's campaign or – one might as well admit it – to the organisations which the Nazis themselves have developed so remarkably in almost every country in the world.' It seemed logical that the weapon of secret warfare could not be neglected by the British, and Dalton stressed: 'This "democratic international" must use many different methods, including industrial and military sabotage, labour agitation and strikes, continuous propaganda, terrorist acts against traitors and German leaders, boycotts and riots.' In total secrecy a resistance network had thus to be installed by daredevils of the British military and intelligence establishment: 'What is needed is a new organisation to co-ordinate, inspire, control and assist the nationals of the oppressed countries who must themselves be the direct participants. We need absolute secrecy, a certain fanatical enthusiasm, willingness to work with people of different nationalities, complete political reliability.'[14]

Under Minister Dalton operational command of SOE was given to Major General Sir Colin Gubbins, a small, slight, wiry Highlander, with moustache who was later to be influential in the build up of the British Gladio.[15] 'The problem and the plan was to encourage and enable the peoples of the occupied countries to harass the German War effort at every possible point by sabotage, subversion, go-slow practices, coup de main raids etc.', Gubbins described the task of SOE, 'and at the same time to build up secret forces therein, organised, armed and trained to take their part only when the final assault began'. SOE was a carbon copy of operation Gladio born in the midst of the Second World War. 'In its simplest terms, this plan involved the ultimate delivery to occupied territory of large numbers of personnel and quantities of arms and explosives', Gubbins summarised the ambitious plan.[16]

Special Operations Executive employed many of the staff of Section D and eventually became a major organisation in its own right with over 13,000 men and women in its ranks, operating on a global scale and in close cooperation with the MI6. Although SOE also carried out missions in Far East Asia, mounted from India and Australia, Western Europe was its main theatre of operation where it focused on establishing of national secret armies. SOE promoted sabotage and subversion in enemy-occupied territory and established nucleus of trained men who could assist resistance groups in the re-conquest of the countries concerned. 'SOE was for five years the main instrument of British action in the internal politics of Europe', the British Cabinet Office report noted, 'it was an extremely powerful instrument' for it could serve a multitude of tasks and thus 'While SOE was at work no European politician could be under the illusion that the British were uninterested or dead.'[17]

Officially the SOE was disbanded after the war in January 1946 and SOE commander Gubbins resigned. Yet Sir Steward Menzies, who headed the MI6 from 1939 until 1952, was not going to throw away such a valuable instrument as the secret army, and as Director of MI6's Special Operations branch made sure that British covert action continued in the Cold War. The formerly secret Cabinet report on SOE concluded 'it is quite certain that in some form SOE must be created again in any future war'.[18] Long-term objectives approved provisionally by the British Chiefs of Staff on October 4, 1945 for SOE and its successor, the Special Operations branch of MI6, therefore directed first the creation of a skeleton network capable of rapid expansion in case of war and, second, the servicing of the clandestine operational requirements of the British government abroad. 'Priority was given in carrying out these tasks to countries likely to be overrun in the earliest stages of any conflict with the Soviet Union, but not as yet under Soviet domination.'[19] Western Europe hence remained a central theatre for British secret warfare also after the end of the Second World War.

After SOE was closed down on June 30, 1946 a new section 'Special Operations' (SO) was erected within MI6 and placed under the command of Major General Colin Gubbins. According to Dutch secret services scholar Frans Kluiters, MI6 actively promoted the setting up of secret anti-Communist armies as 'Special

Operations started to erect networks in West Germany, Italy and Austria. These networks (stay-behind organisations) could have been activated in case of a potential Soviet invasion, in order to collect intelligence and carry out offensive sabotage activities.'[20] Gubbins saw to it that even after 1945, SOE personnel remained in countries including Germany, Austria, Italy, Greece and Turkey; for SOE and its successors had 'political concerns beyond that of simply defeating Germany'. The explicit directive of 1945 'made it clear that SOE's main enemy was Communism and the Soviet Union', for British interests in Europe were seen to be 'threatened by the Soviet Union and European Communism'.[21] A few years later, in an attempt to gain parliamentary support for the ongoing clandestine operations, British Foreign Minister Ernest Bevin in front of the British parliament on January 22, 1948 urged for the creation of specialised armed units to be used against Soviet subversion and Soviet 'fifth columns'. Selected parliamentarians at the time knew that the suggestion was already being implemented.

As Washington shared this enemy of Great Britain, military and secret service cooperation between the two countries was very close. On the orders of the White House in Washington, Frank Wisner, Director of the CIA covert action department Office of Policy Coordination (OPC), was setting up stay-behind secret armies across Western Europe and in his operations collaborated closely with the Special Operations branch of MI6 of Colonel Gubbins. The CIA and MI6 in a first step were to 'neutralise the surviving secret units of the Axis powers in Germany, Austria and northern Italy' and thereafter recruited some of the defeated fascists into the new anti-Communist secret armies as French secret services scholars Roger Faligot and Rémi Kauffer observed. 'And indeed, through the OPC of the CIA and the SOB of the SIS, the secret services of the democratic countries, which have just won the war, have thereafter tried to "return" some of these commandos against their former Soviet ally.'[22]

Next to MI6 and CIA and their respective covert action departments SOB and OPC, the British and American military Special Forces also cooperated closely. The SAS and the American Green Berets, trained to carry out special missions clandestinely in enemy-held territory, were at numerous instances during the Cold War brothers in arms, and among other operations also trained the secret stay-behind armies. Former Royal Marine officers Giles and Preston who had set up the Austrian Gladio confirmed that Gladio recruits were sent to the old Napoleonic Fort Monckton on the waterfront near Portsmouth in England where the MI6 trained its agents together with the British SAS. They themselves had taken part in these Gladio trainings and were given instruction in secret codes, the use of a pistol and covert operations.[23] Among those trained by the British SAS was Decimo Garau, an instructor at the Italian Gladio base Centro Addestramento Guastatori (CAG) on Capo Marargiu in Sardinia. 'I was in England for a week at Poole, invited by the Special Forces. I was there for a week and I did some training with them', Instructor Garau confirmed after the exposure of Gladio in 1990. 'I did a parachute jump over the Channel. I did some training with them and I got on well with them. Then I was at Hereford to plan and carry out an exercise with the SAS.'[24]

The British at the time were the most experienced in the field of covert action and unorthodox warfare. Their SAS Special Forces had been formed in the midst of the Second World War in Northern Africa in 1942 with the task to strike deep behind enemy lines. Arguably the most dangerous enemy of the British Special Forces SAS during the war were the German Special Forces SS headed by Heinrich Himmler and founded already before the beginning of the Second World War. Like all Special Forces also the German SS was an elite combat troop with special insignia – sleek black uniforms, decorated with death's head and silver dagger – who felt superior to the regular forces and gained a reputation as 'fanatical killers'. After the defeat of Nazi Germany the SS Special Forces were declared a criminal organisation and dissolved by the Allied Tribunal in Nürnberg in 1946.

Upon victory the SAS also was disbanded at the end of the war in October 1945. Yet as the need for top-secret dirty tricks and daredevil operation resurfaced as quickly as the global power of the British Empire was declining, SAS was reborn and in 1947 fought again behind enemy lines in Malaysia. From their headquarters 'the Nursery' in Hereford, England, numerous SAS operations on a very low noise followed, amongst which an operation in 1958 in the British client state Oman where SAS units in support of the dictatorial Sultan defeated left-wing guerrillas. The operation allegedly secured the regiment's future funding, for, as a SAS commander saw it, they had shown that 'they could be flown into a trouble spot rapidly and discreetly, and operate in a remote area without publicity, a capability much valued by the Conservative Government of the day'.[25] In its most public operation the SAS in 1980 stormed the Iranian embassy in London, and more secretly in 1982 operated in the Falkland War. In their biggest deployment since the Second World War SAS units served in the Gulf in 1991 and together with the US Green Berets secretly trained and equipped the Kosovo Liberation Army (KLA) forces before and during the 1999 NATO bombardments of Serb's province.

Conservative British parliamentarian Nigel West correctly emphasised that like the US Green Berets, 'Britain's SAS would have played a strategic role in Operation Gladio if the Soviets had invaded Western Europe', with an implicit claim that operational planning extended to the European stay-behind armies.[26] Both paramilitary units cooperated closely. As a sign of intimate cooperation the members of the American Special Forces unit wore the distinctive Green Beret unofficially ever since 1953 in order to imitate their SAS idols who had long used that insignia. The 'foreign' headdress caused much concern for many senior US Army officers. And it was only when President Kennedy, a great enthusiast of covert action and Special Forces, approved it during his visit to Fort Bragg, headquarters of US Special Forces, in October 1961 that the insignia were officially established in the United States and ever since stuck as the label for the most prominent branch of the many US Special Forces. The US esteem for the older and more prestigious SAS endured for many years as SAS headquarters in Hereford were regarded as the 'mother house', and US Special Forces officers gained prestige at home from having graduated at the British secret warfare centre. Returning the respect, the British too cultivated the Special Forces alliance and in

1962 made the commander of the US Green Berets, Army officer Major General William Yarborough, an honorary member of the SAS.

Already two years before the Gladio exposures in 1990 the BBC unveiled the clandestine cooperation between the British and the American Special Forces to the larger public and in a documentary entitled the 'The Unleashing of Evil' revealed how SAS British Special Forces and US Green Berets had used torture against prisoners over the past 30 years in every major campaign from Kenya to Northern Ireland, Oman, Vietnam, Yemen, Cyprus and other countries. Former Green Berets officer Luke Thomson explained in front of the camera to the public that US Special Forces at Fort Bragg share a reciprocal training programme with the SAS. Whereupon journalist Richard Norton Taylor, British producer of 'The Unleashing of Evil' and prominent reporter during the Gladio scandal two years later, concluded that torture is 'more pervasive and a little closer to ourselves than we like to think'.[27] In another top-secret operation US Green Berets trained genocide Khmer Rouge units in Cambodia after the contact had been established by Ray Cline, senior CIA agent and special adviser to US President Ronald Reagan. When the Iran Contra scandal got under way in 1983, President Reagan, fearing another unpleasant exposure, asked British Prime Minister Margaret Thatcher to take over, who sent the SAS to train Pol Pot forces. 'We first went to Thailand in 1984', senior officers of the SAS later testified, 'The Yanks and us work together; we're close, like brothers. They didn't like it any more than we did. We trained the Khmer Rouge in a lot of technical stuff', the officer remembers. 'At first they wanted to go into the villages and just chop people up. We told them to go easy.' The SAS felt uneasy with the operation and 'a lot of us would change sides given half the chance. That's how pissed off we are. We hate being mixed up with Pol Pot. I tell you: we are soldiers, not child murderers.'[28]

'My experience of clandestine operations is that they seldom remain clandestine for long', Field Marshal Lord Carver, Chief of the British General Staff and later Chief of the British Defence Staff mused in what could have been a remark on Gladio. 'Once you take a step down that slippery slope, there is a danger that Special Forces may begin to take the law into their own hands, as the French did in Algeria, and may have done recently in the Greenpeace affair in New Zealand' in which the French secret service Service de Documentation Extérieure et de Contre-Espionnage (SDECE) on July 10, 1985 sank the Greenpeace ship Rainbow Warrior protesting against the French nuclear tests in the Pacific.[29] Slippery indeed was of course the sensitive deployment of SAS units to Northern Ireland where Irish republicans considered the SAS as nothing less than terrorists. 'A very strong case can be made', critics argued, 'that even from a British point of view, the SAS were part of the problem in Northern Ireland rather than part of the solution'.[30]

As the Gladio scandal erupted in 1990 the British press observed that 'it is now clear that the elite Special Air Service regiment (SAS) was up to its neck in the NATO scheme, and functioned, with MI6, as a training arm for guerrilla warfare and sabotage'. Specifically the British press confirmed that 'an Italian stay-behind unit trained in Britain. The evidence now suggests that it lasted well into the 1980s', adding 'it has been proved that the SAS constructed the secret hides where arms were stockpiled in the British sector of West Germany'.[31] Some of the best data on the secret British hand came from the Swiss parliamentary investigation into the secret Swiss stay-behind army P26. 'British secret services collaborated closely with an armed, undercover Swiss organisation [P26] through a series of covert agreements which formed part of a west European network of "resistance" groups', the press informed a stunned public in neutral Switzerland. Swiss judge Cornu was given the task to investigate the matter and in his report 'describes the group's [P26] collaboration with British secret services as "intense", with Britain providing valuable know-how. P26 cadres participated regularly in training exercises in Britain, the report says. British advisers – possibly from the SAS – visited secret training establishments in Switzerland.' Ironically the British knew more about the secret Swiss army than the Swiss government, for 'The activities of P26, its codes, and the name of the leader of the group, Efrem Cattelan, were known to British intelligence, but the Swiss government was kept in the dark, according to the report. It says that documents giving details about the secret agreements between the British and P26 have never been found.'[32]

Swiss Gladiators during the 1960s, 1970s and 1980s trained in Great Britain under British Special Forces instructors. Training, according to Swiss military instructor and alleged Gladio member Alois Hürlimann, also included non-simulated real action operations against IRA activists, probably in Northern Ireland. This Hürlimann carelessly revealed in Switzerland during an English language course conversation hour when in poor English he reported that in May 1984 he had taken part in secret trainings in England which had also included a real, non-simulated assault on an IRA arms depot, in which Hürlimann, fully dressed in battle fatigues, had participated, and in which at least one IRA activist had been killed.[33]

Most interestingly, the Swiss 1991 Cornu investigation revealed that somewhere in England the Gladio command and communications centre equipped with the Gladio typical Harpoon hardware had been erected. In 1984 a 'Joint Working Agreement', complemented in 1987 with a 'Technical Support Memo', specifically 'spoke of training centres in Great Britain, of the installation of a Swiss transmission-centre in England, and of the co-operation of the two services in technical matters'. Unfortunately, as judge Cornu related, 'Both the "Joint Working Agreement", as well as the "Technical Support Memo" could not be found.' The responsible person of the Swiss military secret service UNA declared that 'in December 1989 he had handed them to the British secret services, for reasons which remain unclear, without keeping a copy of the documents'.[34] 'The cadres of the Swiss organisation regarded the British as the best specialists in the field', the Swiss government in its report concluded.[35]

An unnamed former NATO intelligence official after the discoveries of the secret armies in late 1990 claimed that 'there was a division of labour between the British and the US, with Britain taking responsibility for operations in France,

Belgium, Holland, Portugal and Norway and the Americans looking after Sweden, Finland and the rest of Europe'.[36] This division of labour, however, did not come easily in every country as the case of Italy shows. General Umberto Broccoli, one of the first Directors of the Italian military secret service SIFAR, on October 8, 1951 wrote to the Italian Defence Minister Efisio Marras to discuss issues concerning the Italian stay-behind and the training of Gladiators. Broccoli explained that the British had already created such stay-behind networks in the Netherlands, Belgium 'and presumably also in Denmark and Norway'. Broccoli was happy to confirm that Great Britain 'has made its vast experience in the field available to us' and the Americans have 'offered to collaborate actively with our organisation by providing men, material (presumably free of charge or almost free of charge) and maybe funds'. Broccoli highlighted how useful it would be to send seven specially selected Italian officers for special training to England from November 1951 to February 1952, for these officers would upon return direct the training of Italian Gladiators. Chief of the military secret service Broccoli asked Defence Minister Marras to 'give his approval for this course because, unknown to the British, I am in agreement with the American secret service on us going to the course'.[37]

British Gladio training was not for free, but a serious business, and Broccoli confessed that 'one can imagine that the costs will amount to about 500 million Lira which can not be taken on the budget of the SIFAR and which should be dealt with in the budgets of the Armed Forces'.[38] The MI6, as Broccoli specified, had offered the training of Italian Gladio officers on the condition that Italy bought arms from the British. At the same time, however, in what could be interpreted as a combat for spheres of influence the rich CIA was offering Gladio arms for free. In the end the Italians decided to take the best of both. They sent their officers to the highly reputable British Special Training Schools, but at the same time secretly made a deal with the Americans who provided them with arms for free. The British were not amused. And when General Ettore Musco, successor of Broccoli at the head of SIFAR, visited the British Fort Monckton near Portsmouth where Gladio training took place the atmosphere was tense: 'In 1953 the British realised that they have been fooled and angrily reproached General Musco, protesting that "his service was delivering itself hook, line and sinker to the Americans".'[39]

Competition between CIA and MI6 for spheres of influence was not limited to Italy. In late 1990, Belgian Defence Minister Guy Coeme upon discovering the secret army explained that 'The relationship between the British and Belgian intelligence services originates in the contacts which took place between Mr. Spaak and the head of the British intelligence service [Menzies], and in the arrangement between the United States, Great Britain and Belgium.'[40] The ménage à trois had its tricky sides, as MI6 and CIA wanted to make sure that Belgium would not privilege one to the other. Chief of the MI6, Steward Menzies, therefore on January 27, 1949 wrote to the then Belgian Prime Minister Paul Henri Spaak: 'I was delighted to have an opportunity of discussing with you personally certain problems concerning our two countries which I regard as of very real importance and which have been giving me some concern recently.' Whereupon he stressed that both countries should strengthen their cooperation 'on the subject of Cominform and potential enemy activities' and start the 'preparation of appropriate intelligence and action organisations in the event of war'. Specifically 'certain officers should proceed to the United Kingdom in the near future to study, in conjunction with my Service, the technicalities of these matters'. Menzies was very concerned that Spaak would make the Gladio deal with the CIA and not the MI6 and highlighted that he had 'always regarded American participation in the defence of Western Europe of capital importance. I am, however, convinced that all effort, American not excluded, must be integrated into a harmonious whole. Should, therefore, the Americans wish to pursue with your Service certain preparations to meet the needs of war, I regard it as essential – and I understand that I have your agreement – that these activities should be co-ordinated with my own.'

Thereupon Menzies specifically referred to the 'Clandestine Committee of the Western Union' (CCWU), which as of 1948 coordinated non-orthodox warfare until in 1949 the North Atlantic Treaty was signed and NATO took over Gladio coordination. 'Such co-operation', Menzies emphasised in his letter to Spaak, 'moreover will prevent undesirable repercussions with the Western Union Chiefs of Staff. I have already indicated to the Head of the American Service that I am ready to work out plans for detailed co-operation with him on this basis, and I therefore suggest that any projects formulated by them should be referred back to Washington for subsequent discussion between the British and the American Services in London.' Menzies also noted that the Belgian Gladio had to be equipped and that 'Demands for training and material will arise in the near future. I have already undertaken to provide certain training facilities for officers and others nominated by the Head of your Special Service, and I am in a position to provide items of new equipment now in production (such as W/T sets) which will be required for clandestine activities, in the immediate future.' Some of the material, as the chief of the MI6 saw it, could be given for free to the Belgian Gladio while other equipment had to be paid for: 'Such specialised equipment would be given or loaned, but I suggest that should the handling over of more orthodox types of new material arise (e.g. small arms and other military stores), the accountancy should be the subject for friendly negotiation between the British and the Belgian Special Services.' Of course the setting up of the Belgian Gladio had to be carried out in the utmost secrecy and Menzies concluded his letter by stating: 'I need hardly add that I am confident you will share my wish that this correspondence should be regarded as highly secret and that it should not be divulged to a third party without our joint agreement.'[41]

About two weeks later Spaak replied to Menzies stating in his letter that while he was glad to receive the help from the British, he had to inform him that the Americans had also approached Belgium on the subject, and that he therefore thought it important that the British and the Americans first solved this issue amongst themselves. 'I agree with you', the Belgian Prime Minister wrote, 'that it would be highly desirable that the three services (British, American and Belgian) should collaborate closely'. Aware of the competition for influence between the MI6 and the CIA, Spaak noted that, however, 'If two of them, the American and the British, refuse that collaboration, the situation of the Belgian service would be extremely delicate and difficult. I therefore think that it is unavoidable, that on the highest levels negotiations take place between London and Washington to solve this question.'[42]

In Norway secret service chief Vilhelm Evang was the central figure for both the erection of the stay-behind and the creation of the first Norwegian Intelligence Service (NIS). Evang, a science graduate from Oslo, had joined the small intelligence service of the Norwegian government in exile in London in 1942. Back in Norway, Evang with excellent relations to the British built up the post-war NIS in 1946 and led it as Director for 20 years. In February 1947, Evang met an unnamed British MI6 officer with 'close connection with centrally placed defence and military circles' as Evang remembered in his notes. 'Those considerations have led the English to take a strong interest in the build-up of a defence in countries under enemy occupation. It seems as if the Netherlands, France, and Belgium are in the process of setting up a more or less fixed organisation for an underground army.'[43]

Also in neighbouring neutral Sweden the British, together with the US CIA, had played a dominant role in the training of the local Gladio commanders as was revealed in Sweden by Reinhold Geijer, a former Swedish military professional, who in 1957 had been recruited into the Swedish Gladio network and for decades worked as a regional commander. Almost 80-years old, in 1996 Geijer on Swedish television TV 4 recalled how the British had trained him in covert action operations in England. 'In 1959 I went, via London, to a farm outside Eaton. This was done under the strictest secrecy procedures, with for instance a forged passport. I was not even allowed to call my wife' Geijer remembered. 'The aim of the training was to learn how to use dead letter box techniques to receive and send secret messages, and other James Bond style exercises. The British were very tough. I sometimes had the feeling that we were overdoing it.'[44]

As the secret armies were discovered across Western Europe in late 1990 and a beam light focused also on the formerly hidden British hand in the operation, the government of John Major refused to take a stand. 'I'm afraid we wouldn't discuss security matters', spokespersons told the inquisitive British press day after day.[45] The British parliament refrained from an open debate or a parliamentary investigation of the matter and still in summer 1992 journalist Hugh O'Shaughnessy lamented that 'The silence in Whitehall and the almost total lack of curiosity among MPs about an affair in which Britain was so centrally involved are remarkable.'[46] It was left to the British television BBC to observe that 'Britain's role in setting up stay-behinds throughout Europe was absolutely fundamental.' BBC in its Newsnight edition of April 4, 1991 stressed the criminal dimension of the secret armies and reported that as 'the mask is removed, there are horrors to behold'.

BBC correctly found that next to the stay-behind function the secret armies had engaged in political manipulation: 'Just as the Gladiator's sword had a double edge, there were two sides to the story of the modern Gladio'. The question is, the documentary continued, 'was Gladio, with its hidden supplies of arms and explosives used by its mentors... for internal subversion against... the left? Were the agents of the state in fact responsible for an unexplained wave of terrorist killings?' And what was the role of Great Britain? 'We have evidence that right from the beginning of Gladio', Italian parliamentarian Sergio de Julio in front of the camera declared, 'officers were sent to England for training. They were in charge of constituting the first nucleus of the Gladio organisation. So we have evidence for cooperation, let's say, for cooperation between the UK and Italy.'[47]

BBC journalist Peter Marshall interviewed Italian General Gerardo Serravalle, who had commanded the Italian Gladio from 1971 to 1974, and directly questioned him on the role of the British. The Italian General confirmed that cooperation with the British had been intense: 'I invited them [the British] because we had visited their bases in England – the stay-behind bases [of the UK] – and in exchange for this visit I invited them.' Journalist Marshall asked: 'Where is the British stay-behind base?', upon which General Serravalle laughed and replied: 'I'm sorry, I'm not going to tell you where it is, because that enters the area of your country's secrecy.' Then Marshall, in order to get a guaranteed reply, asked: 'But you were impressed with the British?' To which Serravalle replied: 'Yes, I was. Because it's [sic] very efficient, very well organised, and the staff was excellent.'[48]

A year later the BBC took up the Gladio issue once again and broadcasted three excellent documentaries on Gladio by Allan Francovich. Few had as much experience in making documentaries on sensitive issues as filmmaker Francovich who with his 1980 production 'On Company Business' had exposed the dark side of the CIA which won him the International Critics Award for the best documentary at the Berlin Film Festival. Then he investigated Gladio, and thereafter with 'The Maltese Double Cross', Francovich in 1995 presented the connection between the 1988 crash of Pan Am flight 103 over Lockerbie and the accidental shooting down of Iran Air 655 by the American warship USS Vincennes in the same year. 'Rare indeed, outside fiction, are the crusaders of truth who, time and time again, have put themselves in personal danger as Francovich did', his friend Tam Dalyell remembered him after Francovich had died from a heart attack under mysterious circumstances upon entering the United States at the Customs Area of Houston Airport, Texas, on April 17, 1997.[49]

Mainly based on interviews, and focusing almost exclusively on Gladio in Italy and Belgium, Francovich's BBC documentaries feature in front of the camera such key Gladio players as Licio Gelli, head of the P2, Italian right-wing activist Vincenzo Vinciguerra, Venetian judge and Gladio discoverer Felice Casson, Italian Gladio commander General Gerardo Serravalle, Senator Roger Lallemand, head of the Belgian Parliamentary inquiry into Gladio, Decimo Garau, former Italian instructor at the Sardinian Gladio base, William Colby, former Director of CIA, and Martial Lekeu, former member of the Belgian Gendarmerie to name but a few.[50]

'The stay-behind effort, in my view, was simply to be sure that if the worst came to worst, if a Communist Party came into power, that there would be some agents there who would tip us off, and tell us what was happening and be around', Ray Cline, Deputy Director of the CIA from 1962 to 1966, explained for instance in front of Francovich's camera. 'It's not unlikely that some right-wing groups were recruited and made to be stay-behinds because they would indeed have tipped us off if a war were going to begin, so using right-wingers, if you used them not politically, but for intelligence purposes, is o.k.', Cline went on the record.[51] The papers on the next day in London reported that 'It was one of those programmes which you imagine will bring down governments, but such is the instant amnesia generated by television you find that in the newspapers the next morning it rates barely a mention.'[52]

5

THE SECRET WAR IN THE UNITED STATES

After the defeat of Germany and Italy, US President Harry Truman ordered the US Air Force to drop atomic bombs on the cities Hiroshima and Nagasaki whereupon the surrender of Japan ended the Second World War in 1945. While Western Europe was in ruins the economy of the United States was going strong. But despite its military and economic strength the White House feared what it perceived to be an irresistible advance of world Communism. After the United States and Great Britain had invaded the Soviet Union repeatedly but unsuccessfully between 1918 and 1920 the military alliance with the Red Army during the Second World War only served to defeat Hitler and Mussolini and liberate Europe. Immediately after the war the hostilities resurfaced and the former comrade in arms became bitter adversaries in the Cold War. As the United States after the war secured Western Europe and fought the left in Greece, the Soviet Union under Stalin secured its Eastern front from where it had been attacked twice in the century during the two world wars. Truman observed the installation of Communist puppet regimes in Poland, East Germany, Hungary, Romania and Czechoslovakia with great unease as, according to the doctrine of limited sovereignty, Stalin placed the countries of Eastern Europe under the control of local oligarchs, the brutal Soviet military and the Soviet secret service KGB. Likewise Truman was convinced that also in the nominally sovereign democracies of Western Europe the Communist parties had to be secretly fought and weakened.

The CIA also tried to set up a secret army in China in order to stop the advance of Communism but failed as in 1949 Mao and the Chinese Communist Party took over control. Former CIA Director William Colby recalled: 'I have always wondered whether the stay-behind net we built would have worked under Soviet rule. We know that last-minute efforts to organise such nets failed in places like China in 1950 and North Vietnam in 1954.' After the Korean War erupted in 1950 along the fragile border that separated US-controlled South Korea from Communist North Korea, the US army also tried to reduce the influence of Communism in North Korea but failed. Furthermore the CIA attempted to gain control over a number of countries in Eastern Europe with covert action operations and secret armies but failed in these nations also. 'We know that efforts to organise them from outside were penetrated and subverted by the secret police in Poland

51

and Albania in the 1950s', Colby recalled the efforts of the CIA to set up anti-Communist armies.[1]

In the countries known as the 'Third World' in Africa, Latin America and parts of Asia, variations of Communism and Socialism became popular as a means to distribute wealth more equally and gain independence from the industrialised capitalist nations of the 'First World'. In Iran, Mossadegh embarked upon a socialist agenda and attempted to distribute parts of the oil wealth to the population. After India gained independence from Great Britain, Africa also embarked upon a leftist anti-colonial struggle, which peaked in 1960, when Cameroon, Togo, Madagascar, Somalia, Niger, Nigeria, Chad, Congo, Gabon, Senegal, Mali, Ivory Coast, Mauritania and the Central African Republic declared independence. In South East Asia after the withdrawal of the Japanese occupying forces, the Philippines and Vietnam featured strong leftist and Communist anti-colonial movements, which in Vietnam first led to the 'French war' and then to the 'American war', ending only in 1975 with the victory of the Vietnamese Communists.

In the minds of the Cold Warriors in the White House the war therefore did not end in 1945 but simply shifted to a secret low noise level, as the secret services became a prominent instrument of statecraft. US President Roosevelt in late 1944 had followed the suggestion of William Donovan, who during the war had directed the US wartime secret service Office of Strategic Services (OSS), and attempted to establish a US secret service for peacetime to carry out covert action operations in foreign countries against the Communists and other designated enemies of the United States. Yet Edgar Hoover, Director of the US secret service FBI, much resented this plan of Roosevelt and feared that his own FBI intelligence and covert action agency might lose influence. Therefore Hoover leaked copies of Donovan's memo and Roosevelt's executive order to a Chicago Tribune reporter, whereupon on February 9, 1945 the headlines ran: 'New deal plans super spy system – Sleuths would snoop on us and the world – spy on world and home folks – super Gestapo is under consideration'. The Tribune reported that 'In the high circles where the memorandum and draft order are circulating the proposed unit is known as "Frankfurter's Gestapo"' in a reference to Supreme Court Justice Frankfurter and the dreaded German secret service Gestapo. The article revealed that the new secret service was designed to fight a secret war and 'shall perform...Subversive operations abroad...and shall be assigned... such military and naval personnel as may be required in the performance'.[2]

As memoirs of the German secret service Gestapo were still vivid, US citizens were alarmed and the popular outcry effectively killed Donovan's initiative to the amusement of FBI Director Hoover. Yet discussions for a new US secret service continued at high levels under conditions of extreme secrecy. After Roosevelt's death President Harry Truman in January 1946 with a presidential directive established the new Central Intelligence Group (CIG) as the new peacetime US secret service. Celebrating the occasion with a notably eccentric party at the White House, Truman presented his guests with black cloaks, black hats, black moustaches and wooden daggers and announced that the first CIG Director, Admiral Sidney Souers, was to become 'Director of Centralised Snooping'.[3]

The Central Intelligence Group remained a weak interim agency and Truman soon realised that the secret hand of the White House had to be strengthened. Thus in July 1947 the 'National Security Act' was passed which created both the 'Central Intelligence Agency' (CIA) as well as the 'National Security Council' (NSC). This time the 'American Gestapo' was not exposed by the press. Composed by the President himself, the Vice-President, the Foreign Secretary, the Defence Secretary, the Director of the CIA, the National Security adviser, the Chairman of the Joint Chiefs of Staff and other high-ranking personnel and special advisers, 'the National Security Council has evolved into what, without exaggeration, has become the single most powerful staff in Washington.'[4] As has happened repeatedly throughout history, the concentration of power in the White House and the NSC led to abuse. Also in the twenty-first century the NSC remains 'a particular institution, which is known to have been at or across the borderline of legality in the past'.[5]

Most importantly the National Security Act provided a 'legal' basis for US covert action and secret wars against other countries by giving the CIA the duty to 'perform such other functions and duties related to intelligence affecting the national security as the National Security Council may from time to time direct'.[6] No irony intended, this phrase was an almost exact copy of what Hoover had exposed in 1945. The vague formulation on the one hand helped to uphold the pretence that US covert action rested on a solid legal basis, and on the other hand avoided to explicitly contradict numerous US laws including the US constitution and many international treaties. CIA deputy Director Ray Cline rightly called the infamous sentence 'an elastic catch-all clause'.[7] And Clark Clifford later explained that 'We did not mention them [the covert action operations] by name because we felt it would be injurious to our national interest to advertise the fact that we might engage in such activities.'[8]

The first country that the White House targeted with the newly created instrument of CIA covert action was Italy. The first numbered document issued by the NSC, NSC 1/1 of November 14, 1947, analysed that 'The Italian Government, ideologically inclined toward Western democracy, is weak and is being subjected to continuous attack by a strong Communist Party.'[9] Therefore in one of its first meetings the newly created NSC on December 19, 1947 adopted directive NSC 4-A that ordered CIA Director Hillenkoetter to undertake a broad range of covert activities to prevent a Communist victory in the coming Italian election. NSC 4-A was a top-secret document as US covert action in Western Europe was particularly sensitive. There were only three copies, one of which Hillenkoetter had 'closely guarded in the Director's office, where members of his own staff who did not "need to know" could gain no access to it'. A second copy was with George F. Kennan at the State Department.[10] The 'reason for so great secrecy was altogether clear', the official CIA history records, for 'there were citizens of this country at that time who would have been aghast if they had learned of NSC 4-A'.[11]

Operations in Italy weakened the Communists and were a success. President Truman became fascinated with covert action as an instrument of statecraft and urged that the power of the CIA in the field had to be extended beyond Italy. Therefore on June 18, 1948 the NSC passed the notorious directive NSC 10/2 which authorised the CIA to carry out covert action operations in all countries of the world and within the CIA created a covert action branch under the name of 'Office of Special Projects', a label soon changed to the less revealing 'Office of Policy Coordination' (OPC). NSC 10/2 directed that OPC shall 'plan and conduct covert operations'. By 'covert operations' NSC 10/2 designated all activities 'which are conducted or sponsored by this government against hostile foreign states or groups or in support of friendly foreign states or groups but which are so planned and conducted that any US Government responsibility for them is not evident to unauthorised persons and that if uncovered the US Government can plausibly disclaim any responsibility for them'. Specifically covert action operations according to NSC 10/2 'shall include any covert activities related to: propaganda; economic warfare; preventive direct action, including sabotage, anti-sabotage, demolition, and evacuation measures; subversion against hostile states, including assistance to underground resistance movements, guerrillas and refugee liberation groups, and support of indigenous anti-Communist elements in threatened countries of the free world'. The directives of NSC 10/2 thus also covered the setting up of secret anti-Communist Gladio armies in Western Europe but explicitly excluded conventional warfare as well as intelligence and counter-intelligence operations: 'Such operations shall not include armed conflict by recognised military forces, espionage, counter espionage, and covert and deception for military operations.'[12] All in all, the secretive NSC 10/2 differed strangely from the values and principles that Truman had publicly expressed in his much discussed 'Truman Doctrine' in March 1947.

The relatively short period of five years following the end of the Second World War had thus seen the establishment of a US powerful intelligence complex which operates largely beyond the control of US citizens both inside and outside the country. 'I never had any thought when I set up the CIA that it would be injected into peacetime cloak and dagger operations', a fragile Truman claimed after his retirement.[13] And in 1964, eight years before his death, Truman once again insisted that he had never intended the CIA 'to operate as an international agency engaged in strange activities'. Yet by that time the intelligence complex was far beyond his control. 'During his twenty-year retirement Truman sometimes seemed amazed, even somewhat appalled, at the size and power of the intelligence community he had brought into being', British historian Christopher Andrew summarised the feelings of the retired President.[14]

Also George Kennan, covert action fanatic and ardent anti-Communist within the State Department's Policy Planning Staff under the Truman administration, had strongly promoted the passing of NSC 10/2 and CIA covert actions in Italy and beyond. Yet like Truman he was aware of the slippery slope the United States was thus following. 'After all, the greatest danger that can befall us in coping with this problem of Soviet Communism, is that we shall allow ourselves to become like those with whom we are coping', Kennan observed in his famous long telegram on the Soviet Union with a reference to secret government, totalitarian structures and manipulation of foreign governments.[15] Thirty years later Kennan, then an old man, admitted: 'It did not work out all the way I had conceived it.'[16]

In order to guarantee that plausible denial could be upheld, the majority of transcripts of the NSC meetings as well as the majority of NSC assessments and decisions remained inaccessible to researchers. Yet in the aftermath of the Watergate crisis the US parliament critically investigated the CIA and the NSC and found that 'The national elections in Europe in 1948 had been a primary motivation in the establishment of OPC.' The danger of Communism in Western Europe thus directly influenced the beginning of CIA covert action after the Second World War. 'By channelling funds to centre parties and developing media assets, OPC attempted to influence the election results – with considerable success', the US Senators found in their final report which was published in 1976. 'These activities formed the basis for covert political action for the next twenty years. By 1952 approximately forty different covert action projects were under way in one central European country alone.' On the explicit request of the Pentagon the work of the CIA covert action branch OPC also included the setting up of the Gladio secret armies in Western Europe: 'Until 1950 OPC's paramilitary activities (also referred to as preventive action) were limited to plans and preparations for stay-behind nets in the event of future war. Requested by the Joint Chiefs of Staff, these projected OPC operations focused, once again, on Western Europe and were designed to support NATO forces against Soviet attack.'[17]

George Kennan selected Frank Wisner, as the first commander of the CIA covert action unit OPC, Wall Street attorney from Mississippi who had commanded OSS detachments in Istanbul and Bucharest during the Second World War.[18] Wisner and other US OPC officers 'tended to be white [male] Anglo-Saxon patricians from old families with old money . . . and they somewhat inherited traditional British attitudes toward the coloured races of the world'.[19] Wisner guarded the top-secret NSC 10/2 charter closely. 'Whenever someone in the OPC wanted to read 10/2 he had to sign a special access document. Then he would be handed one of the two or three copies of the directive which Wisner kept in a safe in his office.'[20] The spirit in the new US covert action centre OPC was aggressive, enthusiastic, secretive and morally careless, and Wisner insisted in one of the first OPC meetings with Hillenkoetter and Kennan on August 6, 1948 that he be allowed to exploit NSC 10/2 to its full extent and be given a 'broad latitude' in selecting his 'methods of operations'. Wisner wanted to run covert action as he saw it fit without restraint by codes or 'any existing methods'. Hillenkoetter and Kennan assented.[21]

Wisner, Director of OPC, Wisner became the chief architect of the network of secret armies in Western Europe. 'Frank Wisner of the OPC charged his adjoint Frank Lindsay to co-ordinate the stay-behind network in Europe', the Belgian press revealed after the discovery of the secret Gladio armies. Lindsay, as Wisner, had learned his tradecraft in the US secret service OSS during the Second World War in Yugoslavia and knew Communist tactics at first hand. Lindsay, as the Belgian Gladio revelations highlighted, 'sent William Colby (who directed the CIA from 1973 to 1976) to the Scandinavian countries and Thomas Karamessines to Greece where the latter could count on the support of the KYP, the Greek secret service'.[22]

As the United States were intensifying international covert action operations, OPC continued to grow and by the end of Wisner's first year in office he had three hundred employees and seven overseas field stations engaging in numerous different clandestine missions. Three years later, in 1951, OPC had grown to 2,812 full-time people, 47 overseas stations with another 3,142 overseas contract agents and a budget which had grown in the same period from $4.7 to $82 million a year.[23] Even Bedell Smith, who in November 1950 replaced Hillenkoetter as Chief of the CIA, argued in May 1951 that 'the scope of the CIA's covert operations already far exceeded what had been contemplated in NSC 10/2'.[24] The covert action expansion was so drastic that also hard-nosed 'Smith had been concerned about the magnitude and growth rate of the OPC budget.'[25]

Allen Dulles, who replaced Smith as Director of the CIA in 1953, was convinced that covert action was a formidable instrument to combat Communism and clandestinely promote US interests abroad. He monitored the work of OPC Director Frank Wisner and his adjoint Frank Lindsay, who concerning the secret armies collaborated closely with Gerry Miller, chief of the CIA Western Europe desk. Miller, together with other high-ranking CIA officers, recruited CIA agents who were thereafter flown to Western Europe with the task to erect stay-behind nets. Among those recruited was also William Colby, later to become CIA Director. Like many other secret soldiers, Colby during the Second World War had joined the OSS and had been parachuted into occupied France to work with the resistance. During the war he had been exiled again only to be dropped shortly before the end of the war into Norway to blow up transportation lines there. In April 1951 Colby sat in front of Miller's desk. The two men knew each other well, for Miller during the Second World War had been Colby's superior in OSS operations in Norway. According to their understanding the war had never ended and Miller assigned Colby to the unit of Lou Scherer of the CIA's Western Europe Scandinavian Division: 'All right, Bill, get on with it, then'. Miller said 'What we want is a good solid intelligence and resistance network that we can count on if the Russkis ever take over those countries. We have some initial planning, but it needs to be filled out and implemented. You will work for Lou Scherer until we see what more needs to be done.'[26]

Colby was thus instructed by the CIA to support the setting up of the Gladio network in Scandinavia – 'For as it turned out, one of the main fields of the OPC's work then was planning for the not unlikely possibility of a Soviet invasion of Western Europe. And, in the event the Russians succeeded in taking over any or all of the countries of the Continent, Miller explained, the OPC wanted to be in a position to activate well-armed and well-organised partisan uprisings against the occupiers' Colby relates in his memoirs. 'This time Miller said, we intended to have that resistance capability in place before the occupation, indeed even before an invasion; we were determined to organise and supply it now, while we still had the time in which to do it right and at the minimum of risk', Colby described what he perceived to be an honourable operation. 'Thus, the OPC had undertaken a major program of building, throughout those Western European countries that seemed likely targets for Soviet attack, what in the parlance of the intelligence trade were known as "stay-behind nets", clandestine infrastructures of leaders and equipment trained and ready to be called into action as sabotage and espionage forces when the time came.' To this end Miller sent CIA agents to all countries in Western Europe, 'and the job Miller was assigning to me was to plan and build such stay-behind nets in Scandinavia'.[27] The clandestine operations of the United States in Western Europe were carried out 'with the utmost secrecy', as Colby stresses. 'Therefore I was instructed to limit access to information about what I was doing to the smallest possible coterie of the most reliable people, in Washington, in NATO, and in Scandinavia.'[28]

Within NATO the command centre in the Pentagon in Washington was informed in detail about the secret Gladio armies in Western Europe, while in Western Europe the SACEUR, always a US officer, closely supervised the secret army and the command centres CPC and ACC. An internal Pentagon document of 1957, formerly top-secret but declassified in 1978, reveals the existence of a 'CPC charter' which defines CPC's functions within NATO and SHAPE and the European secret services, although unfortunately the CPC charter itself is not part of the declassified document. The document in question is a memorandum for the US Joint Chiefs of Staff written by US General Leon Johnson, US representative to the NATO military committee, on January 3, 1957. In it General Johnson comments on the complaints of the then acting SACEUR General Lauris Norstad concerning the poor quality of intelligence which the latter had received during the 1956 Suez crisis: 'SACEUR has stated a belief that the intelligence received by SHAPE from national authorities during the recent period of tension was inadequate. He states that any re-examination of intelligence support to SHAPE should include the question of increasing and expediting the flow of clandestine intelligence.'

It was in this context that SACEUR Norstad was considering whether the CPC could be used to enhance the situation: 'In addition, SACEUR notes in reference a that there is no provision in reference b, the charter of the SHAPE Clandestine Planning Committee (CPC), which forbids the examination of peace-time clandestine activities. He specifically recommends that the SHAPE CPC be authorised to: a) Examine SHAPE's urgent peacetime intelligence requirements. b) Investigate ways in which the national clandestine services can contribute to an improvement of the flow of clandestine intelligence to SHAPE.' Contrary to NATO's SACEUR Norstad, General Johnson believed that the charter of CPC prevented it from being employed in such a manner. Norstad in his memorandum wrote: 'While there is nothing in reference b [the CPC charter] which clearly forbids the CPC examining the various clandestine intelligence activities, I believe that this would be an unwarranted extension of the CPC activities. It is my interpretation of reference b [the CPC charter] that the CPC was set up solely for the purpose of planning in peacetime the means by which SACEUR's wartime clandestine operational requirements could be met. It would appear to me that any increase in the flow of intelligence to SHAPE, from whatever source, should be dealt with by normal intelligence agencies.' Hence the General concluded: 'I recommend that you do not approve an extension of the scope of activity of the SHAPE CPC...Leon Johnson.'[29]

Next to the Pentagon the US Special Forces were also directly involved in the secret war against the Communists in Western Europe, as together with the SAS they trained the members of the stay-behind network. After the US wartime secret service OSS had been disbanded after the end of the war the US Special Forces were reborn with headquarters at Fort Bragg, Virginia, in 1952. General McClure established a Psychological Warfare Centre in Fort Bragg and in the summer of 1952 the first Special Forces unit, somewhat misleadingly called the 10th Special Forces Group, started its training under Colonel Aaron Bank. The 10th Special Forces Group was organised according to the OSS experience during the Second World War, and directly inherited the latter's mission to carry out, like the British SAS, sabotage missions and to recruit, equip and train guerrillas in order to exploit the resistance potential in both Eastern and Western Europe.[30]

Colonel Bank emphasised that Special Forces training included the 'organisation of resistance movements and the operation of their component networks' as well as 'guerrilla warfare, which in itself is a comprehensive area, including not only organisation, tactics, and logistics, but specialised demolition; codes and radio communication; survival, the Fairbairn method of hand-to-hand combat, and instinctive firing'.[31] The recruitment pamphlet for young men interested to join stressed that US Special Forces applicants ideally should be able to speak European languages. It listed 'a minimum age of twenty-one; rank of sergeant or above; airborne trained or volunteer for jump training; language capability (European) and/or travel experience in Europe; an excellent personnel record; et cetera. All personnel had to volunteer to parachute and operate behind the lines in uniform and/or in civilian attire.'[32]

Defeated Germany was the first nation to which the newly created American Special Forces were deployed. In November 1953 the 10th Special Forces Group erected its first overseas base in a former Nazi SS building that had been set up during Hitler's reign in 1937, the Flint Kaserne at Bad Tölz in Bavaria. Later, headquarters for US Special Forces operations in Latin America were set up in Panama, and Special Forces operations in South East Asia were run by headquarters set up in Okinawa on the territory of defeated Japan. After the Gladio scandal broke in 1990 it was revealed that Gladiators had been trained at the camp of the 10th Special Forces Group at Bad Tölz in Germany and that European Gladiators from numerous countries had received special training from the US Green Berets, allegedly also in Fort Bragg in the USA.[33]

Italian Gladio commander General Serravalle related that in 1972 the Italian Gladiators had been invited by the Green Berets to Bad Tölz.[34] 'I have visited the 10th Special Forces Group at Bad Tölz at the old former SS barracks at least twice. Their commander was Colonel Ludwig Fastenhammer, a Rambo ante-litteram' the Italian Gladio General remembers, 'During briefings in which the missions were explained which I have already mentioned above (counterinsurgency, assistance to local resistance groups etc.) I asked several times whether an operational plan existed between their unit and the various stay-behind units, especially with Gladio.' Serravalle mused that 'You do not need a degree from a Defence College to notice that if unit X is designed to support in times of war in territory Y a resistance movement directed by the secret unit Z, that there should be planning and understandings at least in a very embryonic state between X and Z already during time of peace' and hence the existence of operational plans between US Green Berets and British SAS Special Forces and Gladio were to be expected. 'But on the contrary, they did not exist', Seravalle claimed. 'Thus, in case of war the Special Forces of Bad Tölz would have infiltrated our country to engage in resistance and insurrection operations. How would our Gladiators have welcomed them? With gunfire, of this I am sure, mistaking them for Spetzsnaz, the special forces of the Red Army. Partisan warfare has taught that in case of doubt first you shoot, and then you go and see who lies on the ground.'[35]

At all times the US Special Forces collaborated closely with the covert action department of the CIA. As the Special Forces were set up in Fort Bragg in 1952 the name of the CIA covert action branch changed from 'OPC' to 'Directorate of Plans' (DP), and Wisner was promoted Deputy Director for Plans. Together with CIA Director Allen Dulles he intensified US covert action operations on a global scale. Dulles authorised CIA assassination attempts on Castro and Lumumba as well as the CIA's LSD experiments with unwitting subjects some of whom ended up throwing themselves from skyscrapers. Together with Wisner he organised the overthrow of Iran's President Mossadeh in 1953, and the coup d'état that overthrew the Socialist President Arbenz of Guatemala in 1954. And in 1956 in a reference to left-leaning President Sukarno of Indonesia, Wisner ordered his Far East Division covert action chief Alfred Ulmer that 'It's time we held Sukarno's feet to the fire.'[36] Covert action enthusiasts Wisner and Dulles saw no limits to what they could achieve on a global scale with their secret wars and terrorism, but when clandestine operations against the Cuban government of Fidel Castro failed most prominently with the Bay of Pigs invasion of 1961, President Kennedy angrily fired Dulles and nominated John McCone as the new Director of the CIA.

Allen Dulles during his time as Director of CIA had been the brain behind the secret anti-Communist armies. When the Gladio secret armies were discovered across Western Europe in 1990, an unnamed former NATO intelligence official explained that 'Though the Stay Behind operation was officially started only in 1952, the whole exercise had been in existence for a long time, in fact ever since it was born in the head of Allen Dulles.'[37] During the Second World War CIA chief Allen Dulles had been stationed in Bern in unoccupied Switzerland, and from there had coordinated covert action strategies against Nazi Germany entertaining contacts with both the American OSS as well as with the British secret services. Running secret armies in Western Europe was his training and passion. 'Allen Dulles', reports in Belgium at the time of the Gladio discovery highlighted, 'sees in the [Gladio] project…apart from resisting a Soviet invasion an instrument to stop the Communists from coming to power in the countries concerned!'[38]

As the secret wars of the CIA continued, Wisner increasingly suffered from psychological pain as his soul could no longer find peace. Allan Dulles 'had a theory that Wisner's trouble came from the nature of his job'.[39] Increasingly unable to carry out 'the dirty work' of the CIA in Europe, Africa, Latin America and Asia, Wisner in 1958 was replaced by Richard Bissel who ran the covert action department for the following four years until in 1962 Richard Helms became Deputy Director for Operations. By that time the psychological state of Gladio architect Frank Wisner had seriously deteriorated and in 1965 he shot himself.[40] In the same year Richard Helms was promoted and became Director of CIA and at Wisner's funeral he praised Wisner for his covert action work, ranking him 'Among pioneering men who have had this not always happy responsibility… [to] serve their country in obscurity.'[41] Helms himself in the 1970s faced the unhappy responsibility to testify on the role of the CIA in the coup against leftist President Salvador Allende in Chile. Acting CIA Director Helms bluntly lied to the Senators when he denied that the CIA had attempted to prevent the leftist Allende from being elected President of Chile: 'I had to sign off on all these projects – I would have known.' When the lie was discovered Helms had to resign as Director of the CIA in February 1973 and was fined the amount of $2,000 by the US Senate for perjury.[42]

William Colby due to the details he had offered in his own memoirs until today, has remained the most famous CIA agent involved in operation Gladio. But also his biography ended in tragedy. After having supported the setting up of Gladio networks in Scandinavia, Cold Warrior William Colby in 1953 was transferred to the CIA station in Rome to combat Communism in Italy and promote the clandestine CIA Gladio network. Moving from Cold War battlefield to battlefield, Colby in 1959 left Italy for Saigon and from there ran CIA's covert operations in Vietnam and Laos. Among them CIA's Operation Phoenix devoted to the destruction of the Vietcong's underground organisation and the physical liquidation of its members. In front of the US Congress Colby admitted in 1971 that more than 20,000 Vietcong had been killed while he was in charge of Phoenix but refused to comment whether indeed most of them had died from torture, commenting: 'I would not want to testify that nobody was killed or executed in this kind of programme. I think it probably happened, unfortunately.'[43] In 1973 the CIA's covert action department changed its label to 'Directorate of Operations' (DO) and Colby replaced Thomas Karamessines as the new Deputy Director of Operations. When Helms had to step down, President Nixon in the same year promoted Colby to become Director of CIA, a position which Colby held until he had to resign prematurely in 1976 in the wake of the Watergate scandal. Colby drowned in a river in Maryland in 1996, aged 76.

Colby was succeeded by George Bush Senior as Director of the CIA under President Ford and, in this function, controlled from the White House in Washington the secretive operations of the network in Western Europe. Thereafter George Bush Senior under President Ronald Reagan was promoted to the position of Vice President and continued to sponsor secret wars, most prominently the brutal Contras in Nicaragua. In 1990, as Italian Prime Minister Andreotti revealed the secret CIA armies in Western Europe, George Bush was the acting President of the United States and concerned with preparing the war against Saddam Hussein in Iraq. As the US population remained lukewarm about a war in the Gulf a dirty trick was employed to stir up feelings of hatred and revenge. A 15-year-old girl introduced only as 'Nayirah' testified under tears to the US Congressional Human Rights Caucus on October 10, 1990 that while volunteering as a nurse in a hospital in Kuwait she had witnessed brutal Iraqi soldiers who after the invasion of the country had come to the hospital and taken babies from incubators 'leaving them on the cold floor to die'.[44] The incubator story created an outcry among the US population and President Bush repeated it in numerous speeches, claiming 312 babies had died this way. Bush was so convincing that Amnesty International also reported the story at the time. Only after the war was over it was revealed that the girl had never worked in Kuwait but turned out to be the daughter of the Kuwaiti ambassador to the United States, a fact known by the organisers of the October 10 Congressional hearing. Amnesty International with much regret retracted its support for the story, and Middle East Watch in February 1992 declared that the story had been 'clearly wartime propaganda'.[45] More than a decade later George Bush junior would once again stir up feelings of fear and revenge, by misleadingly claiming that Iraq was developing chemical, biological and atomic weapons, and that President Saddam Hussein had been linked to the terrorist attacks of September 11, 2001.

In December 1990 Bush Senior did not escape sharp criticism from the parliament of the European Union. In a resolution forwarded to the White House and the administration, the EU fiercely condemned the secret war of the United States and the White House. The European Union made it clear that it 'Condemns the clandestine creation of manipulative and operational networks and calls for a full investigation into the nature, structure, aims and all other aspects of these clandestine organisations or any splinter groups, their use for illegal interference in the internal political affairs of the countries concerned, the problem of terrorism in Europe and the possible collusion of the secret services of Member States or third countries'. Above all the European Union 'Protests vigorously at the assumption by certain US military personnel at SHAPE and in NATO of the right to encourage the establishment in Europe of a clandestine intelligence and operation network'.[46]

Due to his large experience in secret operations President Bush Senior was presumably well aware of the most sensitive operations and the terror the secret armies had been involved in and therefore strictly refused to take a stand. Unaware of the dimension of the scandal also the US Congress refrained from asking sensitive questions. Furthermore, also the US media did not carry out critical inquiries. In one of the very few US articles on the subject in the Washington Post, under the headline 'CIA Organised Secret Army in Western Europe. Paramilitary Force Created to Resist Soviet Occupation' an unnamed 'US government official familiar with Operation Gladio' was quoted to have said that Gladio was 'solely an Italian operation. We have no control over it whatsoever', adding, 'If there are allegations that the CIA was involved in terrorist activities in Italy, they are absolute nonsense.'[47] As subsequent investigations revealed in Europe, every single claim in this statement of the CIA was nonsense.[48]

6

THE SECRET WAR IN ITALY

The anti-Communism of the United States dominated the tragic history of Italy's First Republic (1945–1993). The evidence discovered during the last ten years reveals that the Gladio army of the Italian military secret service in alliance with right-wing terrorists was heavily involved in this secret and undeclared war. In the absence of a Soviet invasion the secret anti-Communist paramilitary unit set up by the CIA carried out domestic operations and manipulated the political framework. A parliamentary investigation of the Italian Senate into Gladio and a series of mysterious massacres concluded after the end of the Cold War that in Italy the 'CIA had enjoyed in times of peace maximum discretion' because Italy during the First Republic had lived 'in a difficult and at times tragic situation of frontier'. This Cold War frontier marked the dividing line between the contesting ideologies. On the left side of this frontier stood the exceptionally popular and strong PCI Communist Party, supported with secret funds by the Soviet Union, as well as the strong PSI Socialist Party.[1] On the right side of the frontier operated the CIA and the Italian military secret service with its Gladio army and a number of right-wing terrorists, politically supported by the conservative DCI.[2]

During the Second World War, Italy led by fascist dictator Benito Mussolini sided with Hitler. After the defeat of the Axis Powers, US President Franklin Roosevelt, British Prime Minister Winston Churchill and leader of the Soviet Union Josef Stalin in February 1945 met in the Soviet town Jalta in order to discuss the future shape of Europe and, in a momentous decision for Italy, placed the peninsula under the sphere of influence of the United States. In order to limit the strength of the Italian Communists the CIA sided with the Mafia and right-wing extremists. 'The Mafia', CIA agent Victor Marchetti explained, 'because of its anti-Communist nature is one of the elements which the CIA uses to control Italy'.[3] Already during the Second World War, Earl Brennan, chief of the US wartime secret service OSS in Italy, had advised the US Justice Ministry to reduce the 50-year prison sentence of Mafia boss Charles 'Lucky' Luciano in order to strike a secret deal: In exchange for his liberation, Luciano provided the US army with lists of influential Sicilian Mafiosi who supported the United States when the US army landed in Sicily in 1943.[4] After the war the CIA 'was happy to maintain a clandestine friendship with the Sicilian Mafia' and 'in the name of combating Communism in Italy and

Sicily, the Americans virtually abandoned the island to the Mob rule which persists today'.[5]

The American troops that liberated the country and transformed the dictatorship into a fragile democracy were welcomed by the Italians with flags, bread and vine. Yet the Allies 'were becoming nervous about the conditions of Italian politics, and in particular about the danger of Communist influence growing beyond bounds and reproducing the situations of Greece and Yugoslavia'. Therefore a deliberate change of Allied policy was carried out when London and Washington stopped all supplies to the Communist-dominated Italian partisans who due to their heroic resistance to fascism enjoyed great respect among the Italian population. 'This change of policy was depressing' for American and British liaison officers who behind enemy lines had fought with the Communists against Mussolini and Hitler, 'and for the Italians themselves'.[6] The depression increased as the Italian Communists witnessed how the United States even clandestinely recruited defeated fascists and right-wingers into the security apparatus of the state, 'since virulent anti-Communism, itself a key ingredient of the fascist appeal, was now becoming popular'.[7]

'It's not unlikely that some right-wing groups were recruited and made to be stay-behinds because they would indeed have tipped us off if a war were going to begin', Ray Cline, Deputy Director of the CIA from 1962 to 1966, later confirmed in a Gladio documentary. 'So using right-wingers if you used them not politically, but for intelligence purposes, is o.k.'[8] Far from limiting the influence of the Italian right to information-gathering tasks alone, they were given the keys of power. As a bulwark to Communism the United States founded the Christian Democratic Party DCI, 'riddled through with collaborators, monarchists and plain unreconstructed fascists'.[9] Alice de Gasperi of the DCI was made Prime Minister and from 1945 to 1953 ruled in eight different cabinets. 'A serious purge never occurred, thereby allowing much of the old Fascist bureaucracy to survive.'[10] Prime Minister De Gasperi together with Interior Minister Mario Scelba personally oversaw 'the reinstatement of personnel seriously compromised with the fascist regime'.[11]

Prince Valerio Borghese, nicknamed 'The Black Prince', was among the most notorious fascists recruited by the United States. As the commander of a murderous anti-partisan campaign under Mussolini during the Salo Republic, Borghese with his Decima MAS (XMAS), a Special Forces corps of 4,000 men founded in 1941 and officially recognised by the Nazi High Command, had specialised in tracking down and killing hundreds of Italian Communists. At the end of the war the partisans captured Borghese and were about to hang him when on April 25, 1945 Admiral Ellery Stone, US Proconsul in occupied Italy and a close friend to the Borghese family, instructed OSS employee and later celebrated CIA agent James Angleton to rescue Borghese. Angleton dressed Borghese in the uniform of a US officer and escorted him to Rome where he had to stand trial for his war crimes. Due to the protection of the United States, Borghese was declared 'not guilty' at last resort.[12] CIA agent Angleton received the Legion of Merit from the US Army for his 'exceptionally meritorious' achievements and in subsequent years made a career as chief of CIA counter-intelligence, becoming 'the key American figure controlling all right wing and neo-fascist political and paramilitary groups in Italy in the post-war period'.[13] In a typical development of a Cold Warrior 'only the enemy changed for Jim Angleton' after the defeat of Mussolini and Hitler, as his biographer notes. 'Now the hammer and the sickle replaced the crooked cross.'[14]

In 1947 in Washington the US NSC and the CIA were founded and Italy, due 'to continuous attack by a strong Communist Party', was unfortunate enough to be the first country in the world to be targeted by a silent and undeclared secret war of the CIA. The task of the CIA was straightforward: To prevent the Italian left from winning the first national elections after the Second World War on April 16, 1948. US President Harry Truman was greatly worried because the PCI, the largest Communist Party in Western Europe, and the Socialist PSI for the election had united forming the Popular Democratic Front (Fronte Democratico Popolare, FDP). Observers expected the FDP to gain the majority in the Italian parliament, as in municipal elections preceding the national vote the FDP had shown its muscle, assigning regularly the second rank to the US-supported DCI. Therefore the CIA covert action branch OPC, which under Frank Wisner had set up and directed the secret Gladio armies in Western Europe, pumped ten million CIA dollars into the DCI. At the same time Communists and Socialists were targeted with smear campaigns. Among other dirty tricks the CIA issued anonymous pamphlets which defamed PCI candidates' sex and personal lives, as well as smearing them with the Fascist and/or anti-Church brush. This tactic of targeting specific seats to give control to the DCI rather than going for a complete sweep was successful in all but two of the two hundred plus seats selected. In the final election the DCI with 48 per cent of the vote won 307 seats of the Italian parliament, while the leftist FDP coalition unexpectedly polled but 31 per cent, and with 200 seats was left defeated.[15] Protests of the population and the left were answered with heavy-handed repression leading to a 'strikingly high number of victims during demonstrations and land occupations'.[16]

US President Harry Truman was pleased and became a covert action enthusiast. In his much discussed 'Truman Doctrine' in March 1947 he had insisted that 'we shall refuse to recognize any government imposed upon any nation by the force of any foreign power', declaring that US foreign policy was based on 'righteousness and justice' with no 'compromise with evil'.[17] Yet had the Italian election resulted in anything else but a victory for the US-sponsored conservative DCI, Italy might indeed have faced a civil war along the Greek experience in the same period. Both during and after the election US warships were in the area and US armies still on the ground. George Kennan, chief of the State Department's Policy Planning Staff with the task to develop long-term programmes for the achievement of US objectives in US foreign affairs, recommended outright American military intervention should the Italian Communists win.[18] Italian President Francesco Cossiga confirmed after the Gladio discoveries that during the elections of 1948 a paramilitary branch of the DCI had been ready to intervene in case of a Communist victory. Armed with a Stern machine gun, magazines and 'various hand grenades', Cossiga had been personally part of the paramilitary unit. 'I was armed to the teeth, and I wasn't the only one.' The DCI paramilitaries had arms 'bought with funds put at the disposition of the party'.[19]

After the PCI had been successfully excluded from the government, Italy under the US-supported DCI party was allowed to join the newly created NATO on April 4, 1949 as a founding member. Only a few days earlier, on March 30, 1949, the first post-war military secret service had been created in Italy in close collaboration with the CIA. Placed within the Defence Ministry the clandestine unit was labelled SIFAR and General Giovanni Carlo was nominated to be its first Director. SIFAR during Italy's First Republic repeatedly manipulated Italian politics and through its branch 'Office R' ran and directed the anti-Communist Gladio stay-behind army.[20] 'The contemporaneous joining of NATO and reinstalement of an intelligence capability was more than mere coincidence', secret services expert Philipp Willan correctly observed, 'and gives an insight into the fundamental purpose of the post-war Italian secret service in the intentions of those who sanctioned its rebirth'.[21]

The Secret Service SIFAR was from the very beginning 'regulated by a top-secret protocol imposed by the United States which constitutes a real and complete renunciation of the Italian sovereignty'. According to this protocol, which was coordinated with NATO planning, the obligations of SIFAR towards the CIA headquarters in the United States allegedly included the making available of all intelligence collected and the granting of supervision rights to the United States, above all concerning the choice of SIFAR personnel which at all times had to be CIA approved.[22] SIFAR, in effect, was not a sovereign Italian service but was heavily influenced by the CIA. Or as Paulo Taviani, Italian Defence Minister from 1955 to 1958, during the Gladio investigation put it: The Italian secret services were bossed and financed by 'the boys in Via Veneto', i.e. the CIA in the US embassy in the heart of Rome.[23] Also the Italian Senators did not fail to notice the dominance of the CIA and recorded that 'Gladio was established through an agreement between two secret services, a very important one, the US secret service, and a much less important one, the Italian secret service.'[24]

In 1951 General Umberto Broccoli was made Director of SIFAR and as a member of a 'Secret Committee' regularly met with CIA representatives, the representative of the NATO Command for southern Europe, as well as the representatives of the Italian Army, Navy and Air Force.[25] SIFAR had to guarantee Italy's stability as NATO feared the strong Italian PCI. The Gladio secret army was the central element to achieve this aim. On October 8, 1951 Broccoli wrote to Italian Defence Minister Efisio Marras concerning the training of Gladiators in Great Britain and the supply of arms and explosives from the CIA. Broccoli in his letter explained that the British SIS had offered the training of Italian Gladio officers on the condition that Italy buys arms from the British. At the same time the CIA had offered the weapons for free, but was not as experienced in training as the British. The Italians decided to take the best of both and sent SIFAR Gladio officers to the highly reputable British Special Training Schools while secretly taking the arms from the United States. In 1953 the British realised that they had been fooled and angrily reproached General Musco, successor of Broccoli at the head of SIFAR, protesting that 'his service was delivering itself hook, line and sinker to the Americans'.[26]

Promoting NATO's clandestine anti-Communist policy, representatives of SIFAR regularly participated in the secret Gladio meetings of the NATO command centres ACC and CPC. Shortly before his resignation, Italian President Cossiga in a large television interview elaborated that 'concerned with what might happen to Europe if it were invaded', the secret Gladio army had allegedly been set up in Italy in 1951. 'It was agreed that three countries, the United States, Great Britain and France, would be permanent members, and the rest would be associate members that meant Denmark, Norway, Holland, Belgium, Luxemburg, Greece and Turkey', Cossiga explained with reference to the NATO-linked Gladio command centre CPC. 'Italy was invited to become an associate member. Italy turned down this invitation and instead asked to become a permanent member but did not get an answer at the time. In 1956 Germany joined.' The President insisted that these operations were carried out under the strictest secrecy. 'It was standard policy of NATO to deny the existence of anything that it had been agreed to keep secret.'[27]

In a top-secret document of the US National Security Council signed by Truman on April 21, 1950 the president insisted that 'Italy is a key country for American security' and hence the United States 'has to be prepared to use all their political, economic and, if necessary, military might' in order to stop the PCI. 'In case that the Communists successfully enter the government by legal means, and also in the case that the government should no longer show a strong opposition to both the domestic and foreign Communist threat, the United States have to be prepared to take counter measure', explicitly including an invasion if 'parts of Italy fall under Communist control after an armed insurrection'. US military planning for the upcoming Italian election envisaged that in phase one the 'US military presence in the Mediterranean' would be strengthened. In phase two, the 'alarm phase', US troops would invade Italy upon 'request of the Italian government and after consultation with Great Britain and the other NATO countries'. The troops were to be deployed 'into those zones of the peninsula which are controlled by the government as a demonstration of force'. Finally in 'phase three, red alarm', US 'armed forces in sufficient numbers' were to 'land in Sicily or Sardinia, or in both regions' in order 'to occupy the territory against the indigenous Communist resistance'.[28]

The fears of Washington mounted when on election day in June 1953 despite CIA covert action operations the US-sponsored DCI with 40 per cent of the vote lost 43 seats in parliament compared to its 1948 result and was back to 261. The leftist coalition of Socialists and Communists increased their strength to 35 per cent of the vote and 218 seats. The CIA intensified its secret war for 'there was good reason to fear that if the voting trend between 1948 and 1953 were allowed to continue . . . the combined Communist and socialist vote would grow to become the largest political force in Italy', as William Colby, later to become Director of the CIA under Nixon, rightly analysed.[29] As a first step a more aggressive chief of SIFAR had to be installed. In 1955 high-ranking CIA officer Carmel Offie, a close collaborator of acting CIA chief Allen Dulles, came to Italy and at the US embassy together with CIA Chief of Station (COS) Gerry Miller instructed Claire Boothe Luce, the good-looking US ambassador in Rome, to pressure Italian Defence Minister Paolo Emilio Taviani to promote General Giovanni De Lorenzo. As of January 1956 General De Lorenzo, a solid anti-Communist asset of Washington, directed SIFAR and its Gladio secret armies.[30]

With his moustache, the spectacles and the harsh military appearance, De Lorenzo represented the stereotype of a General of the old school. In a top-secret document dated November 26, 1956 and signed by De Lorenzo he confirmed 'former agreements' between the CIA and SIFAR and stressed that operation Gladio was progressing well.[31] The document contained highly sensitive data and was withheld from the Italian Senate investigation. 'The agreement between SIFAR and the CIA of 1956 concerning the stay-behind organization can not, as of now, be made public as it is a bilateral agreement classified top-secret', acting SIFAR chief Admiral Fulvio Martini explained to the startled Italian Senators who had wrongly worked upon the assumption that SIFAR was answerable to the Italian legislative and not to the CIA. 'The declassification of the document, which I have already requested on December 13, 1990', Martini reasoned, 'is necessarily subordinate to the agreement of the other party involved'.[32]

Among the most important projects of SIFAR Director De Lorenzo ranged the construction of a new headquarters for the secret army for which the CIA had provided 300 million Lira. SIFAR and CIA had agreed that for reasons of secrecy and functionality the Gladio centre should not be erected on the Italian mainland, but on one of the larger islands off the Italian west coast in the Mediterranean. Sardinia was chosen and land was bought. SIFAR Colonel Renzo Rocca, Chief of Office R that ran Gladio, was given the responsibility to supervise the construction of the new Gladio base where secret anti-Communist soldiers were equipped and trained by experts of the American and the British Special Forces.[33] The Gladio headquarters, baptised 'Saboteur's Training Centre' (CAG), was located at Capo Marragiu near the village Alghero. Behind walls and high security electric fences a little harbour was built, underground bunkers erected, strong long-distance radio transmitters were set up, sub-water facilities for frogmen training were installed, and two small runways for planes and a landing area for helicopters were built. Several other specialised buildings were added, serving for shooting and explosives training as well as for ideological lectures.[34]

'I was at Capo Marragiu for the first time in 1959', Gladiator Ennio Colle testified after the discovery of the secret army. On November 27, 1990, Colle had received a letter of SISMI Director to inform him that 'the stay-behind structure has been dissolved'. Gladiator Colle testified that the members of the secret unit were kept in the dark on the larger international framework and had not even known where they were trained: 'I didn't know where I was because we were transported in planes with blacked out windows.' Decimo Garau, a Gladio instructor at CAG who had been trained in Great Britain confirmed to journalists that Italian Gladiators were literally kept in the dark: 'They arrived in a disguised plane and were transferred to a disguised coach. They were then dropped off in front of their quarters. Then training would start.'[35]

'My job, simply put, was to prevent Italy from being taken over by the Communists in the next 1958 elections', CIA agent William Colby revealed and in his memoirs. In autumn 1953 he came to Rome to serve under COS Gerry Miller. With the Gladio secret armies the CIA wanted to 'prevent the NATO military defences from being circumvented politically by a subversive fifth column, the Partito Communista Italiano (or PCI)' in what according to Colby was 'by far the CIA's largest covert political action program undertaken until then'. Next to the Communists the Italian Socialists were also attacked by the CIA with smear campaigns as Washington continued to fund the DCI. 'I had to agree that we will not turn from the Christian Democrat bird in the hand to the socialist birds in the bush.' Colby was successful and in 1958 the DCI gained strength with 42 per cent of the vote and 273 seats, while the Communists received 23 per cent and 140 seats with the Socialists polling but 14 per cent and 84 seats.[36]

Colby much like US President Dwight Eisenhower was fascinated with covert action after the CIA together with the MI6 in 1953 had overthrown the Mossadegh government in Iran and in 1954 toppled Socialist Arbenz in Guatemala. In Italy the manipulation of the election and the secret funding of the DCI 'was so effective that often the Italian recipients of our aid themselves were not certain where the aid was coming from', Colby proudly related. 'CIA's Italian political operations, and several similar ones that were patterned after it in subsequent years, notably Chile, have come under scorching criticism', Colby said in retrospect. 'Now, there can be no denying that "interference" of this sort is illegal. Under the laws of most countries, as under American law, a foreign government is strictly prohibited from involving itself in that nation's internal political process.' However, the Cold Warrior reasoned, the 'assistance to democratic groups in Italy to enable them to meet the Soviet supported subversive campaign there can certainly be accepted as a moral act'.[37]

Sharing in this assessment the Pentagon ordered in a top-secret directive that in 'Operation Demagnetize' the CIA together with the military secret services in Italy and in France start 'political, paramilitary and psychological operations' in order to weaken the Communists in the two countries. The directive of the US Joint Chiefs of Staff dated May 14, 1952 insisted sensitively enough that 'The limitation of the strength of the Communists in Italy and France is a top priority objective. This objective has to be reached by the employment of all means' including by implication a secret war and terrorist operations. 'The Italian and French government may know nothing of the plan "Demagnetize", for it is clear that the plan can interfere with their respective national sovereignty.'[38]

As Colby left Italy for the CIA station in Vietnam, SIFAR Director De Lorenzo in Italy continued his battle against the PCI and the PSI. Under the title 'The Special Forces of SIFAR and Operation Gladio' a top-secret document of the Italian

Defence Department dated June 1, 1959 specified how NATO military planning for unorthodox warfare and anti-Communist covert action operations was coordinated by the CPC directly linked to SHAPE. The document stressed that next to a Soviet invasion, NATO feared 'internal subversion' and, in Italy, specifically an increase of power of the PCI. 'On the national level, the possibility of an emergency situation as above described has been and continues to be the reason for specific SIFAR activities. These special activities are carried out by the section SAD of the Ufficio R', the document explained with reference to the secret Gladio army. 'Parallel to this decision the chief of SIFAR decided, with the approval of the Defence Minister, to confirm the previous accords agreed upon by the Italian secret service and the American secret service with respect to the reciprocal co-operation in the context of the S/B operations (Stay Behind), in order to realize a joint operation.' De Lorenzo's Gladio document concluded that the agreement between CIA and SIFAR with date of November 26, 1956 'constitutes the basis document of Operation "Gladio" (name given to the operations developed by the two secret services)'.[39]

When John F. Kennedy became president in January 1961 the policy of the United States towards Italy changed because Kennedy unlike his predecessors Truman and Eisenhower sympathised with the PSI. He agreed with a CIA analysis that in Italy the 'strength of the socialists, even without aid from outside, means that left-wing sentiment looked forward to a democratic form of socialism'.[40] Yet Kennedy's plans for reform met with stiff resistance from both the US State Department and the CIA. Secretary of State Dean Rusk with horror related to Kennedy that for instance Riccardo Lombardi of the PSI had publicly asked for the recognition of Communist China, had asked for the withdrawal of the American military bases in Italy including the important naval NATO base in Naples and had declared that capitalism and imperialism must be fought. 'Should this be the party with which the United States should deal?'[41]

Ambassador Frederick Reinhardt at the US embassy in Rome together with COS Thomas Karamessines debated how Kennedy could be stopped. Vernon Walters advised them, a notorious CIA Cold Warrior 'who has been involved directly or indirectly in the overthrow of more governments than any other official of the US government'.[42] Walters declared that if Kennedy allowed the PSI to win the elections the US should invade the country. Karamessines, more subtly, suggested that the forces within Italy that opposed the opening to the left should be strengthened.[43] 'The absurd situation developed in which President Kennedy found himself up against the Secretary of State and the Director of the CIA.'[44]

On election day in April 1963 the CIA nightmare materialised: The Communists gained strength while all other parties lost seats. The US-supported DCI fell to 38 per cent, its worst result since the party had been created after the war. The PCI polled 25 per cent and together with the 14 per cent of the triumphant PSI secured an overwhelming victory as for the first time in the First Republic the united left dominated parliament. The supporters of the Italian left celebrated in the streets the novelty that the Socialists were also given cabinet posts in the

Italian government under Prime Minister Aldo Moro of the left-wing of the DCI. President Kennedy was immensely pleased and in July 1963 decided to visit Rome to the great delight of many Italians. The airport was crowded and once again the Americans were greeted with flags and cheers. 'He is a wonderful person. He seems much younger than his real age. He invited me to visit the United States', Pietro Nenni, the leader of the PSI with much enthusiasm declared.[45]

Kennedy had allowed Italy to shift to the left. As the Socialists were given cabinet posts the Italian Communists, due to their performance at the polls, also demanded to be rewarded with posts in the cabinet and in May 1963 the large union of the construction workers demonstrated in Rome. The CIA was alarmed and members of the secret Gladio army disguised as police and civilians smashed the demonstration leaving more than 200 demonstrators injured.[46] But for Italy the worst was yet to come. In November 1963, US President Kennedy was assassinated in Dallas, Texas, under mysterious circumstances. And five months later the CIA with the SIFAR, the Gladio secret army and the paramilitary police carried out a right-wing coup d'état which forced the Italian Socialists to leave their cabinet posts they had held only for such a short period.

Code-named 'Piano Solo' the coup was directed by General Giovanni De Lorenzo whom Defence Minister Giulio Andreotti of the DCI had transferred from chief of SIFAR to chief of the Italian paramilitary police, the Carabinieri. In close cooperation with CIA secret warfare expert Vernon Walters, William Harvey, chief of the CIA station in Rome, and Renzo Rocca, Director of the Gladio units within the military secret service SID, De Lorenzo escalated the secret war. Rocca first used his secret Gladio army to bomb the offices of the DCI and the offices of a few daily newspapers and thereafter blamed the terror on the left in order to discredit both Communists and Socialists.[47] As the government was not shaken, De Lorenzo in Rome on March 25, 1964 instructed his secret soldiers that upon his signal they were to 'occupy government offices, the most important communication centres, the headquarters of the leftist parties and the seats of the newspapers closest to the left, as well as the radio and television centres. Newspaper agencies were to be occupied strictly for the time only that it takes to destroy the printing machines and to generally make the publication of newspapers impossible.'[48] De Lorenzo insisted that the operation had to be carried out with 'maximum energy and decisiveness, free of any doubts or indecisiveness' and, as the Gladio investigation put it, made his men 'feverish and biting'.[49]

The Gladiators equipped with proscription lists naming several hundred persons had the explicit order to track down designated Socialists and Communists, arrest and deport them to the island of Sardinia where the secret Gladio centre was to serve as a prison. The document on 'The Special Forces of SIFAR and Operation Gladio' had specified that 'As for the operating headquarters, the Saboteur's Training CAG is being protected by a particularly sensitive security system and equipped with installations and equipment designed to be useful in case of an emergency.'[50] In an atmosphere of greatest tension the secret army was ready to start the coup. Then, on June 14, 1964, De Lorenzo gave the go-ahead and with his troops entered Rome with tanks, armoured personnel carriers, jeeps and grenade launchers while NATO forces staged a large military manoeuvre in the area to intimidate the Italian government. Cunningly the General claimed that the show of muscle was taking place on the eve of the 150th anniversary of the founding of the Carabinieri and, together with feverishly anti-Communist Italian President Antonio Segni of the right-wing of the DCI, saluted the troops with a smile. The Italian Socialists noted that somewhat unusually for a parade the tanks and grenade launchers were not withdrawn after the show but stayed in Rome during May and most of June 1964.[51]

Prime Minister Aldo Moro was alarmed and secretly met with General De Lorenzo in Rome. It was of course a 'highly unusual meeting between a Prime Minister in the midst of a political crisis and a General planning to replace him with a sterner regime'.[52] After the meeting the Socialists silently abandoned their Ministerial posts and sent their most moderate Socialists for a second government under Moro. 'Suddenly the political parties realized that they could be replaced. In case of a power vacuum resulting from the failure of the Left, the only alternative would have been an emergency government', Pietro Nenni of the Socialist party recalled years later, this 'in the reality of this country would mean a right-wing government'.[53] After the coup the Gladio traces were covered up. Several years later, in July 1968, investigators wanted to question Gladio commander Renzo Rocca. The Gladiator was willing to cooperate but the day before his testimony was found dead, shot with a pistol through his head, in his private apartment in Rome. A judge who started to follow the assassination track was taken off from the case by higher authorities.[54] 'There is no doubt that the operation corresponded to the interests followed by sectors of the administration of the United States', the Italian Gladio investigation was left to lament, while historian Bernard Cook correctly labelled Piano Solo 'a carbon copy of Gladio'.[55] Italian Gladio scholar Ferraresi after the discovery of the secret army concluded that 'the plan's truly criminal nature has finally been recognized today' and lamented that Piano Solo had had an immense influence 'in obstructing and voiding the content of the first Left coalition – perhaps the only genuine attempt at a reformist government in the entire post-war period'.[56]

Next to staging the coup, General De Lorenzo on the orders of COS Thomas Karamessines secretly monitored the entire Italian elite. Above all he gathered data on 'irregular behaviour', such as extramarital relationships, homosexual relationships and regular contacts with feminine and masculine prostitutes. In the slang of Langley this allowed the CIA and SIFAR to have the Italian elite 'by the balls', and the threatened exposure of compromising details in subsequent years helped to influence politicians, clerics, businessmen, union leaders, journalists and judges alike. De Lorenzo went as far as to install microphones in the Vatican and in the Palace of the Prime Minister in order to allow the CIA to monitor and record top-level conversations in Italy. The discovery of the secret operation came as a massive shock to the Italian population as a parliamentary investigation into the SIFAR revealed that files containing text and pictures on the lives of over

157,000 persons had been set up. Some files were enormous. The dossier on professor Amintore Fanfani, a DCI Senator who had held numerous Ministerial posts including the one of Prime Minister, consisted of four volumes, each as fat as a dictionary.

'The persons were spied upon with cameras making close up pictures from afar, secret systems with which their correspondence was controlled, recordings of what they had said in their phone calls, documentation with pictures of their extramarital relationships or sexual habits.' The parliamentary commission under General Aldo Beolchini did not fail to notice that 'especially data, which could be used as instruments of intimidation' was recorded.[57] In front of the parliamentary investigation De Lorenzo was forced to admit that the United States and NATO had ordered him to set up the files.[58] This confession met the fierce criticism of the parliamentary commission. 'The gravest aspect of this whole affair consists in the fact that a significant part of the secret service activity of SIFAR', the parliamentarians noted, 'consisted in collecting information for the NATO countries and for the Vatican'. The Senators were shocked. 'This situation is incompatible with the constitution. It is an open violation of the national sovereignty, a violation of the principles of liberty and the equality of the citizens, and a constant menace for the democratic balance of our country.'[59]

The silent war of the CIA, however, was beyond the control of the Italian parliamentarians. As the name of the discredited military secret service after the scandal was changed from SIFAR to SID and General Giovanni Allavena was appointed its new Director the parliamentarians ordered De Lorenzo to destroy all secret files. This he did, after he had given a copy both to COS Thomas Karamessines and to SID Director General Giovanni Allavena. It was a remarkable gift, which allowed its possessor to clandestinely control Italy from within. In 1966, General Allavena was replaced as Director of SID by General Eugenio Henke but remained active in the clandestine battle against the Italian left. In 1967, Allavena joined the secret anti-Communist Masonic Lodge organisation of the Freemasons in Italy called 'Propaganda Due', or in short P2, and to its Director Licio Gelli as a very special gift gave a copy of the 157,000 secret files.

Years later it was revealed how much P2 Director Licio Gelli and the CIA had manipulated Italian politics in order to keep the Communists out of power. Gelli was born in 1919 and only partly educated – having been expelled from school at the age of 13 for striking the headmaster. He enrolled at 17 as a volunteer in the Black Shirts and went to fight for Franco in the Spanish Civil War. During the Second World War he was a Sergeant Major in the fascist German Hermann Goering division of the SS and only narrowly escaped the Italian left-wing partisans at the end of the war by fleeing to the US Army. Frank Gigliotti of the US Masonic Lodge personally recruited Gelli and instructed him to set up an anti-Communist parallel government in Italy in close cooperation with the CIA station in Rome. 'It was Ted Shackley, director of all covert actions of the CIA in Italy in the 1970s', an internal report of the Italian anti-terrorism unit confirmed, 'who presented the chief of the Masonic Lodge to Alexander Haig'. According to the document

Nixon's Military adviser General Haig, who had commanded US troops in Vietnam and thereafter from 1974 to 1979 served as NATO's SACEUR, and Nixon's National Security Advisor Henry Kissinger 'authorized Gelli in the fall of 1969 to recruit 400 high ranking Italian and NATO officers into his Lodge'.[60] Gelli's contacts with the United States remained excellent throughout the Cold War. As a sign of trust and respect Gelli was invited in 1974 to the Presidential inauguration ceremonies of Gerald Ford and again in 1977 was present at the inauguration ceremony of President Carter. When Ronald Reagan became President in 1981 Gelli was proud to sit in the first row in Washington. He was Washington's man in Italy and, as he saw, it saved the country from the left: 'I deserve a medal.'[61]

In April 1981, Milan magistrates in the context of a criminal investigation broke into the villa of Licio Gelli in Arezzo and discovered the files of the P2 the existence of which had been unknown. A parliamentary investigation under Tina Anselmi thereafter to the massive surprise of most Italians revealed that the secretive anti-Communist P2 member lists confiscated counted at least 962 members, with total membership estimated at 2,500. The available member list read like a 'Who is Who in Italy' and included not only the most conservative but also some of the most powerful members of the Italian society: 52 were high-ranking officers of the Carabinieri paramilitary police, 50 were high-ranking officers of the Italian Army, 37 were high-ranking officers of the Finance Police, 29 were high-ranking officers of the Italian Navy, 11 were Presidents of the police, 70 were influential and wealthy industrialists, 10 were Presidents of banks, 3 were acting Ministers, 2 were former Ministers, 1 was the President of a political party, 38 were members of parliament and 14 were high-ranking judges. Others on lower levels of the social hierarchy were mayors, Directors of hospitals, lawyers, notaries and journalists. The most prominent member was Silvio Berlusconi, who was elected Prime Minister of Italy in May 2001, by coincidence, almost exactly 20 years after the discovery of the P2.[62]

'We have come to the definite conclusion that Italy is a country of limited sovereignty because of the interference of the American secret service and international freemasonry', Communist member of the Anselmi commission, Antonio Bellocchio, later emphasised and lamented that at the time of the administration of Ronald Reagan the Italian parliamentarians had shied away from investigating the links of P2 to the USA. 'If the majority of the commission had been prepared to follow us in this analysis they would have had to admit that they are puppets of the United States of America, and they don't intend to admit that ever.'[63] The investigation noted that while other Masonic Lodges exist in Germany, Spain, France, Argentina, Australia, Uruguay, Ireland, Greece, Indonesia and most other countries of the world, the headquarters of the Freemasons was in the United States, counting around 5 million members.[64] 'If democracy is a system of rules and procedures which define the parameters within which political action can take place, what happens when alongside this system there is another one whose rules are mysterious, its procedures unknown, its power immense and which is able to protect itself against the formal institutions of democracy by a wall of secrecy?', the parliamentarians asked the obvious question and sharply criticised this 'dangerous side of extra parliamentary activity'.[65]

The US-funded anti-Communist parallel government P2 and the US-funded anti-Communist parallel army Gladio cooperated closely during Italy's First Republic. Licio Gelli, who after the discovery of the P2 had escaped arrest and fled to South America, after the end of the Cold War was happy to confirm that the secret army was made up of staunch anti-Communists. 'Many came from the ranks of mercenaries who had fought in the Spanish Civil War and many came from the fascist republic of Salo. They chose individuals who were proven anti-Communists. I know it was a well-constructed organization. Had Communist strength grown in Italy, America would have assisted us, we would have unleashed another war and we would have been generously supplied with arms from the air.'[66] Gladiators were paid well, Gelli elaborated, for the US spent a lot of money on the network: 'The Americans paid them large sums of money, the equivalent of an excellent salary. And they guaranteed the financial support of the families in case the Gladiator was killed.'[67]

'The aim of Gladio and other similar organizations which existed in all countries of Western Europe was to counter the invasion of the Red Army or the coming to power by coup d'état of the Communist parties', Gelli stressed the twofold function of the secret network. 'That PCI, during all those years, has never come to power, although they have tried to do so repeatedly, is the merit of the Gladio organ-ization.'[68] Gladio researcher Francovich, with an implicit reference to the numerous massacres Italy had suffered from, asked Gelli: 'How far would you have gone in your campaign against Communism?' to which Gelli vaguely replied: 'Ah, number one enemy was Communism [silence] – We were an association of believers – We did not admit non believers – We wanted to stop Communism in its track, eliminate Communism, fight Communism.'[69]

As after the death of Kennedy too, during the administration of President Lyndon Johnson, the Italian Communists and Socialists remained very popular and upheld a strong performance during national elections, the Italian right together with the CIA continued its secret war. Following the success of the Piano Solo coup Gladio commander Renzo Rocca on the orders of the CIA and SIFAR in 1965 organized a public congress of the extreme right in Rome on the topic of 'Counter Revolutionary Warfare' and 'the defence of Italy from Communism by all means'. The Alberto Pollio Institute, a right-wing think tank, fronted for the SIFAR and the CIA as the conference was held at the luxurious Parco dei Principi hotel in Rome from May 3 to May 5, 1965. The right-wing extremists at the meeting endorsed the view that 'the Third World War is already under way, even if it is being fought at a low level of military intensity'. Amongst the speakers, right-winger Eggardo Beltrametti stressed that 'It is a struggle to the last drop of blood and our aim is to eliminate the Communist threat by whatever means. We would prefer non-violent methods but we must not refuse to consider other forms of struggle.'[70] The Italian parliamentary investigation into Gladio found that right-wingers during the now infamous Parco dei Principi conference had repeatedly referred to a mysterious armed parallel structure, only later discovered to be Gladio.[71]

Richard Nixon, who in January 1969 became president of the United States, as well as Richard Helms, who directed the CIA from June 1966 to February 1973 and during his time in office in a right-wing coup d'état installed dictator Pinochet in Chile, shared the analysis of right-wing extremists in Italy. For in yet another nightmare for the CIA in the US embassy in Rome during the elections of 1968 the combined votes of the Socialists and the Communists had once again defeated the DCI while the anti-Vietnam War and anti-violence demonstration of the flower power movement dominated the streets. The backlash came when Junio Valerio Borghese, a leading Italian fascist saved by CIA agent James Angleton after the Second World War, in close collaboration with the CIA in Rome on the night of December 7, 1970 started the second right-wing Gladio coup d'état in Italy. The secret operation was code-named 'Operation Tora Tora' after the Japanese attack on the US ships in Pearl Harbour which had led the United States to enter the Second World War on December 7, 1941. The plan of the coup in its final phase envisaged the involvement of US and NATO warships which were on alert in the Mediterranean.

Exactly like Piano Solo in 1964 the operation called for the arrest of left-wing political and trade union leaders as well as leading journalists and political activists who were to be shipped away and locked up in the Gladio prison on Sardinia. Several hundred armed men under Borghese's commando spread across the country with elite units gathered in Rome. In the dark of the night under the command of notorious international right-wing extremist Stefano Delle Chiaie, one paramilitary unit succeeded in entering the Interior Ministry through the complicity of the police guards. The conspirators sized a consignment of 180 machine guns and sent them out from the ministry in a lorry for their associates. A second unit, as the parliamentary investigation into Gladio found, under right-winger and parachutist Sandro Saccucci had the task to arrest political functionaries. A third armed group, among them Carabinieri of Piano Solo fame, waited in a gym in Rome's Via Eleniana, ready for action. A clandestine unit under the command of General Casero was about to occupy the Defence Ministry in Rome. A squad of fully armed men under the command of General Berti equipped with hand cuffs was only a few hundred meters away from the radio and television headquarters. A group of conspirators under Colonel Amos Spiazzi that night was on its way to occupy Sesto San Giovanni, a working-class suburb of Milan and heartland of Communist electoral support where the CIA expected heavy resistance.[72]

Italy was on the brink of a right-wing coup d'état. But it did not come. Shortly before one o'clock in the dark morning hours of December 8, coup leader Borghese received a mysterious phone call and the Gladio coup was stopped. The conspirators returned to their barracks, and strategic posts already occupied were abandoned. In Chile and in Greece, right-wing governments were installed with a coup d'état after the political left had significantly increased its power. Why had the right-wing coup been stopped in Italy? Members of the Italian Mafia, which the CIA had recruited to support the conspirators, later testified on trial that Soviet intelligence had learned about the planned coup whereupon both Washington and NATO had noticed that numerous Soviet ships were cruising in the Mediterranean. 'Nothing was done and the coup came to nothing, partly because there were a lot of Soviet ships cruising in the Mediterranean at the time', Mafia super grass Tommaso Buscetta testified to anti-Mafia judge Giovanni Falcone in 1984.[73] While Mafia super grass Luciano Liggio lamented: 'They told me that the secret services and the Americans were in favour. I told them to get lost and as a result I was given life sentence at Bari.'[74]

According to the plan of the CIA and Borghese, Italy and the world would have woken up on December 8, 1970 to find a new right-wing conservative government installed in the peninsula. 'The political formula which has governed us for twenty-five years and brought us to the verge of economic and moral collapse has ceased to exist', Borghese planned to greet the population on that morning on television. 'The armed forces, the forces of order, the most competent and representative men in the nation are with us and we can assure you that the most dangerous enemies, to be clear, those who wanted to enslave the fatherland to the foreigner, have been rendered inoffensive.' After that Borghese and his conspirators had intended to implement their governmental program which envisaged: 'Maintenance of the present military and financial commitment to NATO and the preparation of a plan to increase Italy's contribution to the Atlantic Alliance', as well as the appointment of a special envoy to the United States to organise an Italian military contribution to the Vietnam War![75]

Who had made the mysterious phone call after midnight that had stopped the Gladio army? CIA Director William Colby implicitly suggested that it had been President Nixon himself. Colby in his memoirs confirmed that 'Certainly, in Track II in 1970 it [the CIA] sought a military coup, at the direct order of President Nixon.'[76] To Nixon the world was a battlefield where the Communists threatened to take over command and with few scruples at the time of the Tora Tora operation Nixon, next to Vietnam, was also bombing neutral Cambodia killing thousands.[77] The involvement of Nixon was also alleged in Italy by Remo Orlandini, a right-wing wealthy Italian businessman closely involved in the Tora Tora operation. At the headquarters of the SID in 1973 he discussed the coup in confidence with Captain Antonio Labruna. Labruna asked Orlandini about 'the support from abroad'. Orlandini's answer was short, but revealing: 'NATO. And [West] Germany. At the military level, because we don't trust the civilians'. Labruna insisted: 'You must tell me the names, everything, because I know a lot about the international scene', upon which Orlandini replied: 'Look, for America there's Nixon, as well as his entourage.' The signal to stop the Gladio coup had allegedly come from high-ranking NATO officials, Orlandini testified and to Labruna insisted: 'That's why I tell you that you don't have the slightest idea of the scale and the seriousness of the thing.'[78]

Giovanni Tamburino, an investigative magistrate of the Italian city Padua, critically investigated the Tora Tora operation and to his massive surprise already at the time discovered the involvement of a mysterious secret army, later discovered to be Gladio. Thereafter he arrested Vito Miceli, the acting Director of the SID who before had directed NATO's Security Office in Brussels. Tamburino charged Miceli with 'promoting, setting up, and organizing, together with others, a secret association of military and civilians aimed at provoking an armed insurrection to bring about an illegal change in the constitution of the state and the form of government'.[79] His data suggested that a mysterious armed organisation existed within the SID, and as its real code name Gladio had not yet been discovered the structure during questionings was referred to as 'Super-SID'. On trial on November 17, 1974 an angry Miceli shouted: 'A Super SID on my orders? Of course! But I have not organized it myself to make a coup d'état. This was the United States and NATO who asked me to do it!'[80] As the trial dragged on Miceli in 1977 was forced to elaborate: 'There has always been a certain top-secret organization, known to the top authorities of the state and operating in the domain of the secret services, involved in activities that have nothing to do with intelligence gathering . . . If you want details, I can not give them to you.'[81] In 1990 when Prime Minister Andreotti revealed the Gladio secret in front of the Italian parliament, Miceli was greatly annoyed and shortly before his death he shouted at Andreotti's revelation.[82]

Next to Miceli Colonel Amos Spiazzi was also locked up because on the night of the Borghese coup he had gathered his Gladiators in Milan to squash the Communist unions. 'The day of the Borghese Coup, on the evening of December 8, 1970, I received an order to carry out an exercise in the maintenance of public order, using reliable men', Spiazzi in a BBC documentary on Gladio recalled the coup. 'We were to guard certain predetermined locations which could be vulnerable in an uprising' he declared sitting in his home in front of a picture of himself in uniform with erected right hand making the Hitler salute. 'At the time I only knew of a structure made up of people which were certainly anti-Communists, but which could be activated only in the event of an invasion of the nation' the right-winger elaborated on the secret Gladio army. 'I was arrested in 1974 and found myself in an embarrassing situation. The judge was persistently interrogating me until I realized that this judge was probing into something what he thought was something revolutionary or unconstitutional. To me it was an organization for national security.'[83] Right-winger Spiazzi was confused. 'My superiors and the judge belonged to the same system. Could I tell the judge certain things? No, because of military secrecy.' Thus Spiazzi asked the judge to be allowed to talk to SID Director Vito Miceli who clumsily forbade Spiazzi to tell the truth on Gladio. 'He made signs not to say anything [Spiazzi moves his hand imitating the no signal Miceli made in court]. The Judge noticed it. So he was actually saying "yes" [to the existence of Gladio] whilst signalling "no".'[84] In the end 145 Tora Tora conspirators were charged with crimes, of which only 78 were actually brought to trial, of which again only 46 were convicted by a Roman court, only to be acquitted on appeal by a higher court. In what amounted to a massive juridical scandal all Gladiators walked free.

To the distress of the CIA and the Nixon administration, the aborted Tora Tora coup d'état did not stop the Italian left. In the national elections of 1972 the

US-supported DCI with 39 per cent of the votes secured only a very slim advantage over the Communist PCI and Socialist PSI that together held 37 per cent.[85] This despite the fact that on the orders of Nixon, US ambassador Graham Martin in Rome had invested 10 million dollars for covert operations, bribes and support of the DCI, as an investigation of the United States parliament into the CIA under Congressman Ottis Pike found. While Moscow financially supported the PCI, Washington generously supported the DCI, as Pike found: 'CIA reports total US election financing over a previous 20 year period at some 65 million dollars.'[86]

As the Italian Communists and Socialists remained very strong at the polls and controlled large segments of the Italian parliament, it was obvious that they should have been included in the government. Yet it was equally clear that US President Nixon categorically opposed such an opening towards the left for he feared the exposure of NATO secrets. Following the Watergate scandal, covert action enthusiast Nixon was forced to resign on August 8, 1974 and Vice President Gerald Ford entered the White House the next day to declare 'Our long national nightmare is over.'[87] The word was also heard in Italy where many hoped for a new start and therefore acting Italian Foreign Minister Aldo Moro of the DCI together with Italian President Giovanni Leone in September 1974 flew to Washington to discuss the inclusion of the Italian left in the government. Their hopes were shattered. Ford pardoned Nixon for all crimes he had committed during his time in the White House and kept key players of the Nixon administration in office. In a heavy confrontation with Henry Kissinger who under Nixon had served as the President's National Security Advisor and now under Ford held the powerful position of Foreign Minister, the Italian representatives were told that under no circumstances must the Italian left be included in the Italian government. Italy had to remain firmly and strongly within NATO. The visit weighed heavily on Aldo Moro who had already lived through both the Piano Solo Gladio coup and the Tora Tora Gladio coup and hence had no illusions concerning the influence of the United States on Italy's First Republic.

Upon his return to Italy, Moro was sick for days and contemplated his complete withdrawal from politics. 'It's one of the few occasions when my husband told me exactly what had been said to him, without telling me the name of the person concerned', Moro's wife Eleonora later testified. 'I will try and repeat it now: "You must abandon your policy of bringing all the political forces in your country into direct collaboration. Either you give this up or you will pay dearly for it."'[88] In the national elections of June 1976, the PCI secured its best ever result at the polls, 34.4 per cent, and clearly defeated the DCI. Consequently, acting president of the DCI Aldo Moro found the courage to defeat the USA's veto. On March 16, 1978 he packed the documents of the 'historical compromise' (compromesso storico) into his suitcase and ordered his driver as well as his bodyguards to bring him to the palace of the Italian parliament in Rome where he was determined to present the plan to include the Italian Communists in the executive. Moro's car was approaching a crossroads, where Via Mario Fani meets Via Stresa in the residential suburb of Rome where he lived, when a white Fiat suddenly reversed around the corner and blocked the path. Moro's driver had to break abruptly and the escort car following close behind rammed into the back of them. Two men form the white car and a further four who had been waiting in the street opened fire on Moro's five bodyguards. Moro after his return from Washington had become uneasy and had asked for a bulletproof car, yet the request had been turned down. And thus the shots went through the car and his bodyguards were killed right away. One was able to return two shots but together with the two other bodyguards still alive was finished off at close range. Moro himself was captured and held hostage in central Rome for 55 days. Thereafter Moro's bullet ridden body was found in the boot of an abandoned car in central Rome symbolically parked halfway between the headquarters of the DCI and the headquarters of the PCI.

Italy was in shock. The military secret service and acting Prime Minister Giulio Andreotti immediately blamed the left-wing terrorist organisation Red Brigades for the crime and cracked down on the left. 72,000 roadblocks were erected and 37,000 houses were searched. More than 6 million people were questioned in less than two months. While Moro was held captive his wife Eleonora spent the days in agony together with her closest family and friends and even asked the Pope Paul VI, a long-standing friend of her husband, for help. 'He told me he would do everything possible and I know he tried, but he found a lot of opposition.'[89] Captured Moro himself understood that he was the victim of a political crime in which the political right and the United States were instrumentalising the Red Brigades. In his last letter he requested that nobody of the corrupt DCI was to be present at his funeral. 'Kiss and caress everyone for me, face by face, eye by eye, hair by hair', he wrote to his wife and his children fully aware that he was going to die. 'To each I send an immense tenderness through your hands. Be strong, my sweet, in this absurd and incomprehensible trial. These are the ways of the Lord. Remember me to all our relatives and friends with immense affection, and to you and all of them I send the warmest embrace as the pledge of my eternal love. I would like to know, with my small, mortal eyes, how we will appear to one another afterwards.'[90]

The Senate commission investigating Gladio and the massacres suspected the CIA and the Italian military secret service including its Gladio hit squads to have organised the Moro crime. It therefore reopened the case but found with much surprise that almost all files on the Moro kidnapping and murder had mysteriously disappeared from the archives of the Ministry of the Interior. The files contained all official logs of phone calls, letters which had been exchanged between Moro and the government, contacts with the security forces and minutes of meetings made during the 55 days of Moro's kidnapping. The Senate commission sharply criticised that 'the documents of the crisis committee of the Interior Ministry disappeared', highlighted that 'the reflection on the Moro affair must be seen inserted in an evaluation of a broader contest' as 'the phenomena must be considered in the historical reality of the period' and concluded that the Moro assassination was 'a criminal project in which the Red Brigades most probably were instruments of a larger political framework.'[91] The Senate observed with criticism that in 1978 'the administration of the United States first refused to help at all in the investigations on the hostage taking, and later sent one single expert on hostage taking who worked under the direction of the Interior Ministry.'[92]

The tragic history of Italy reached its climax when during Nixon's time in office the political right spread terrorism, blood and panic in Italy and brought the country to the brink of civil war. The terrorists planted bombs in public places and blamed them on the Italian Communists in order to weaken the Communists and the Socialists at the polls. 'The suggested link with the Bologna massacre is potentially the most serious of all the accusations levelled against Gladio', the British press headlined when in 1991 the Italian parliamentary commission investigating Gladio and the massacres had received an anonymous memorandum which suggested that the Bologna bomb had come from a Gladio arsenal.[93] General Gerardo Serravalle, who had commanded the Gladio units within the SID in Italy from 1971 to 1974, later confirmed with much regret that at times some Gladio members 'could pass from a defensive, post-invasion logic, to one of attack, of civil war'.[94] When in a BBC interview he was asked why, given this manifest danger, he did not decide to close down the network, Serravalle replied: 'Well, closing down is a political decision, it is not in my sphere of competence to close down the Gladio operation.'[95]

It was the CIA that controlled the Italian secret army and as General Serravalle raised his concerns regarding the domestic operations of the secret army, he met the fierce opposition of the Chief of the CIA station in Rome, Howard Stone, who stopped to send CIA supplies. 'When I took over command I noticed that the American financing, agreed in bilateral accords and in particular the shipping of material and armaments to us had stopped.' Serravalle was angered and asked Stone to come to the Gladio headquarters in Sardinia. The COS came with CIA officer Mike Sednaoui, and Serravalle according to his own testimony said to them: 'This is our training etc., you could help us achieve our full potential. So why cut your aid? If this is your government's position, we accept it. But you owe us an explanation.' Thereafter he realised 'that the CIA interests, as represented by these officials weren't really concerned with the level we had reached in training but rather on the subject of internal control. That is, our level of readiness to counter street disturbances, handling nation-wide strikes and above all any eventual rise of the Communist Party. Mr Stone stated, quite clearly, that the financial support of the CIA was wholly dependent on our willingness to put into action, to program and plan these other – shall we call them – internal measures.'[96]

'It emerges without the shadow of a doubt that elements of the CIA started in the second half of the 1960s a massive operation in order to counter by the use of all means the spreading of groups and movements of the left on a European level', the official Italian Senate investigation into Gladio and the massacres concluded in 1995 in its 370-pages strong final report. 'The final picture which emerges from the analysis is one of a country which for more than 40 years has lived through a difficult frontier situation. Obviously, the tensions which have characterised these 40 years and which were the object of the analysis had also social and therefore internal roots. However, such tensions would never have lasted so long, they would not have taken on such tragic dimensions as they did, and the path towards the truth would not have been blocked so many times, if the internal political situation would not have been conditioned and supervised by the international framework into which Italy was integrated.'[97]

Due to the brutality of the history of Italy's First Republic – which according to official figures in the terror years between 1969 and 1987 had claimed the enormously high death toll of 491 civilians, while 1,181 were left injured and maimed – this was too weak a formulation for those Senators in the parliamentary Gladio committee belonging to the Italian left. Under the chairmanship of Senator Pellegrini they therefore continued to investigate, heard witnesses and evaluated documents. In June 2000 they presented their final report on 326 pages and concluded that 'those massacres, those bombs, those military actions had been organized or promoted or supported by men inside Italian state institutions and, as has been discovered more recently, by men linked to the structures of United States intelligence.'[98]

In order to support this far-reaching conclusion, the Gladio report 2000 included the testimonies of selected Gladiators. Secret soldier Giuseppe Tarullo, who had entered the SIFAR in 1961, had testified to the Senators that next to the invasion preparations it had been their task to control the Italian Communists: 'We among us also spoke of the internal task of Gladio. It was said that the structure and its foreign connections would also have been activated against a domestic subversion by support of the Special Forces. By domestic subversion we understood a change of government which did not respect the will of the ruling authority.'[99] Gladiator Giuseppe Andreotti to the Senators put it like that: 'The Gladio structure was the answer to an internal logic, in that sense, as I have already said, that it had to react against the taking of power in Italy of regimes hated by the population . . . thus dictatorships of the right or the left.'[100]

Gladiator Manlio Capriata, who in the SIFAR in the rank of General had directed office R from February to June 1962, testified to the Senators: 'I confirm that the V section, thus the organisation S/B [stay-behind] and thus the CAG [Gladio centre Centro Addestramento Guastatori in Sardinia] had an anti-subversive function for the case that the forces of the left should come to power.'[101] By now enough evidence had surfaced and member of the commission Senator Valter Bielli drew the conclusion: 'I am convinced that the intervention of the Americans in Italy is now a historically proven fact.' The Clinton administration in Washington was embarrassed and in summer 2000 refused to comment while in Rome at the US embassy a source which wished to remain unnamed declared: 'These are allegations that have come up over the last 20 years and there is absolutely nothing to them.'[102]

Senator Bielli remained firm and made it clear that: 'They interfered to prevent the Communist party from achieving power by democratic means. The Communist threat no longer exists and it would be appropriate if the Americans themselves helped us to clarify what happened in the past.' As the Soviet Union opened its archives the United States remained tight-lipped. 'During the Cold War the east was under Communist domination, but the west too had become, in a certain sense, an American colony', Bielli lamented. Aldo Giannuli, a historian working as a consultant to the parliamentary commission on Gladio and terrorism correctly stressed that the stay-behind now had to be investigated internationally based on NATO documents: 'The real issue today is gaining access to NATO's archives.'[103]

7

THE SECRET WAR IN FRANCE

The invasion and occupation of France by the German army in the Second World War represented the most traumatic experience of France in the last century. Already on June 14, 1940 Paris had fallen. While right-wing segments of the French military and political elite under General Philippe Pétain collaborated with Hitler's occupation army and set up a fascist government in Vichy, French General Charles de Gaulle fled to London and on radio declared to the French population that he represented the legitimate French government. De Gaulle insisted that the war against the occupiers must and will continue. In order to collect intelligence in France, make liaison with the local French resistance and carry out sabotage operations in enemy-held territory General de Gaulle in London created the French secret service BCRA (Bureau Central de Renseignement et d'Action). BCRA agents were dropped by parachute into France and carried out their secret missions at the cost of very high casualties. In its mission, training and equipment, the BCRA, which was closed down before the war had ended, was a forerunner of the French secret army and many secret soldiers of the Cold War had formerly fought as BCRA agents. After the Normandy invasion on June 6, 1944 and the liberation of France led by the United States, General de Gaulle triumphantly re-entered Paris and became Prime Minister. General Pétain who had collaborated with Hitler was sentenced to death, then pardoned and imprisoned for life.

With the end of the Second World War the Fourth French Republic (1945–1958) was born, characterised by a highly unstable political and military situation in which the various parties competed for influence.[1] On the left the French Communist Party (PCF), above all due to its leading role of resisting the fascist Vichy collaborators during wartime, was very popular among the population and locked for power in the post-war government. 'The PCF had gained enormous prestige and a sort of moral pre-eminence for having spearheaded the Resistance... its patriotic credentials were unchallenged.'[2] On the right, Vichy collaborators in the military and powerful groups within the French business society most vehemently rejected the idea of seeing France coming under Communist control, no matter whether such a situation would be reached by a Communist coup d'état, or by a democratic election victory of the PCF. Most importantly the United States as well as Great Britain were strictly opposed to the PCF whom they considered to

THE SECRET WAR IN FRANCE

be strongly dependent on Moscow. Therefore, similar to Italy, a secret war continued also in France after 1945 roughly along the lines of PCF and Communist labour unions on one side against the CIA and segments of the French political, military and police apparatus on the other side.

'To start with, they [the CIA] want to stop the left from coming to power, and want even more to stop Communist participation in the government. For the CIA this is evidently the priority of priorities, as it is in all the countries of the Atlantic alliance', former CIA agent Philip Agee later commented on this secret Cold War in France.[3] For nowhere in Western Europe, with the exception of Italy, were the Communists as strong as in France in the post-war years. Washington feared that Moscow might urge the PCF to seize power in France with a coup. But Stalin, the leader of the Soviet Union, did not encourage the PCF to follow such a strategy and although young and enthusiastic French Communists anticipated something more adventurous, the old and established PCF leadership did not plan to take power by force. They rightly saw that this would relegate them to the political ghetto, if they were not simply crushed by the American Army, which after the liberation of Western Europe was still stationed in France. The PCF had more to win if it stuck to democratic election procedures.

Prime Minister de Gaulle included two Communist Ministers in his newly founded cabinet and at the same time in November 1944 was able to convince the strong French Communist resistance army to peacefully hand over their arms in return for a promise for fair and democratic elections. The municipal elections in the spring of 1945 brought an overwhelming victory for the PCF, which polled strongest and secured 30 per cent of the vote. The two other competitors, the newly founded MRP party (Mouvement Républicain Populaire) and the French Socialists, came second and third, with 15 and 11 per cent respectively. This pattern was confirmed in the first national elections on October 21, 1945 when the victorious PCF got 26 per cent of the vote and 160 seats in the Constituent Assembly, while the Socialists came in second with 24 per cent and 142 seats, while the MRP ranked third with 23.6 per cent. Together the two left-wing parties had a bare majority.

Despite the clear election victory of the PCF and despite his promises, Prime Minister de Gaulle refused to give the PCF key ministries in his cabinet. The PCF protested loudly when they were assigned but four minor posts including Economy, Armaments, Industrial Production and Labour, with Communist Secretary-General Maurice Thorez named as Minister of State. In a dramatic showdown the Communists used their power in parliament and sharply condemned the ongoing French War to regain control over the Vietnam colony. Communist parliamentarian Jeannette Vermeersch criticised that in burning Vietnamese villages the French were 'committing the same kind of atrocities' the Nazis had committed in France but a few years earlier. The remark left the French parliament in tumult and its president insisting: 'Madame, I tell you very politely that ... you intolerably insult both this Assembly and the Nation!' As Vermeersch insisted, the president of the assembly in consternation uttered: 'Madame, I never believed a woman capable of such hatred.' To which Vermeesch responded: 'Yes, I hate. I do when I think of the millions of workers you exploit. Yes, I hate the majority of this Assembly!'[4]

Conservative members of the French society were greatly worried about the radicalism of the PCF and shocked when the latter in protest of their unfair representation in the executive proposed two bills, one of which limited the powers of the executive while the other cut the military budget by 20 per cent. When the two bills passed the Communist-dominated parliament, De Gaulle resigned dramatically on January 20, 1946. But the struggle for power in France continued as the PCF proposed to divide the ministries of the executive among the Communists and the Socialists, for indeed nothing else would have reflected the will of the French people as expressed at the democratic elections more adequately. Yet the French Socialists objected. They realised clearly that France, much like Italy at the same time, had but limited sovereignty, as the USA would not give a leftist French regime the Marshall plan economic aid France so desperately needed.

The position of the White House in Washington increasingly contradicted the democratic will expressed at the polls in France as on November 10, 1946 in the national elections for the French parliament the PCF once again emerged as the leading party, securing almost 29 per cent of the vote, their highest total ever, while both the MRP and the Socialists declined slightly. The fascination and strength of Communism in France remained unbroken. In Western Europe in terms of size and influence the PCF were only equalled by the strong PCI in Italy. In Switzerland the Communist Party had been outlawed, the British Communist Party was only very small and subordinate to the strong British Labour Party, and also in Belgium the comparatively influential Communists only held minor posts in the ministry. Yet the PCF could claim around one million members. Its daily newspaper, *L'Humanité*, was, together with its evening counterpart, *Ce Soir*, the most widely read paper in France, and the PCF controlled the nation's largest youth organisations (including the 'Union des Jeunesses Républicaines') as well as the largest and biggest Labour unions (including the large Confederation Generale du Travail, CGT).

The US ambassador to France, Jefferson Caffrey, a staunch anti-Communist, week after week sent alarming reports to US President Truman in the White House. Washington and the US secret service were convinced that the PCF had to be attacked and defeated in a secret war. General Hoyt Vandenberg, Director of CIG (predecessor of the CIA), on November 26, 1946 in a memorandum warned Truman that due to their strength the PCF could seize power whenever they wanted: 'In discounting the possibility that a French Government could be formed excluding the Communists, Ambassador Caffrey asserts...that the Communists now have sufficient strength to seize power in France whenever they may deem it desirable to do so.' Vandenberg highlighted that US intelligence indicated that, however, the PCF did not intend to use its strength to seize power in France by coup d'état. 'The failure of the Communists to seize power in these circumstances', Vandenberg continued, 'is attributed to (1) their appreciation that it is preferable to attain it by legal processes, and (2) the fact that to do so would be contrary to the present policy of the Kremlin'.[5]

On the initiative of the US and the British Special Forces SAS a secret army was set up in France under the cover name 'Plan Bleu' (Blue Plan) whose task was to secretly prevent the powerful PCF from coming to power. The Blue Plan, in other words, aimed to prevent France from turning red. Victor Vergnes, one of the French secret soldiers who were recruited for the Plan Bleu army, recalled that in the immediate post-war years the stimulus had come from the British. 'At the time I lived in Sète in the house of commander Benet, a DGER officer formerly active in missions in India. Numerous meetings took place during that time in his house.' The SAS, specialised in secret warfare, contacted the newly created French secret service Direction Generale des Etudes et Recherches (DGER) and agreed with them to set up a secret army in northern France across the Channel in the Bretagne. 'One day', Vergnes recalled, 'after he had been visited by lieutenant Earl Jellicoe of the SAS, he said to me: "We are setting up a secret army, especially in the Bretagne area".'[6]

The cells of the secret army soon spread across all of France. Involved were numerous agents and officers of the DGER. It was noteworthy that the DGER under Director André Devawrin included also members of the Communist resistance. Conservative agents and above all the United States considered the presence of Communists in the DGER to represent a security risk. This applied above all to top-secret operations targeting the French Communists such as Plan Bleu. Therefore the DGER was closed down in 1946 and replaced by a staunch anti-Communist new military secret service SDECE under Henri Alexis Ribiere. With the replacement of the DGER by the SDECE, the Communists lost an important battle in the secret war in France as the SDECE became its most dangerous opponent. Trained anti-Communists from the civil war in Greece were recruited as the SDECE shifted to the right. 'The Anglo-Americans were in close contact with the conspirators, above all with Earl Jellicoe, who had just come back from his anti-Communist operations in Greece.'[7]

As France suffered from large Communist strikes which paralysed the entire country, Plan Bleu agents secretly collected money from wealthy industrialists to fund their anti-Communist secret war. 'I met the Peugeot brothers in their offices', agent Vergnes recalled his clandestine contacts to the French automobile industry. 'We discussed what should be done in case of occupation and general strikes in the firms. For two months we have worked on the details of an action plan. We were divided into sections. We had cars, garages and hotels.'[8] When a massive strike at the Renault car manufacturing plant occurred supported by the PCF and the CGT union, the tensions in France increased. Socialist Prime Minister Paul Ramadier ordered a freeze on wages contrary to the workers, demand for more money. It was eyeball to eyeball. The Communists voted against Ramadier's freeze on wages, while the Socialists urged Ramadier not to resign whereupon in an unexpected manoeuvre Prime Minister Ramadier on May 4, 1947 with his powers as Prime Minister ousted the Communist ministers from his cabinet. Very surprised, the latter took the operation stoically and left, believing it to be only temporary. Yet for over 30 years the PCF was not to return to the council chamber of the French executive. Only later it was discovered that Washington had been secretly involved in the silent coup. 'General Revers, the French Chief of Staff, later reported that the American government had urged Ramadier to remove the PCF Ministers.' Specifically, 'the Socialists discussed the matter beforehand with Ambassador Caffery' who had made it clear to the French Socialists that American economic aid would not be forthcoming as long as the Communists remained in the executive.[9]

One month after having ousted the Communists from the government the French Socialists attacked the military right and the CIA and exposed the Plan Bleu secret army. On June 30, 1947 French Socialist Minister of the Interior Edouard Depreux lifted the secret and declared to a baffled population that a secret right-wing army had been erected in France behind the back of the politicians with the task to destabilise the French government. 'Towards the end of 1946 we got to know of the existence of a black resistance network, made up of resistance fighters of the extreme-right, Vichy collaborators and monarchists', Depreux explained. 'They had a secret attack plan called "Plan Bleu", which should have come into action towards the end of July, or on August 6 [1947].'[10]

According to the far-reaching allegations of the French Interior Minister the CIA and the MI6 together with French right-wing paramilitaries had planned to stage a coup d'état in France in summer 1947. In the wake of the revelations several arrests and investigations followed. Among the arrested conspirators was Earl Edme de Vulpian. His castle 'Forest' close to Lamballe in the north of France had served as the headquarters for the final coup preparations. Investigating commissioner Ange Antonini found 'heavy weapons, battle orders, and operation plans' on the castle. The plans revealed that as an essential component of the secret war the Plan Bleu conspirators had intended to escalate the already tense political climate in France by committing acts of terror, blame them on the left, and thus create suitable conditions for their coup d'état, a 'strategy of tension' also carried out during the secret anti-Communist wars in Greece, Italy and Turkey. 'It was even planned to assassinate de Gaulle in order to increase the public resentment', French secret service expert Faligot relates.[11]

While admitting that a secret war was being waged in France in the post-war years, other sources have categorically rejected the claim that the conspirators would indeed have staged a right-wing coup d'état in 1947. 'When Minister of the Interior Depreux revealed the Plan Bleu dossier, his intention was to deal out a blow to the right, after having previously dealt a blow to the left', Luc Robet, himself directly involved with the conspiracy, claimed with reference to the ousting of the Communists from the executive in the previous month. 'Furthermore it was a move to weaken the French army, which had a mentality of making its own politics.'[12] Surprisingly the investigation of the role of the SDECE in the conspiracy was lead by SDECE Director Henri Ribiere himself. He concluded that the CIA and the MI6 were to blame as they had promoted Plan Bleu, although they had allegedly never envisaged a coup d'état. 'The arms which were found all over the country had been paid in parts by London and Washington. Yet they had been provided to resist the Communists, and not to stage a coup d'état', the investigators concluded.[13]

On the suggestion of US ambassador Caffery, who closely supervised the secret war against the Communists in France, the CIA, following the coup that had ousted the Communists from the executive in late 1947 targeted the strong Communist labour union CGT, the very backbone of Communist strength in France. US General Vandenberg in his memorandum to President Truman had correctly emphasised that the Communist's 'capabilities of economic pressure through the CGT or of resort to force are, as Ambassador Caffery suggests, significant principally as guarantees against their exclusion from the Government'.[14] The CIA succeeded to create a schism in the Communist-dominated CGT, splitting away the moderate Force Ouvrière, which by the early 1950s it supported with more than one million dollars per year.[15] The secret operation greatly diminished the strength of the PCF.

Last but not least the secret war of the CIA in the Fourth Republic targeted also the French police. After in the spring of 1947 the Communist Ministers had been expelled from the French government the whole administration was purged from Communists while the anti-Communists were promoted in the police forces. Prominent among them was commissar Jean Dides who during the Second World War had closely cooperated with the OSS and now was promoted to become the commander of a clandestine French paramilitary anti-Communist police unit operating under Interior Minister Jules Moch. The embassy of the United States was pleased with the progress made and in early 1949 cabled to the US State Department in Washington that in order 'to fight the danger of Communism, France has organised cells of restrained but efficient policemen . . . Also Italy is erecting such anti-Communist police squads under the control of Interior Minister Mario Scelba, using commanders of the former fascist police.'[16]

Together with other commanders of anti-Communist police forces engaged in the secret war in Western Europe, Dides regularly took part in the meetings of 'Paix et Liberté', a large CIA front under the leadership of French anti-Communist Jean-Paul David.[17] American historian Christopher Simpson estimated that covert action units such as 'Paix et Liberté' were funded by the CIA during the secret war against the Communists with 'well over a billion dollars yearly'.[18] With branches in several European countries, 'Paix et Liberté' carried out CIA operations in psychological warfare in Western Europe and spread anti-Communist propaganda by printing posters, sponsoring a radio program, publishing printed material in various outlets and organising occasional demonstrations. In Italy the CIA branch of Paix et Liberté directed by Edgardo Sogno was called Pace e Liberta with headquarters in Milan. In 1995 the Italian Senate investigation into Gladio and secret warfare found that Paix et Liberté had operated on the direct orders of NATO. Allegedly French Foreign Minister Georges Bidault had in 1953 suggested in NATO's Atlantic Council that Paix et Liberté should head a reorganisation of NATO's Intelligence Service and serve as a centre and motor for the coordination of international actions against Cominform.[19] Irwin Wall in his history of the influence of the United States on post-war France judged that along with Force Ouvrière 'Paix et Liberté accounted for the major part of the CIA's effort to promote mass non-Communist organisations in France during the 1950s.'[20]

The secret war against the Communists did not end when Plan Bleu was exposed and closed down in 1947. Much to the contrary, French Socialist Prime Minister Paul Ramadier saw to it that his trusted chiefs within the military secret service were not removed by the scandal. When the storm had passed he ordered Henri Ribiere, Chief of SDECE, and Pierre Fourcaud, deputy Director of the SDECE, in late 1947 to erect a new anti-Communist secret army under the code name 'Rose des Vents' (Rose of the Winds, i.e. Compass Rose), the star-shaped official symbol of the NATO. The code name was well chosen, for when NATO was created in 1949 with headquarters in Paris the SDECE coordinated its anti-Communist secret war closely with the military alliance.[21] The secret soldiers understood that within its maritime original context the compass rose is the card pattern below the compass needle according to which the course is set, and according to which corrections are undertaken if the ship is in danger of stirring off course.

As the secret cooperation with the United States intensified in April 1951 the French SDECE opened a station in Washington.[22] According to the overall CIA and NATO planning for anti-Communist secret warfare in Western Europe the Rose des Vents army within the SDECE had the task to locate and fight subversive Communist elements within the French Fourth Republic. Furthermore it had to undertake evacuation preparations and provide for a suitable exile base abroad. The Rose des Vents secret army was trained to undertake sabotage, guerrilla and intelligence-gathering operations under enemy occupation. France was divided into numerous geographical stay-behind zones, to which secret cells were allocated, with each zone being supervised by an SDECE officer. An exile base for the French government was installed in Morocco in northern Africa, and the SDECE sent some of its microfilmed archives to Dakar in Senegal.[23]

Maybe the most famous member of the French secret anti-Communist Rose des Vents army was Francois Grossouvre who in 1981 became the adviser of Socialist President Francois Mitterand for secret operations. During the Second World War Grossouvre had enrolled in a fascist Vichy-backed militia that he later claimed to have infiltrated on behalf of the resistance. After the war the military secret service recruited him for the Rose des Vents secret army. SDECE agent Louis Mouchon who had himself recruited many secret soldiers for the network recalled how Grossouvre had been contacted: 'Our responsible man in Lyon, Gilbert Union, who during the war had carried out missions for the BCRA, was a passionate car driver and at that time had died on the road. To replace him, the SDECE had recruited, in 1950, Francois de Grossouvre.' Mouchin elaborated that Grossouvre was not only chosen for his wartime experience but as well for his contacts: 'His business, the A. Berger et Cie Sugar company, offered ample opportunities to stage fronts. He really had excellent contacts.'[24]

As special adviser of President Mitterand, Grossouvre influenced French secret warfare in the beginning of the 1980s but was eased out of his main responsibilities in 1985 as his cloak-and-dagger style became intolerable to Mitterrand's staider colleagues. Yet the personal relations to Mitterand allegedly remained good and when in late 1990 after the pan European Gladio discoveries President Mitterand in the midst of the scandal had to close down the French Gladio network 'he had first consulted his "grey eminence", Francois Grossouvre'.[25] By the time of Grossouvre's death his participation in the secret war was no longer a secret. 'He was recruited into the French espionage service and helped to organise Gladio, an American-backed plan to create an armed resistance movement in Western Europe against a Russian invasion', the British Economist noted in his obituary after Grossouvre, aged 76, had dramatically shot himself in the Elysée Palace on April 7, 1994.[26]

Retired CIA officer Edward Barnes during the French Fourth Republic had served as liaison officer to the French stay-behind Rose des Vents and left the country in 1956. After the discovery of the secret armies in 1990 he recalled how not only Washington but also many Frenchmen had been greatly concerned that the strong French Communists should come to dominate the country. 'There were probably a lot of Frenchmen who wanted to be ready if something happened.' Resisting a Soviet occupation according to Barnes was the primary motivation of the French Gladio, while promoting anti-Communist political activity in France 'might have been a secondary consideration'.[27] According to Barnes the French stay-behind program consisted of 'several dozen' men individually recruited by the CIA, each of whom was to build a small network of his own recruits. If in analogy to other Gladio countries each Gladiator recruited and trained another ten men then Barnes might have been implying that the French Gladio program numbered around 500 secret soldiers.

The exact number of participants in the secret war against the Communists is very hard to specify. The Paris-based *Intelligence Newsletter* reported after the discovery of the secret CIA armies that 'a director of French intelligence at the time had offered to place at the disposal of the CIA some 10,000 trained and armed "patriotic" troops, outside the ranks of the French armed forces' trained to intervene in a secret war 'in case a Communist government came to power'. According to Barnes the CIA 'had no record of how many people would come out of the woodwork. There was no way to calculate that. Those I met were farmers, townspeople, trades people.' Many did not need much training as they were war veterans and during the Second World War had served in the BCRA secret operations unit behind enemy lines.[28]

In order to guarantee the material independence of the secret soldiers the CIA together with the SDECE set up secret Gladio arms caches across the country. 'All kinds of things were stuck away in remote places, almost anything people would think might be needed', including arms, explosives, gold coins and bicycles, while radio equipment and codes were the top priority. In order to keep the network top-secret the need-to-know principle limiting information to the smallest number of people possible was strictly followed. Barnes stressed that he could only meet with about ten CIA recruits 'for fear of blowing me and blowing them. You couldn't go out and just say "Dig this stuff up, Joe." There were probably all kinds of things that went awry. Some of those guys didn't bury things where they said they did.'[29]

The Italian Defence Ministry knew that the SDECE together with the CIA was running a secret army to oppose the Communists. General Umberto Broccoli in October 1951 wrote to Defence Minister Marras that secret armies existed in the Netherlands, Belgium, Norway, Denmark, and also 'France has already organised such operations in Germany and Austria, as well as on its own national territory up to the Pyrenees.'[30] How far the French secret army spread into the zones of Austria and Germany occupied after their defeat in the Second World War remains unclear, but estimates are that secret operations were limited to the respective sectors controlled by the French troops until the allied forces withdrew from the two countries. Italian Prime Minister Giulio Andreotti in October 1990 in his report 'The so called "Parallel SID" – The Gladio Case' confirmed that the secret anti-Communist armies had standing links to NATO and elaborated that 'Resistance networks were organised by Great Britain in France, the Netherlands, Belgium and probably also in Denmark and Norway. The French took care of the German and Austrian territories under its control, as well as of its own territory up to the Pyrenees.'[31]

A top-secret memorandum of the US Joint Chiefs of Staff, dated May 14, 1952 and entitled 'Operation Demagnetise', detailed how 'political, paramilitary and psychological operations' shall be employed according to the directive in order 'to reduce the strength of the Communist Party in Italy' and also 'in order to reduce the strength of the Communist Party in France'.[32] 'The final aim of the plan is to reduce the strength of the Communist parties, their material resources, their influence in the Italian and French governments and particularly in the unions', the secret Pentagon paper specified, 'in order to reduce as much as possible the danger that Communism could gain strength in Italy and France and endanger the interests of the United States in the two countries'. The secret CIA armies run by the SDECE were instructed and trained within this strategic context, for, as the document specified, 'the limitation of the strength of the Communists in Italy and France is a top priority objective. This objective has to be reached by the employment of all means'. The war had to remain strictly secret and 'the Italian and French government may know nothing of the plan "Demagnetise", for it is clear that the plan can interfere with their respective national sovereignty'.[33]

Training of the Rose des Vents secret soldiers took place in various parts in France and abroad in close cooperation with French Special Forces. Above all the highly trained French special operations parachute commando regiment '11th Demi-Brigade Parachutiste du Choc' or, in short, 11th du Choc was directly involved. The relationship with the secret army was intimate and in several cases officers of the 11th du Choc served also as members of the secret Rose des Vents army. As the British SAS carried out secret operations and dirty tricks for the MI6, the French 11th du Choc after the Second World War served as the iron fist of the SDECE. According to French Gladio author Brozzu-Gentile 'the instructors of the French stay-behind were all members of the SDECE, or close to the service'.[34] At the time of the 1990 Gladio scandal the French press revealed that the French Gladiators had received their training on the use of arms, the manipulation of explosives, and the observation and usage of transmitters in the Centre d'Entrainement des Reserves Parachutistes (CERP) of the 11th du Choc in Cercottes, near Orléans in the south of Paris, in the 11th du Choc training centre Fort Montlouis in the Pyrenees mountains, close to the French Spanish border, as well as in the training centre of the 11th Choc in Calvi on the northern coast of the French Mediterranean island Corsica, close to the Italian Gladio headquarters on the island Sardegna.[35]

As the leading military unit in secret warfare and dirty tricks the 11th du Choc operated above all in Indochine and Africa as France after the Second World War struggled in vain to hold on to its colonies Vietnam and Algeria. 'The unit to carry out the dirty tricks, the iron spear of the secret war in Algeria from 1954 to 1962, was clearly the 11th battalion Parachutiste du Choc', French secret service author Roger Faligot observed.[36] By 1954, 300 men of this special force had arrived in Algeria. Most of them had extensive covert action and anti-guerrilla experience as they came directly from Vietnam after France had lost its colony Indochine in the same year after the battle of Dien Bien Phu. One of the most prominent members of the 11th du Choc was Yves Guerain-Serac, a notorious secret soldier who had served in Korea and Vietnam and later became directly involved in the operations of the Portuguese secret anti-Communist army. Italian secret Gladio soldier and right-wing terrorist Vincenzo Vinciguerra from behind prison bars admired Guerain Serac as a fascinating personality and unmatched strategist of terror.[37]

As the secret war against the Communists in France and the secret war against the Algerian Liberation Front FLN in northern Africa intensified, the dangers of secret warfare became apparent when the politicians in Paris lost control over their secret soldiers and the entire country was dragged into a major crisis that culminated with the end of the Fourth Republic. In May 1958 the independence fight of the French colony Algeria started in earnest. The weakened government of the French Fourth Republic was unsure how to react while the French secret service and military were firmly committed to keeping Algeria a French colony. Many of the politicised men within the ranks of the military and the SDECE viewed the politicians of the Fourth Republic as 'weak, potentially or actively corrupt, a pusillanimous category of humanity whose predisposition was to cut and run in Algeria'.[38] When the first French prisoners were killed by the FLN in Algeria, secret war experts within the French secret services and military started to plan for a coup d'état to overthrow the government in Paris and install a new regime.

Within this process the 11th du Choc played a central role on both sides of the battle. On May 24, 1958, elements of the 11th du Choc based in Calvi on the northern shores of Corsica started the coup by leading the occupation of the entire island by paratroops. Soon the news spread that the secret soldiers intended to overthrow the elected government and bring retired General Charles de Gaulle back into power. As other members of the 11th du Choc disagreed with such an undemocratic secret war against Paris, they left their Cercottes training base near Orléans on the same day and gathered in order to protect targets designated by Gaullist plotters and the paramilitary units that supported them.[39] One of the targets of the Gaullist plotters was the chief of the SDECE himself, General Paul Grossing. When the latter caught wind of the plan, he immediately surrounded the SDECE headquarters on Paris' boulevard Mortier with members of the 11th du Choc loyal to him.

France in that May 1958 sank into chaos. The chief of the powerful French domestic secret service DST (Direction de la Surveillance du Territoire), Roger Wybot, was about to activate a secret anti-Communist plan called 'Operation Ressurection'. The plan that parachutists foresaw including members of the 11th du Choc falling from the sky would within very few hours take over control of the vital centres of Paris: The Interior Ministry, the police headquarters, communication centres including television and radio stations, electricity production plants and other strategically vital areas of the capital. 'The plan also foresaw the arrestation of a certain number of politicians, among which Francois Mitterand, Pierre Mendès France, Edgar Faure, Jules Moch, as well as the entire direction of the French Communists.'[40]

But on May 27, 'just hours before Operation Resurrection was to break upon the French capital', de Gaulle announced that he had 'begun the regular process necessary to the establishment of a Republican government'.[41] Thereafter a succession of rapid and far-reaching actions ended the Fourth Republic. On May 28, Prime Minister Pierre Pflimlin resigned. On the morning of May 29 the President of the Republic, René Coty, made public the fact that he had invited Charles de Gaulle to form a government. Only 24 hours later the General appeared before the National Assembly and demanded full powers to rule by decree for six months, and enforced four months of 'holiday' for the deputies, and authority to submit himself a new constitution. De Gaulle's requests were voted 329 to 224. 'The Fourth Republic had chosen suicide over assassination by . . . the army and its security services.'[42]

Many within the military and the secret services who had supported the coup of de Gaulle expected that the General would firmly support a policy of 'Algerie Francaise', i.e. that he would do everything to keep Algeria under French colonial rule. To their surprise, however, de Gaulle with the backing of many politicians of the Fourth Republic embarked on a policy of Algerie Algerienne, which led to the independence of Algeria in 1962. The secret soldiers were furious. 'Increasingly, Presidents of the Fifth Republic, led by de Gaulle, came to distrust their secret services, regarding them as liabilities rather than assets.'[43] The secret soldiers were in disagreement on whether they should follow the orders of de Gaulle and withdraw from Algeria or whether they should fight against the government of France. The final split of the 11th du Choc came in 1961 when most of its members chose Algeria Francaise and in order to promote their politics together with French officers fighting in Algeria founded the clandestine and illegal Organisation Armee Secrete, in short OAS. The two declared aims of the

OAS were to first of all keep French control over colonial Algeria – and thus continue to fight the FLN liberation movement by all means no matter what Paris directed – and secondly, to overthrow the Fifth Republic of President De Gaulle and replace it with a militantly anti-Communist authoritarian French state.

The OAS coup came on April 22, 1961 when four French Generals under the leadership of General Challe seized power in Algeria in an attempt to maintain the country's union with France. Allegedly, secret soldiers of the CIA-supported NATO stay-behind army who had joined the OAS were directly involved. The secret soldiers 'supported a group of generals who were resisting, sometimes violently, de Gaulle's attempts to negotiate Algerian independence and end the war', US author Jonathan Kwitny related in his article on the secret armies in Western Europe.[44] Obviously more research is needed on the involvement of the French stay-behind in the 1961 coup d'état as it figures amongst the most sensitive dimensions of the history of the secret war in France. As of now the evidence suggests that the stay-behind armies were involved in successful coup d'états in Greece in 1967 and in Turkey in 1980, and in the coup against the French government in 1961 which failed.

The CIA and its Director Allen Dulles together with militant secret soldiers of NATO and the Pentagon in Washington had allegedly supported the coup against de Gaulle. Immediately after the coup 'minor officials at the Elysée Palace itself' had given 'to understand that the generals' plot was backed by strongly anti-Communist elements in the United States Government and military services', as the *Washington Star* reported. 'Both in Paris and Washington the facts are now known, though they will never be publicly admitted', an article of Claude Krief revealed already in May 1961 in the widely read French weekly *L'Express*. 'In private, the highest French personalities make no secret of it. What they say is this: The CIA played a direct part in the Algiers coup, and certainly weighted heavily on the decision taken by ex-general Challe to start the putsch.' Shortly before the coup General Challe had held the position of NATO Commander in Chief Allied Forces Central Europe, cultivating close contacts not only with the Pentagon and US officers but also with the NATO secret stay-behind army, maintaining daily contact with US military officers. General Challe, as Krief concluded, had acted directly on CIA orders: 'All the people who know him well, are deeply convinced that he had been encouraged by the CIA to go ahead.'[45]

When Krief wrote his article on the CIA-supported coup against de Gaulle, the existence of the secret stay-behind armies of NATO in all countries of Western Europe had not yet been revealed. But with a focus on the international secret war, Krief relates that ten days before the coup, on April 12, 1961, a clandestine meeting had taken place in Madrid, with the presence of 'various foreign agents, including members of the CIA and the Algiers conspirators, who disclosed their plans to the CIA men'. During that meeting the Americans allegedly angrily complained that de Gaulle's policy was 'paralysing NATO and rendering the defence of Europe impossible', assuring the putsch generals including Challe, that if they and their followers succeeded, Washington would recognise the new Algerian Government within 48 hours.[46] De Gaulle, who through a number of manouvres and strategies was indeed attempting to make France and Europe less dependent on the United States and NATO, was furious about the recklessness of the CIA. Whether US President Kennedy – who exactly at the same time was overseeing the secret coup against Cuban President Fidel Castro and the Bay of Pigs invasion which started on April 15, 1961 – had been informed about the coup in Algeria remains unclear. But it is known that Kennedy was furious when the CIA coup in Cuba failed, and that also the recognition of Washington of the Generals in Algeria was not forthcoming. In Algeria the coup d'état by the secret soldiers held out for four days only and then collapsed. The French leading daily *Le Monde* critically summarised that 'the behaviour of the United States during the recent crisis was not particularly skilful. It seems established that American agents more or less encouraged Challe', while 'Kennedy, of course, knew nothing of all this.'[47]

After the failed coup, the secret soldiers were completely out of control. OAS outrages soon escalated to assassinations of prominent government officials in Algiers, random murders of Muslims, and bank raids.[48] By November 1961 the secret OAS soldiers operated at will in Algiers and killed repeatedly to sabotage the beginning of the peace process that should have led to Algerian independence. The battle of the French security and military apparatus against the OAS proved very difficult because many only half heartedly engaged in it, or even sabotaged it, as they were sympathetic of the OAS and its political aims. As the violence escalated, the OAS carried the secret war to France and killed the mayor of Evian south of Lake Geneva where peace talks between the French government and FLN representatives were being held. Furthermore the secret soldiers targeted the government in Paris, and de Gaulle only narrowly escaped an assassination attempt at Pont-sur-Seine. Paris hit back with a vengeance and in November 1961 six prominent cafés in Algiers frequented by OAS sympathisers were ripped apart by explosions.

Next to France the secret soldiers of the OAS from their bases in Algeria carried their secret war to other European countries including Spain, Switzerland and Germany where special squads of the 11th du Choc engaged in assassination operations of FLN leaders as well as their financial contributors and arms suppliers.[49] In Germany the secret soldiers allegedly cooperated with the German secret soldiers of the stay-behind network and the German secret service BND. The Germans allowed the 11th du Choc to carry out its operations against the FLN using the German parachute-training centre in Altenstadt in Bavaria as a secure camouflaged operation base. 'Gladio members and many BND members were recruited there also for other secret services operations', BND expert Erich Schmidt Eenboom observed. The French assassins of FLN activists in Germany were never caught. 'The police seemed unable to catch the members of the hit and run teams', Eenboom relates.[50]

The secret war dragged France into a nightmare of violence with brutality escalating on all sides. At the height of the tensions in Paris, police chief Maurice Papon imposed a curfew in the capital after the murder of 11 of his officers. The FLN, which had orchestrated the attacks, responded by organising a protest march, and up to 40,000 Algerians answered the call to demonstrate in Paris on October 17, 1961. Papon, a notorious racist who during the Second World War had been involved in the deportation of more than 1,500 Jews to Nazi death camps, ordered his officers to brutally smash the demonstration whereupon a massacre ensued.[51] According to the 1988 testimony of Constantin Melnik at least 200 – and probably closer to 300 people – were slaughtered by police officers who were eager to avenge the deaths of their colleagues.[52] Melnik had been the security adviser for de Gaulle's government and chief of all French secret services from 1959 to 1962. When asked about the stay-behind network Melnik had highlighted the inherent danger of secret armies when he declared that 'any group with radios and training would be very dangerous for the security of France'.[53]

'I saw people collapse in pools of blood. Some were beaten to death. The bodies were thrown onto lorries and tossed into the Seine from the Pont de la Concorde' Saad Ouazene, a 29-year-old foundry worker and FLN sympathiser later remembered the massacre in Paris. 'If I hadn't been strong I'd never have got out alive', Ouazene who escaped with a fractured scull testified. 'As Algerians got out of the buses at the Porte de Versailles, they were clubbed over the head', French policeman Joseph Gommenginger, on duty that night, recalled the 1961 massacre. 'Those carrying out the attacks even threatened me. They had all removed their numbers from their uniforms. I was revolted. I never thought police could do such things.' In the days following the massacre, dozens of bodies were taken from the Seine as far down river as Rouen.[54] In the absence of an official investigation the magazine of distinguished French philosopher Jean-Paul Sartre *Temps Modernes* called the episode a pogrom.[55]

The secret war of the OAS, which had involved secret soldiers of the NATO stay-behind, in the end failed to both overthrow de Gaulle and prevent Algeria from becoming independent. The agreement for peace in Algeria and the independence of the country was signed between the FLN and the government of de Gaulle in Evian in March 1962, whereupon also the OAS collapsed about a year after its creation declaring truce on June 17, 1962. Only a fraction of OAS diehards led by Colonel Jean-Marie Bastien-Thirty were unwilling to give up and carried out another ambush on President de Gaulle near Paris on August 22, 1962. De Gaulle, who survived after having displayed as always little concern for his own safety, was outraged that the OAS assassins had attacked him while in the company of his wife and made the operation a personal affair. In September the OAS men involved in the assassination operation were captured in Paris, all were sentenced to death, but only Bastien-Thirty was executed.[56] The larger part of 11th du Choc, many of whom had joined the OAS, saw their career at an end. The remaining units of the 11th du Choc were put under close Gaullist control.

The secret CIA army designed by NATO as an anti-Communist stay-behind had thus during the Algerian crisis on the ensuing chaos and violence allegedly been involved in domestic operations in the total absence of any Soviet invasion. The danger of secret warfare consisted then, as now, in the lack of control that the democratic institutions including parliament and at times also the government had over the secret soldiers. Admiral Pierre Lacoste who directed the French military secret from 1982 to 1985 under President Mitterand confirmed after the discovery of the secret Gladio networks in 1990 that some 'terrorist actions' against de Gaulle and his Algerian peace plan were carried out by groups that included 'a limited number of people' from the French stay-behind network. However, Lacoste insisted that the Algerian anti de Gaulle operations had been the only case when the French Gladio had become operational inside France and stressed that he believed that Soviet contingency plans for invasion nevertheless justified the stay-behind program also during his time in office as chief of the military secret service.[57]

Like few others Charles de Gaulle had been at the centre of secret warfare in France for most of his lifetime until in April 1969 when he was replaced peacefully by Georges Pompidou and died a year later at the age of 80 in his home, allegedly watching a sentimental television serial. De Gaulle had led the resistance of France against Hitler in the Second World War, had employed secret warfare to reach power as the Fourth Republic ended and during the Fifth Republic became the target of coup d'états and assassination operations. Long before the public exposure of the secret stay-behind armies of NATO, de Gaulle was envious of the United States, when he considered to have too stray a position in Western Europe, and suspicious of the CIA, whom he suspected to engage in manipulation and secret warfare. Upon coming to power de Gaulle had made it plain that he intended to carry out his foreign policy with his diplomats, not his 'irresponsible secret services', who were ordered to sever all relations with the CIA, upon whom they depended for much of their intelligence.[58] As de Gaulle saw it, 'the French state was under assault by secret forces. Who was to blame? The CIA certainly, believed de Gaulle.'[59]

When NATO was founded in 1949, its headquarters, including the SHAPE, were built in France. France was therefore particularly vulnerable to NATO and CIA secret warfare as de Gaulle lamented – for together with NATO also the secret Gladio command centre CPC was located in Paris as the Italian document 'The special forces of SIFAR and Operation Gladio' of June 1959 revealed: 'On the level of NATO the following activities must be mentioned: 1. The activity of the CPC of Paris (Clandestine Planning Committee) attached to SHAPE.'[60] Furthermore also the secret Gladio command centre ACC repeatedly met in Paris. It came as a massive shock to the White House in Washington when de Gaulle in February 1966 – due to a number of strategic and personnel motives that historians still struggle to explain – decided to challenge the United States head-on, and ordered NATO and the United States either to place their military bases in France under French control, or to dismantle them. The United States and NATO did not react to the ultimatum whereupon in a spectacular decision de Gaulle took France out of NATO's military command on March 7, 1966 and expelled the entire NATO organisation together with its covert action agents from French territory. To the anger of Washington and the Pentagon the European headquarters of NATO had to move to Belgium. In Brussels, Mons and Casteau, new European

NATO headquarters were being erected where they have remained until today. The Belgium parliamentary investigation into Gladio and secret warfare later confirmed that 'in 1968 the Chair of CPC moved to Brussels'.[61] Research in Belgium furthermore revealed that the ACC secret warfare centre held a meeting with international participation in Brussels as late as October 23 and 24, 1990.[62]

Belgium Gladio author Jan Willems drew attention to the sensitive fact that when de Gaulle withdrew the French army from the military-integrated command of NATO, some of the secret agreements between France and the United States were cancelled. 'On this occasion it was revealed that secret protocols existed concerning the fight against Communist subversion, signed bilaterally by the United States and its NATO allies.'[63] De Gaulle denounced the protocols as an infringement of national sovereignty. Similar secret clauses were also revealed in other NATO states. In Italy Giuseppe de Lutiis revealed that when becoming a NATO member Italy in 1949 had signed not only the Atlantic Pact, but also secret protocols that provided for the creation of an unofficial organisation 'charged with guaranteeing Italy's internal alignment with the Western Block by any means, even if the electorate were to show a different inclination'.[64] And also US journalist Arthur Rowse in his article on Gladio claimed that a 'secret clause in the initial NATO agreement in 1949 required that before a nation could join, it must have already established a national security authority to fight Communism through clandestine citizen cadres'.[65]

It might come as a surprise that after the thoroughly disturbing experiences during the Algerian crisis the secret stay-behind armies were not closed down for good in France but were merely reformed. In 1998 secret service expert Jacques Baud correctly observed that 'although proofs are missing, certain experts have suggested that the activities of the French stay-behind network have been carried out under the cover of the Service d'Action Civique'.[66] Allegedly, after the OAS had collapsed de Gaulle saw to it that the Rose des Vents stay-behind network was weakened while the 'Service d'Action Civique', or in short SAC, was strengthened. The secret SAC army became a sort of Gaullist praetorian guard, a refuge of Gaullist purity which reflected the General's distrust of all political parties, including his own. The self-proclaimed mission of SAC was accordingly to support the action of General de Gaulle.[67] Founded in the immediate post-war years, SAC was the iron arm of de Gaulle's RPF party (Rassemblement du Peuple Francais), which after the war had competed in vain against the strong French Communists and Socialists. Officially a 'service d'ordre', SAC in reality was the anti-Communist hit gang of the RPF that had to carry out the dirty work. SAC units engaged in secret operations to break strikes or faced Communist militants whose speciality was to silence Gaullist orators by hurling lug nuts from the floor. Furthermore SAC units protected Gaullist politicians or groups putting up Gaullist political posters.[68]

Neither de Gaulle's RPF party nor its iron fist SAC were successful during the Fourth Republic and the RPF was dissolved in 1954. But the faithfuls of the SAC allegedly stayed in touch and supported the coup that in 1958 ended the Fourth

Republic and brought de Gaulle back into power. Jacques Foccart, the Director and spiritual father of the SAC, as a secret warrior and supporter of de Gaulle, allegedly played an active coordinating role through military, secret service and old Resistance contacts in the very beginning of the coup when on May 24, 1958 the secret soldiers of the 11th du Choc based in Calvi occupied the island.[69] The SAC and Foccart, secret services expert Porch concluded, helped 'to play midwife to de Gaulle's return to power in 1958'.[70]

Foccart has remained a shadowy and ill-defined player in the French secret war. 'The extent of Foccart's powers are almost as mysterious as the question of how he came to acquire them in the first place.'[71] A native of the French Caribbean colony Guadeloupe, Foccart had been mobilised at the outbreak of the Second World War in 1939 but had managed to evade capture during the Fall of France. He cooperated with the German army but towards the end of the war once again changed sides and joined the French as an activist in the Normandy resistance and was awarded the Medal of Freedom from the US Army.[72] After the war Foccart entered de Gaulle's inner circle and set up the SAC. The secret warfare school that he established at Cercottes near Orléans 'became a place of pilgrimage for SAC members in the 1950s'.[73] SAC in the post-war years had a membership of nearly 8,000 'reservists', including active members of the SDECE covert action department Service Action, and the SDECE elite combat unit the 11th du Choc. Together they all trained in Cercottes, and in the wake of the 1990 Gladio discoveries the secret warfare centre was revealed as one of the places where the French Gladiators had received their training.[74]

Due to the absence of an official investigation into the history of the French secret army it remains difficult for researchers to outline in detail the differences between the French stay-behind army Rose des Vents, and the French stay-behind army SAC, and clearly more research is needed. Allegedly also the French stay-behind SAC in the absence of a Soviet invasion had engaged in numerous secret anti-Communist operations. But only the coming to power of the Socialists under President Francois Mitterand in 1981 finally shifted the balance of power and allowed for a parliamentarian investigation. When a former chief of SAC in Marseilles, police inspector Jacques Massié, was murdered with his entire family in July 1981, Communist deputies in the French National Assembly demanded for an investigation of SAC. After listening to six months of testimony, the parliamentary committee concluded in December 1981 in a voluminous report that the actions of the SDECE, SAC and the OAS networks in Africa were 'intimately linked'. The parliamentarians found that SAC had financed itself in mysterious ways, including through SDECE funds and drug trafficking.[75]

'A typical case in which a "Gladio" network should have intervened was during the student riots in France in 1968', *Intelligence Newsletter* reported after the discovery of the secret armies.[76] The parliamentary committee convened to investigate SAC had discovered that indeed SAC had hit its membership peak during the May 1968 troubles, when it might have counted as many as 30,000 members. It might have intervened during the student riots in 1968. In 1981, SAC claimed

10,000 adherents. 'An estimated 10 to 15 percent were in the police. Opportunists, gangsters, and men with extreme-right-wing views were also well represented.'[77] The committee denounced SAC as a dangerous secret army, which had served as a parallel police, had infiltrated the public organisation in order to influence decisions, and had carried out acts of violence. In what remained the most detailed parliamentarian investigation into any of the French secret armies so far, the parliamentarian committee deemed the continued existence of SAC 'incompatible with the laws of the Republic', whereupon the government of Francois Mitterand ordered the SAC to be disbanded in July 1982.[78]

The Mitterand government, increasingly unsure about the role of secret services in modern democracies, targeted the French military secret service, which for decades had been at the heart of France's secret warfare. A 1982 parliamentarian investigation into secret service activity led by Socialist party deputy Jean-Michel Bellorgey concluded that intelligence agents driven by Cold War phobias and obsessed with the 'enemy within' had broken the law repeatedly while the secret service had accumulated a record of 'failures, scandals, and doubtful operations'.[79] After this shattering conclusion Mitterrand supported the demand of the Communists, which for a long time already together with a group of Socialists had asked quite simply for the dissolution of the military secret service SDECE.

In the end this far-reaching step was not taken and the SDECE was not closed down but merely reformed. Its name changed to Direction Generale de la Securite Exterieure (DGSE) and Admiral Pierre Lacoste became its new Director. Lacoste continued to run the secret Gladio army of the DGSE in close cooperation with NATO and after the discovery of the network in retrospect insisted that Soviet contingency plans for invasion had justified the stay-behind program also during his time in office.[80] 'Operation Satanique', the covert action operation of the DGSE, which on July 10, 1985 with a bomb sank the Greenpeace vessel *Rainbow Warrior* that had protested peacefully against French atomic testing in the Pacific, ended the career of Admiral Lacoste. He was forced to resign after the crime had been traced back to the DGSE, Defence Minister Charles Hernu and President Francois Mitterrand himself.

In March 1986 the political right won the parliamentary elections in France and as a result Socialist President Mitterrand had to govern together with Gaullist Prime Minister Jacques Chirac. When the secret Gladio armies were discovered across Europe in 1990, Chirac was less than eager to see the history of the French secret army investigated. For such an investigation could have ruined the very successful political career of Chirac who later moved on to become President of France. As still in 1975 Chirac had directed the SAC secret army as president.

France therefore had extreme difficulties in facing the history of its secret anti-Communist war. There was no official parliamentarian investigation. And officials of the government attempted to minimise the damage with lies and half-truths. Defence Minister Jean Pierre Chevènement on November 12, 1990 reluctantly confirmed to the press that 'it is correct, that a structure has existed, erected in the beginning of the 1950s, to enable liaison with a government forced to flee abroad in the hypothesis of an occupation', whereupon the Defence Minister wrongly claimed that 'this structure was dissolved on the order of the President of the Republic. As far as I am aware it never had more than a sleeper's role and a role of liaison.'[81] A day later President Mitterand had to face the extremely curious press in Paris. 'When I arrived', Mitterand wrongly claimed, 'I didn't have much left to dissolve. There only remained a few remnants, of which I learned the existence with some surprise because everyone had forgotten about them.'[82] Prime Minister Chirac did not take a stand. But Italian Prime Minister Giulio Andreotti was not amused to see how the French government denied and played down their role in the Gladio affair and contradicted his claim that Gladio had existed in most countries of Western Europe. Thus Andreotti let the press know that far from having been closed down long ago, representatives of the French secret army also had taken part in the ACC meeting in Brussels as recently as October 24, 1990, which caused considerable embarrassment in France.

8

THE SECRET WAR IN SPAIN

In Spain the battle of the militant right against the Communists and the left was carried out not clandestinely but as an open and brutal war, which lasted for three years and led to a total of 600,000 casualties, equalling those of the American Civil War. Historian Victor Kiernan wisely observed that an 'army, supposed to be the nation's protector, may really be a watchdog trained to bite some of those under its protection'. Kiernan, obviously, could have been speaking of the secret stay-behind armies. But he made the remark when describing the beginning of the Spanish Civil War that started on July 17, 1936 when a group of army conspirators attempted to take power into their own hands as 'Spanish generals, like their South American cousins, had tenacious habits of intervention in politics.'[1]

The military coup of General Franco and his associates came after a leftist reforming government under Manuel Azana had won at the polls on February 16, 1936 and had begun numerous projects many of which benefited the weakest members of the society. Yet in the eyes of the badly controlled powerful army, Spain after the elections was slipping into the embrace of Socialists, Communists, anarchists and church-burners. Many within the military forces were convinced that they had to save the nation from the red menace of Communism that during the very same years in the Soviet Union under Stalin led to fake trials and assassinations on a large scale. Historians, including Kiernan, have been less generous in their evaluation of the beginning of the Spanish Civil War. To them 'the rights and wrongs couldn't have been clearer...There was a classic simplicity about Spain. A democratically elected government was overthrown by the army. The battle lines were clear. On one side stood the poor and against them were fascism, big business, the landowners and the church.'[2]

Whereas in Greece in 1967 the military coup established the power of the armed forces in less than 24 hours, in Spain in July 1936 civilian opposition to the military coup was so massive that the republic fought for three years before the military dictatorship under Franco was installed. The battle was long and intensive, not only because large segments of the Spanish population took up arms against the Spanish military, but also because 12 so-called International Brigades formed spontaneously to stiffen the Republican resistance to Franco. Idealistic young men and women, drawn from more than 50 countries around the world, in a unique moment in the history of warfare volunteered to join the International Brigades, which eventually numbered to some 30,000–40,000 members. Most of them were workers, but also teachers, nurses, students and poets took a train to Spain. 'It was terribly important to be there', nurse Thora Craig, born in 1910, from Great Britain judged 60 years later, 'a bit of history, and helping. It was the most important part of my life.' Plasterer Robert James Peters, born in 1914, declared for the record: 'If I ever did anything useful in my life, this is the one thing I have done.'[3]

In the end the Spanish Socialists and Communists together with the International Brigades were unable to stop the coup of Franco because Hitler and Mussolini supported the fascist General while the governments of Great Britain, France and the United States opted for non-intervention. They feared Spanish Communism more than a Spanish fascist dictator and thus silently consented to the death of the Spanish republic. While in the context of the prelude to the Second World War much has been written on the failure of British Prime Minister Chamberlain and French Prime Minister Daladier to stop Hitler and Mussolini in Munich in September 1938, the silent support of London and Paris for Italian and German anti-Communism in Spain and beyond has attracted much less attention. While the Soviet Union armed the Spanish Republicans, Hitler and Mussolini sent more than 90,000 trained and armed German and Italian soldiers to Spain. Moreover the German air force dropped horrors on Spain, a fact immortalised in Pablo Picasso's protest painting of the Nazi-bombed Guernica village. Thereafter on February 27, 1939 the British Government ended the struggle of the Spanish Republic when it announced its recognition of Franco as the legitimate leader of Spain. Hitler and Mussolini had secured their Western flank and agreed with Franco that Spain would stay neutral during the Second World War. As the fight against Communism continued on a large scale with Hitler's repeated invasions of the Soviet Union, all of which failed but led to a terrible death toll, dictator Franco returned the favour to Mussolini and Hitler and sent his Blue Division to fight with the Wehrmacht on the Russian front.

After the Second World War the fight against the Communists in Western Europe was often referred to as a fight against 'Fifth Columns'. The term originally referred to secret fascist armies and originated from the Spanish Civil War where it had been, coined by Franco's General Emilio Mola. When in October 1936, three months after the military coup, Spain's capital Madrid was still held by the Republicans and the International Brigades, Franco ordered his General Mola to conquer the capital with overwhelming force and secret warfare. Only hours before the attack Mola in a legendary psychological warfare operation announced to the press that he had four army columns waiting outside the city, but in addition a 'Fifth Column' of Franco supporters inside Madrid. Wearing neither uniforms nor insignias, and moving among the enemy like the fish moves in the water, the secret members of this 'Fifth Column' allegedly were the most dangerous, as Mola claimed.

The strategy was successful for it spread fear and confusion among the Communists and Socialists in the city. 'Police last night began a house-to-house search for rebels in Madrid', the *New York Times* reported the search for the mysterious

Fifth Column the day after Mola's press conference. Orders for these raids 'apparently were instigated by a recent broadcast over the rebel radio station by General Emilio Mola. He stated that he was counting on four columns of troops outside Madrid, and another column of persons hiding within the city who would join the invaders as soon as they entered the capital.'[4] Although the attack of Mola was defeated, the fear of the right-wing secret Fifth Column remained throughout the war. Mike Economides, a Cypriot commander in the International Brigades, used to inform every newcomer that the war in Spain was being waged in two directions, 'the enemy in front, and the Fifth Column in the rear'.[5]

The term 'Fifth Column' survived the Spanish Civil War and has ever since been used to designate secret armies or groups of armed subversives which clandestinely operate in an enemy's zone of influence. During the Second World War, Hitler set up Nazi Fifth Columns which as secret armies in Norway and beyond prepared and supported the invasion of the regular German army. When Germany was defeated the West and NATO conquered the language, shifted the meaning from the political right to the political left, and used the term 'Fifth Columns' in the Cold War context to designate the secret armies of the Communists. Soon secret warfare experts denounced 'the Free World's readiness to let Communist fifth columns flourish in its midst'.[6] Only in the Gladio scandal in 1990 it was discovered that maybe the biggest network of secret Fifth Columns has until today remained the stay-behind network of NATO.

Franco ruled with an iron fist and between 1936 and the dictator's death in 1975 no free elections were held in Spain. Amidst arbitrary arrests, fake trials, torture and assassinations the danger of Communists or Socialists gaining positions of influence therefore remained minimal. Hence when in late 1990 Calvo Sotelo, Spanish Prime Minister from February 1981 to December 1982, was questioned on the existence of Gladio in Spain, he observed with bitter irony that during Franco's dictatorship 'the very government was Gladio'. Alberto Oliart, Defence Minister under the Sotelo government, made the same point when he declared it to be 'childish' to claim that an anti-Communist secret army had been set up in Spain in the 1950s because 'here Gladio was the government'.[7]

Within the Cold War context Washington did not embrace the bloody hands of Franco from the very beginning. Much to the contrary, after Hitler and Mussolini were dead, segments of the US wartime secret service OSS considered it to be only logical that as the culmination of the anti-Fascist combat dictator Franco had to be removed. And hence in 1947, as the CIA was being created, the OSS started 'Operation Banana'. With the aim to overthrow Franco, Catalan anarchists were equipped with weapons and landed on the shores of the peninsula. However, there does not seem to have existed a solid Anglo-Saxon consensus on the political desirability of removing Franco, as segments in both Washington and London considered him a valuable asset. In the end the British MI6 betrayed Operation Banana to Franco's secret service. The subversives were arrested and the counter coup failed.[8]

Franco strengthened his position internationally when in 1953 he sealed a pact with Washington and allowed the United States to station missiles, troops, airplanes and Signals Intelligence (SIGINT) antennas on Spanish soil. In return the United States saw to it that Franco's fascist Spain, against the opposition of many countries including prominently the Soviet Union, could overcome his international isolation and became a member of the World Peace Organisation UNO in 1955. As a public sign of support for the Spanish 'bulwark against Communism' US Foreign Minister John Foster Dulles, brother of CIA Director Allen Dulles, met with Franco in December 1957 and Franco's trusted aid, Marine Officer Carrero Blanco, thereafter skilfully cultivated the contacts of the dictatorship with the CIA. By the end of the 1950s, 'the ties had strengthened, making Franco's secret service community one of the best allies of the CIA in Europe'.[9]

Franco, together with a series of dictators in Latin America, had become Washington's ally. From the top floors of the American Embassy in Madrid, behind the tightly locked doors of the so-called Office of Political Liaison, the CIA station chief and his clandestine action team closely watched and influenced the evolution of the political life in Spain. Franco in the manner of a classical oligarch increased his wealth and conserved his power by constructing a pyramid of privilege and corruption. His top generals were allowed to make millions from shady business, their officers in turn got their cut, and so on down the line. The entire structure of military power was co-opted by the Caudillo and depended on him for its survival.[10]

Within that framework the military and secret service apparatus flourished beyond control and engaged in arms trade, drugs trade, torture, terror and counter-terror. A bit of a constitutional curiosity, under Franco's dictatorship, totalitarian Spain featured not one single Defence Ministry but three, one each for the Army, the Air Force and the Navy. Each of these three Defence Ministries ran its own military secret service: Segunda Seccion Bis of the Army, Segunda Seccion Bis of the Air Force and Servicio Informacion Naval (SEIN) for the Navy. Furthermore the Spanish Chiefs of Staff (Alto Estado Mayor, AEM), placed directly under Franco, also ran their own secret service, the SIAEM (Servicio de Informacion del Alto Estado Mayor). Furthermore the Interior Ministry also operated two secret services, the Direction General De Seguridad (DGS) and the Guardia Civil.[11]

In 1990 it was revealed that segments of the Spanish secret services together with the CIA had been running a Spanish Gladio cell in Las Palmas on the Spanish Canary Islands in the Atlantic. The base had allegedly been set up as early as 1948, and was operative throughout the 1960s and 1970s. Above all members of the Army secret service Buro Segundo Bis had allegedly been strongly involved in the secret stay-behind network. Andre Moyen, a 76-years-old retired agent who from 1938 to 1952 had been a member of the Belgian military secret service SDRA, alleged that the Segundo Bis secret service of the Army had always been 'well up to date on Gladio'.[12] French researcher Faligot supported this claim and highlighted that the Spanish secret army in the 1950s had been run by the Dutch Consul Herman Laatsman, 'closely linked, as well as his wife, to Andre Moyen'.[13] Further confirmation came from Italy where Colonel Alberto Vollo testified in 1990 'that in the 1960s and 1970s in Las Palmas on the Canary Islands a Gladio training base existed, which was run by US instructors. On the same location existed also US SIGINT installations.'[14]

Andre Moyen was interviewed by journalists of the Belgian Communist newspaper *Drapeau Rouge*. As the Cold War had ended, Moyen confirmed to his former adversaries that during his active years he had been intimately involved with operation Gladio and secret operations against the Communist parties in numerous countries. The former agent signalled his surprise that the secret services of Spain had not been investigated more closely, for he knew first hand that they had played 'a key role in the recruitment of Gladio agents'.[15] According to Moyen's own testimony, Belgian Interior Minister Vleeschauwer had in September 1945 sent him to his Italian colleague, Interior Minister Mario Scelba, with the task to find ways to prevent the Communists from coming to power. Thereafter also France became interested and French Interior Minister Jules Moch linked Moyen to the Director of the SDECE, Henri Ribiers. Most sensitively Moyen according to his own testimony in the 1950s in the same context also met with high-ranking military officers in neutral Switzerland.[16]

Moyen testified that his first contacts to the Spanish branch of the Gladio network had taken place in October 1948 when 'a cell of the network operated in Las Palmas' on the Spanish Canary Islands in the Atlantic. At that time SDRA agent Moyen had allegedly been sent to the Canary Islands in order to investigate a fraud involving fuels which had been transported by ship from Belgium to the Congo via the Canary Islands. 'The fraud', Moyen testified, 'enriched highly placed Spanish authorities, and furthermore we uncovered a massive drugs trade'. When the secret drugs business was exposed by Belgium, dictator Franco sent 'two agents of the Buro Segundo Bis' of the military chiefs of staff in order to help with the investigation. 'They were well informed men, who helped me greatly', Moyen recalls, 'we talked of many things, and they could show me that they were well up to date on Gladio'.[17]

In 1968 also Franco was faced with international revolutionary student protests. Fearing large public protests the Spanish Education Minister asked the chief of the SIAEM, General Martos, to carry out secret operations against the universities. Admiral Carrero Blanco, closely connected to the CIA, in October 1968 created a new special unit for the secret war called OCN within the ambit of SIAEM, targeting students, their professors and the entire social revolutionary movement. After a number of successful operations, Blanco in March 1972 decided to transform the SIAEM subsection OCN into a new secret service, which he labelled SECED (Servicio Central de Documentación de la Presidencia del Gobierno), placed under the command of Jose Ignacio San Martin Lopez, who had directed OCN ever since 1968.[18] According to Gladio author Pietro Cedomi, SECED cultivated very close links to the Spanish secret Gladio army with many agents being members of both secret armies as the stay-behind in Spain brutally cracked down on student protests and outspoken professors.[19]

Franco's dictatorship during the Cold War served as a safe haven for many right-wing terrorists who had taken part in the secret anti-Communist war in

Western Europe. Italian right-wing extremist Marco Pozzan, a member of the Italian right-wing organisation Ordine Nuovo, in January 1984 revealed to judge Felice Casson, who later discovered the Gladio secret army, that a whole colony of Italian fascists had installed themselves in Spain during the last years of Franco's rule. More than 100 complotters had fled Italy after Prince Valerio Borghese had organised a neo-fascist attempt to overthrow the Italian government on December 7, 1970. The right-wing extremists, who included Borghese himself as well as Carlo Cicuttini and Mario Ricci, regrouped in Spain under the leadership of notorious international right-wing terrorist Stefano Delle Chiaie, who during the coup with his men had occupied the Interior Ministry.

In Spain, Delle Chiaie linked up with right-wing extremists from other European countries including Otto Skorzeny, a former Nazi, and Yves Guerain Serac, a French former officer of the illegal Organisation Armee Secrete (OAS) and Gladio-linked leader of the Portugal-based CIA front Aginter-Press. Skorzeny was employed by Franco's secret service as a 'security consultant' and hired Delle Chiaie to target opponents of Franco in both Spain and abroad, whereupon Delle Chiaie carried out well over a thousand bloodthirsty attacks, including an estimated 50 murders. The secret war in Spain was characterised by assassinations and acts of terror. Members of Delle Chiaie's secret army, including Italian right-winger Aldo Tisei, later confessed to Italian magistrates that during their Spanish exile they had tracked down and killed anti-Fascists on behalf of the Spanish secret service.[20]

Marco Pozzan, who himself had fled to Spain in the early 1970, revealed that 'Caccola', as Delle Chiaie was nicknamed, was well paid for his services in Spain. 'He made very expensive trips. Always by plane, including transatlantic flights. Caccola received the money above all from the Spanish secret service and the police.' Among the targets of the right-wing terrorist ranged the terrorists of ETA (Euskadi Ta Askatasuna) who were fighting for Basque independence. The unit and their supporters were under the command of Caccola infiltrated by agent provocateurs. 'We know that Caccola and his group had operated on the orders of the Spanish police against the Basque autonomists', Pozzan recalled. 'I remember that during a manifestation in Montejurra, Caccola and his group organised a clash with opposed political groups. In order that the Spanish police could not be accused of unjustified violent repressive intervention, Caccola and his group had the task to provocate and create disorder. In this particular instance there were even casualties. This was in 1976.'[21]

After Franco's death in 1975, Delle Chiaie decided that Spain was no longer a safe place and left for Chile. There CIA-installed right-wing dictator Pinochet recruited him to haunt and kill Chilean oppositionals in 'Operation Condor' across the Americas. Thereafter Caccola moved to Bolivia, set up death squads to protect the right-wing government and engaged once again in 'murder unlimited'. Stefano Delle Chiaie, born in Italy in 1936, remains the best known terrorist member of the secret armies who clandestinely fought Communism in Europe and abroad during the Cold War. The right-wing terrorist remained a danger to left-wing movements across the world but after having fled from Spain only rarely came back to the

Old Continent with the exception of 1980, when he was suspected by the Italian police to have come back to Italy in order to carry out the bloody Bologna railway massacre. Aged 51 the untouchable was finally arrested on March 27, 1987 in the capital of Venezuela by the local secret service. Only hours later, agents of the Italian secret service and the CIA were present on the scene. Cacolla did not express regret for his actions but, with few words, drew attention to the fact that in his secret wars against the left, he had been protected by a number of governments, which in turn wanted him to carry out certain actions, which he then carried out: 'The massacres have taken place. That is a fact. The secret services have covered up the traces. That is another fact.'[22]

As Franco vaguely anticipated the end of his days he promoted his CIA liaison officer and secret services master architect Carrero Blanco to the post of Spanish Prime Minister in June 1973. Yet Blanco due to his brutality was hated by large segments of the population and in December of the same year his car drove upon an ETA land mine and he was blown apart. Previously perceived as 'folklorist' the Spanish and French terrorist organisation ETA, fighting for Basque independence, with the assassination of Blanco established itself as a dangerous enemy of the state.

After Franco's death on November 20, 1975, the transformation of Spain's dreaded security apparatus proved difficult. SECED (Servicio Central de Documentacion de la Defensa), the most prominent Spanish military secret service, changed its label to CESID (Centro Superior de Informacion de la Defensa). Yet its first Director, General Jose Maria Burgon Lopez-Doriga, saw to it that it was made up mostly by ex-members of the SECED. Thus the secret war in cooperation with Italian right-wing extremists was allowed to continue as the press reported during the discovery of the secret Gladio armies in 1990: 'A week ago the Spanish newspaper El Pais discovered the last known link between Spain and the secret network. Carlo Cicuttini, linked to Gladio, took active part in the Atocha massacre in January 1977 in Madrid', the press reported on the secret war. 'Then an extreme right-wing Commando had attacked a lawyer's office closely linked to the Spanish Communist party, killing five people. The attack caused panic, for it fell right into Spain's transition movement, and it was feared to be the start of further attacks, attempting to stop Spain's transition to democracy.'[23]

Secret warrior and right-wing terrorist Cicuttini had fled to Spain on board a military plane after the 1972 Italian Peteano bomb which years later was traced back to right-wing terrorist Vincenzo Vinciguerra and the secret army by judge Felice Casson and started the discovery of the Gladio network across Europe. In Spain Cicuttini engaged in secret warfare for Franco who in turn protected him from the Italian justice. In 1987, Italy condemned Cicuttini to life imprisonment for his role in the Peteano massacre. But Spain, now a democracy, in an illustration of the continued influence behind the scene of the military apparatus refused to hand him to the Italians as the right-winger had married the daughter of a Spanish General and had become a Spanish citizen. Only in April 1998, aged 50, right-wing extremist Cicuttini was arrested in France and handed to Italy.[24]

Like all other secret armies in Western Europe, Spain's anti-Communist network at times cultivated close contacts with NATO. Italian General Gerardo Serravalle, who commanded the Italian Gladio from 1971 to 1974, after the discovery of the network in 1990 wrote a book about the Italian branch of the NATO secret army.[25] In his book the General relates that in 1973, NATO's secret army commanders met in the CPC in Brussels in an extra ordinate meeting in order to discuss the admission of Franco's Spain to the CPC. The French military secret service and the dominant CIA had allegedly requested the admission of the Spanish network while Italy represented by Serravalle had allegedly opposed the suggestion, for it was well known that the Spanish network protected wanted Italian right-wing terrorists. 'Our political authorities', the General reasoned, 'would have found themselves in a situation of extreme embarrassment before the Parliament' if it had been revealed that Italy not only ran a secret army but furthermore also closely cooperated with the Spanish secret network which harboured and protected Italian terrorists. Hence Spain was not officially admitted to the CPC.[26]

In a second CPC meeting, this time in Paris, members of Franco's secret service were once again present. They argued that Spain should be allowed to become an official member of the Gladio command centre because Spain had for a long time given the United States the right to station US nuclear missiles on its soil and military ships and submarines in its harbours, but was getting nothing in return from NATO. Sheltered behind the Pyrenees and far away from the Soviet border, the stay-behind post-invasion function seemed not to have been the first thing on the mind of the Spanish secret service agents attending the meeting. Rather they were interested to have a secret network in place to fight the Spanish Socialists and Communists. 'In all meetings there is "an hour of truth", one must only wait for it', Serravalle relates to the meeting in his book. 'It is the hour in which the delegates of the secret services, relaxed with a drink or a coffee, are more inclined to speak frankly. In Paris this hour came during the coffee break. I approached a member of the Spanish service and started by saying his government had maybe overestimated the reality of the danger of the threat from the East. I wanted to provocate him. He, looking at me in complete surprise, admitted that Spain had the problem of the Communists (los rojos). There we had it, the truth.'[27]

Spain became an official member of NATO in 1982, but Italian General Serravalle revealed that unofficial contacts had taken place much earlier. Spain, as the General put it, 'did not enter the door, but came through the window'. The Spanish secret army had for instance taken part in a stay-behind exercise commanded by the US forces in Europe in Bavaria, Germany, in March 1973 following an invitation of the United States.[28] Furthermore the Spanish secret army seems under the code name 'Red Quantum' also to have been a member of the second NATO-linked command centre, the ACC. 'After Spain's entry into NATO in 1982, the stay-behind structure linked to the CESID (Centro Superior de Informacion de la Defensa), successor of the SECED, joined the ACC', Gladio author Pietro Cedomi reported. 'This has lead to disputes in the ACC, above all from the Italians of the SISMI [Italian Military Secret Service], who accused the

Spanish of supporting Italian neo-fascists indirectly through the stay-behind "Red Quantum". '[29]

Whether the Spanish Socialists under Prime Minister Felipe Gonzalez, who had reached power in 1982, were aware of this secret cooperation with NATO remains doubtful. For the relationship with the CESID headed by Colonel Emilio Alonso Manglano was characterised by distrust and powerlessness of the new democratic government. In August 1983 it was revealed that CESID agents were secretly monitoring the conversations of the Socialist government, operating from the cellars of the government building. Despite the scandal which ensued, CESID Director Manglano was not fired. When Spain in 1986 after its truly remarkable peaceful transition from a dictatorship to a democracy was welcomed as a new member of the European Union, many hoped that the secret service apparatus was finally defeated and under solid democratic control. Yet such hopes, as in several other democracies in Western Europe, were shattered also in Spain as the discovery of the secret armies across Western Europe highlighted.

As the press started to report on the secret armies in late 1990, Spanish Communist member of parliament Carlos Carnero raised the well-founded suspicion that Spain might have functioned as a major Gladio base, harbouring neo-fascists from numerous countries, protected under the Franco apparatus. His concerns were confirmed by Amadeo Martinez, a former Colonel in the Spanish military who had been forced to leave the army due to his critical remarks, who declared to the press in 1990 that of course a Gladio-linked structure had existed under Franco also in Spain, which among other sensitive operations had spied on opposition politicians.[30] Also Spanish state television thereafter broadcasted a Gladio report in which it confirmed that Gladio agents had trained in Spain during Franco's dictatorship. An Italian officer involved with the secret armies testified that soldiers of the secret NATO army had trained in Spain from at least 1966 to the mid-1970s. The former agent said that he himself together with 50 others had been instructed at a military base in Las Palmas on the Spanish Canary Islands. According to the source the Gladio instructors were mostly from the United States.[31]

Others were less well informed. Javier Ruperez, first Spanish ambassador to NATO from June 1982 to February 1983, explained to the press that he had had no knowledge of Gladio. Ruperez, at the time of the Gladio discoveries a member of the Spanish conservative Partido Popular Party (PP) and Director of the Defence Commission, declared: 'Never have I known anything about this topic. I did not have the vaguest idea about what I am now reading of in the papers.' Also Fernando Moran, first Spanish Socialist Party (PSOE) Foreign Minister, in office until July 1985, testified for the record that he knew nothing of Gladio: 'Not during my time as minister, or at any other moment, was I aware of the slightest information, indication or rumour on the existence of Gladio or of anything similar.'[32]

Parliamentarian Antonio Romero, a member of the Spanish United Left opposition party (IU), became interested in the mysterious affair and contacted former agents of the secret trade whereupon he became convinced that this secret network had operated also in Spain and had 'acted against militant Communists and anarchists, such as against the miners of Asturias and the Catalan and Basque nationalists'.[33] On November 15, 1990, Romero thus asked the Spanish government under Socialist Prime Minister Felipe Gonzalez and Defence Minister Narcis Serra to explain exactly what role, if any, the country had played with respect to operation Gladio and the secret stay-behind armies of NATO. Already a day later Spain's Prime Minister Felipe Gonzalez claimed in front of the press that Spain 'was not even considered' for a role in Gladio.[34] But Romero wanted a more specific answer and posed three questions, of which the first one was: 'Does the Spanish government intend to ask NATO, as a member, for explanations on the activity and existence of a Gladio network?' The second question also aiming at the NATO alliance, Romero wanted to know, whether the Spanish executive 'will start a debate and a clarification on the activities of Gladio on the level of the Defence Ministers, the Foreign Ministers, and the Prime Ministers of the NATO members?' And finally Romero wanted to know, whether the Spanish government was considering the possibility of NATO disloyalty, in so far as 'some allied countries had illegally operated through Gladio, without that Spain was informed of this when it entered NATO [in 1982]?'[35]

The next day the Spanish newspapers headlined that 'The Spanish secret service cultivates close links to NATO. [Defence Minister] Serra orders investigation on Gladio network in Spain.' Within Spain's fragile post-fascist political area the topic was of course highly explosive because the press based on unnamed sources revealed that Gladio 'activists were recruited among military men and members of the extreme-right'. Serra became very nervous and in the first reply to journalists was eager to point out that 'when we came to power in 1982, we did not find anything of that sort', adding, 'probably because we entered NATO very late, when the Cold War was calming down'. Furthermore Serra assured the Spanish press that in response to parliamentarian Romero's question he had ordered an investigation to be carried out in his Defence Department on the potential connections of Spain to Gladio. However, sources close to the government revealed to the press that the in-house investigation was designed to hide more than it would reveal, as 'it aimed to confirm that this specific organisation did not operate in Spain'.[36] Tellingly Serra, aiming for a cover-up, had trusted the CESID with the investigation, and thus, technically, the suspect was investigating the crime.

It did not amount to a massive surprise when on Friday November 23, 1990, in response to Romero's question, Narcis Serra in front of parliament claimed that based on the CESID investigation Spain had never been a member of the secret Gladio network, 'either before or after the Socialist government'. Then Serra cautiously added that 'it has been suggested there were some contacts in the 1970s, but it is going to be very difficult for the current secret service to be able to verify that type of contact'. Serra, increasingly vague in his statement, referred to 'common sense' instead of using documents, testimonies, facts and figures: 'Since Spain was not a NATO member at the time, common sense says there could not have been very close links.' The Spanish press was not amused and criticised that the Defence Minister either was spreading propaganda, or had no knowledge nor control over the Department which he presided.[37]

Above all, Romero was also not satisfied with the answers provided by Serra and insisted that the acting Director of the CESID had to be questioned. 'If the CESID knows nothing on this, then General Manglano must be sacked', Romero concluded in front of the press. For General Manglano was not only the acting Director of the CESID, but also the Spanish delegate to NATO for security affairs. The Gladio scandal culminated in Spain when General Manglano despite the request of the legislative simply refused to take a stand. Angrily Romero concluded that obviously in Spain also 'high ranking military personnel is involved with the Gladio affair'.[38]

After the failure of the acting government to shed light on the secret affair the Spanish press questioned the most prominent retired governmental official of the young democracy and asked him whether he knew more about the mysterious affair. Calvo Sotelo, Spanish Prime Minister from February 1981 to December 1982, who during his time in office had nominated General Alonso Manglano as Director of the CESID claimed that Gladio did not exist in Spain: 'I do not have any knowledge that here something like that has ever existed, and without any doubt, I would have known, if it had existed here.' When the journalists insisted that Gladio armies had existed secretly across Western Europe Sotelo angrily explained that the Gladio network was both 'ridiculous and also criminal', adding that 'If they had informed me of such a crazy thing, I would have acted.'[39]

Sotelo confirmed that when Spain had embarked upon its democratic new experiment as a toddler nation after Franco's death, there had been fears about what the Spanish Communist Party (PCE) might do. But 'the modest result of the PCE in the first elections, and the even more modest result in the following elections, calmed our fears'. Sotelo at the time had been a prominent promoter of Spain's NATO membership. But to the press he stressed that Spain upon its entry had not been informed in writing by NATO on the existence of a secret Gladio network: 'There has been no written correspondence on the topic', adding enigmatically, 'and therefore there was also no need to talk about it, if indeed that should have been of what one would have talked'. Sotelo explained that there had been only a few meetings with NATO personnel before Spain joined the Alliance in May 1982, stressing that already at the end of the same year the PSOE had come to power and he had been replaced as Prime Minister by Felipe Gonzalez. There was no Spanish parliamentary Gladio investigation and no detailed public report.

9

THE SECRET WAR IN PORTUGAL

In May 1926 General Gomes da Costa staged a military coup d'état in Portugal, abolished both the constitution and the parliament, and turned the country into a dictatorship. In his wake dictator Salazar came to power. During the Spanish Civil War, Salazar supported right-wing dictator Franco in neighbouring Spain with troops and supplies. Thereafter the two dictators in a strategic right-wing alliance which effectively protected large parts of the Western front guaranteed to Hitler and Mussolini that Portugal would also stay neutral during the Second World War. The four dictators were in agreement that Communism both in the Soviet Union and in their own countries had to be fought and defeated.

As the Soviet Union emerged victorious from the Second World War and both Hitler and Mussolini were defeated, Salazar as well as Franco found themselves in a delicate situation in 1945. Yet as the United States under President Truman continued the fight against Communism on a global scale, both the dictators on the Iberian Peninsula gained at least the silent support of Washington and London. Despite Salazar's support for the coup in Spain and his alliance with Hitler and Mussolini, to the surprise of many, Portugal in 1949 was able to figure among the founding members of NATO. Thereafter Salazar ruled Portugal almost single-handedly for almost four decades until he died in 1970, whereupon the country was able to begin its transition towards a democratic state and became a member of the European Union.

As in right-wing dictatorships in Latin America and Franco's Spanish police state, Portugal's population was also being controlled through a security apparatus operating without transparency and beyond legal or parliamentarian control. Secret warfare against the political opposition and the Communists was therefore wide-spread throughout Salazar's rule. Operations were carried out by a number of services and organisms but most prominently by the Portuguese military secret service PIDE (Policia Internacional e de Defesa do Estado).

In the absence of a detailed investigation into the right-wing networks and secret operations of Portugal's dictatorship, the links to the anti-Communist NATO stay-behind army remain vague and mysterious. The existence of secret CIA and NATO-linked armies in Portugal was revealed for the first time in 1990 following the exposure of the Italian Gladio stay-behind. 'In Portugal a Lisbon radio station has reported that cells of the network associated with Operation Gladio were active during the 1950s to defend the rightist dictatorship of Dr. Salazar', the international press revealed.[1] And five years later US author Michael Parenti, without giving any further sources, claimed that Gladio operatives 'helped prop up a fascist regime in Portugal'.[2]

More specifically the local press claimed in 1990 that the secret army in Portugal was allegedly called 'Aginter Press'. Under the headline ' "Gladio" was active in Portugal', the Portuguese daily O Jornal informed a stunned audience in the country that 'The secret network, erected at the bosom of NATO and financed by the CIA, the existence of which has recently been revealed by Giulio Andreotti, had a branch in Portugal in the 1960s and the 1970s. It was called "Aginter Press" ' and was allegedly involved in assassination operations in Portugal as well as in the Portuguese colonies in Africa.[3]

Aginter Press was no press at all. The organisation did not print books or anti-Communist propaganda leaflets but trained right-wing terrorists and specialised in dirty tricks and secret warfare in Portugal and beyond. The mysterious and brutal organisation was supported by the CIA and run by European right-wing officers who with the help of the PIDE recruited fascist militants. The investigation of the Italian Senate into Gladio and the secret war and massacres in Italy discovered that Italian right-wing extremists had also been trained by Aginter Press. While in Portugal it was revealed that a sub-branch of Aginter Press called 'Organisation Armée contre le communisme International' (OACI) had also operated in Italy. The Italian Senators found that the CIA supported Aginter Press in Portugal and that the secret organisation was lead by Captain Yves Guillon, better known by his adopted name of Yves Guerin Serac, a specialist in secret warfare who had received war hero medals from the United States including the American Bronze Star for his involvement in the Korea War. 'Aginter Press', the Italian Gladio report concluded, 'in reality, according to the latest documents acquired by the criminal investigation, was an information centre directly linked to the CIA and the Portuguese secret service, that specialized in provocation operations.'[4]

While the government of Portugal shied away from investigating the history of the sinister Aginter Press and the secret war, the Italian Senate Commission investigating Gladio and the massacres in 1997 continued its research and questioned Italian judge Guido Salvini. With expert knowledge on right-wing terrorism in Italy and beyond, Salvini had also studied in detail the available documents on Aginter Press. 'Is the American secret service CIA', member of the Gladio commission Senator Manca asked Salvini, 'according to your analysis, directly responsible for the operations carried out by Aginter Press?' Judge Salvini replied: 'Senator Manca, you have asked a very important question now' and due to the political sensitivity of his answer demanded that he may give his answer during a secret session only. This was agreed, and the documents remain inaccessible as of now.[5]

Publicly judge Salvini stressed that 'it is difficult to give a precise definition of Aginter Press', while at least in vague terms he suggested the following: 'It is an organisation, which in many countries, including Italy, inspires and supports strategies of selected groups, which intervene according to a defined protocol against the situation they want to combat.' The anti-Communist secret CIA army Aginter Press operates, as Salvini continued, 'according to its aims and values, which in their essence are the defence of the Western world against a probable and imminent invasion of Europe by the troops of the Soviet Union and the Communist countries'.[6] The Portuguese secret army Aginter Press, according to judge Salvini, hence carried out like most other secret Gladio armies in Western Europe a twofold task. The stay-behind network clandestinely trained for the eventuality of a Soviet invasion, and, in the absence of such an invasion during the Cold War, targeted political groups of the left according to the strategies of secret warfare in several countries in Western Europe.

While many members of Aginter Press had been active in the secret anti-Communist war under different labels in previous decades, Aginter Press was officially founded in Lisbon only in September 1966. Domestic operations much rather than the fear of a Soviet invasion seem to have dominated the strategic thinking of its founders and the CIA at the time. For the period was characterised by large-scale left-wing protests in numerous countries in Western Europe against the Vietnam War and the US support of right-wing dictatorships in Latin America and Western Europe, including Portugal. Both dictator Salazar and the PIDE feared the potentially destabilising effects of the social movement and amongst other instruments relied upon Aginter Press to combat the movement.

Most of the secret soldiers that in the second half of the 1960s joined the secret CIA army Aginter Press in Lisbon had previously fought in Africa and Southeast Asia attempting in vain to prevent the loss of European colonies to strong independence movements. Aginter Press Director Captain Yves Guerin Serac himself, a catholic militant and anti-Communist recruited by the CIA, was an ex-French army officer who had seen France defeated by Hitler in the Second World War. He was a veteran of the French Vietnam War (1945–1954), a veteran of the Korean war (1950–1953) and a veteran of the French War in Algeria. Guerin Serac had served in the notorious 11th Demi-Brigade Parachutiste du Choc, a special dirty tricks unit of the French secret service SDCE closely linked to the French stay-behind, and in 1961 together with other battle-hardened 11th du Choc officers had founded the clandestine and illegal Organisation Armee Secrete, in short OAS, in order to keep French control over colonial Algeria and to overthrow the French government of President De Gaulle and replace it with a militantly anti-Communist authoritarian French state.

Even after Algeria gained its independence in 1962 and De Gaulle closed down the OAS, former OAS officers including Guerin Serac were in great danger. They fled from Algeria and in exchange for asylum and other amenities offered their remarkable skills in secret warfare, covert action, counter-terrorism and terrorism to dictators in Latin America and Europe.[7] The OAS diaspora strengthened militant right-wing networks internationally and in June 1962 Yves Guerin Serac was hired by dictator Franco to employ his skills together with the Spanish secret army

116

against the Spanish opposition. From Spain Guerin Serac moved on to Salazar's Portugal, as the country according to his analysis was not only the last remaining colonial empire, but also the last bulwark against Communism and atheism. A convinced anti-Communist Cold Warrior, he offered his services to Salazar: 'The others have laid down their weapons, but not I. After the OAS I fled to Portugal to carry on the fight and expand it to its proper dimensions – which is to say, a planetary dimension.'[8]

In Portugal Guerin Serac linked up with French right-wingers and OAS fugitives, whereupon former Petainist Jacques Ploncard d'Assac introduced him to the right-wing establishment and the PIDE. Due to his extensive experience Guerin Serac was recruited as an instructor for the paramilitary Legiao Portuguesa and for the counterguerilla units of the Portuguese army. It was within this context that he erected Aginter Press as an ultra secret anti-Communist army with the support of both the PIDE and the CIA. Aginter Press set up training camps in which it instructed mercenaries and terrorists in a three-week course in covert action techniques including hands-on bomb terrorism, silent assassination, subversion techniques, clandestine communication and infiltration and colonial warfare.

Next to Guerin Serac, Italian right-wing terrorist Stefano Delle Chiaie was among the founding fathers of Aginter Press. 'We acted against the Communists and against the bourgeois state, against the democracy, which deprived us from our liberty. And thus we had to use violence', Delle Chiaie later reasoned. 'We were considered to be criminals, but in reality we were but the victims of an anti-Fascist liberal movement. Thus we wanted to make our ideas public, we wanted to be heard all over the world.' Aged 30, Delle Chiaie in the mid-1960s together with Guerin Serac and the support of the CIA set up the Aginter secret army. 'Together with a French friend of mine [Guerin Serac] I decided back then [1965], to establish the press agency Aginter Press, in order to be able to defend our political views.'[9] In the years that followed Delle Chiaie became maybe the most brutal right-wing terrorist directly linked to the secret war. In Italy he engaged in coup d'états and massacres, including the Piazza Fontana massacre of 1969, and in Latin America together with Nazi Klaus Barbie, the 'butcher of Lyon', he propped up right-wing dictatorships.[10]

'Our number consists of two types of men: (1) Officers who have come to us from the fighting in Indo-China and Algeria, and some who even enlisted with us after the battle for Korea', Aginter Director Guerin Serac himself described the anti-Communist secret army. '(2) Intellectuals who, during this same period turned their attention to the study of the techniques of Marxist subversion.' These intellectuals, as Guerin Serac observed, had formed study groups and shared experiences 'in an attempt to dissect the techniques of Marxist subversion and to lay the foundations of a counter-technique'. The battle, it was clear to Guerin Serac, had to be carried out in numerous countries: 'During this period we have systematically established close contacts with like-minded groups emerging in Italy, Belgium, Germany, Spain or Portugal, for the purpose of forming the kernel of a truly Western League of Struggle against Marxism.'[11]

Coming directly from war theatres, many secret soldiers, and above all their instructors, including Guerin Serac, had little respect for or knowledge of non-violent conflict solutions. Guerin Serac himself, together with many others, was convinced that in order to defeat Communism in Western Europe secret terrorist operations were necessary: 'In the first phase of our political activity we must create chaos in all structures of the regime' he declared without specifically indicating the state targeted. 'Two forms of terrorism can provoke such a situation: The blind terrorism (committing massacres indiscriminately which cause a large number of victims), and the selective terrorism (eliminate chosen persons)'. In each case the terror carried out secretly by the extreme right had to be blamed on the left, as the master and eminence grise of anti-Communist terrorism insisted: 'This destruction of the state must be carried out as much as possible under the cover of "Communist activities".' The terrorist attacks of the secret armies are designed as a means to discredit the ruling government and force it to shift to the right: 'After that, we must intervene at the heart of the military, the juridical power and the church, in order to influence popular opinion, suggest a solution, and clearly demonstrate the weakness of the present legal apparatus . . . Popular opinion must be polarised in such a way, that we are being presented as the only instrument capable of saving the nation. It is obvious, that we will need considerable financial resources, to carry out such operations.'[12]

The CIA and Salazar's military secret service PIDE provided the finances for the terrorism of Captain Guerin Serac. An Aginter document, entitled 'Our Political Activity' and dated November 1969, was found in late 1974. It describes how a country can be targeted with secret warfare: 'Our belief is that the first phase of political activity ought to be to create the conditions favouring the installation of chaos in all of the regime's structures'. As the most essential component of the strategy the violence inflicted had to be blamed on the Communists and traces had to be planted accordingly. 'In our view the first move we should make is to destroy the structure of the democratic state under the cover of Communist and pro-Chinese activities.' The document continued to stress that left-wing militant groups had to be infiltrated and manipulated: 'Moreover, we have people who have infiltrated these groups and obviously we will have to tailor our actions to the ethos of the milieu – propaganda and action of a sort which will seem to have emanated from our Communist adversaries.' Such false flag operations, the secret soldiers concluded, 'will create a feeling of hostility towards those who threaten the peace of each and every nation', i.e. the Communists.[13]

During the early phase of Aginter Press one of the main efforts of its officers and trained mercenaries and terrorists was to weaken and destroy the national liberation guerrilla groups operating in Portuguese colonies. Thus in the mid-1960s the first theatre of operations for Aginter Press was not Europe but Africa where Portugal in its colonies fought against the national liberation movements. Aginter dispatched its operation chiefs to the countries bordering Portuguese Africa. 'Their aim included the liquidation of leaders of the liberation movements, infiltration, the installation of informers and provocateurs, and the utilisation of false liberation movements.'[14] The secret wars were carried out in coordination with the PIDE and other branches of the Portuguese government. 'Aginter Press had written contracts with PIDE to carry out special operations and espionage missions.'[15]

The most prominent victims of the political assassinations carried out by Aginter secret soldiers in Portugal and the colonies allegedly included Humberto Delgado, Portuguese opposition leader, Amilcar Cabral, one of Africa's foremost revolutionary figures and Eduardo Mondlane, leader and President of the Mocambique liberation party and movement FRELIMO (Frente de Liberacao de Mocambique), killed in colonial Mocambique in February 1969.[16] Despite the brutality employed, Portugal was unable to prevent its colonies from becoming independent. Goa became a part of India in 1961. Guineau-Bissau became independent in 1974. Angola and Mocambique reached their independence in 1975 while East Timor was invaded in the same year by Indonesia.

Next to the colonial wars Aginter also directly influenced the secret wars against the Communists in Western Europe. The evidence available as of now on the NATO stay-behind armies and the secret war in Western Europe suggests that maybe more than any other secret army the Lisbon-based Aginter Press was responsible for much brutality and bloodshed in Portugal and beyond. The secret soldiers of Aginter Press operated with a different mentality. Unlike the secret soldiers of, for instance, the Swiss stay-behind P26 or the Norwegian stay-behind ROC, the members of the Portuguese stay-behind Aginter Press were engaged in real wars in the colonies, killed repeatedly and were lead by a captain who viewed violence as a primary tool to solve conflicts after having served in Vietnam, Korea and Algeria.

Maybe the best-documented atrocity carried out by the secret soldiers in Western Europe in their anti-Communist battle is the Piazza Fontana massacre which hit Italy's political capital Rome and Italy's industrial capital Milan shortly before Christmas on December 12, 1969. On that day four bombs exploded in Rome and Milan killing 16 citizens indiscriminately, predominantly farmers who after a day on the market wanted to deposit their modest earnings in the Banca Nationale Dell' Agricultura at Piazza Fontana in Milan, while 80 were maimed and wounded. One bomb in Piazza Fontana did not explode because its timer had failed, yet upon arriving on the scene the Italian military secret service SID together with the police immediately destroyed the compromising evidence and made the bomb go off after its discovery. The massacre was carried out exactly along the secret warfare strategies drafted by Guerin Serac. The Italian military secret service blamed the massacre on the left and planted parts of a bomb as evidence in the villa of well-known leftist editor, Giangiacomo Feltrinelli, and arrested immediately numerous Communists.[17]

A classified internal report of the Italian military secret service SID dated December 16, 1969 had already alleged at the time that the massacres of Rome and Milan had been carried out by the political right with support of the CIA.[18] Yet the Italian public had been made to believe that the strong Italian Communists had begun using violence to achieve power. Presumably the massacre had been carried out by the Italian right-wing groups Ordine Nuovo and Avanguardia Nazionale which cooperated closely with the stay-behind armies in the secret war. Italian right-wing extremist Guido Giannettini who was directly involved in the massacre cooperated closely with the Lisbon-based Aginter Press. 'In these investigations data has emerged which confirms the links between Aginter Press, Ordine Nuovo and Avanguardia Nazionale' judge Salvini explained to the Italian Senators investigating the secret war in Italy and beyond. 'It has emerged that Guido Giannettini had contacts with Guerin Serac in Portugal ever since 1964. It has emerged that instructors of Aginter Press... came to Rome between 1967 and 1968 and instructed the militant members of Avanguardia Nazionale in the use of explosives.' Judge Salvini concluded that based on the available documents and testimonies it emerges that the CIA front Aginter Press had played a decisive role in secret warfare operation in Western Europe and had started the great massacres to discredit the Communists in Italy.[19]

This fact was further confirmed in a far-reaching testimony in March 2001 by General Giandelio Maletti, former head of Italian counter-intelligence, at a trial of right-wing extremists accused of killing 16 in the Piazza Fontana massacre. Maletti testified in front of a Milan court that 'The CIA, following the directives of its government, wanted to create an Italian nationalism capable of halting what it saw as a slide to the left, and, for this purpose, it may have made use of right-wing terrorism.' It was a far-reaching testimony confirming that the CIA is a terrorist organisation. 'Don't forget that Nixon was in charge', Maletti elaborated, 'and Nixon was a strange man, a very intelligent politician, but a man of rather unorthodox initiatives'.[20] Italian Judge Guido Salvini confirmed that the traces lead to 'a foreign secret service'. 'By saying "foreign secret service", do you mean the CIA?' Italian journalists inquired, to which Salvini cautiously replied: 'We can say that we know very well who assisted in the preparations for the massacres and who sat at the same table from where the orders for the massacres have been given. That is the truth.'[21]

Apart from fighting Communism in Italy Captain Guerin Serac made it a point that the anti-Communist struggle had to be carried out on a global scale. Therefore Aginter operatives, including American Jay Sablonsky, together with the CIA and US Green Berets Special Forces participated in the notorious Guatemalan counter-terror of 1968–1971, in which some 50,000 people, mostly civilian, were estimated to have been killed. Furthermore Aginter operatives were present in Chile in 1973 and were involved when the CIA ousted elected Socialist President Salvador Allende and replaced him with right-wing dictator Augusto Pinochet.[22] From its safe haven in Portugal's right-wing dictatorship Aginter was able to dispatch its secret soldiers to numerous territories across the globe.

This changed only when in May 1974 Portugal's 'Revolution of the Flowers' finally abolished the dictatorship and paved the way for a democratic transition of the country. The secret soldiers of Aginter knew that the survival of their organisation depended upon the survival of the right-wing dictatorship. Upon learning that left-wing officers within the Portuguese military were planning a coup to start the 'Revolution of the Flowers', Aginter operatives plotted with right-wing General Spinola against the Portuguese centrists. Their plan was to occupy the Portuguese Azores islands in the Atlantic and use them as an independent territory and offshore base for covert operations against the Portuguese mainland.

Unable to realise their plan Aginter Press was swept away together with the dictatorship when on May 1, 1974 the left-wing of the Portuguese military took over power and ended the dictatorship which had lasted for almost half a century. Three weeks after the revolutionary coup, on May 22, 1974, special units of the Portuguese Police on the orders of the new rulers broke into the Aginter Press headquarter in the Rua das Pracas in Lisbon in order to close down the sinister agency and confiscate all material. But by then the premises were deserted. With good relations to the intelligence community all Aginter Press agents had been warned and had gone underground and nobody was arrested. Leaving their offices in a hurry some documents were left behind. The special police units were able to collect a large amount of criminal evidence, proving that the CIA front Aginter Press had very actively engaged in terrorism.

As the young democracy was attempting to cope with the security apparatus left behind by the dictatorship, the military secret service PIDE as well as the Legiao Portuguesa were being dissolved. The 'Commission to dissolve the PIDE and the Portuguese Legion' (Comissao de Extincao da PIDE e da Legiao) quickly learned that PIDE with the support of the CIA had ran a secret army labelled Aginter Press and thus demanded that it be provided with the files which had been compiled on Aginter Press after its headquarters had been ambushed and which contained all the relevant evidence. The history of the secret army of Portugal was about to be investigated for the first time when suddenly the files disappeared. 'The dossier "Aginter-Press" was taken away from the Commission to dissolve the PIDE and the Portuguese Legion, and vanished thereafter', the Portuguese daily *O Jornal* related the scandal years later with much regret in its article on the Gladio network.[23]

How could this happen? Why had the commission not been more careful with its sensitive data? Italian journalist Barbachetto of the Milan-based political magazine *L'Europeo* later recalled: 'Three of my colleagues were present back then during the confiscation of the Aginter archive. They managed to take pictures of parts, only of very small parts, of the large amount of confiscated data.' Under the headings 'Mafia' or 'German financial contributors' the confiscated documents indicated the cover names of Aginter supporters. 'The documents were destroyed by the Portuguese military,' Barbachetto recalls, 'because obviously they feared diplomatic complications with the governments of Italy, France and Germany, if the activities of Aginter in the various European countries would be revealed'.[24]

PIDE was replaced by a new Portuguese military secret service labelled SDCI which investigated the secret Aginter army and concluded that the sinister organisation had had four tasks. First, it had been an internationally well-connected 'espionage bureau run by the Portuguese police and, through them, the CIA, the West German BND or "Gehlen Organisation", the Spanish Direccion General De Seguridad, South Africa's BOSS and, later, the Greek KYP'. Next to this intelligence-gathering task Aginter Press had secondly functioned as a 'centre for the recruitment and training of mercenaries and terrorists specialising in sabotage and assassination'. According to the SDCI document, Aginter Press had thirdly been a 'strategic centre for neo-fascist and right-wing political indoctrination operations in sub-Saharan Africa, South America and Europe in conjunction with a number of sub-fascist regimes, well-known right-wing figures and internationally active neo-fascist groups'. Fourth, Aginter had been a secret anti-Communist army, an 'international fascist organisation called "Order and Tradition" with a clandestine paramilitary wing called OACI, "Organisation Armée contre le communisme International"'.[25]

After the fall of the Portuguese dictatorship Guerin Serac and his militant anti-Communists had fled to neighbouring Spain and protected by Franco re-established headquarters in Madrid. True to their trade, Aginter secret soldiers in exchange for asylum agreed with Franco's secret service to hunt down and assassinate leading members of the Bask separatist movement ETA. Furthermore they continued their clandestine operations abroad and amongst others attempted to discredit the Algerian liberation movement. 'I can provide you with another very interesting example', Italian judge Salvini related to the Italian Senators, whereupon he explained that from their Spanish base in 1975 the group of Guerin Serac, together with the American Salby and militant French, Italian and Spanish rightists, had organised a series of bomb attacks each time leaving the signal SOA, which signifies 'Algerian Opposition' in order to discredit a group of the Algerian opposition.

'The bombs were planted at Algerian embassies in four different countries, France, Germany, Italy and Great Britain' and made the Algerian opposition look bad, while 'in reality the bombings were carried out by the group of Guerin Serac, who thus demonstrated his great camouflage and infiltration capabilities'. The bomb in front of the Algerian embassy in Frankfurt did not blow up and was meticulously analysed by the German police. 'In order to understand the links of Guerin Serac and Aginter Press, it is important to notice the complex fabrication of the bomb', judge Salvini highlighted. 'It contained C4, an explosive exclusively used by the US forces, which has never been used in any of the anarchist bombings. I repeat, this was a very sophisticated bomb. That Aginter had C4 at its disposability, certainly shows which contacts it enjoyed.'[26]

When the Spanish right-wing dictatorship collapsed with the death of dictator Franco on November 20, 1975, Guerin Serac and his secret army were once again forced to flee. The Spanish police took its time to investigate what Aginter had left behind and only in February 1977 staged a razzia in Madrid's Calle Pelayo 39, where at Aginter headquarters they discovered arms caches with rifles and explosives. By this time Delle Chiaie, Guerin Serac and their secret soldiers had long left Europe for Latin America, where in Pinochet's Chile many found a new secure operational base. Guerin Serac was last seen in Spain in 1997.[27]

Public attention was once again drawn to the history of the secret and mysterious anti-Communist army in Portugal when in late 1990 Italian Prime Minister Giulio Andreotti revealed that NATO-linked secret stay-behind armies existed in Italy and beyond. On November 17, 1990 the European discoveries reached Lisbon where the Portuguese daily *Expresso*, under the headline 'Gladio. The Cold War Soldiers', reported that 'The scandal has transgressed the frontiers of Italy and until now the existence of secret Gladio networks has been confirmed officially in Belgium, France, Holland, Luxemburg, Germany, and semi-officially in Sweden, Norway, Denmark, Austria, Switzerland, Greece, Turkey, Spain, United Kingdom and Portugal.'[28]

Greatly worried, Portuguese Defence Minister Fernando Nogueira on November 16, 1990 declared to the public that he had no knowledge of the existence of any kind of Gladio branch in Portugal and claimed that there existed neither in his Defence Ministry nor in the General Staff of the Portuguese Armed Forces 'any information whatsoever concerning the existence or activity of any "Gladio structure" in Portugal'.[29] The Portuguese newspaper *Diario De Noticias* lamented that 'the laconic position now put forward by Fernando Nogueira is being confirmed, in one way or another, by former Defence Ministers, such as Eurico de Melo and Rui Machete, as well as by [former Foreign Minister] Franco Nogueira and by Marshall Costa Gomes, who confirmed to DN that they had absolutely no knowledge on the issue. The same position has also been taken by oppositional parliamentarians in the Parliamentary Defence Committee.'[30]

Costa Gomes, former Portuguese liaison officer to NATO, insisted that he had no knowledge of a secret network linked to NATO, 'despite the fact that between 1953 and 1959 I have taken part in all reunions of the Alliance'. At the same time he admitted however that a Portuguese Gladio could have been linked to the PIDE or to certain persons in Portugal who were not members of the government. 'Such links', Costa Gomes explained, 'if they indeed existed, would have run parallel to the official structures', and were thus unknown to him. Similar to Costa Gomes, Franco Nogueira, who had been foreign minister under Salazar, claimed: 'Never have I had the slightest idea that this organisation existed. Not even during the time that I was foreign minister and was in contact with NATO officials, nor during the time thereafter.' He explained that if Gladio had been active in Portugal, 'the activity would certainly have been known to Dr. Salazar'. Salazar would of course, as Nogueira implied, have communicated this information to his foreign minister: 'It would be very difficult for me to believe that the network would have had connections to the PIDE or to the Legiao Portuguesa. Therefore I am convinced that this Gladio did not exist in our country, despite of course, that all is possible in life.'[31]

While governmental officials were unable to provide information on the secret war, the Portuguese press observed the obvious and lamented that 'obviously various European governments have not controlled their secret services', criticising NATO for having followed 'a doctrine of limited trust. Such a doctrine claims that certain governments would not act sufficiently against Communists, and were thus not worth being informed on the activities of NATO's secret army'.[32] Only one senior Portuguese military officer was willing to lift parts of the secret if allowed to remain unnamed. A Portuguese General, who had been Chief of the Portuguese Chiefs of Staff, confirmed to *O Jornal* that 'a parallel operation and information service had indeed existed in Portugal and its colonies, the financing and command of which escaped the Armed Forces, but was dependent on the Defence Ministry, the Interior Ministry, and the Ministry for Colonial Affairs. This parallel operation and information service, the General confirmed, was also directly linked to PIDE and to the Legiao Portuguesa.'[33] There was no parliamentary investigation into the affair, let alone a parliamentary report and with these vague confirmations the matter rested.

10

THE SECRET WAR IN BELGIUM

In the Second World War Belgium was defeated and occupied by German troops. The Belgian government was forced to flee to London and remained in exile until the Allied Forces liberated Europe. During the traumatic exile in London the Belgian government and military established close ties with the British when the two nations cooperated in order to set up secret armies in occupied Belgium. As of summer 1942 the British SOE had established arms dumps in Belgium and erected and trained a secret army. The British managed the availability of radios and aeroplanes to transport men and material, and from London controlled the logistics and directed the training and debriefing of the agents who were sent secretly to occupied Belgium. Next to carrying out sabotage operations against the German occupiers the secret Belgian army collected information which the agents transmitted to London by radio, writing or microfilm. The overall impact of the network was marginal but the strategy served as an example: 'Towards the end of the hostilities, the activities of this first stay-behind were well organised and admired by the British and American secret service.'[1]

As the enemy changed from Nazi Germany to Soviet Communism the secret armies were created anew after the war. The stay-behind network which during the Cold War operated in Belgium, as the Senate investigation found, had two branches: SDRA8 and STC/Mob. SDRA8 was the military branch located within the military secret service, Service General du Renseignement (SGR), under the direction of the Defence Ministry. The branch SDRA8, also spelled SDRA VIII, stands for 'service de documentation, de renseignement et d'action VIII' (service for documentation, intelligence and action). The members of SDRA8 were military men, trained in combat and sabotage, parachute jumping and maritime operations. SDRA8, next to information gathering, was trained to organise evacuation routes if an occupation of Belgium should occur. If the entire territory were occupied, some SDRA8 agents had to accompany the Belgian government abroad and liaise with the secret agents who remained in Belgium to combat the enemy.[2]

The civilian branch STC/Mob of the Belgian stay-behind was located within the civilian secret service Security of the State (Sûreté de L'Etat, short Sûreté) under the direction of the Justice Ministry. STC/Mob stands for 'section training, communication and mobilisation'. The members of the civilian STC/Mob were technicians trained to operate a radio station. Predominantly recruited from groups 'with strong religious convictions as a guarantee for their anti-Communism' the STC/Mob men, according to the Belgium Gladio investigation, were 'calm fathers [pères tranquilles], at times even a bit naive'.[3] STC/Mob 'had the mission to collect intelligence under conditions of enemy occupation which could be useful to the government. Furthermore STC/Mob had the task to organise secure communication routes to evacuate the members of the government and other people with official functions.'[4] In order to coordinate the coexistence of the two Belgian stay-behinds an 'Inter-Service' coordination committee was created in 1971. Reunions took place every six months, with the presidency rotating between SDRA and the Sûreté d'Etat. The reunions helped to assure a common position in the international meetings of NATO's secret warfare centre Allied Clandestine Committee.[5]

The somewhat unusual twofold structure of the Belgian secret army resulted directly from its origins in the Second World War. The units which during the war had collected intelligence which then had been sent by radio, by writing or by microfilm to London had been commanded by M. Lepage who directed the Sûreté within the Belgian Justice Ministry. This branch became STC/Mob. The Belgian agents who during the war were sent from London by parachute into the occupied country to engage in covert action and sabotage operations were coordinated by the Belgian army. They formed SDRA8. 'It therefore follows from the above explained', the Belgian Senate report on Gladio observed, 'that Belgium, in contrast to other countries, has had right from the beginning a civilian and a military stay-behind organisation'.[6]

The members of the Belgian secret army were 'on the whole Royalist in politics' and thus did not include members of the Belgian Communist resistance, as a formerly classified British SOE report stresses.[7] After D-day and the liberation of Belgium both the United States and England were concerned about the strength of the Belgian Communists. As in Italy and France, in Belgium too the Communists were widely respected by the population for their courage and prominent role in the resistance battle against the Nazis. Therefore British and Belgian authorities in late 1944 were anxious to disarm the Resistance and to arm the police as quickly as possible.[8] 'After the war a rather powerful Communist party arose having, I think, twenty one members of parliament, which was unique in Belgium', Belgian historian Etienne Verhoyen later highlighted the delicate period in a Gladio documentary on BBC. 'It had never happened before and given the international context of Communism, right-wing people were of course afraid of what they called "Communist Danger" in Belgium.'[9]

Julian Lahaut was the charismatic leader figure of the Belgian Communists. After his arrest by the Germans, Lahaut had spent the war in captivity and upon his liberation in 1945 was appointed honorary President of the Belgian Communists. Lahaut openly and prominently agitated against the return of the Belgian king Baudouin, whom he and other leftists considered to be a puppet of the Belgian centre-right and the United States. 'The left-wing was opposed to the return of the

King, so the right-wingers were for the return of the king and some of these groups established in 1948 their first contacts within the American embassy', historian Verhoyen related in the Gladio documentary. The Belgian right in the US embassy made contacts with an officer called Parker, allegedly working for the CIA. Parker, according to Verhoyen, 'insisted on not only the Leopoldist agitation, he insisted also on the formation of stay-behind groups to assure anti-Communist resistance'.[10]

When King Baudouin returned to Belgium and in August 1950 took his oath, Lahaut shouted in protest in the Belgian Parliament 'Long live the Republic!' Many on the Belgian right considered this to have been an unforgivable action and feared that the Belgian Communists might radically alter the established system. The political climate in the country become very tense. Two weeks later, on August 18, 1950, two men shot Lahaut dead in front of his house. The assassination left large parts of the Belgian society in shock. The extreme right and its clandestine network had eliminated the most popular Belgian Communist.[11]

Whether the Belgian secret anti-Communist army was responsible for the assassination remains unclear. But it has been alleged that by the time of Lahaut's assassination the Belgian stay-behind was operational. Stewart Menzies, the chief of the MI6, in a letter dated January 27, 1949 to Belgian Socialist Prime Minister Paul Henri Spaak, had urged that the existing secret collaboration between the United Kingdom and Belgium started during the Second World War must continue. 'It was agreed', Menzies in his letter summarised a meeting which he had had with Spaak, 'that Anglo-Belgian co-operation between the special services should be pursued on the basis of those traditions which date from the First World War, and which were reaffirmed in discussions between both M. Pierlot [H. Pierlot, Belgian Prime Minister 1939–1945] and M. Van Acker [A. Van Acker, Belgian Prime Minister 1945–1946, predecessor of Spaak] and myself during the periods that they held office as Prime Minister.' Specifically Menzies stressed that 'the preparation of appropriate intelligence and action organisations in the event of war', thus the running of a Belgian Gladio, had to be continued. 'Demands for training and material will arise in the near future', Menzies explained in his letter and offered his assistance: 'I have already undertaken to provide certain training facilities for officers and others nominated by the Head of your Special Service, and I am in a position to provide items of new equipment now in production.' Menzies urged Spaak to keep the letter top-secret. Above all he urged Spaak not to collaborate with the CIA exclusively and suggested that 'certain officers should proceed to the United Kingdom in the near future to study, in conjunction with my Service, the technicalities of these matters'.[12]

Belgian Prime Minister Spaak replied to MI6 chief Menzies that he was glad to receive help from the British, but since the American CIA had also approached him on the subject he thought it important that the British and Americans cooperated so that Belgium would not get into an uncomfortable position of having to choose between them. 'I agree with you', Spaak wrote to Menzies, 'that it would be highly desirable that the three services (British, American and Belgian) should collaborate closely. If two of them, the American and the British, refuse that collaboration, the situation of the Belgian service would be extremely delicate and difficult. I therefore think that it is unavoidable, that on the highest levels negotiations take place between London and Washington to solve this question.'[13]

After high-level negotiations had taken place the American, British and Belgian secret services created an organisational body labelled 'Tripartite Meeting Brussels' (TMB) at times also called 'Tripartite Meeting Belgian' to oversee the creation of the Belgian stay-behind. Spaak was rewarded for his loyalty and in 1957 became NATO Secretary-General, the highest civilian position within the military alliance, a post which he held until 1961. Eleven years later Spaak died and could thus no longer be questioned by the Belgian Gladio investigation. 'Several documents establish thus that the responsible politicians of the time were aware of the gravity of the situation and endorsed the idea of negotiations in favour of close collaboration with the American and British secret services', the Belgian Senate report on Gladio summarised the period. 'This cooperation gained even further solid basis with the creation of the Tripartite Meeting Belgian/Brussels towards the end of the 1940s.'[14]

Most of the details on the secret warfare command centres remain unavailable as of now, but it is known that next to TMB other centres were also created which carried the acronyms CCUO, CPC, ACC and SDRA11. The Gladio evidence available as of now suggests that in the immediate post-war years trilateral structures were favoured, for at the same time the United Kingdom and the United States had also formalised their secret cooperation with the Dutch Gladio in a Tripartite Committee Holland (TCH), in which the United Kingdom, the United States and the Netherlands each had a seat.[15] Furthermore such a trilateral secret agreement seems to have existed also between the British and the French, who on May 4, 1947 had signed a pact on secret stay-behind collaboration.[16] In addition to these secret warfare centres on March 17, 1948 the so-called Western Union Clandestine Committee (WUCC) was founded. With the task of carrying out peacetime preparations against an eventual Soviet invasion, it was a clandestine Gladio coordination centre in which five nations had a seat: the United Kingdom, Belgium, the Netherlands, Luxemburg and France.[17] 'Other countries thus also followed such policies; they formed a unit which was independent from the TMB, with the aim to develop a common policy as far as the peacetime preparations for an eventual war were concerned', the Belgian Senators noted while observing that the United States allegedly became a member of the WUCC only in 1958.[18]

According to Belgian Gladio author Jan Willems, the creation of WUCC in spring 1948 had been a direct consequence of a public speech by British Foreign Minister Ernest Bevin held in London on January 22, 1948. In front of the British parliament Bevin had elaborated on his plan for a 'Union Occidental', an international organisation designed to counter what he perceived to be the Soviet threat in Europe, which consisted not only in the Red Army, but above all also in the Communist subversion of Western Europe. Together with Washington, as a US memorandum of March 8, 1948 indicates, Bevin was in agreement that 'The problem of the moment consists not so much any longer that we must prepare against a foreign aggressor, but that we must prepare internally against a fifth column, supported by a foreign power.'[19] WUCC, at times also labelled CCWU, had two missions on the security level: Guarantee that political and military discussions could be carried out in secrecy; and to develop forms of cooperation in the fight against subversion and infiltration activities. 'The aim was to develop mechanisms that allow to eliminate Communist candidates from the command of political institutions; this aim, according to the American documents, was realised.'[20]

After the creation of NATO in Paris in 1949 the WUCC, as the Belgian Senate found, was in April 1951 firmly integrated into the military alliance and changed its label to 'Clandestine Planning Committee' (CPC). 'In conclusion', Belgian Gladio author Willems stresses, 'The fight against the internal enemy has been an integral part of the NATO pact ever since it was signed in 1949.'[21] As NATO intensified secret warfare next to the CPC a second secret command centre was established within the military alliance, the Allied Clandestine Committee (ACC), which allegedly held its first meeting in France on April 29 and 30, 1958, under the presidency of France. When NATO had to leave France, the ACC moved to Brussels in 1968 and the clandestine ACC was, as section SDRA11, located administratively within the Belgian military secret service SGR with its headquarters in Evere, directly behind NATO installations. SDRA11, a front for ACC, was 'financed by NATO', as the Belgian Gladio report revealed while SDRA8, the covert action branch of the Belgian Gladio was paid by the Belgian Defence Department.[22] The last confirmed meeting of the Gladio command centre ACC took place in Brussels on October 23 and 24, 1990 under the presidency of Belgian SGR Director General Raymond Van Calster who was furious when journalists started to ask questions about the secret centre.[23]

Michel Van Ussel, alias Georges 923, a member of the Belgian Gladio in the 1980s, explained in his book on the Belgian Gladio in 1991 that ACC had, above all, a coordination task. 'The activities which needed to be co-ordinated were debated in the ACC. The issues included the use of the radio systems, the marking of areas where parachuted agents would land, the ways by which agents would recognise each other, the transferral of agents across national boarders, etc.' Van Ussel elaborated that the military secret services used the ACC to exchange ideas and discuss clandestine operations: 'Within the fields of intelligence gathering, escape and evasion operations, as well as the air and sea operations, each ACC member country followed the same rules, which had furthermore been established by common agreement between the participants. Yet each member country was also free to carry out other "activities", which obviously were not mentioned at the reunions, or, if at all, only secretly at the side among instructors.'[24]

The Belgian Senate faced great difficulties to clarify the facts when it came to the secret NATO centres. General Raymond Van Calster deliberately misled the Senators during his interrogation when he failed to mention the existence of SDRA11, a front for the ACC, within the Belgian military secret service.[25] Furthermore some Belgian military officers flatly rejected to testify to the Belgian Senators by stating that they had agreed to a Gladio secret which read: 'I hereby declare that I will never discuss such information and material outside a secure area, nor with those unauthorised to receive it even after my retirement or release from the service of my Country, unless freed from this obligation by specific, unmistakable and categorical official notice.' The Senators were frustrated and noted for the record that their investigation into the secret war of NATO 'has been hindered gravely by the refusal of the concerned military personnel who referred to obligations towards NATO secrecy which also covered the activities which they had carried out in the CPC.'[26]

Senator Cecile Harnie of the Belgian Green Party, later criticised that the Belgian Gladio commissar of which she was a member commission had been unable to find the truth on the Brabant massacres and that above all the links to NATO had not been clarified. Witnesses, she correctly highlighted, often hid behind NATO secrecy in refusing to answer questions about the links between the two international secretariats of the Gladio networks – the ACC and the CPC – and NATO's Supreme Allied Headquarters Europe (SHAPE). After the termination of the Belgian Senate inquiry into Gladio in October 1991, Madame Harnie therefore called for a further investigation focusing on the role of NATO. Given that NATO's European headquarters are located in the cities Brussels, Mons and Casteau, Belgium was arguably in an ideal position among European countries to investigate NATO's secret armies in more detail. But despite this advantageous position Harnie's request was turned down.[27]

During their investigation, the Belgian parliamentarians noted with surprise how well hidden the secret army (SDRA8) was within the Belgian military secret service (SGR). At the time of the discoveries of the secret network, the military secret service was divided into five departments, one of which was SDRA which employed around 150 of the total 300 full-time SGR employees. SDRA had been created in the beginning of the 1950s by Colonel Charlier, who had before served in the British SAS Special Forces and at the time of the Gladio exposure was Lieutenant Colonel and Chief of Staff of the Belgium army. SDRA was again subdivided into 8 units, and next to the top-secret stay-behind SDRA8 included under the label SDRA6, for instance, the Belgian Gendarmerie. Only later the Senators learned that in most countries the paramilitary secret army had been hidden within the military secret service like Russian 'babushka dolls', where the first and smallest doll is contained inside the second larger doll, the second inside the third, the third inside a fourth and so on making it almost impossible for the legislative and its parliamentarians to carry out its constitutional duty to oversee, control and, in case of need, investigate the secret services.[28]

SDRA8 like all other stay-behind networks in Europe was made up of instructors and agents with the former training the latter. Allegedly the number of instructors was but ten at a certain time, while 'there were a total of about 40 agents. As a general rule, the instructors made contact with their agents twice a month.'[29] Advisors to the Senate investigation judged that the suggested total of 50 SDRA8 members was probably too low, yet as many relevant documents had been destroyed the issue could not be clarified. Like all stay-behind networks the SDRA8 and the civilian STC/Mob functioned according to the cell principle. In case of occupation the instructors would go abroad, while their agents were to remain in the occupied territory and recruit their own networks: 'The agents were trained so they themselves could recruit other agents in case of occupation of the country, with the aim of building up a network of which they were the chiefs. The recruitment strategy followed a pyramid structure. This way, the network could be expanded five times.'[30]

In STC/Mob each instructor knew his own agents, but did not know the agents of the other instructors, and the agents did not know each other. The 'need to know principle' was rigorously applied to enhance the secrecy of the stay-behind, and only the Director of the Sûreté within the Justice Ministry knew the names of both the STC/Mob instructors and agents. M. Raes, powerful Director of the Sûreté from 1977 to 1990, in front of the Senate investigation, claimed that he had 'forgotten' the names of the agents, while insisting that he had studied their file for security reasons.[31] Justice Minister Wathelet claimed that STC/Mob counted but seven instructors in November 1990. 'Each instructor recruited, formed and trained a maximum of 10 voluntary agents', the Senate investigation found and maintained that the section counted 45 agents in late 1990.[32] If these numbers are correct then the Belgian Gladio STC/Mob was made up of a modest number of 7 instructors and 45 agents in November 1990, thus a total of 52 men.

At least as of 1951 the missions of the Belgian Gladios SDRA8 and STC/Mob were outlined in writing to the Gladiators in a secret letter dated September 28, 1951 and signed by Belgian Prime Minister Van Houtte, Belgian Justice Minister Moyersoen and Belgian Defence Minister De Greef. In it the Prime Minister wrote: 'I have to specify to you the nature and the idea of the mission which the government has assigned to you. The mission basically consists in the co-ordination of the resistance activities against the enemy on the occupied national territory.' The letter continued: 'In times of peace your mission is to 1) study the conditions under which the resistance to the enemy could develop 2) Oversee the co-ordination of the general plans prepared to this purpose 3) Select the persons ... who would remain in Belgium to continue in the occupied territory your work under your authority ... 4) Be informed ... on all the suggestions, dispositions and decisions taken on international and national levels on the subject of the defence in occupied territory.' The fact that the mission also included the order to react to international decisions worried some of the Belgian Senators investigating the secret army, for this implied that NATO and foreign countries including the US and the UK were in a position to influence the Belgian stay-behind. 'The chiefs of the two services [SDRA8 and STC/Mob] have the obligation', the letter continued, 'on all which concerns the preparations of military and civilian resistance in occupied territory, to keep you informed on the plans which they have elaborated, the activities which they will take, the general directives which they give to their subordinates, or the general directives which they receive from national and international authorities'.[33]

Then the letter went on to specify the missions in case of war. SDRA8 has to engage in: 'a) intelligence gathering for the military; b) counter-intelligence; c) actions: sabotage of military objectives, collaboration with elements of the Allied Forces [Special Forces], paramilitary actions, secret army and guerrilla;

d) organisation of liaisons and evacuation lines.' While STC/Mob had the following tasks: 'a) information gathering on political, economical and social topics; b) liaison work between the government in exile and the civil resistance networks in the country; c) psychological warfare, and above all secret press and radio; d) counter information activity, aimed at the protection of the activities above mentioned; e) organisation of the liaisons and the evacuation routes which are necessary to fulfil the above mentioned missions.'[34]

In order to be able to operate independently of the regular forces the Belgian secret army like all stay-behinds across the continent was equipped with secret arms caches spread across the country containing guns, munitions, gold coins and explosives. Furthermore the Belgian secret army, as all other NATO stay-behinds in Western Europe as of the mid-1980s, was equipped with a total of 79 'Harpoon' communication centres that the government had purchased for a total of 155 million Belgian Francs. Belgian Justice Minister M. Wathelet, in front of the Senators, testified that NATO had suggested that the expensive Harpoon equipment should be bought by each state for the secret armies. 'Given the existing danger of detection or repair of the old machines, it was decided in ACC to develop a new type of radio machine', Wathelet explained. 'The project "Harpoon", often mentioned in the Sûreté de l'Etat, was thereafter realised by the German firm AEG Telefunken' on the orders of the Gladio command centre ACC.[35]

The powerful Harpoon machines operating on short waves with high frequency were able to communicate with another station 6,000 km away without the help of satellites by having the radio waves rebound on the natural ionosphere which surrounds the world. Using highly sophisticated encoding systems they produced messages which were practicably undecodable.[36] Michel Van Ussel, a member of STC/Mob in the 1980s, recalls that 'these little technical wonders' were a 'huge technical jump forward: Without exaggeration, the Harpoon system is the military radio system of the year 2000, of which there existed, when it was first put into service, in the whole world no similarly powerful equivalent.' The portable Harpoon transmitters weighed only 8 kg, batteries included, and came 'in an elegant briefcase protected by a number lock'. The Harpoon systems were able to automatically, with no agent present, receive and decode, as well as encode and send messages at high speed. The agents no longer had to use Morse as in the previous decades, and could even be absent while sending their communication.[37]

The Belgian Senate investigation found that STC/Mob agents were trained in Belgium and sometimes also 'went abroad to follow courses'.[38] The stay-behind strongly relied on international contacts, and agents had to lead a double life. 'As far as I am concerned, we [my radio instructor and I] saw each other about once a month. The training took place in my house, usually on a Friday evening, after the children had gone to bed', former STC/Mob member Michel Van Ussel relates, adding that 'some agents did not dare to welcome their instructors at home, for they had not informed their wives about their secret double life'.[39] During international stay-behind exercises STC/Mob agents had, for instance, to establish a secure radio connection with the French Gladio.[40]

'One day a man came to my house and asked me if I would accept a confidential mission', Van Ussel related his recruitment. 'He said that it was something within the framework of NATO. As I could still refuse his offer he didn't explain much. It was advisable not to be too specific, because this was one of the most secret organisations that has ever existed.' In the end Van Ussel agreed to become a secret soldier. 'We had a radio at our disposition. Our base was near London with a second base near Boston in the United States.'[41] 'Above all, it was pure curiosity which made me do it', Van Ussel reflects upon his motives to become a Gladiator, 'to penetrate this strange world, which one depicts as made up of silhouettes, trench coats, and false beards'. As he saw it most Gladiators were simply curious and adventurous. 'This is a far cry', he notes in his book, 'from such noble motives as honour, sense of duty, or patriotism... which some have wanted to see as the motive of members, which in fact they did not even know'. Van Ussel thought that the best way to prevent dark conspiracies from spreading was for the secret Belgian soldiers to step out of the dark and explain their side of the story for 'now nothing prevents them from testifying themselves'.[42]

Van Ussel stressed that the names of the secret soldiers were kept top secret by the CIA and the MI6. 'Exactly as in the best spy novel each Gladio agent had a code-name and a number. These were systematically used, above all during exercises.' Van Ussel himself was given the Gladio code name 'Georges 923', while other secret soldiers used such names as 'Charles', 'Isabelle', 'Pollux' and 'King-Kong'. The real name to which the cover name corresponded 'was known only by two or three persons', Van Ussel alias Georges 923 explains, among which the officer who had recruited the Gladiator, as well as the officer whom he met for instructions at regular intervals.[43] A personal file existed at CIA and MI6 headquarters on each Gladiator, 'some sort of curriculum vitae' in which the real name of the Gladiator, his work, his address, his family and some other information 'including a complete set of fingerprints!' were included. Also the encryption codes used by that specific agent were noted in the personal file as well as activation code words and the exact location of the secret arms caches assigned to the agent. 'This file was encoded and one copy was in the countries where the radio bases are located', thus in England and the United States. 'The chief of SDRA8 went there regularly to update the files.'[44] Van Ussel explained that 'The British and the Americans were privileged correspondence partners, because the radio bases were (and still are) installed on their territory.'[45]

Most members of SDRA8 were recruited in the Belgian army among the parachutists. Training took place in the Meerdaal army camp, the training with explosives was carried out at the Polygone in Brasschaat. The recruited agents wore uniforms during the training and Belgian instructors took courses in Great Britain and British instructors came to Belgium to give courses.[46] In order to camouflage their secret mission within the military secret service SGR, members of SDRA8 pretended to train different techniques allegedly for regular warfare. These activities consisted above all in scuba-diving and parachute jumping.[47] Cooperation between SDRA8 and the Belgian Gendarmerie, officially integrated into the SDRA as section SDRA6, was close. The chief of the Gendarmerie testified that before 1990 the helicopter Puma of the Gendarmerie was regularly used by the SDRA for dropping missions in blackout situations.[48]

The Belgian stay-behind agents themselves knew very little about the larger Gladio framework. The agents were told that they were part of a European organisation with bases in Washington and London. The structure of the entire organisation was not revealed.[49] As in all secret armies the Belgian secret soldiers were also 'thoroughly anti-Communist', as the Senate investigation found.[50] In joint exercises members of the Belgian stay-behind met with British and US officers and trained with other Gladiators. SDRA8 agents took part in several national and international exercises over the years, both inside and outside of Belgium. In how many exercises SDRA8 participated in total could not be clarified as the Belgian Senate commission only received 'an incomplete list' of the requested data, as allegedly 'the documents were often destroyed once the exercise had been carried out'. The Commission could, however, confirm that 'per year several exercises were organised'.[51]

As these exercises had to be carried out in total secrecy, agents were issued special identification cards, to be shown in case of arrest. 'All participants were given an exercise card, which they had to show in case of an accident, in order to prove that they were taking part in an official exercise. These cards gave the permanent phone number of SDRA, who in turn was ordered to contact the chief of SDRA8.'[52] Exercises included the gathering of information and international escape and evacuation operations. In one exercise SDRA8 agents had to observe for instance Soviet ships coming and leaving Belgian ports and communicate the information to headquarters. Such international stay-behind exercises took place during the entire Cold War. They included submarine operations on the Mediterranean French island Corsica where SDRA8 trained with the French secret stay-behind army. These exercises continued until 1990. Around April 1990, General Charlier, Chief of Staff, informed Defence Minister Coeme that he had ordered to terminate a series of activities of the section SDRA8 'regarding above all the scuba diving and the exercises organised in Corsica'.[53] Yet operations of SDRA8 outside Belgium were not limited to the Mediterranean, as the Belgian Senators found with much surprise. Members of the Belgian secret army much like their colleagues of the secret Portuguese army had also operated in the Belgian colonies in Africa. 'It has been confirmed by a responsible authority of SDRA8 that the para-commando instructors have participated in operations of the Belgian army in Zaire in the 1970s (Kisangani, Kitona) and in Rwanda', the Senators found. 'These interventions are in flagrant contradiction to the affirmed rules, according to which, for reasons of total secrecy, the instructors and the agents should not mix with military or social activities in times of peace.'[54]

During international escape and evacuation missions in Europe SDRA8 agents and their international Gladio colleagues passed on persons along secret lines from save house to save house and effectively brought them secretly in and out of a country. 'Often these exercises were organised on an international level and trained the reception and exfiltration of a shot down pilot, or of foreign agents who landed in the country with a special mission (intelligence, sabotage), to be carried out in a specified place.' The pan-European Gladios system worked remarkably well as the Belgian Senators learned with some surprise: 'One must note two points regarding these exercises. First of all, we are dealing here with an international network which could evacuate clandestinely a person from Norway to Italy. This implies a very close collaboration and strict co-ordination on an international level between a series of secret services', the Senators noted in their report. 'What secondly is astonishing is the perfect technical infrastructure which the stay-behind was equipped with: The persons and the material were moved on or intercepted by sea, by air, by parachute. Their arrival zones were marked and controlled. The persons were housed in secure buildings.'[55]

STC/Mob agent Van Ussel, alias Georges 923, relates that for scuba-diving operations the favourite territory was the Mediterranean and the Solenzara military base in Corsica which 'was therefore well known by the families of Belgium military personnel on holidays'.[56] Van Ussel stressed that the secret armies cooperated closely in Europe and took only about one month to move an agent clandestinely from Norway to Italy without him having ever to face customs or police controls: 'One of the exercises carried out was the following: On a moonless night an English submarine surfaced on the coast of Norway and a small raft carried the agent discretely to the main land, guided by the light signals of the agent of the local network on the beach', Van Ussel recalled. 'As the raft returned to the submarine, the "visitor" was taken over by a civilian agent who questioned and searched him, in order to verify that indeed this was the expected person. Inserted into the network the "visitor" was thereafter transported on foot, on horse and by car from network to network until he reached Kristiansand' on the southern coast of Norway. 'From there a fisherman who worked for the network transported him to Alborg' on the northern coast of Denmark, 'where the Danish network took over. In this way, after a month of travelling, he passed the Netherlands, Belgium and France to reach on a beautiful morning the Frioul area in Italy, without having ever undergone not even the smallest customs or police control. The latter was in fact one of the aims of the exercise', Van Ussel stressed. 'Constantly watched, he had been guided by several dozen evacuation networks.'[57]

SDRA8 officers were trained in the United Kingdom and also received training in the United States together with US Special Forces as the Belgian Gladio investigation found: 'The Commission could establish that several members of SDRA8 have profited from a Special Forces training in the United States' and participated in NATO exercises carried out in Europe with the participation of US Special Forces. 'The United States thus disposed as of 1947', the Senators critically observed, 'over an important instrument which allowed the United States to act on the domestic situation of a country in their sphere of influence'.[58] Today, the most sensitive Gladio question in Belgium and elsewhere in Europe therefore is: Have the United States made use of this instrument also in the absence of a Soviet invasion? Has the Belgian Gladio used its arms and explosives in Belgium during times of peace, or, alternatively, did it assist clandestine right-wing groups which engaged in such military operations?

After their investigation of the secret army the Belgian Senators answered this sensitive question in the affirmative. They were able to reconstruct at least one case, the so-called Vielsalm incident. In 1984 a squad of US Marines had set out from an airport north of London. Above Belgium they parachuted into a designated area and were met by a local Belgian agent from SDRA8 who offered them guidance. Living off the land for a fortnight, hiding from the Belgian population, the US Special Forces and the Belgian secret soldiers prepared for their mission: To attack the police station in the sleepy southern Belgian town of Vielsalm. Stealthily the US Marines approached their objective and opened fire. A Belgian warrant officer at the Vielsalm station was killed, and one US Marine lost an eye in the operation.[59]

The attack, as the Senators found, had been part of a so-called Oesling exercise. The forces of the national army and sections of the US Special Forces carried out these exercises, taking place at least once every year. 'The Commission has asked several times whether SDRA8 or its instructors have taken part in Oesling exercises.' 'Let us remember', they stressed in their report, 'that it was during one of these exercises, in 1984, that weapons were stolen from the arsenal of the Vielsalm station'. Initially Belgian stay-behind members claimed they had not been involved. 'The last commander of SDRA8 has denied all participation of his service in exercises of this kind, as they were not part of the mission of his unit and as the risk for his agents was too high', the Senate Gladio report notes. 'Contrary to this declaration a former chief of SDRA11 and former commander of the entire SDRA unit has confirmed that the network could participate in Oesling exercises. Another official has confirmed that the network took part in two Oesling exercises.'[60]

'For months the explanation the civilian authorities gave us was that the attack was the work of common criminals or of terrorists', Belgian journalist Rene Haquin remembers the Vielsalm terror operation. 'It was several months before I received a telephone call. That's how I went to France and met Lucien Dislaire who gave me his report and talked to me at length. He told me he had taken part in a secret manoeuvre which was to reproduce the operations of the resistance and of support for the resistance as it was done at the end of war.'[61] When in 1990 the entire stay-behind network was exposed, Belgian secret soldier Dislaire explained in front of the camera in a Gladio documentary that next to Vielsalm there had also been other exercises with US Special Forces. 'I am originally from the north of the province of Luxemburg', Dislaire explained in the documentary. 'At that time I was manager of a bank as well as an ex-paracommando. One day some people came to my house and asked for help with some special manoeuvres in co-ordination with American Special Forces', he explained. 'The Belgian commandos were told to recover American paratroopers. After this operation they were to go to pre-determined spots and attack barracks belonging to the Gendarmerie. I had with me the supplies, the weapons and the radio transmitter for co-ordinating it all.'[62]

Rene Haquin recalls that the Vielsalm operation was but one among several other operations during which US Special Forces had clandestinely operated on Belgian soil. 'We read in the papers about the attack on a military camp of the Chasseur Ardennes here in Belgium. I went there along with other journalists', Haquin remembered in a Gladio documentary. 'They had cut the fences, attacked the armoury, wounded the guard and left with a certain number of weapons. I was able to get into the camp because I knew some people there. Inside I saw foreign military personnel, notably Americans.'[63] Belgian Gladiator Dislaire confirmed to journalist Haquin that US Special Forces had repeatedly been involved in clandestine operations in Belgium. 'There had been some trouble a few days before' the attack on the Vielsalm barrack, Dislaire recalls. 'The Americans had gone too far. These were people in their forties, officers, tough guys. They took the game too far. They had attacked barracks before. They had even thrown a grenade near the Attorney Generals office.' Dislaire alleged that the violent procedure of the US Special Forces had greatly angered those Belgians who knew of the clandestine operations: 'The civilian authorities reacted, saying this was too much. It was then that the planned attack on Vielsalm barracks was cancelled. The day of the attack we were told that it was cancelled.' Yet the US Special Forces could not be stopped. Dislaire recalls: 'But the Americans asked me to drive them to the camp as a stand-by. The next morning I went with my wife to Namur. I heard on the radio that the barracks had been attacked at midnight. I can't say what happened, because I had left at 8 p.m. that evening. I wasn't supposed to stay.' Dislaire was informed of what had happened the next morning. 'The following day the commander of Vielsalm barracks called me and updated me on the operation. He told me to tell the Belgian commando that the guard wasn't dead, he was in hospital, seriously wounded.'[64] Later that guard died.

Belgian authorities covered up the traces after the mysterious operations in the 1980s and sensitive questions were not answered. The secret Belgian army was not exposed and only some attacks were confirmed. 'The American and Belgian authorities who were questioned, ended up admitting, after months, that there had been an exercise and admitted that certain attacks had taken place', Haquin recalls. 'I remember, for example, one attack on a military fuel depot in Bastogne. Another attack on a police station at Neufchateau. Gradually, the military admitted that there had been certain attacks.' Yet details on the Vielsalm incident were not available. 'Their last version of Vielsalm was that an attack had been planned but had been cancelled at the last moment' Haquin recalls, stressing that sensitively enough the arms stolen had been planted among a mysterious leftist group in order to blame the Communists for the crime: 'Some of the arms stolen at Vielsalm were found in a flat belonging to the Cellules Communistes Combattantes (CCC, Fighting Communist Cells).'[65]

Why were these operations carried out? And why were guns stolen in the Vielsalm operation by the US Special Forces later planted in the Brussels squat used by a Belgian Communist group? 'The objective of the exercise had been twofold: to jolt the local Belgian police into a higher state of alert, and, no less important, to give the impression to the population at large that the comfortable and well-fed Kingdom of Belgium was on the brink of red revolution', British journalist Hugh O'Shaughnessy suggested in an article on Gladio.[66] The Belgian Communists, as in Italy, were discredited by these false flag operations carried out by US Special Forces together with the Belgian stay-behind. This thesis was supported when it was revealed that the alleged Communist terror group CCC in reality had been set up by the extreme right. Between October 1984 and fall 1985 the CCC was responsible for 27 attacks. CCC was lead by Pierre Carette and targeted, with well-planned explosions, classical capitalist symbols including American installations linked to NATO, banks and military installations. On December 17, 1985 the leaders of CCC were arrested and the unit was closed down in the biggest military and police round up that Belgium had seen ever since the arrest of the Nazis after the Second World War. The Communists were discredited at least until journalists discovered that CCC leader Pierre Carette had in the beginning of the 1980s erected a terrorist network made up of agents linked to the extreme right. His principal aide, Marc De Laever, had later joined a German extreme right-wing group.[67]

'In Belgium there have been a number of unexplained events – an armed band committed numerous murders in the mid-eighties and we still know nothing about this', Belgian Defence Minister Guy Coeme speculated on a connection between the secret Belgian stay-behind army and acts of terrorism in Belgium when the Gladio network was discovered in late 1990.[68] 'I have asked the chief of the army, Lieutenant General José Charlier, whether there existed in Belgium a Gladio like organisation', Defence Minister Coeme explained in his first public information statement during the Gladio revelations on Belgian television on November 7, 1990 to a stunned TV audience. He stressed that despite his position as Defence Minister he had never heard of the secret NATO Gladio army before. 'Furthermore I want to know whether there exists a link between the activities of this secret network, and the wave of crime and terror which our country suffered from during the past years.'[69]

The Defence Minister was referring to the so-called Brabant massacres, a series of brutal and mysterious terrorist attacks carried out in the geographic area around Brussels called Brabant between 1983 and 1985 in which 28 people had died and many more were injured. The Brabant massacres had left the country in shock and remain the most traumatic episode of Belgium's most recent history. The Brabant massacres range among the worst cases of terrorism that Western Europe has seen in the second half of the twentieth century. All in all 16 armed assaults are subsumed under the term 'Brabant Massacres'. The first one took place on August 14, 1982 and was an armed attack on a food shop in the Belgian city Maubeuge in Brabant county. The last one, an attack on the supermarket chain Delhaize, took place on November 9, 1985 in the Belgian city Aalst, also in Brabant county. The other 14 attacks, all taking place in Brabant county, had targeted twice a restaurant, once a taxi driver, once a jeweller's store, once a textile factory, once a food store, and five times a Delhaize supermarket in five different towns. The police noticed that in all attacks only very small amounts of money, often less than £5,000, had been stolen while at the same time massive brutality and professionalism was employed.[70]

The Brabant massacres were designed to strike fear to the bones of the Belgian population. This aim was accomplished, as the raid on the Delhaize super-market in Aalst on November 9, 1985 illustrates. A prominent date of the Christmas season, November 9 is St Martin's day in Belgium, the local Santa Claus, and children on the night before leave carrots in front of the house for the horse of St Martin and go to bed with wishes for wonderful Christmas presents. The next morning, a busy Saturday, people hurried to the Delhaize supermarket to make their last minute purchases. What happened thereafter was reconstructed from the testimony of witnesses. A Volkswagen GTI was parked outside the supermarket and three armed men with hoods over their heads came out of the car. The tallest of the three produced a pump-action shotgun, opened fire at point blank range and finished off in cold blood two shoppers instantly. Upon reaching the checkout counter he began to fire ran-domly at anything that moved. 'I saw three masked men coming out at the rear. A man said to his child "Drop down! There they are!"', an unnamed witness recalls the terror in a Gladio documentary shown on BBC. 'One bystander who tried to flee was shot at, seven or eight bullets through his car and a shot grazing behind the ear.' Total panic reigned. 'One woman whose face was covered in blood, was screaming something about her child. I don't know exactly what.'[71] There was little cover or shelter for the terrified shoppers in the aisles of the supermarket from the three masked gunmen. In the ensuing massacre eight people, including a whole family, died, and seven more were injured. A husband and wife and their 14-year-old daughter were finished off in cold blood at the supermarket checkout. Another father and his nine-year-old daughter were killed in their car trying to flee. The takings from the raid amounted to a meagre couple of thousand pounds, found later in a canal in an unopened sack. The killers escaped without a trace and have not been identified, nor arrested, nor tried ever since. The actors behind the series known as the Brabant massacres remain unidentified until today.[72]

After the massacre Justice Minister Jean Gol went on television to promise greater security to the terrified population. The repeated terror reduced Belgium to a state of panic. Police outside supermarkets were reinforced with paratroopers and Jeeps mounted with light artillery. Witnesses and experts agreed that these massacres were not the work of petty criminals, but bloody operations of elite professionals. This applied both to the calm and professional way in which they had handled the situations and their arms, as well as how recklessly they had sped away with their GTIs under the very noses of the Belgian police. Always operating in very small groups, the tallest man also present in Aalst, whom witnesses and journalists started to call 'the giant' turned up time and time again in the attacks, giving orders and firing with his Italian made SPAS 12 shotgun. Brutality was their trademark. In one attack on September 30, 1982 a policemen was laying wounded on the wet pavement. He was finished off in cold blood at close range. In another attack on March 3, 1983 in a food store in Nivelles the killers – after having assassinated a couple and having set off the alarm – instead of fleeing waited for the police to arrive. The police ran right into the ambush.

'Have certain relationships existed between this network and the acts of terrorism and large scale banditry, as carried out in Belgium during the last ten years?', the Belgian parliament had ordered its select committee on Gladio to find out. Having otherwise carried out excellent work the Senators failed to answer this crucial question. The regrettable failure came largely because SDRA8 and STC/ Mob strictly refused to disclose the identity of their members. 'The Commission has found no indications which would allow to conclude that there has been any link whatsoever between the network and acts of terrorism and large-scale banditry', the Senators noted in their final report. 'The refusal, however, of the responsibles of SDRA8 and STC/Mob to provide the expert judges with the identity of all civilian agents has not allowed to carry out the verifications, which, probably, could have eliminated all doubt.'[73] Equally the group of judges who advised the Senate Commission was unable to prove that the Belgian stay-behind had been linked to the Brabant massacres. 'The expert judges have until now [1991] no element which would allow to believe that members of SDRA8 and STC/Mob could have played a role in the criminal activities which have greatly moved public opinion.' Like the Senators the judges also had not been able to investigate the mater sufficiently: 'The judges regret that they are not able to answer this question with more certainty: The silence which has been kept on the identity of the agents does not allow the judges to carry out the necessary verifications in order to establish the whole truth.'[74]

If the secret army has nothing to hide, then it must reveal the identities of its members, the Belgian press reasoned as the Senators faced stonewalling. Yet the two Gladio chiefs within the Belgian executive, M. Raes as powerful Director of the Sûreté de l'Etat from 1977 to 1990 and thus chief of STC/Mob, and Lieutenant Colonel Bernard Legrand, chief of the Belgian military secret service, and thus chief of SDRA8, categorically and repeatedly refused to make the names available. The categorical refusal of the executive to answer the questions of the legislative and judicative sent storms of protest through the Belgian democracy. The refusal of Raes and Legrand to cooperate was illegal, because Justice Minister Wathelet, the superior of Raes, and Defence Minister Coeme, the superior of Legrand, had explicitly and imperatively ordered their subordinates to cooperate with the stay-behind investigation and had ordered them to hand out the names. However, without success.

As the question of the Brabant massacres remains the most sensitive dimension of the history of the Belgian secret war the Senate commission had agreed with the Defence and Justice Ministers that the available names of the persons which were or are part of the stay-behind network would only be communicated to the three judges, who in turn would deal with the material confidentially. The magistrates would only reveal specific names if any of the persons were implicated in the grave actions which took place in the 1980s.[75] Thus privacy was guaranteed, unless stay-behind soldiers could be linked to the Brabant massacres. It seemed like a fair suggestion. But Raes and Legrand insisted that they were never going to reveal names. Thereafter it was suggested that if not the names then at least the birth dates of the secret soldiers should be made available, in order to allow the judges to compare them with terrorist suspects of the Brabant massacres. But that also was declined.

'Whatever the Minister says, there remain very good reasons not to reveal the names of the clandestines. For different reasons, of social and family contexts, the clandestines rely upon the promise given to them', commander Legrand explained. 'I will remain firm. I will not give any names of the clandestines, unless proofs can be shown' he insisted, although he knew that proofs could only be found if names were available. 'This is a valuable organisation. I do not understand why such a lot of noise is being made on the subject', Legrand lamented. 'When I read the articles in the press, I can not believe that one can be so intensively interested in such problems, while there are so many other important things.'[76] The Senators and judges kept up the pressure for three more months. It was eyeball to eyeball. But in the end Raes and Legrand won the contest. The names were not revealed. And on March 28, 1991 the leading Belgian daily Le Soir printed the following encoded statement: '"Give us the names!" "Never!" reply the "Gladiators". The hour of truth [l'heure du choc] has come. This is Brussels calling. Dear friends in Operation Stay Behind, section SDRA8 assures you of its very high esteem and thanks you for your devotion to your country. They guarantee that the pressures and threats will be empty and that undertakings will be honoured. Adolphe is looking well!'[77]

The Gladio commission was humiliated. It was left to the Senators to establish that the article in Le Soir had been printed on the orders of Legrand and that 'it can be considered as a form of collective resistance against the intention of the commission to get hold of the names'.[78] The phrase 'Adolphe is looking well!' served to indicate that the statement indeed came from the highest stay-behind authorities. Both Raes and Legrand had to resign over the affair and their public careers in Belgium were over. On November 23, 1990, the Belgian government decided to close down its secret army and to terminate all collaboration with analogous foreign networks. What angered the Belgian Senators most, however, was the fact that the CIA and the MI6 as commanders of the European stay-behind networks were also in possession of the names of the Belgian Gladiators, but despite the most serious suspicions in the context of the Brabant terror, together with Raes and Legrand, had refused to cooperate. The Senate commission found that 'the names of the agents were kept in sealed envelopes in boxes kept in Washington and London by the respective secret services'.[79]

While the Belgian press concluded that the British and the US secret service were responsible for the mysteries that continued to surround the Brabant massacres, the Belgian Justice Ministry in 1996 asked academics Fijnaut and Verstraeten of Louvain University to investigate why the secret could not be lifted in Belgium. Yet after only two months of research the professors resigned, lamenting that a serious lack of cooperation from the Belgian government institutions had made it impossible for them to continue.[80] Thereafter yet another parliamentary committee was formed to investigate why the Belgian democracy was unable to clarify the Brabant massacres. In October 1997 the commission presented a damning report of 90 pages. Detailing a litany of official incompetence in the investigations that had followed the Brabant massacres in the 1980s, the report accused the Belgian police of a dislocated and inefficient inquiry during which documents had been lost or destroyed, leads not pursued and information not passed on to the neighbouring forces.[81]

New light was suddenly shed on the Brabant massacres when Gladio researcher Allan Francovich successfully followed the thesis that segments of the Belgian secret army might have cooperated with the Belgian extreme right-wing organisations Westland New Post (WNP). Already in 1988 British investigative journalist John Palmer had reported that evidence for the Brabant massacres 'now points to the not insignificant extreme right-wing, including the neo-Nazi group called Westland New Post (WNP)'.[82] In 1974 the Belgian ultra right-wing organisation Front de la Jeunesse (FJ) had been founded. Five years later WNP was created within FJ as the armed and highly militant branch of the right-wing organisation. 'The Front de la Jeunesse was born in 1974 and existed until the 1980s. At times it was a political group, at times militant', Francis Dossogne, head of the FJ, described his organisation in the Gladio documentary of Francovich. 'Extreme right wing', he confirmed it was, adding that it 'was essentially a youth movement and a militant movement'.[83] Dossogne confirmed that FJ had resorted to violence in numerous cases: 'The Front de la Jeunesse carried out actions which upset things. It put many things into question, things which were well established. The Front really upset things so much that they wanted to destroy it.' Carrying out their paramilitary training more and more openly the FJ started to face criticism. 'The Front were condemned for their camps. In fact, all we did was what scouts do. What certain companies do in incentive courses goes much further.'[84]

Most sensitively Dossogne admitted in the Gladio documentary that within FJ they had set up a militant branch made up almost exclusively of members of the Belgian Gendarmerie. As SDRA6 the Gendarmerie was part of the Belgian military secret service SGR which under the label SDRA8 also directed the secret armies. The new branch within FJ was first labelled 'G' for Gendarmerie and later became WNP. 'Group G was a section of the Front in the Gendarmerie. As Gendarmes they didn't want to be mixed up with the rest – and risk being involved during demonstrations and so on', Dossogne relates. Gendarme Martial Lekeu played a prominent role in Group G and later in WNP. 'Lekeu was part of Group G, he was one of its first members', Dossogne explained in the Gladio documentary. 'He was so much part of Group G that he later informed the Chief of Staff of the Gendarmerie of their existence.'[85]

Lekeu served as a Belgian Gendarme from 1972 to 1984. Thereafter he fled to Florida in the United States. In the Gladio documentary he testified in poor English that elements of the Belgian military secret service and the security apparatus were linked to the Brabant massacres: 'My name is Martial Lekeu, I used to be with the Belgian Gendarmerie. I left Belgium in August 1984 after precise death threats against my kids', Lekeu testified. 'In the beginning of December 1983 I did go personally to the BSR [Brigade Spéciale des Recherches, branch of Gendarmerie] of Wavre who were doing the investigation about the [Brabant] killing.' Lekeu had discovered that the massacres were linked to groups within the security apparatus. 'I was surprised that no arrests had been made and I know that I did report myself what was going on – we were respecting killing like that – random killing or going into supermarket and killing people, even kids. I believe they kill about thirty people. So I told a gentleman I met: "Do you realise members of the Gendarmerie of the army are involved in that?" His answer was "Shut up! You know, we know. Take care of your own business. Get out of here!" What they were saying was that democracy was going away the leftists were in power the socialists and all this and they wanted more power.'[86]

A Belgian parliamentary report on the Brabant massacres published in 1990 only months before the discovery of the Belgian secret army supported this finding. 'According to the report, the killers were members or former members of the security forces – extreme right-wingers who enjoyed high-level protection and were preparing a right-wing coup.' 'It is now believed', British newspapers reported after the parliamentary report had been presented to the public, 'that the Brabant killings were part of a conspiracy to destabilise Belgium's democratic regime, possibly to prepare the ground for a right-wing coup d'état'.[87] 'The terrorist line was followed by camouflaged people, people belonging to the security apparatus, or those linked to the state apparatus through rapport or collaboration', Italian right-wing terrorist Vincenzo Vinciguerra observed on maybe the most sensitive feature of the secret stay-behind armies. Right-wing organisations across Western Europe 'were being mobilised into the battle as part of an anti-Communist strategy originating not with organisations deviant from the institutions of power, but from the state itself, and specifically from within the ambit of the state's relations within the Atlantic Alliance'.[88] Following this suggestion parliamentarian Agalev Hugo Van Dienderen attempted to find out more about the clandestine operations in Belgium by contacting NATO. Two years before the Gladio discoveries he asked in writing in 1988 whether NATO had some secret 'Security Committee'. NATO first inquired why he was asking this, and then refused to hand out any specific information on the subject.[89]

Suspicions mounted that the right-wing organisation WNP enjoyed special protection from NATO when in October 1990 seven WNP members charged with having stolen hundreds of NATO and Belgian army documents in the early 1980s were acquitted mysteriously by the highest military court in Belgium. This despite the fact that the documents had been found in the WNP offices and the con-firmation of the WNP activists that the top-secret material belonged to them. At the same time the accused strongly rejected the charge that the documents had been stolen. 'We only followed the wishes of authority!', accused WNP member Michel Libert explained, stressing that when he had gotten hold of the material he had acted out of patriotism and with authorisation from NATO superiors. Fellow WNP right-winger Frederic Saucez protested: 'If I stole any NATO telexes, it was on the orders of state security.' The state, as Vinciguerra had correctly predicted, proved unable to punish itself. First the trial was dragged on and on, with the accused appealing always to higher instances, whereupon in October 1990 finally the highest military tribunal, The Council of War, ruled that the offences happened too long ago for any sentence to be passed on the seven WNP members. The court added that the crime was mitigated by the fact that it had been committed when the Cold War was 'more than just a phrase'. The WNP members were ordered to hand over the stolen NATO and Belgian army documents to the Justice Ministry and walked free.[90]

One of the accused, right-winger Michel Libert, a WNP member from 1978 to the 1980s, thereafter confirmed in a Gladio documentary that higher officers had protected them during their operations. 'The fittest members', Libert proudly spoke of the WNP, 'can form an action branch'. Head of WNP Paul Latinus gave the orders for covert action operations. 'When an operation was to be carried out, Latinus was given the job. To get us to do it he had to have an aide in case of problems.' Protection by higher echelons was mandatory. 'You can't send young members into the field. Within two hours they would have a bullet between the eyes. There were always risks. They could be stopped by the local police for an identity check. The police turn up like a hair in the soup. One can't say: "We're here on such and such a mission." "Doing what?" "Can't tell you." Click, the handcuffs and that's it.'[91]

Was right-wing extremist Libert willing to confirm that WNP and the Belgian security apparatus had been involved in the Brabant massacres, investigative journalist Allan Francovich wanted to know in his Gladio documentary? Was Brabant one of their 'missions'? 'One received orders. We can go back to, say, 1982. From 1982 to 1985' Libert replied, referring to the period in which the Brabant massacres were carried out. 'There were projects.' Very sensitive projects Libert admitted. According to his own testimony he had been told: 'You, Mr. Libert, know nothing about why we're doing this. Nothing at all. All we ask is that your group, with cover from the Gendarmerie, with cover from Security, carry out a job. Target: The supermarkets. Where are they? What kind of locks are there? What sort of protection do they have that could interfere with our operations? Does the store manager lock up? Or do they use an outside security company?' The operation was top-secret and right-wing extremist Libert followed the order: 'We carried out the orders and sent in our reports: Hours of opening and closing. Everything you want to know about a supermarket. What was this for? This was one amongst hundreds of missions. Something that had to be done. But the use it was all put to, that is the big question.'[92]

'If the object was to sow terror', journalist Davison observed, 'the killers chose the perfect targets: Women, children and the elderly, cut down by rapid gunfire while wheeling their trolleys through a local supermarket.'[93] In this chain of command WNP right-wing extremist Michel Libert was on the lower end. He received his orders from WNP commander Paul Latinus. 'It is clear that Latinus is one of the most interesting pieces of the puzzle in order to understand the political-juridical mysteries of the 1980s', journalists of the Belgian magazine *Avancées* judged after having compiled an entire dictionary on the Belgium terror years. He was, the Belgian journalists concluded, the link 'between the extreme-right, the classical right, and the foreign and Belgian secret services'.[94]

Paul Latinus was a high-ranking European right-wing terrorist. According to his own testimony he was, amongst other sources, paid by the military secret service of the Pentagon, the US Defence Intelligence Agency (DIA). A former nuclear science technician and informer for the Belgian Sûreté Latinus had been recruited in 1967, aged 17, by the DIA. Later NATO trained him. Belgian journalist Haquin who had written a book on terrorist Latinus relates that 'during a juridical investigation in which he was involved, Latinus named this foreign organisation: It was the Defence Intelligence Agency (DIA), the military equivalent to the CIA.'[95] In the 1970s Latinus became a member of the Brabant Reserve Officers Club (BROC), a conservative military organisation created in 1975 and obsessed with the 'red peril'. In 1978 Latinus joined the right-wing organisation FJ and within that organisation set up the WNP covert action department. With excellent contacts Latinus during the same period worked in the Belgium government as Assistant Adviser to the Labour Minister and counsellor to several committees. When in January 1981 the left-wing magazine *Pour* exposed the right-winger in the government, Latinus abandoned his public offices and fled to Pinochet's Chile. Yet after not even two months in exile Latinus due to his excellent contacts came back to Belgium exactly at the time when the Brabant massacres began. He reassumed the command of the WNP and among other activities collaborated with the Sûreté in the anti-Communist struggle by providing the Justice Ministry with data on the left.[96]

'Latinus had been implanted into Front de la Jeunesse with a specific task' Jean-Claude Garot, editor of the magazine *Pour*, recalls: 'To teach the Front de la Jeunesse how to carry out violent attacks, attacks on immigrant Arab cafes, how to organise military training camps, how to carry out surveillance.'[97] Journalist Garot while investigating the Belgian extreme right had followed the Latinus trace to covert action training camps of WNP. 'In the training of their groups for active intervention, para-military groups, they had to form and train elements from the extreme-right, ex para-commandos, ex militaries (gendarmes), militant rightists', Garot discovered long before the Belgian secret army was exposed in 1990. 'This kind of exercise involves the firing of machine-guns and the throwing of grenades. This makes noise and attracts attention. We knew that this camp was taking place. We knew about it and organised the necessary photographic equipment in order to record part of the action.'[98] The training camp was located in the Ardennes and instructors from different secret services were present during the trainings. 'These people gave courses in recruitment, surveillance and arms. "Robert" gave courses on explosives, on arms and shooting, and in how to kill without leaving a trace.'[99]

When Garot published his findings, officials were alarmed and tried to cover up. 'With friends from radio and TV, we interviewed General Beaurir. At that time he was number one in the hierarchy of the Gendarmerie', Garot recalls. 'In the interview he said "That never happened." The same day the examining judge intervened. But where? Here [in the office of the journalist]. They searched the premises and made a statement "Jean-Claude Garot has lied. He has fabricated uniforms, photos and arms, it's all a masquerade."''[100] In retrospect it was revealed that Garot had discovered the extreme right-wing branch of the Belgian stay-behind SDRA8 which allegedly included right-wing extremists of WNP. Paul Latinus commanded the terrorist hit squad. Belgian journalist Haquin personally interviewed Latinus who confirmed to him that he was a member of a clandestine anti-Communist network. 'Latinus was charged with forming a group, an army on the model of the SS', Haquin explains. 'They had a secret service, a security service in the group. Each member had a double name, a code-name, usually in German. The members didn't know the others.' Haquin recalls: 'I contacted Paul Latinus again. We met in a country restaurant and talked all night. Certain authorities, he wouldn't say which at first, had given him the job of creating a secret resistance group in Belgium. It was to fight certain Soviet penetration, and stop certain Belgian authorities form collaborating with the Soviets.'[101]

Former WNP member and former Gendarme Martial Lekeu in Florida confirmed to Gladio researcher Francovich that the secret army in Belgium had been involved in the Brabant terror massacres in order to discredit the Belgian left. 'The guns they were using were coming from far away and that's exactly what we had planned, to organise gangs and groups like that and let them go by themselves, but make sure they will survive and make sure to supply them and you know just to create a climate of terror in the country', Lekeu explained. 'They'd have two plans. The first one was to organise gangs to do hold up of hostage, you know, killing; the second one was to organise the so called "Left movement" who will do a terrorist attempt just to make believe, make the population believe that these terrorist attempts were done by the Left.'[102]

Was this terror supported and encouraged by the administration of US President Ronald Reagan, who during the same time brutally cracked down on the Sandinistas in Nicaragua, Gladio researcher Francovich wanted to know from WNP member Michel Libert. Libert, who had gathered the data on the supermarkets on the orders of WNP chief Paul Latinus reluctantly confirmed that his chief had collaborated very closely with the United States: 'He [Latinus] met people from the [US] Embassy, but I never met them like we meet now', thus face to face in the interview. 'That wasn't in my domain. His was, you might say, the domain of diplomacy, that is, relations with foreign authorities. Our sole concern was with action', terrorist Libert recalls. 'We knew we were protected, by all the possible authorities depending on the type of mission. Was he [Latinus] paid by the Americans? I can't say, but he was in contact with them.'[103] Senator Roger Lallemand, head of the Belgian Gladio investigation, had thus drawn the correct historical analysis when he summarised that the Brabant massacres had been 'the work of foreign governments, or of intelligence services working for foreigners, a terrorism aimed at destabilising democratic society'.[104]

Senator Lallemand was cautious in his wording and refrained from accusing the United States directly, while he insisted that the terror had to be seen in a Cold War anti-Communist political context: 'This gratuitous killing of people could have a political motive, one recalls what happened in Italy. At the station at Bologna 80 innocent people died. We think a political organisation was behind the Brabant-Wallon killings.'[105] It was Haquin who later provided the missing link in his interview with US-sponsored WNP terrorist Paul Latinus: 'When we met up in the following days and weeks, I asked Latinus who had asked him to build the group. He mentioned State Security. He talked of foreign military authorities. I pushed him and he eventually said American military secret services.'[106] At the end of the Brabant massacres Paul Latinus was arrested. Yet before he could speak out the right-wing commander was found hanged by a telephone cord in his prison cell with his feet on the ground on April 24, 1985. 'In the circles around Paul Latinus all, or almost all, remain convinced that the boss of WNP had not committed suicide, but that he had been liquidated.' 'Each time when they attempted to reconstruct the suicide, the telephone cord broke.' Haquin wondered: 'If the United States have nothing to do with the massacres, why then do they not communicate, keep silent, and leave suspicions grow?'[107]

11

THE SECRET WAR IN THE NETHERLANDS

As in neighbouring Belgium, the stay-behind secret army of the Netherlands originated from the country's Second World War occupation experience. The Netherlands, as Dutch strategists later lamented, had not erected a stay-behind before the Second World War due to lack of money, lack of visions and concerns in the context of neutrality. Then in May 1940 the Netherlands were occupied by the German Army and the Dutch government together with the Dutch royals and privileged figures of the political, military and economic sphere had to leave Dutch soil hastily and chaotically for Great Britain. GS III, the Section Intelligence of the Dutch General Staff, had warned too late of the German attack and had thus failed bitterly in what would have been its most important task. Due to the hasty retreat there was logistic distress in many areas, and the Dutch ministers who in May 1940 arrived in London could hardly carry out their work for a lack of crucial documents. For many within the military and security services it was clear that such a chaotic escape was never to happen again and that after the war preparations against a potential future invasion had to be taken very seriously.

After the chaotic escape of the government in May 1940 the homeland was occupied for almost five consecutive traumatic years by the Germans. The Dutch government in London, which almost completely lacked reliable intelligence on its occupied home country, sent agents into the Netherlands with the task of collecting intelligence, organising resistance and engaging in small-scale covert action operations. As in Belgium these Dutch operations were carried out in close cooperation with the British, above all together with the newly created British Special Operations Executive (SOE). However, the Germans with disastrous effects quickly infiltrated the hastily created units. In one of the greatest disasters for the SOE, the so-called Englandspiel, the Dutch section of SOE was secretly penetrated by the Germans who thereafter controlled the transmitters and read the communication. Dozens of agents fell straight into enemy hands as a result and never returned.

During the war the Dutch and the British established intimate ties and London advised the Dutch on the reorganisation of their destroyed and chaotic secret service apparatus. According to the advice of the British two new services were created in the early 1940s during the London exile. The Bureau Inlichtingen (BI) was established in November 1942 with the task of collecting intelligence. And the Bureau Bijzondere Opdrachten (BBO) was created with the task of carrying out special operations. Together with the British SOE special units, the BBO parachuted into the occupied country. When the war was over both the BI and BBO were closed down. But in subsequent years much of their personnel was directly involved in setting up the Dutch stay-behind.

BI member C. L. W. Fock had insisted during the war that in the future the Netherlands had to be better prepared and in peacetime a stay-behind should be erected in the country. Also his superior J. M. Somer, chief of the BI in London, was convinced that after the end of the German occupation a stay-behind had to be erected in the Netherlands. 'I remember how Somer, Charles van Houten (Liaison officer between BI and Dutch Queen Wilhelmina), and I in 1944 already agreed that something like that must never happen again' Fock, aged 87, remembered during a Gladio interview in his apartment in the Hague in 1992. Looking back almost half-a-century later, Fock recalled: 'In this conversation it became clear that it would be better for the Netherlands to prepare for a new war. It was necessary to take actions into that direction as soon as possible.'[1]

At the time of the liberation of the Netherlands in 1945 BI chief Somer figured amongst the most experienced men in the secret trade. Before the war he had served in the pre-war Dutch secret service GS III. During the war he had engaged in resistance operations on Dutch soil and in March 1942 had narrowly escaped the German Sicherheitsdienst, reaching safe haven London after an adventurous excursion. In London, Somer served as the first chief of the newly created Dutch wartime secret service BI. After the war Somer, now promoted to the rank of Colonel, put down his stay-behind thinking on paper and presented them to General J. Kruls, who in November 1945 had become Chief of the Dutch Chiefs of Staff. Somer's memorandum to Kruls was entitled: 'Lessons to be drawn from the period 1940–1945 in the field of Intelligence and Security Services.' A former involved remembers that 'It was one of the first pieces which Kruls as new chief of the Chiefs of Staff had to deal with in his new office.' Kruls was immediately won over for the idea. Fascinated by covert action Kruls in his book 'Peace or War' (Vreede of Oorlog) which he published a few years later during the time of the Korean War stressed that the 'greatest possible attention' had to be given to the 'preparations for covert action warfare'. As Kruls saw it Western Europe had to face 'the hard facts', meaning that if there should soon be a war, 'then the underground operations might be the decisive factor'.[2]

With the support of Kruls, Somer in September 1945 presented the stay-behind plan to Dutch Defence Minister J. Meynen. Somer did not stress the covert action and sabotage operations of a potential secret army but suggested the creation of an intelligence collection unit 'which should be able to collect military, political and economic information and to send them by courier or on wireless networks' to the military command outside the occupied country. Somer explained that men should be recruited and trained in radio communication and encryption techniques, and insisted that these men should not be part of the regular Dutch military for only then they would be available for special operations in case of an invasion.[3] Defence Minister Meynen agreed with the plan and Somer became the first commander of the Dutch stay-behind with the specific task to set up a secret army. At the same time Somer was given the task of closing down the wartime secret service IB that he had previously directed. The task gave him the perfect cover for his clandestine preparations. He attached the new stay-behind service to the old pre-war Dutch military secret service GS III and therefore the first Dutch stay-behind received the cover name GIIIC.

After some months Somer started to dislike the organisational structure. He resented that his stay-behind network GIIIC was placed under the command of the Chiefs of Staff. Somer, little inclined to tolerate a section chief above him, stressed that such a structure represented a secrecy risk. 'Somer was of the opinion that his top-secret unit must exist, but can not officially appear', Dutch scholar Koedijk described the situation.[4] In January 1948 it was therefore decided that the stay-behind section should no longer be mentioned in organisational charts of the Defence Ministry and the clandestine army came under the direct command of Somer. Furthermore the label of the Dutch Gladio was changed from GIIIC to G7. Somer furthermore insisted that his Gladio headquarters could no longer be in the headquarters of the Dutch General Staff which was located in the Prinses Juliana military complex half way between the Hague and the Dutch village Wassenaar. He was therefore allowed to search for an adequate building not too far from the headquarters of the Dutch General Staff. With less than total emphasis on secrecy he decided upon House Maarheeze in Wassenaar, an architectonic highlight and impressive villa built in 1916 by a Dutch businessman who had become wealthy in Indonesia. Located within an acceptable distance of five minutes' driving from the headquarters of the General Staff, Somer in May 1945 took up residence in the Villa Maarheeze, still officially under BI activities. In 1946 the Dutch Gladio GIIIC, shortly thereafter renamed G7, also moved into the same building.

Somer insisted that secrecy was of the utmost importance for the clandestine army. While he was in command no Roman Catholics for instance could become members of the secret unit, for Somer believed that their duty for confession stood in contrast to the principle of secrecy within the service. At the same time Somer made sure that the Dutch executive was informed of his clandestine preparations. Assisted by the Chief of Staff Kruls he debriefed Dutch Prime Minister Louis Beel when the latter took office in July 1946 to head the Dutch executive until 1948. Beel was soon convinced of the values of a stay-behind, and thus consented to the secret operation despite the fact that he considered the scenario of a Soviet invasion to be rather unlikely.

As BI was being closed down by Somer, Villa Maarheeze, next to being the headquarters of the Dutch stay-behind G7, potentially provided enough space also for other branches of the Dutch secret service establishment. The Dutch Second World War secret services BI and BBO were closed down. In their place two new Dutch Cold War secret services were created: The domestic secret service BVD, short for Binnenlandse Veiligheidsdienst, and the Dutch foreign secret service IDB, short for Inlichtingendienst Buitenland.[5] On the orders of the Prime Minister the task to set up the foreign secret service IDB was given to C. L. W. Fock, who during the war under Somer had been Vice Director of BI in London. When Fock was promoted to become first Director of IDB Somer asked him whether he was interested in erecting the new headquarters of his service in the Villa Maarheeze. Fock agreed and the IDB came into the villa and paid 60 per cent of the rent, while Somer's G7 paid the rest. Villa Maarheeze in subsequent decades became a symbol of clandestine operations and was strongly compromised when it was discovered that IDB had carried out illegal domestic operations and had cultivated links with Dutch right-wing circles during the Cold War. When it was furthermore discovered in 1990 that the mysterious Gladio secret army had been located in the same house as the IDB, Villa Maarheeze became a symbol of intrigues and manipulations. The Dutch foreign secret service IDB was closed down in 1994 by Prime Minister Lubbers and most of its functions were transferred to the domestic secret service BVD.[6]

From his headquarters in Villa Maarheeze stay-behind commander Somer travelled extensively through the Netherlands to recruit members for his secret army. Most of these early Dutch Gladiators shared a common Second World War experience. Many were drawn from the BBO units that during the war together with the British SOE special units had parachuted into the occupied country to carry out covert action operations. Other recruits were drawn from the wartime Dutch resistance OD (Ordedienst), which Somer had commanded during the war in the Dutch province West Brabant before he had been forced to flee to London in 1942. 'Somer searched the whole country for this purpose', a former agent remembers. 'He visited for instance an old commander of the OD, or a member of the illegal wartime intelligence unit Albrecht, met with them in hotel rooms, and there briefly discussed matters.' Obviously this was not the sort of fieldwork the chief of a super secret organisation would be expected to carry out himself. Yet as the personal contacts were the central elements of the operation, Somer insisted stubbornly that his recruitment tactic was the most efficient, while the former agent reasoned: 'In retrospect you can question such proceedings of course.'[7]

At all times Somer cultivated his clandestine contacts with the MI6 and CIA. When Somer asked the Dutch Ministry of Traffic and Energy as well as the Dutch General Directory of Telecommunications for a licence to operate radio receivers and transmitters and permission for several defined frequencies he highlighted the need for 'a fast secret and independent connection with the English and American officials abroad'.[8] Somer in his request made it clear that the 'desirability of such proceedings' had been requested by the United Kingdom and the United States, whereupon the transmitters were quickly installed in the villa Maarheeze.

At the same time as Somer was setting up the G7 a second stay-behind was being secretly erected in the Netherlands, independent of G7. Immediately after the Second World War Dutch secret service circles under the influence of the British MI6 had approached Prince Bernhard with the suggestion of erecting a stay-behind in the country with the tasks of sabotage, liquidation and armed resistance in case of invasion. Sympathetic to the suggestion Prince Bernhard saw to it that Louis Einthoven, the first chief of the Dutch post-war domestic security service BVD was to carry out the preparations. Einthoven with the consent of Dutch Prime Minister W. Schermerhorn set up the Dutch stay-behind code-named 'O', recruited and trained agents and erected secret arms caches.[9]

Born in 1896 Louis Einthoven had served as a senior officer with the Rotterdam police before the war and during the war was an active resistance fighter against the German occupation. Until his death in 1973 he remained an ardent Cold Warrior, repeatedly stressing the danger of Communism. He introduced 'security checks' in order to control the ideological reliability of his Gladio and BVD agents. Einthoven's position as chief of the BVD provided him not only with the perfect cover for his top-secret function as chief of the secret army. It also gave him during the 16 years that he directed both units, at least potentially, the opportunity to use the Gladiators domestically also in the absence of an invasion. Einthoven was constantly alert that his secret army could be infiltrated by agents of the Soviet Union and thus placed much emphasis on counter-intelligence. 'The double function of Einthoven as chief BVD and of O was of course very valuable for us', a former Dutch Gladiator remembers.[10] For as most domestic secret services, the BVD had the task to spy upon elements of the Dutch society that could pose a threat to the state and government and to collect and monitor political movements including that of the far right and the far left. As of now no documents or testimonies are available on Einthoven's secret army and what it did remains almost completely in the dark.

The two Dutch secret armies, the one commanded by Einthoven directly integrated into the BVD, and the other commanded by Somer located in Villa Maarheeze, in 1948 reached a formal agreement of cooperation with the MI6. A similar agreement on clandestine stay-behind cooperation was reached with the newly created CIA in 1949. Whether the agreements, as in other stay-behind countries, directed the two Dutch secret armies to fight Communism and political parties on the left also in the absence of a Soviet invasion, has still not been clarified.[11] But when the Dutch stay-behind network was discovered in 1990 these secret agreements lead to much criticism in the Netherlands as the argument was raised that MI6 and CIA had controlled the Dutch secret army, a suggestion which was unacceptable to most Dutch politicians valuing their sovereignty. In 1992 an unnamed former member of the Dutch Gladio insisted therefore that despite the close contacts with both London and Washington the Dutch secret armies had always been sovereign: 'Neither the British nor the American secret service should have been able to locate an agent of our stay-behind. That's the way it had to be. For if you pass the permission to use the network to, for instance, the British, nobody would want to be part of it any longer.'[12] Another former Dutch agent claimed, after the discovery of the secret army, that 'The CIA had only a general idea of the strength of the stay-behind in our country.'[13] Contrary to these claims rumours surfaced at the same time that the top-secret identity of all secret soldiers in all countries in Western Europe, including the Dutch stay-behind agents, was known to the CIA and the MI6.

In 1948 dramatic events overseas drew commander Somer away from his stay-behind activities in the Netherlands. Indonesia, the richest and oldest colony of the Netherlands, was at that time desperately and successfully fighting for independence, similar to many other European colonies. On the orders of General Spoor, covert action specialist Somer therefore left for the Far East and in late spring 1948 became Director of the dreaded NEFIS, the Dutch military secret service in Indonesia. NEFIS engaged in brutal covert action operations but was unable to stop Indonesia from becoming independent from the Netherlands in 1949. Somer returned to the Netherlands and wrote a book about 'his' service, the IB and his wartime memoirs. Published in 1950 under the title *Zij sprongen buj nacht* (They jumped by night), the book contained names of numerous agents and descriptions of several covert action operations. The Dutch Defence Department later criticised Somer for these disclosures.

'The Government knew of nothing', a former secret soldier highlighted the secrecy of both Dutch stay-behinds, adding that 'only very few Secretary Generals within the Executive were informed, as the Ministers above them could change quickly'.[14] The evidence available suggests that those who knew of the secret army included at times the civilian Prime Minister, the Defence Minister and the Secretary-Generals if the stay-behind commanders trusted them, as well as regularly the military Chief of Staffs and the Directors of the foreign and domestic Dutch secret services. 'Politics can at times nominate strange people', another anonymous stay-behind agent reflected. 'But it is only normal that a new official is being informed on everything. Yet for these sensitive issues the civil servants make an exception and first observe what kind of meat they have in their bowl.'[15] Parliament and its specialised committees were kept in the dark. Neither the secrecy bound 'Permanent Commission for secret service and security services', nor the 'Ministerial Commission for secret service and security' of the Dutch parliament were informed on the existence of the stay-behinds before the 1990 revelations.[16]

To replace Somer as commander of the secret army J. J. L. Baron van Lynden, a 35-year-old instructor with the Dutch cavalry was selected. Finding a successor had not been easy. Most former senior BI members refused, for they had simply no intention to again lead a secret life with all its awkwardness and double standards. When Baron van Lynden on June 1, 1948 officially replaced Somer as chief of the Dutch stay-behind G7 quite a few within the intelligence community were surprised about the choice. For van Lynden in total contrast to his predecessor

Somer was a complete newcomer to the field. He had been suggested by IDB Director Fock, who 40 years later recalled 'I am a bit proud of this finding of mine', praising the Dutch stay-behind commander's excellent character traits.[17] Van Lynden's glory was based on his wartime resistance. In 1940 he had belonged to a small unit of 50 Dutch senior officers who in a group of 2,000 had refused to promise to the Germans that they would do nothing against the occupiers, whereupon he had been sent to a German prisoners of war camp. In the Stanislau prison in Poland he met with British War hero Airey Neave, a contact which both cultivated also after the war. For Neave after the war directed the SAS which in numerous instances trained with the national secret armies in Europe, until he was killed by an IRA car bomb in the parking of the British parliament in March 1979. At the time of van Lynden's nomination as stay-behind commander the Baron was working for Prince Bernhard, the husband of Queen Wilhelmina. Van Lynden continued his bonds with the Queen and the cavalry, both of which served as a handy cover for his secret main function as commander of the Dutch secret army. In 1951 he was nominated adjutant of the Queen, and several times a week he travelled to the royal palace in The Hague. The Baron was a very gifted horseman, a passion he shared with Prince Bernhard. In The Hague in 1951 van Lynden became Dutch champion in horseback riding and in Rotterdam in 1955 he was a member of the Dutch equip which won the international jumping contest, a success he was particularly proud of.

Although scepticism had surrounded the start of the newcomer, van Lynden took off well in the secret services community. 'He was a natural talent in security affairs', an admirer recalled. And people who knew him in his job and outside sketch a picture of a strong but friendly personality that united 'character, knowledge and expertise'. Van Lynden's phlegmatic and philosophical views – during his time in the prisoner of war camp he had 'studied' with a woman who later was to become professor of philosophy – were not typical for the military and secret services field.[18] When speculations arose in the community what exactly the mysterious G7 unit was doing in Villa Maarheeze next to the IDB of Fock, the Baron for secrecy reasons on July 1, 1949 changed the label of G7 to SAZ, short for Section for General Affairs (Sectie Algemene Zaken), which he thought sounded harmless. Van Lynden also thought that after an invasion it would have been comparatively easy for the Soviets to identify former resistance and secret service members and he therefore made it an imperative to recruit new faces and unknown names, replacing most of the former colleagues of Somer with unknown men.

During his time in office van Lynden stressed that he needed more money to pay for the technical equipment of his stay-behind. Especially communication machines were expensive. Chief of the General Staff Kruls had asked already in 1946 for such funds. The money came in 1948 after Lynden had replaced Somer as chief of SAZ and sophisticated equipment was thereafter being developed in cooperation with departments of the Dutch technology firm Phillips. In exchange for their cooperation van Lynden saw to it that leading Phillips technicians involved in the development of SAZ high-tech equipment were not sent to the brutal colonial battle in Indonesia.[19] Interestingly enough van Lynden, leader of the SAZ stay-behind, was being kept unaware of the second and more mysterious stay-behind that his fellow Dutchman and BVD commander Einthoven was running. Tellingly it was the British who in 1949 informed van Lynden in London that a second parallel stay-behind network under the command of Einthoven existed in the Netherlands.[20] Van Lynden, who was mightily surprised, immediately insisted that both secret armies must be coordinated, for otherwise serious complications could result. This advice was followed and van Lynden's SAZ was fused with Einthoven's stay-behind into the Dutch secret army 'Intelligence and Operations' (Intelligence en Operations), short I&O, the label under which the Dutch stay-behind also became known in 1990. The two branches were nevertheless kept apart. The SAZ net became synonymous with the I unit, while Einthoven's stay-behind was the O unit. According to internal sources, Einthoven who followed his own secretive agenda allegedly strongly resented the cooperation of his unit with van Lynden's SAZ and little cooperation between Intelligence and Operations took place as long as Einthoven was in command of Operations.[21]

As the Dutch secretly agreed with the British, I&O had the general task to function as a stay-behind in case of foreign occupation of the Netherlands. 'The main attitude at the time was that we were both [British and Dutch] facing difficult times, and that the British would solve it all, as they had the expertise in the field', a former Dutch agent later recalled.[22] Within the Dutch stay-behind tasks were split. The Intelligence (I) unit under van Lynden was responsible for the collection and transmission of intelligence from occupied areas, preparations and running of exile bases and evacuation operations of the royalty, the government and the security apparatus including personnel of I&O. The Operations (O) unit under Einthoven had to carry out sabotage and guerrilla operations, strengthen the local resistance and create a new resistance movement. Most sensitively O also had the task to make people sensitive to the danger of Communism during times of peace. O was therefore trained in covert action operations, including the use of guns and explosives, and possessed independent secret arms caches.[23] Most of the costs of the Dutch stay-behind were covered by a secret budget of the Dutch Defence Ministry with the spendings being controlled personally by the chairman of the General Accountancy Department (Algemene Rekenkamer).

During his time in office, Van Lynden actively sought a suitable exile base, where his SAZ Gladio unit would have taken the Dutch government and other selected individuals in the event of an occupation. England, a safe place during the Second World War, could not be assumed to be a safe place in a future war. Lynden searched for a suitable place for a long time. In the end he decided that in Europe only Great Britain and the Iberian Peninsula were potentially suitable, while more secure overseas bases included the Dutch colony Curacao in the Caribbean, as well as the United States and Canada. In the early 1950s van Lynden made several trips to the United States. The base could not be situated close to a strategic area, such as an industrial zone, or an important military facility, for these would have ranged among the first Soviet targets. While the location of the base in the USA remains unknown it is known that van Lynden found a base and that important documents of the Dutch executive were copied and transferred to the secret exile base. The Dutch stay-behind headquarters had been set up in the USA with the consent of the CIA. A former Dutch official relates how reluctant the CIA was on the topic: 'When the time comes, one can speak about that', he recalls the first contacts. 'But we insisted that we had to talk now. Finally the CIA agreed after a few months to give us what we wanted', whereupon a Dutch stay-behind command centre was set up in the USA.[24]

Furthermore van Lynden set up a secret exile base in Spain then ruled by fascist dictator Franco. 'If he had allowed us we would have build our exile base even in Franco's very home', a former Dutch secret soldier remembers.[25] Stay-behind commander van Lynden convinced stay-behind commander Einthoven to carry out the sensitive mission, whereupon the latter disguised as tourist in 1959 travelled to Spain and with the help of the contacts of former Dutch ambassador to Spain, W. Cnoop Koopmans, set up a secret Dutch exile base. The evidence remains fragmentary and further contacts concerning an exile base seem to have taken place with Canada and Great Britain. The post-invasion escape preparations were taken very seriously, and ships and airplanes were kept ready for that task. 'I remember that around 1950 I had to test and judge quite a few yachts whether they were seaworthy', a former member of the Dutch Marine and stay-behind officer recalled after the discovery of the network in 1990.[26]

Symbolising its strong connection to the British the official SAZ insignia of the Dutch Gladio featured the Tudor rose next to the motto of Somer 'We will never give up.' 'We had no intention of fighting the next war under British command', a former Dutch secret soldier nevertheless highlighted Dutch independence. 'Van Lynden was very strong. They could not push him aside. Neither could later the Americans do that as towards the end of the 1950s they started to play an increasingly important role. But van Lynden understood that a certain consensus had to be reached between the parties, and in his mind it was up to the respective chiefs who had to determine how they wanted to work together while keeping at the same time their own sovereignty.'[27] In the top-secret meetings in the NATO stay-behind coordination and planning centres ACC and CPC, the Dutch Gladio I&O at all times aimed to present itself as a single harmonic unit with two branches. The Dutch had some experience on how to work with the dominant MI6 and CIA, for after the war the United Kingdom and the United States had formalised their secret cooperation with the Dutch in a trilateral secret forum labelled TCH, in which the United Kingdom, the United States and the Netherlands each had a seat. Parallel to the creation of this secret coordination committee on March 17, 1948 the so-called WUCC had been erected with the task of carrying out peace time preparations in the United Kingdom, Belgium, the Netherlands, Luxemburg and France against an eventual Soviet invasion. In April 1951 the early stay-behind command centre WUCC handed over its functions to the CPC, closely linked to NATO, within which the Dutch secret service also had a seat.[28]

Van Lynden during his time in office very actively promoted the contacts between the European secret services and their secret armies and insisted that cooperation was mandatory when it came to the erection of international escape and evasion routes. To this purpose the Baron travelled Europe extensively for numerous years after having become commander of the Dutch secret army. He was much praised for his efforts among the security services and with this encouragement admitted that he would much like to become the first secretary of the CPC. Yet the British who distrusted the liberal and open-minded van Lynden blocked his nomination.[29] In 1957 CPC members Great Britain, the United States, France, Belgium, Luxemburg and the Netherlands under the participation of van Lynden erected the so-called Six Powers Lines Committee, which like the CPC had the task to organise and coordinate stay-behind preparations with a focus on international communication and escape lines. The Six Powers Lines Committee became the ACC, which was founded in 1958 in Paris. ACC coordinated the international Gladio exercises which were carried out clandestinely with the participation of the different networks. In case of an invasion there was an ACC basis in the United States, and one in the United Kingdom from where the units in the occupied territory could be activated and commanded. ACC manuals instructed stay-behind soldiers on common covert action procedures, encryption and frequency-hopping communication techniques, as well as air droppings and landings. The chairmanship of ACC changed every two years. Through the TCH, the CPC and the ACC, the Dutch Gladio I&O had standing contacts with both the CIA and the MI6.[30]

The CIA and the MI6 by the 1950s collaborated closely in covert action operations and in 1953 overthrew the Iranian government of Mossadegh who had attempted to distribute parts of the oil wealth to the population. At the same time the CIA and MI6 feared that European Communists and the Soviet secret service might apply the same techniques to Western Europe and hence they attributed much importance to their secret armies on the old continent. In 1953 the CIA instructed van Lynden that several changes had to be carried out in order to make his units more professional. 'It was literally a blue print, a collection of thick blue books' which were given to the Baron, a former agent recalls. 'Van Lynden studied the texts extensively. They contained information on take over techniques which the Soviets had practised in Eastern Europe. The examples illustrated which sort of persons the Soviets were particularly focusing on. Consequently such persons could obviously not be recruited as secret agents. On this basis van Lynden had to terminate the contact to a certain number of agents, which had been recruited by Somer.'[31]

Yet it was not only from the CIA but also from within the Dutch security apparatus that van Lynden faced pressure. In February 1951 General Kruls, who had been actively involved in the erection of the Dutch stay-behind as the superior of both Somer and van Lynden, was replaced after serious disagreements with

Defence Minister H. L. Jakob on the future task and organisation of the Dutch army. To the surprise and dislike of many inside the Dutch army, General B. R. P. F. Hasselman succeeded Kruls as new Chief of the Dutch Chiefs of Staff. Van Lynden personally resented Hasselman. Already before the war Hasselman had been known for his pro-German attitudes. After the war rumours claimed that Hasselman had been a traitor within the Dutch General Staff before the German invasion of 1940. After the capitulation of the Netherlands Hasselman had cooperated with the Germans and had urged other officers including van Lynden to do the same. Van Lynden had refused. During a harsh consolidation effort of the German occupying army in 1942 a large segment of Dutch officers including Hasselmann were transferred to prisoner of war camps. In Stanislau Hasselman met van Lynden. Again Hasselman collaborated and the Germans promoted him to a leading position within the prison. After the war Hasselman was dismissed from the Dutch army for having cooperated with the German invaders. Yet he successfully appealed against this decision and to the surprise of many was promoted steadily, throwing an unfavourable light on the Dutch Defence Department.

Upon the nomination of Hasselmann in 1951, the Dutch cavalry, to which van Lynden belonged, had decided that none of its members was to shake hands with the compromised General, even if now nominally he was their boss. As section chief van Lynden had to meet his new commander during official procedures. He was so worried that he considered resigning. In the end he went to the meeting and General Hasselmann was smart enough not to stretch out his hand himself.[32] Hasselmann in subsequent years repeatedly blocked the promotion of van Lynden to higher ranks. Serious infighting resulted and Fock, then Secretary-General within the Ministry of General Affairs, had to intervene. 'I have spoken to Hasselmann in quite a rough and direct manner then', Fock recalled many years later, whereupon the two men in subsequent years kept their distance.[33] Despite the in-house fighting in the Defence Department, van Lynden remained focused on his task. 'I still remember the invasion of Hungary in 1956', a former Dutch secret soldier recalled a well-known operation of the Soviet forces. 'On that day van Lynden came into the office where much confusion and excitement reigned. He calmly said: "We have been building up this thing for years now. Why are you all so nervous?" Indeed I believe that we could have become operational in 1956.'[34]

Another historical moment in the Cold War saw van Lynden more distressed. When in 1961 it was revealed that the British agent George Blake had worked for the Russians ever since the early 1950s there was not only horror in London, but also considerable panic in the Dutch secret army. 'Van Lynden was scared to death when this was revealed', a former Dutch stay-behind soldier recalled. For as part of the intense cooperation with the British, Blake had spent a few months in The Hague immediately after the end of the Second World War engaging in clandestine operations. During that time Blake was also in Villa Maarheeze in Wassenaar, headquarters of the Dutch domestic secret service and the 'I' branch of the Dutch stay-behind. Van Borssum Buisman, later to become Gladio commander, had talked to Blake. Allegedly 'Blake knew locations and persons' of the Dutch secret army, an unnamed Dutch agent later claimed. Contrary to this claim Blake himself in 1992 from his Moscow exile claimed in a conversation with former SAZ members: 'I have never known of these [stay-behind] activities. And I was never asked about them by the Soviets. Thus they [Dutch secret soldiers] need not worry. The name van Borssum Buisman says nothing to me at all.'[35]

After having commanded the SAZ or 'I' branch of the Dutch Gladio I&O for 14 years van Lynden resigned in March 1962. He went back to the Royal Palace for a full-time profession which the Queen had asked him to carry out. Van Lynden died in September 1989 aged 76. At the time of the Cuban missile crisis when the Cold War reached its climax in 1962 the command of the Dutch stay-behind I&O was restructured as both units received new commanders. The O branch of the Dutch secret army had been commanded for 14 years by Louis Einthoven who at the age of 66 left the BVD and retired. At the same time he also gave up his function as leader and commander of the top-secret O branch of the Dutch stay-behind. Twelve years later he died. General Major M. De Boer replaced him in April 1962. Chief of the Dutch General Staff van den Wall Bake had specifically instructed De Boer to ameliorate the relationship between I and O which had suffered under Einthoven. Two years later a commission within the Defence Department under the chairmanship of Dr Marius Ruppert investigated whether De Boer had successfully carried out his task. The commission was made up of three men and next to Ruppert included Fock and Lieutenant Admiral Propper.

Ruppert, a member of the Dutch Parliament and a senior adviser to the crown, presented his report on the cooperation of the two Dutch secret armies in 1965. His findings were shattering. Given the poor cooperation between the two branches of the Dutch stay-behind, Ruppert suggested that the position of 'Co-ordinator of I&O' should be created and assigned this position to himself. Furthermore Ruppert advised to replace De Boer as chief of O and again assigned the job to himself. On the directive of Dutch Prime Minister J. Zijlstra, it was Ruppert who in 1967 became chief of the O branch of the Dutch stay-behind, a position he held until 1975.[36] When Fock was interviewed after the Gladio revelations in the 1990s, he confirmed that he had been a member of the secret commission, but claimed that he could not remember what was being discussed. He only recalled that they had met several times in the villa of Ruppert in the Dutch village Zeist.

Ruppert's manoeuvre was a shock for the SAZ, the I branch of the Dutch stay-behind. Much resentments arose between the unequal parts of the Dutch stay-behind, above all due to the fact that Ruppert, in his dual role of commander of O and coordinator of O&I, increased the strength and position of O at the expense of I. Ruppert saw to it that O lead the representation of I&O in the international ACC and CPC NATO-linked stay-behind committees. Cooperation between I and O remained less than perfect also in the years to come. Tensions concerning Ruppert's dual role relaxed only when a new coordinator for I&O replaced

Ruppert. The position was, after Ruppert, repeatedly given to retired Marine Officers who retire already at the age of 55, early enough for a second career in the underground. In 1975 Th. J. A. M. van Lier who, somewhat unusual for the overall Gladio pattern, was a Socialist replaced Ruppert as commander of O. After the war van Lier had sat in the Dutch parliament for the Workers Party, and later was chief of the illegal secret service Albrecht, a function for which he was later arrested. At the time of van Lier I&O allegedly had an annual budget of around 3 million Dutch Guilders. But thereafter the units grew in size, and also cooperation between the two Dutch stay-behind increased. It is unknown who commanded the Dutch Gladio in the 1980s until the discovery of the network in 1990 as the names of the commanders are being kept secret as with all probability they are still alive and hold offices.

Not only the O branch but also the I branch of the Dutch Gladio featured significant changes in 1962. After Somer and van Lynden, van Borssum Buisman took over command of the I branch of the secret army in March 1962. With his moustache and fair hair the tall cavalerist van Borssum Buisman to many looked like the typical Dutchmen. During the Second World War he had been a liaison officer between the Dutch wartime secret service BI (Bureau Inlichtingen) and the Dutch resistance organisation OD (Ordedienst) under P. J. Six. In this function van Borssum Buisman was captured by the Germans in February 1944, made a tour through several German prisons, but survived several questionings without revealing the identity of the members of the Dutch resistance. After having been sentenced to death by the Germans, he was able to escape from a running train heading for Germany. Injured, he made his way to Holland and re-established contacts with Six, whereupon some Germans considered van Borssum Buisman to have been the best Dutch secret agent.

Also after the war van Borssum Buisman did not leave the secret trade and was first stationed in Ceylon for some time, where he waited in vain with a special unit for employment in Indonesia. Back in the Netherlands the first commander of I, Somer, recruited Buisman into the secret stay-behind network. During van Lynden's time in the 1950s Buisman was vice commander of SAZ. Among his primary tasks ranged the design of escape routes from Holland to Franco's Spain through Belgium and France. Along the route he recruited agents and trained them, in France often exile Dutchmen, or Frenchmen who had once lived in Holland. He held the position of chief of I until May 1970, whereupon he retired and died in February 1991 aged 77. After the discovery of the secret Gladio networks in Europe in 1990 it was revealed that after Buisman the commander of O had been J. W. A. Bruins who directed the clandestine army from May 1970 to December 1981. The names of more recent commanders of I&O, who presumably are still alive, were not revealed.[37]

Personal strength of the I&O still remains somewhat vague. 'The building up of a stay-behind always takes years and consumes large investments in the form of training and schooling. Thus you must handle your agents carefully, use them as you would use your best troops, which you also save for the decisive battle', a former member of the Dutch secret army explained after the cover of the network had been blown.[38] SAZ allegedly had a standing body of but 25 staff members, plus an additional 150 trained SAZ agents. O had a standing body of but 20 staff members, plus an additional 150 trained O agents with expertise in guerrilla warfare, explosives and sabotage operations. According to these figures, the Dutch stay-behind I&O thus possessed a nucleus of 350 members who in case of war would have enlarged the secret army by recruiting and training new members. In order to be able to bargain under occupation conditions commander van Lynden had equipped his agents with gold and diamonds. Commander Einthoven had bought gold at the Dutch national bank which he transferred to the exile bases in Spain and the United States.

As a rule not even the wives and closest relatives of the Gladiators were allowed to know of the existence of the secret stay-behind armies. Van Lynden therefore advised his people to cultivate extensive hobbies, which could function both as a cover and a compensation for the awkward secret life. He himself cultivated horse riding, but also developed extensive skills as a bird specialist. Commander van Borssum Buisman for his part loved numismatics and pretended to develop an expertise in coins. All agents were strictly ordered to follow the need to know principle and thus active stay-behind agents often only had a vague idea of the overall pattern and structure of the secret European army they were a part of. Foreign secret warfare experts, above all the British, were involved in the training. 'Me too I have been on a little [British] island', a Dutch wartime veteran remembered his contact with the British. 'But there I did not learn anything, which I did not already know from my time in the resistance.'[39]

During training the secret soldiers had to refer to each other with cover names. 'The training had to take place completely during the leisure time', a former Dutch secret soldier remembered. 'Together with the instructor an adequate training program was set up. Several different training locations had to be frequented, for you cannot do things like that on the attic. The training could not take place at regular intervals because that would have been too obvious.'[40] Motivation at times was a problem: 'The difficult dimension was that you had to prepare for a situation that might only take place in ten years time', a former Dutch secret soldier recalled. 'You had to keep motivation burning like a religion. Especially during times of relaxation and peaceful coexistence, that was very difficult. Also the other side [the Communists] were fighting a psychological battle. Thus the instructors had to be kept alert with the help of objective information [on the danger of Communism], which they in turn handed over to the agents in the field.'[41]

Of the twofold clandestine Dutch stay-behind I&O the mysterious O branch was the top-secret branch and still today only very limited data exists on it. 'The difference between I and O is that O must not "exist", it was a different affair', a former involved explained after the existence of the network was discovered in 1990.[42] During exercises of the Dutch secret army the members of O allegedly felt superior to I agents and in the evenings after the training refused to socialise. 'They often considered themselves as the top of the top who would carry out the real work in case of an occupation.'[43] In order to keep O as secret as possible all contacts to Dutch officials were carried out through I, which was not always appreciated by I. O was partly financed from private sources, above all multinational firms and the CIA. Apart from these funds O also received Dutch public funds which were covered as funds for I. The very few senior officials within the Dutch Defence Ministry who were aware of the secret I and its budget wrongly, and much to the resentment of van Lynden, thought that I was quite an expensive secret army. 'It [O] seemed a little bit like a 15th century nunnery', a former I agent recalls. 'You were not allowed to see each other, and everybody sat alone in his cell.'[44]

I was used as a front if O wanted a printing press, explosives or other devices. In these cases I was informed where a specific delivery, which in most cases came from England, had arrived. A military van then transported the material to a specified site of I where O agents took over the material. But if something went wrong the official Dutch secret services had to shoulder the blame as the existence of neither I nor O could be publicly admitted. In the 1980s stay-behind arms caches were discovered by accident in the Netherlands. In 1983 Defence Minister J. de Rujiter had to answer questions in front of TV cameras after a mysterious arms cache had been discovered in Rozendaal. De Ruijter at the time had asked the newspapers to give him some time for internal investigations and was briefed extensively. Towards the public the domestic secret service BVD shouldered the blame. Thereafter within the BVD everybody wanted to know which colleagues had such arms caches, and thus the version for internal BVD consumption was that a secret unit I was responsible. This of course was yet another lie, for in truth all weapons belonged to the top-secret O sabotage and covert action unit.

'While I was a politically independent unit O was known to be more ideologically oriented' a former Dutch agent testified, implying that O was an anti-Communist armed unit similar to the SDRA8 in neighbouring Belgium. This, however, does not mean that O was an illegal anti-Communist hit squad, another former O member was eager to stress: 'We based our struggle on the defence of values which were written down in the constitution.'[45] Dutch stay-behind expert Paul Koedijk found that O units also during times of peace specialised in what they called 'immunising' Dutch citizens. 'Against what exactly the citizens had to be immunised was more than clear: Communism in all its appearances.' O engaged in black propaganda and fake smear stories against Communists as part of its ideological struggle and to this purpose possessed a printing network. 'The assumption within O was that a Soviet occupation would be much worse than the German occupation which the Netherlands had experienced', a former involved recalls. 'Because also the few values which the Germans left untouched, for instance family and religion, would have been threatened under Soviet occupation. We expected radical changes.'[46]

When in late 1990 Italian Prime Minister Giulio Andreotti revealed the existence of secret anti-Communist armies across Western Europe, the cover of the Dutch network was also blown. A former Dutch stay-behind member mused: 'We actually were surprised as well that we could work so long undisturbed.'[47] Dutch Prime

Minister Ruud Lubbers of the Dutch DCI, in office ever since 1982, on November 13, 1990 confirmed in a letter to the Dutch parliament that also the Netherlands had a secret army, a 'mixed civilian and military group', and that this army was still active. Lubbers in his letter claimed that 'there was never any NATO supervision over this organisation' and with reference to the classical stay-behind function declared that 'contacts with other NATO countries, some of which had other structures, was limited on the Dutch side to how those goals could be achieved'.[48] Parliamentarians of both government and opposition parties agreed that Lubbers' letter was not good enough on explanation. Some of the parliamentarians remembered that in the 1980s mysterious arms caches containing grenades, semiautomatic rifles, automatic pistols, munitions and explosives had accidentally been discovered and requested more information on the alleged links to the secret army. Other parliamentarians critically insisted that the government should at least have informed the secrecy-bound Parliament Intelligence and Security Committee about the existence of the secret army.

Lubbers and Dutch Defence Minister Relus Ter Beek thereafter briefed the Parliament Intelligence and Security Committee behind closed doors for the first time on the Dutch stay-behind I&O and hours later Lubbers addressed parliament. He confirmed that the secret arsenals discovered in the 1980s had belonged to the secret army. Lubbers highlighted that the Dutch stay-behind was responsible jointly to the Prime Minister, thus himself, and the Defence Minister, Ter Beek. 'Successive Prime Ministers and Defence Ministers have always preferred not to inform other members of their cabinets or Parliament.'[49] The Prime Minister took pride in the fact that some 30 Ministers had kept the secret, while some members of the Dutch parliament thought that this had been a violation of the Dutch constitution. Many parliamentarians did not reject stay-behind emergency preparations on general grounds. But they did object to having been kept in the dark. Dutch Labour Party MP Maarten van Traa in a representative statement declared: 'We need more clarification on what structures there are, and to what extent they have collaborated or still collaborate with NATO.' Ton Frinking, a member of Lubbers' Christian Democrats said he also wanted more information on the 'NATO perspective' of the Gladio group. He said he had noted Belgium's recent admission that they had chaired the last secret stay-behind meeting. 'The question is what that Belgian chairmanship really means', Frinking said.

Lubbers thereafter admitted that the Dutch secret army was still a member of the secret NATO committee that coordinated the stay-behind armies in Western Europe. Hans Dijkstal of the opposition Liberals said, 'I don't particularly worry that there was, and perhaps still is, such a thing. What I do have problems with is that until last night Parliament was never told.'[50] Some parliamentarians wanted to know who was a member of the secret army. Lubbers in response claimed that he had no personal knowledge who was part of the secret organisation. Some parliamentarians thought this to be a contradiction to his earlier statement in which he had maintained that it was his task together with the Defence Minister to control the secret soldiers. But Lubbers insisted that the need for secrecy would make it 'pretty much lethally dangerous if the prime minister ... were to investigate everyone personally'.[51] In response to specific questions of parliamentarians Lubbers was forced to confirm that members of the Dutch secret army had taken part recently in a training exercise on the Italian island Sicily at the headquarters of the Italian Gladio.[52]

There was no parliamentary investigation nor a public report and only in April 1992 the Dutch secret army I&O was closed down. Defence Minister Relus Ter Beek in his personal letter thanked the secret soldiers for their services to the country.[53] The ghosts of the past came to haunt the Netherlands in December 1993 when a court in The Hague sentenced a 38-year-old man to three years prison. Together with him a 44-year-old Major of the Dutch Army was also found guilty for having blackmailed the Dutch baby food manufacturer Nutricia in spring 1993 for five million Dutch Guilders. Interestingly enough the lawyers acting on behalf of the defendants claimed that the two men were members of the top-secret Dutch stay-behind organisation which had been set up by the secret services in the Netherlands and other European countries. The Major of the Dutch Army during his defence claimed that in the past stay-behind agents apprehended by the police could rely on an agreement between the justice and defence authorities, whereby no action was taken against them. He alleged that a number of Gladio missions had failed in the past without any charges being issued against those involved, implying that Dutch Gladiators had also operated beyond oversight and legal limitations. The Major did not specify what kind of missions he was referring to.[54]

12

THE SECRET WAR IN
LUXEMBURG

Of all three Benelux countries Luxemburg is by far the smallest state. Exactly like Belgium and the Netherlands the country was invaded and occupied during the Second World War by the German army. Yet unlike Belgium where a Senate commission had investigated the secret army or unlike the Netherlands where the academic community had researched the network in Luxemburg only a very limited amount of information on the national stay-behind has been made available so far.[1]

As Prime Minister Jacques Santer stressed in front of his parliament on November 14, 1990, in reply to a priority request posed by parliamentarian Charles Goerens of the Democrat Party, small countries also had been integrated into the continental network of secret stay-behind armies. As in Belgium and the Netherlands the idea had been derived from the experiences of the Second World War during which similar networks had existed also in Luxemburg to fight with limited success the German occupation forces. Luxemburg had joined NATO at its foundation in 1949 and thereafter the secret networks were coordinated by the military alliance.

'The word "Gladio" is a term used for the Italian structure. The term used internationally and inside NATO is "Stay-Behind"', the Prime Minister explained the terminology of the secret army to the astonished parliamentarians. 'This term reflects the concept of an organisation designed to become active behind the fronts of a military conflict, thus in case of enemy occupation of the territory. This concept has been designed by NATO. The idea has been derived from the experiences of World War Two, during which similar networks were established during occupation periods, thus in a particularly difficult environment and under enemy control.' Never again, the Prime Minister presented the rationale of the secret network, should a country be so ill-prepared before a war and a potential occupation: 'In order to avoid in the future the same preparation gap, it was decided to prepare the foundations of such an organisation already in peace time.'

While certain members of parliament thought that the secret NATO-directed army had violated the sovereignty of European states Prime Minister Santer, who later served as president of the EU commission, claimed that this had not been the case: 'All NATO countries in central Europe have taken part in these preparations, and Luxemburg could not have escaped this international solidarity. Each member state was allowed to define its own structures. Thus, although NATO was the initiator and coordinator of the stay-behind network, each country remained the director of its own national component.' By implication the stay-behind network of Luxemburg was also coordinated by NATO and hence took part in the secret meetings of the ACC and the CPC, including the ACC meeting under Belgian General Van Calster in Brussels on October 23 and 24, 1990.

Neither the names nor the number of agents belonging to the secret stay-behind army in Luxemburg were revealed, and the Prime Minister only confirmed that the secret service of Luxemburg, the Service de Renseignements, had been running the network. 'The agents of this stay-behind network were recruited by the secret service on a voluntarily basis and according to criteria relating to their profession and place of living.' The Prime Minister implied that the stay-behind of Luxemburg in the 1980s had also been equipped with the modern Harpoon communication stations: 'These persons, directed through radio communications, had the task to carry out clandestine missions at their own risk and in a context of enemy control of the area.' The Prime Minister did not elaborate on the role of MI6 or CIA in Luxemburg but confirmed that in case of war the secret army would have cooperated with Special Forces, presumably including the British SAS and the US Green Berets. 'The essence of their mission was to inform NATO on the political and military situation of their region, to organise escape routes out of the occupied territory, and to support the special forces of the military.'

In the midst of revelations in Europe that the secret armies had not only been a prudent precaution but also a source of terror, the Prime Minister was eager to emphasise that the 'mission was only to be carried out in case of invasion and enemy occupation of the territory'. Jacques Santer knew that in numerous other countries, including most prominently neighbouring Belgium as well as Italy, Greece, Turkey, France, Spain and Portugal, evidence was surfacing which linked the secret stay-behind soldiers to massacres and other forms of terrorist manipulation of the political climate. Thus he stressed: 'As far as Luxemburg is concerned, it is clear that these missions were really only reserved to the above mentioned forms of assistance to the NATO authorities. The only activities of these persons – and this is the case for the entire time period in which this network has existed – have been limited to the training in preparation of their missions, including the training of how to behave individually in a hostile environment, and how to coordinate efforts with allied countries.'

In the absence of an independent enquiry the words of the Prime Minister were accepted at face value despite the fact that also in Luxemburg a number of parliamentarians felt that it had been a mistake that parliament had never been informed of the secret warfare preparations. The Prime Minister only very briefly touched upon the topic of parliamentary oversight of such a secret structure within the state by dismissing the thought that such parliamentarian oversight would even have been possible. Santer, who himself had been a member of the Luxemburg parliament from 1974 to 1979, supported the assumption, widespread in secret services circles, that parliamentarians are too talkative and hence unable to keep a secret. Even against their best intentions they would have betrayed the top-secret network. 'It is unnecessary to mention again the secrecy that must characterise such operations by their very nature', Santer told parliament without explaining who had assured civilian control of the secret army. Prime Minister Santer concluded his short speech in front of parliament by admitting that also he, and with all likelihood his entire government, had been completely unaware of the secret NATO network within the country. 'I can answer that I did not have any personal knowledge of the existence of the network, and exactly like the Minister of Belgium, I was surprised to learn about its existence. I do not think that another member of the government could have guessed its existence. Obviously, I can not make this declaration also in the name of my predecessors, for I did not have the time to consult them before my answer.'

This was not good enough an explanation for certain members of parliament. For the far-reaching confession amounted to the fact that a secret army had operated in Luxemburg not only beyond the knowledge and control of parliament, but also beyond the knowledge and control of the government. The Prime Minister was unable to solve this delicate issue and indirectly blamed NATO for the fact that a secret army had been set up in the country: 'In conclusion I repeat that it was only in the context of Inter Allied agreements that Luxemburg contributed through its own and only secret service to the erection of the discussed network under the coordination of NATO authorities.' At no time, Santer was eager to convince his parliament, had the network used its arms or explosives, nor engaged otherwise in illegal activities during peacetime, for 'the Luxemburg network has never known a military entanglement and it has never been used for other purposes than those for which it had been created!' The Prime Minister stressed that 'the very principle of a secret patriotic resistance organisation for the case of an enemy occupation of the territory, must not be questioned' and informed his parliament that 'it is only normal that I have ordered the secret service to close down immediately the stay-behind network, in the expectation that the NATO countries will define their new strategy in a completely changed Europe'.

The history of the Gladio network in Luxemburg remains classified and fragmentary. The numbers and exact contents of the arms caches and their location were not revealed, nor the dates or terms of cooperation between Luxemburg's stay-behind and NATO, CIA and MI6. As numerous questions remained, parliamentarian Jean Huss of the Luxemburg Green Alternative Party together with coalition partners after Santer's declarations asked first of all for an open debate in parliament on the issue, and secondly for the establishment of a parliamentary commission of inquiry into the topic. Yet both suggestions were declined by the Luxemburg parliament in a majority decision.

13

THE SECRET WAR IN DENMARK

The Danish secret stay-behind army was code-named 'Absalon'. Nomen est omen, the code name, highlighted the anti-Communist task of the unit for; Absalon was the name of a medieval Danish Bishop who with the sword in his hand had defeated the Russians in the Middle Ages. A large bronze statue of Absalon on horseback in battle gear is still standing in the Danish capital Copenhagen and received a sudden increase of attention when the Danish press in November 1990 headlined that 'The group "Absalon" erected by the CIA and supported by NATO prepared against a Communist take over of power in Denmark.'[1]

The history of Absalon remains fragmentary because the Danish parliament upon discovery of the network in 1990 had decided to discuss the top-secret affair behind closed doors with no official reports for the public. According to a former unnamed member of the network, the secret army had been created after the traumatic occupation experience during the Second World War and allegedly numbered not more than 360 core members. As in all stay-behind countries the network would have been enlarged in case of occupation. 'The organisation was naturally copied after the resistance movement. There were twelve districts, structured according to the cell principle, but not as tightly organised as during the War', the unnamed Danish secret soldier revealed to the Danish press. 'Each district had up to 30 members in its inner circle.'[2]

According to several anonymous sources, E. J. Harder had for numerous years been the chief of the Danish stay-behind. 'Harder had the nickname "Bispen" ', Danish for 'Bishop', in memoria of the medieval bishop Absalon, a former Danish stay-behind member related.[3] Next to running the Danish secret army, Harder cultivated close contacts with NATO. He worked at NATO head-quarters from 1966 to 1970, the period when NATO had been forced to set up new headquarters in Belgian after French President De Gaulle had expelled the military alliance from French soil. Danish stay-behind Director Harder already during his time at NATO headquarters in Valenciennes in France, as well as after the expulsion from France during his time at the new NATO headquarters in Brussels, was informed of the details concerning NATO secret warfare.

Harder, in his political views, followed a right-wing agenda and to many in Denmark was a compromised figure. Erik Ninn Hansen, a member of the Conservative Party and Danish Defence Minister from 1968 to 1971, attempted to distance himself from the stay-behind commander when interviewed by the press in 1990. 'Several groups were formed after World War II. It could be true that Absalon was a group connected to the resistance movement', former Defence Minister Hansen cautiously replied to the questions of the journalists. 'I can also well remember Harder who had held many lectures. But if anybody thinks that I had expressed any sympathies with his thoughts then this is wrong. He was too chauvinistic for my taste. I have never thought of Absalon as being very influential and have never thought of it in connection with the work of the secret services.' Harder himself after the discovery of the secret armies in 1990 was not available for an interview.[4]

In 1978 – in the wake of US President Nixon's Watergate scandal and the CIA's covert war against Chile which had lead to the death of Socialist President Salvador Allende and the installation of dictator Augusto Pinochet in 1973 – former CIA Director William Colby published a book attempting to correct the heavily compromised public image of the US foreign secret service CIA. In this book Colby revealed to the public that he himself had engaged in setting up the stay-behind networks in Scandinavia when based as junior operative at the CIA headquarters in Stockholm. 'The situation in each Scandinavian country was different. Norway and Denmark were NATO allies, Sweden held to the neutrality that had taken her through two world wars, and Finland was required to defer in its foreign policy to the Soviet power directly on its borders', Colby related. 'Thus, in one set of these countries the governments themselves would build their own stay-behind nets, counting on activating them from exile to carry on the struggle', Colby implicitly referred to NATO countries Denmark and Norway. 'These nets had to be co-ordinated with NATO's plans, their radios had to be hooked to a future exile location, and the specialised equipment had to be secured from CIA and secretly cached in snowy hideouts for later use. In the other set of countries' the CIA operative continued with implicit reference to neutral Sweden and Finland, 'CIA would have to do the job alone or with, at best, "unofficial" local help, since the politics of those governments barred them from collaborating with NATO, and any exposure would arouse immediate protest from the local Communist press, Soviet diplomats and loyal Scandinavians who hoped that neutrality or nonalignment would allow them to slip through a World War III unharmed.'[5]

'Berlingske Tidende can reveal that Absalon is the Danish branch of the international Gladio network. This has been confirmed by a member of Absalon to Berlingske Tidende who wishes at present to remain unnamed', a Danish daily newspaper sensationally headlined its discoveries in 1990.[6] The source, named Q by the newspaper, confirmed what Colby had revealed in his book. 'Colby's story is absolutely correct. Absalon was created in the early 1950s', the source Q related. The network, according to Q, was composed of right-wing men in order to guarantee staunch anti-Communism. 'Colby was a member of the world spanning laymen catholic organisation Opus Dei, which, using a modern term, could be called right-wing. Opus Dei played a central role in the setting up of Gladio in the whole of Europe and also in Denmark', Q claimed. 'The leader of Gladio was Harder who was probably not a Catholic. But there are not many Catholics in Denmark and the basic elements making up the Danish Gladio were former [World War II] resistance people – former prisoners of Tysk Vestre Faengsel, Froslevlejren, Neuengamme and also of the Danish Brigade.'[7]

The Danish newspapers contacted Colby again in late 1990 and found that the Gladio secrets were still being guarded very closely. Then aged 70 and living in Washington, the retired CIA Director went on the defensive and claimed: 'I really know nothing on the Danish organisation. I have never been in contact with them. I don't believe so. In any case I don't remember.'[8] The Danish journalist insisted: 'But in your book it says that you were building CIA organisations in four countries!?' Colby replied: 'I have forgotten whether I have spoken of four or three or any other number. All which I could have known back then must really have been second hand knowledge. But the book was correct, judged on my knowledge at the time.' Unwilling to accept Colby's 'fading memory', the Danish journalist insisted, whereupon the former CIA Director explained: 'I think people have put more into it than they should have. A Soviet invasion was a real danger according to the understanding of many people and the co-operation with the resistance movements in Norway and France was a very natural way to defend the country.' He declined to comment on alleged terrorist operations or manipulation of the political climate.[9] When another group of Danish journalists insisted to be given at least the name of a Danish CIA contact person, Colby revealed that 'his Danish contact person' for the Gladio net had been Ebbe Munck, a central figure of the Danish secret service and a former member of the resistance movement who later had entered diplomacy to become an adviser to the Danish Queen Margarethe.[10]

As in all Gladio countries, in Denmark too the secret army was integrated into the military secret service FE (Forsvarets Efterretningstjeneste). According to an unnamed source, the clandestine right-wing army was staffed by military officers: 'Ninety five per cent were military people. Also many leading members of the Territorial Units were members. Furthermore a very useful extra potential to draw upon was the Reserve Officers Federation.' Allegedly selected Danish politicians were informed about the existence of the secret army for according to Q the 'connection to the conservative popular party was very close. The ideological basis was strongly anti-Communist. We were Danish and had strong national feelings based on Christian ideology. It was very important to us that it would not take two to three years as in 1940 until a resistance unit was organised.' The secret army, as Q related, had the twofold task to act in case of invasion or if the Communists seized power in Denmark without the help of the Red Army and to collect information on leftist organisations: 'It was during the time of the Cold War and a Russian invasion or take-over of power by the Danish Communists was – we felt – a clear and present danger.'[11] Despite its rightist conservative leanings Absalon would not recruit every right-wing activist, as a former agent was eager to stress: 'Not everybody could become a member. Among other things the right-wing activist Hans Hetler wanted to become a member. But we did not want him. He had been compromised and we did not think that he had the necessary qualities.'[12]

Former CIA Director Colby was correct to highlight that, as all secret armies, the Danish stay-behind Absalon also had independent supplies. 'Also a number of arms caches were erected across Denmark. I do not want to say how many. But they were less than ten', former Danish Gladiator Q claimed. 'Two of them were for instance in big forests, Bribskov and Dronninglund Storskov. I do not want to say how the arms were hidden and whether they still exist.'[13] Unlike Italy the arms and explosives in Denmark were never used for domestic terror operations as Q stressed: 'Such things have never happened in Denmark. We have never used weapons. But we have taken part in military exercises. For instance in a military exercise on the northern flank of NATO in Troms [Norway].'[14] During such international exercises the officers of the Absalon stay-behind together with other secret armies from other countries and personnel from NATO, CIA and MI6 trained covert action operations and secret warfare. Furthermore, as the Danish press was surprised to learn, the secret army Absalon had engaged in sensitive covert action operations on the other side of the iron curtain in the Communist countries 'in Eastern Europe'.[15] Absalon member Q confirmed: 'Absalon had all kinds of functions. First and foremost it had to be ready in case of a Russian invasion or a Communist take-over. But it also gathered information on leftist organisations and gathered intelligence in Eastern Europe.'[16]

When the secret army was set up at the end of the Second World War, arms and explosives to supply the unit were readily available. 'The weapons holdings resulted from the unequal distribution of arms after the liberation of Denmark, when several military groups received a large number of Swedish arms, while the Communists received none,' Q said. Later the CIA sent further equipment to the Danish stay-behind, as the former agent carefully suggested. 'I do not want to exclude the possibility that new equipment was added later. These were probably American.'[17] The claim was confirmed in 1991 when the Danish press headlined 'CIA sent weapons to Denmark' quoting from a document on CIA arms shipping found in the US national archives. The handwritten memorandum of US General G. C. Steward, who in the 1950s had been responsible for US military aid to Europe, was dated February 10, 1953 and directed to the chief of the Military Assistance Advisor Group (MAAG) in Copenhagen. The MAAG at the time possessed a whole fleet of ships to transport military equipment and brought arms from the United States to Denmark. The Steward memorandum was entitled 'Concerns the assistance of the CIA in special deliveries to Denmark through channels of the MAAG'. The document did not specify exactly what material was sent to which group in Denmark. 'The Danish government until now has declined allegations that the CIA in the early 1950s had set up a network of arms caches and men designed to fight a Soviet invasion of Denmark', the Danish press lamented. While as late as February 1991 Defence Minister Knud Enggaard in an ill-advised cover-up claimed that 'The government has no knowledge of such an organisation in Denmark.'[18]

The members of the Danish secret army like most of their colleagues in the secret armies of other countries were secretly trained in the United States, presumably at CIA covert action training centres or at the headquarters of the US Special Forces in Fort Bragg. 'Several members of the Danish Gladio allegedly took part in CIA training courses relating to intelligence and sabotage in the United States', the Danish press revealed without giving the exact location of the secret trainings in the United States.[19] Next to the CIA also contacts to NATO were intimate. For the Danish military secret service FE, next to directing the Absalon stay-behind, was also revealed to have linked the stay-behind network to NATO in very much the same manner as in Italy, Belgium and France where the military secret services guaranteed the cooperation of the secret armies with the NATO Special Forces command. Erik Fournais, Director of the Danish military secret service FE form 1963 to 1973, allegedly held a prominent role within the Danish secret army Absalon. He left his position as chief of FE in 1973 to become coordinator of the NATO intelligence services in Brussels, an office he held until 1977. An anonymous former member of Absalon stressed: 'Also Fournais was in the very inner circle of the organisation Absalon. I do not exactly know whether Fournais was a direct member. But he led a shadow existence in close vicinity of Absalon. He must have been in the very inner circle.' Gladio commander Harder, who had worked at NATO headquarters from 1966 to 1970 and functioned as the contact person between NATO and Absalon during that time, allegedly was replaced in that function by Fournais in the early 1970s. 'When Fournais got a top post within NATO he replaced Harder as the contact person between Absalon and NATO', Q relates.

Fournais, confronted with the allegations of Q by journalists in 1990, nervously denied that he had had any connection to the secret right-leaning army, while wrongly stressing that NATO was definitely not involved in secret stay-behind operations: 'I and the military secret service kept a ten feet distance from Absalon. Absalon had no contact whatsoever to NATO and the Danish military secret service', Fournais claimed. 'But I have heard of Absalon, especially because politicians have stressed that we [of the Danish secret service] should also keep an eye on the right-wing groups. But we did not observe and investigate Absalon. That would have been ridiculous.'[20] Indeed it would have been unusual if Fournais the military secret service Director, had investigated Fournais the Absalon member, to report on alleged illegal activities of the latter.

Within the Danish military secret service FE the stay-behind army was set up within the secret covert action department, the Special Operations (SO) unit directed by Gustav Thomsen. 'FE had a secret Special Operations (SO) department the tasks of which were not even known to other personnel within FE outside the Special Operations department', a former Danish secret soldier revealed. 'When bugging had to be undertaken SO provided the equipment. The chief of SO was Gustav

Thomsen.'[21] Also former anonymous Absalon member Q confirmed that the Danish stay-behind was linked through SO to the military secret service: 'I do not want to mention a name. But this is correct. It was there [in the SO] through which we had the contact.'[22] Former SO Commander Gustav Thomsen was less inclined to speak about the secrets of the state and in 1990 explained: 'I went into retirement in 1975. Since then many years have gone by. I remember nothing.'[23]

In the absence of an official investigation by the Danish parliament, specific trainings and operations carried out by SO and Absalon during the Cold War remain largely unknown. But allegations have been made that secret operations, as in other countries, included the supervision of Danish Communists and left-wing organisations and the setting up of personal files. Based on unnamed sources the Danish press reported that 'Absalon had among other tasks the order to collect information on leftist organisations.'[24] In the late 1950s FE agent Arne Sejr caused a scandal in the country after it was discovered that he had been bugging and observing the prominent leading Danish Communist Alfred Jensens.[25] Allegedly this and other domestic operations had been carried out with the support of SO and Absalon, although already at the time the secret army 'did everything to escape media attention'.[26] After Absalon had lain dormant in the early 1950s the domestic operations allegedly increased towards 1960. Absalon commander Harder allegedly had his difficulties and 'could not make Absalon function well in the 1950s. It was only in 1960 and 1961 that the dynamics increased', former Danish Gladiator Q relates. 'This happened after 18 Danish Absalon members had been to a meeting at the NATO headquarters then located at Valensciennes near Paris.'[27]

As the secret army operated in the dark its traces were covered up. The only time when the wider public also noticed domestic operations of Absalon was in 1974. In that year Absalon had tried in vain to prevent a group of leftist academics from becoming members of the directing body of the Danish Odense University which the secret army considered to be left leaning. When the cover of this Absalon operation was blown, it caused much media attention and a hype over this 'mystic underground organisation'. At the time nobody was able to reveal the links between NATO, the CIA and the international stay-behind framework.[28] After the Odense University scandal Absalon allegedly withdrew to the underground and formed front organisations to promote its ideology. 'This [the Odense operation] means that Absalon withdrew from the public. Instead a new organism, called Pindsvinet (hedgehog) was created to put forward the legitimate arguments of Absalon in the public debate' Q remembered, explaining that the symbol hedgehog was chosen to underline the ideological links to NATO: 'Pindsvinet is the name of an operation of General Eisenhower but also the symbol of the Atlantic Union. The Defence of Denmark after 1981 also used the hedgehog as a symbol.'[29]

The next shock for the Danish secret army came but four years later. In 1978 a huge stay-behind arms cache was discovered in neighbouring Norway and Norwegian Defence Minister Rolf Hansen was forced to confirm the existence of a secret NATO army in front of the Norwegian parliament. This was a highly critical moment for the secret Absalon stay-behind as revelations in Norway could easily have blown also the cover of the Danish network. According to Absalon member Q, the secret army thereafter was scaled down considerably in 1978 and 1979. At that time Danish Gladio chief Harder and his assistant Flemming Norgaard emigrated to Spain 'and we were all getting older', as Q claims.[30] Q himself alleged that Absalon after 1978 had been replaced by a new organisation with new people. And the academic Nils Gleditzch of the Oslo-based International Peace Research Institute observed in 1990 with reference to the 1978 Norwegian exposures that, 'It is a little surprising that no one in the other NATO countries picked up on it and raised questions about their own countries.'[31]

Harder's assistant Flemming Norgaard, as Q stressed, had been an important member of the Absalon network, functioning above all as 'an important money collector for the organisation'. Norgaard, who had emigrated to France, in 1990 was confronted by Danish journalists with the allegations of Q. Norgaard confirmed that he had been a member of Absalon but insisted that there had been no connection between Absalon and the compromised Italian secret army Gladio. Furthermore Jorgen Svenne, who died recently, had allegedly been an important figure of the inner circle of Absalon with excellent international contacts and close ties to the Danish Conservative Party. 'Svenne was the grey eminence who travelled a lot', Q recalled. 'Nobody really knew what he did. But hardly ever the most visible are the most important.'[32]

At the time of the discovery of the Italian Gladio army in 1990 the Danish secret network was still active and therefore Danish Defence Minister Knud Enggaard was forced to take a stand in front of the surprised and curious Danish parliament Folketing. On November 21, 1990 the Defence Minister in the first public official statement on the secret Danish army claimed that it was not true that 'any kind' of NATO-supported CIA organisation had been erected in Denmark. Thereafter, to the confusion of the parliamentarians, he said: 'Further pieces of information on a secret service operation in case of an occupation is classified material even highly classified material, and I am therefore prohibited from giving any further information in the Danish parliament'. Member of Parliament Pelle Voigt who had raised the Gladio question thought the Defence Minister's answer to be 'contradictory and an indirect confirmation of the fact that Denmark, too, had its secret network'.[33]

As the press started to question former Ministers, journalists found that they were most reluctant to talk about the sensitive affair. Erling Brondum, Defence Minister from 1973 to 1975, claimed in 1990 that 'So many years have gone by. The name Absalon says nothing to me.'[34] Thereafter the press was happy to highlight that in 1974 Brondum had in front of parliament used the name 'Absalon' that he now no longer remembered while refusing allegations concerning connections between the Danish stay-behind and the Defence Department. Social Democrat Poul Sogaard, Danish Defence Minister from 1978 to 1982, remembered his time in office more clearly and stated unambiguously: 'I can well remember Absalon. It was a circle of regular officers', the former Defence Minister claimed. 'In case Defence lacked in one or another equipment then Absalon could provide money for the purchase of these things. I have been briefed in this way by General Andersen.' However, General Andersen, who according to Sogaard had been part of the Gladio conspiracy, issued a denial and declared to the press: 'Poul Sogaard must be mistaken in his recollections. The name Absalon says nothing at all to me.'[35]

At the insistence of acting Defence Minister Enggaard, the stay-behind matter in 1990 was moved for further debate to the committee of the Danish parliament concerned with the supervision of the Danish secret service whose records are classified and not accessible to the public. Thus only selected parliamentarians were informed while the public was being kept in the dark. 'All ministers knew of the activities of Absalon. This is a hundred and twenty percent sure. We had a member highly placed in the ministry who in turn was in contact to the Prime Minister', former Danish stay-behind member Q emphasized. 'What we did was right. But now so many years have passed that for history's sake it is right now to reveal the main features.'[36]

14

THE SECRET WAR IN NORWAY

Hitler's armies invaded Norway in April 1940 and occupied the country for the next five years until the end of the Second World War. Similar to other countries in Western Europe, the traumatic occupation experience shaped Norwegian understanding of security policy profoundly and directly influenced the creation of a stay-behind network after the war. The Norwegians who secretly erected the stay-behind in their country were mostly people who had seen Nazi troops sweep away their ill-prepared resistance in the Second World War and who feared that the Cold War could bring a Soviet invasion. 'To establish a stay-behind organisation in Norway was not a question of shall, or shall not. It was a question of timing', Norwegian stay-behind authors Ronald Bye and Finn Sjue relate the feeling at the time. After all, NATO was insisting on the clandestine network. 'If the starting shot was not fired in 1947/48, it would have in 1949 with the NATO membership. Because a precondition for the membership was that the members should have, or promptly establish instruments for "unorthodox warfare"', Bye and Sjue explain with reference to an undated 'NATO/SACEUR Directive for Unorthodox Warfare.'[1]

Vilhelm Evang, the Director of the Norwegian secret service after the Second World War, and Jens Christian Hague, the first post-war Norwegian Defence Minister, were the two central figures for both the erection of the stay-behind and the creation of the Norwegian Intelligence Service (NIS) after the war. Evang, a science graduate from Oslo, had joined the small intelligence service of the Norwegian government in exile in London in 1942 while Hague had been the wartime leader of the Norwegian military resistance organisation. Back in Norway Evang, with the support of Hauge, built up the post-war NIS in 1946 and lead it as Director for 20 years. The US intelligence community was critical of Evang because of his known sympathies with the left in Norwegian politics, and particularly because of his membership in the Communist 'Mot Dag' movement in his younger days in the 1930s. In 1966 Evang had to leave the service after the so-called Lygren Affair.[2] To soften his exit the Norwegian Defence Minister transferred Evang to NATO headquarters in France as National Military Representative. He served first in Paris, then in Brussels until 1969. Evang resigned from civil service on reaching retirement and died in 1983 aged 74.

During his time in London Evang had established close ties with the British intelligence community. He shared the conviction of MI6 officers that Norway should never again come under enemy occupation without being prepared. As he was setting up the stay-behind network Evang in February 1947 visited an unnamed interlocutor of the MI6 with 'close connection with centrally placed defence and military circles' – presumably Director of MI6 Sir Steward Menzies himself – and presented to him the Norwegian stay-behind plan. Evang and Menzies agreed that the Soviet Union and the spread of Communism in Western Europe represented a real and present danger. 'Those considerations have led the English to take a strong interest in the build-up of a defence in countries under enemy occupation', Evang noted in his diary. 'It seems as if both the Netherlands, France, and Belgium are in the process of setting up a more or less fixed organisation for an underground army.'[3]

Next to the British MI6 the US CIA was also directly involved in the operations that lead to the creation of the Norwegian secret army. Already in 1946 Evang had sent Major Kaj Martens to New York to establish liaisons with the developing US intelligence community. Then in November 1947, after the CIA had been created, Evang visited the United States himself and discussed the issue of secret unorthodox warfare presumably with Frank Wisner, Director of CIA's Office of Policy Coordination (OPC) which was erecting the stay-behind net in Western Europe. As in Italy the CIA eventually became more important than the MI6 as the power of the United States increased to the degree that the power of the former empire Great Britain declined. 'Co-operation with the United States', Norwegian scholar Olav Riste observes, was 'by far the most important aspect of NIS foreign relations'.[4] In order to coordinate the clandestine cooperation, Norwegian, British and American secret service officers met in London in 1948. A secret service memorandum records that during the meeting it was decided 'to establish an apparatus in Norway whose task would be in the event of a complete or partial enemy occupation to communicate intelligence reports by radio or other means to an allied headquarters inside or outside the country'. The memorandum highlights that NIS was proud to inform both CIA and MI6 that in a secret NIS operation code-named SATURN such a secret army had already been set up. 'Colonel Evang was able to inform our allies that an apparatus which could be made to serve such a purpose was practically ready and at his disposal.'[5]

It was Norwegian intelligence officer Alf Martens Meyer who allegedly secured the contacts with the CIA, was himself on the CIA payroll and generally 'ran most of Norwegian intelligence operations in the 1950s and 1960s', as former Norwegian Intelligence officer and author Christian Christensen relates.[6] 'It has also been proven that Martens Meyer and his collaborators had regular contacts with MI6 and CIA "undercover" representatives at the British and American embassies in Oslo', Gladio journalists Bye and Sjue claimed in the 1990s.[7] As in other countries also in Norway the purchase of radio transmitters ranged among the largest and most conspicuous investments of the secret army. Evang in this context in a confidential letter in May 1948 asked Defence Minister Hauge for money in order to be able to purchase 50 radio transmitters for the Norwegian stay-behind. 'The transmitters will be securely stashed away, and will only be activated if parts of the country become occupied by a foreign power', Evang explained and highlighted that the secret NATO army might also be used domestically in the absence of an invasion in the case of a coup d'état by the Norwegian Communists: 'In case of an internal coup d'état individual transmitters may be activated by special agreement with the Defence Staff.' Evang highlighted that 'Preparations for the establishment of this network are well in hand' and specified that as operators of the transmitters 'we intend to select suitable persons who did not during the last war engage in similar underground activities and who are not identified as radio operators'.[8] Defence Minister Hauge was pleased with the development of the top-secret operation and supported the funding.[9]

Highlighting the domestic function of the secret army, Evang in his letter to Hauge stressed that private groups from selected industries had with the consent of Norwegian industrialists under NIS direction been trained and were in place to guard against 'fifth-column (Communist) subversive activities in certain industries'. Probably aware of the potential danger that such private armed groups uncontrolled by parliament pose, Evang in a report to Defence Minister Hauge in October 1948 insisted that the groups were made up of loyal and disciplined collaborators. When Norway joined NATO in April 1949 special posters were printed against fifth-column activity to be displayed on the wall of every military office. The posters instructed military officers to cooperate with the police and secret services in preventive measures against 'fifth columnists', defined as 'Norwegians or foreigners who within the nation's borders work for a foreign power through illegal intelligence activities, planning and carrying out sabotage, assassinations, etc.' After Norway's entry into NATO, lists of Norwegians and foreigners who would have been arrested and detained in an emergency were compiled and stored by the Security Police.[10]

Hauge, who had become Norwegian Defence Minister in 1945 at the relatively tender age of 30 mainly because of his credentials as wartime leader of the military resistance organisation, strongly supported the stay-behind army and in his first post-war plan for the reconstruction of the Norwegian armed forces, in front of the Norwegian parliament, in autumn 1946 emphasised that 'in the light of our wartime experience, a determined will to fight on even after military defeat and occupation is an essential part of a small country's defence preparedness'.[11] Hague decided that the main radio station of the NIS in the Oslo area was to function as the central station of the Norwegian stay-behind communication network and ordered that a reserve station be set up in the interior of the country.

On October 25, 1948 Defence Minister Hague passed a governmental directive officially establishing the Norwegian stay-behind. In a top-secret letter in the same month Hauge ordered the Chief of Defence Staff, Lieutenant-General Ole Berg, to establish 'an FO 4 preparedness'. Berg knew exactly what Hauge meant, for 'FO 4' during the Second World War had been the section of Norway's Defence High Command in exile charged with planning and carrying out sabotage and other underground activities in occupied territory together with British SOE. 'Free Norwegian authorities must be able to organise sabotage and "small war" activity against targets of military significance in areas of Norway that may temporarily be occupied by the enemy (communications, industrial plants, military stores, units, etc.)', Hague ordered. 'It will be necessary to carry out such measures as part of an armed struggle in Norway. The apparatus must therefore have a high preparedness already in peacetime.'[12]

Based on his own experience Hague wished for small action groups of two to four men, operating with access to secret arms caches containing guns, explosives, radio transmitters and other supplies. The secret soldiers were to be recruited from the Norwegian army and Home Guard. They woe to have local knowledge of their area of operations. Veterans of the Second World War Norwegian military resistance were to be used only as instructors, for the latter could most easily be identified and eliminated by an invading enemy and his local informers. A secret independent radio network, Hague wished, was to provide the communication channel for the stay-behind. Operation SATURN progressed well and FO4 preparedness was soon reached, whereupon the Norwegian stay-behind was given the new cover name Rocambole, or short, ROC. 'The "philosophy" behind ROC was clearly based on the lessons learnt during the German occupation a few years earlier', historian Olav Riste summarised the attitude of ROC operatives.[13]

In September 1952 the Norwegian Defence Ministry carried out an assessment of the secret army and in this context repeated both definition and tasks of the Norwegian stay-behind. 'ROCAMBOLE is a strictly top-secret military organisation under the direct command of the Defence Chief (Chief of Defence Staff), whose task will be to perform isolated missions of particular military importance on occupied Norwegian territory', the memorandum read. 'It is a condition that each single action will be on a direct order from the Defence Chief, and that the task can be performed by a few determined and hardy persons who have been organised, trained and equipped for such missions.' In times of war ROC, according to the document of the Defence Ministry, had three main tasks: '1. Destruction of material targets, by explosives or in other ways. 2. Protection of installations or communications on a temporary basis in connection with the liberation of a given area, or 3. Other missions like the organisation of larger secret groups, reception of airlifted personnel and supplies, reconnaissance, special intelligence tasks, guerrilla actions, coups, assassinations, etc.'[14] Domestic control operations 'in case of an internal coup d'état', as Evang had foreseen them, or missions 'to guard against fifth-column (Communist) subversive activities' were not listed by the document but presumably remained valid.

ROC headquarters were established in a house in Smestad in 1950 and arms caches were erected across the country while a government bunker in Cort Adeler Street in central Oslo was chosen as a central repository for ROC equipment. Jens Nordlie, a close wartime resistance collaborator of Defence Minister Hauge, was chosen to be the first chief of the Norwegian stay-behind ROC. Already in

February 1949 Nordlie had met with officers of the MI6 in London where an agreement had been reached to accelerate the build-up of the Norwegian secret army ROC and the intention was confirmed 'to establish 15 five-man groups before the end of the year'.[15] The British provided the necessary equipment including radio transmitters and explosives. In case of war and occupation of Norway, Britain was to function as the wartime stay-behind headquarters. Allegedly there were some doubts on the Norwegian side concerning the wisdom of letting the British have the names of all ROC personnel, for thus the secret army was not only under Norwegian, but also under foreign control. Collaboration of ROC with the CIA was equally close. With the approval of Defence Minister Hauge ROC leaders regularly met with the American official Harold Stuart, a representative of the US National Security Council. Information and money was exchanged and presumably also the CIA possessed lists with the names of ROC members.[16]

A survey from the end of 1949 showed that stay-behind training had been completed for nine group leaders and seven radio operators. Arms caches had been erected containing arms and equipment for the secret groups with sufficient supplies for a 12-month period without reprovisioning. By 1952, 32 ROC units counting five members each had been established, with plans to continue building up the secret army to at least 40 units or 200 core members. Hauge praised ROC chief Nordlie for the progress being made, but questioned whether not too many ROC units had been stationed in the very north of Norway, including the so-called Finnmark area, closest to the Soviet Union. 'It is probably mainly foreign interests, such as in connection with bombing raids across Finnmark against the Soviet Union etc., which are served by our being so strongly committed in Finnmark', Hauge in March 1952 wrote to Nordlie. 'Viewed in the light of a more general ROC concern, I am inclined to believe that we would achieve greater results in the south of Norway. In accordance with this line of argument, we should, therefore, be careful not to mismanage our resources by allocating too much of them to Finnmark.'[17]

Defence Minister Hauge was well aware of the fact that Washington and London had strategic interests in northern Norway. For during the entire Cold War, Norway guarded the 192-km long sparsely populated and icy most northern frontier of NATO with the Soviet Union. The strategic importance of Norway to NATO was, similar to that of Turkey in the south, that the country reached like a long arm over neutral Finland far into the east and was therefore closer to Moscow than any other northern NATO country. Hence the country could be used as a listening post and departure area for CIA spy planes and, at least potentially, NATO bombers, as Hague indicated in his letter. The resistance preparations against a foreign occupier, however, were according to Hague more useful in the more densely populated south of Norway.

Hague was not exactly satisfied how the secret army was being financed, insisting that Norway was covering too much of the bill. According to an agreement amongst the three parties involved in the Norwegian secret army ROC radio equipment was being provided free of charge by the United States and

Great Britain, whereas Norway paid 50 per cent of all other equipment and furthermore covered all training expenses. Hague reached the conclusion 'that the operations under the ROC arrangements ... were more in the interests of the Allies than in Norway's interest'.[18] Hague found that Norway was paying for two-thirds of the total costs of ROC, while the CIA and the MI6 covered the rest, and that above all the expenses for ROC were consuming over 50 per cent of the entire budget of the Norwegian secret service NIS. Therefore Hauge suggested in a memorandum in 1950 that in addition to providing ROC radio equipment free of charge the United States and Great Britain, who were so eager to erect a stay-behind in Norway, should also cover the costs of all other equipment. Norway in turn would pay for the ROC people and arrange for their training. It seems that the suggestions of Hauge were accepted in the White House and in London and Norway's bill was reduced. For 1952 the total ROC costs amounted to 1.5 million Norwegian Kroner that were split equally between the three secret services NIS, CIA and MI6. The yearly costs thereafter seem to have remained stable, for 13 years later, in the 1965 budget, the third that Norway had to cover amounted to 600,000 Kroner.[19]

As in all countries of Western Europe information on the secret anti-Communist army was limited according to strict 'need to know' principles. While ROC was being built up, there were staff meetings at least once every week with ROC chief Jens Nordlie and often in the presence of NIS chief Evang. From late autumn 1950 onwards the national representatives of the CIA and the MI6 also regularly took part in these Norwegian Gladio meetings. Contact with the Norwegian Minister of Defence was sporadic, and mostly in the form of informal conversations between Hague and Evang or Hauge and Nordlie. Not even the Norwegian Security Police, comparable to the American FBI, was informed of the top-secret stay-behind. And as in all other Gladio countries the Norwegian parliament, representing the Norwegian people, knew nothing of the secret army.[20]

During an ROC meeting in October 1951 the issue of reporting to Defence Minister Hauge as well as to London and Washington was specifically raised. Nordlie suggested that Hauge should receive but a short summary at regular intervals on the Norwegian stay-behind, 'since it must be assumed that he is so overburdened with work that he cannot be expected to have the time to read the relatively lengthy summary'.[21] It was agreed that CIA and MI6 should regularly receive the detailed reports on the secret army, allegedly also in order to give the two foreign secret services an idea concerning 'the seriousness and the hard work involved in the distribution of more than thirty tons of equipment', while Hauge was only provided with the lengthy summary upon request and otherwise was debriefed with the short summary. In January 1952 Hauge resigned. It is unclear how, and to what degree, subsequent Norwegian Defence Ministers were informed of the top-secret ROC.[22]

In April 1949 Norway together with 11 other nations founded NATO and signed the North Atlantic Treaty. Thereafter the secret army of Norway was more closely coordinated with the special warfare department of the military alliance. The written records of the Norwegian Defence Ministry concerning ROC confirm that in August 1951 NATO's Supreme Commander for Europe (SACEUR) established the so-called CPC to plan secret operations and direct the European stay-behind network.[23] In April 1952 NIS Director Evang was informed that SACEUR had given the order to CPC to summon representatives of the secret services of the NATO countries to CPC. Together with other European secret services chiefs Evang received an invitation to a CPC meeting in Paris on May 7, 1952 for a briefing on the stay-behind situation and a discussion of ROC's relationship to the CPC, presumably with the presence of SACEUR US General Matthew Ridgway of the US Army.

Prior to the meeting Evang contacted his Danish counterpart in order to establish a common approach to the expected NATO questions. Evang and the chief of the Danish secret service agreed to make it clear to the CPC that the Norwegian secret army ROC and the Danish secret army Absalon were only to be used 'in the event of a total occupation or a static partial occupation'. It was out of the question to make use of the organisation under what Evang called 'normal fighting', a vague term which maybe also included domestic unrest or a coup d'état.[24] Evang was particularly sensitive as to the potential subversion of Norwegian sovereignty by NATO's US-dominated CPC as his notes of the meeting indicate. 'Agreement was reached, moreover, that Stay Behind was first and foremost an instrument at the disposal of the national governments wherever they might happen to be, and that its primary task was to form the nucleus for the recapture of temporarily lost areas.' Evang in his notes stressed that 'it is our job to see that it is the respective governments which, in the last instance, exercise control over' the secret armies. 'It was clear that this could only be done if one controlled communications, and that the individual operator's identity was not known to anybody but a small minority of the person's own countrymen. This viewpoint must not, however, be revealed in international discussions.'[25]

In November 1952, NATO's secret warfare centre CPC presented a basic document that was circulated among the chiefs of the national secret services for comments. The CPC plan aimed at a whole range of 'unorthodox warfare' activities to be carried out by the national secret services and their stay-behind armies. The planning and preparation for such unorthodox warfare, as the CPC document insisted, had to be carried out by the national secret services and their stay-behind units. In peacetime the CPC in close collaboration with the SACEUR would have a coordinating responsibility. In the 'active phase', probably meaning several possible stages from domestic coup d'état to full Soviet invasion of the territory, the SACEUR would assume direct control of such sections of the national secret services including the stay-behind, as were placed at the disposal of NATO. The Norwegian representatives were worried that the secret army could become an instrument of Washington and London and the NIS insisted that there should be an agreement that the Norwegian Government retained 'the right to deal with the political situation in Norway whatever the circumstances', as well as the 'sovereign right to control and manage the clandestine effort which it deems necessary to exercise political control in Norway'.[26]

The idea of a CIA secret army in Norway under the control of a US SACEUR remained unacceptable to the majority of officers within the Norwegian secret service. 'During the last war, the Norwegian government was located outside the boundaries of the country, but its constitutional powers remained in legal order and it exercised its functions as government throughout the enemy's occupation of Norway', a NIS memorandum dating from January 1953 on the CPC summarised the wartime experience. 'Under the influence of these experiences the Norwegian government views it as self-evident that it should retain responsibility for the political leadership in the country – also in occupied parts of the country.' Hence the suggestion that in case of emergency NATO and its American SACEUR should take over control of the Norwegian secret army was a most sensitive issue. 'That the leadership of the resistance movement should be subordinated to an American general and his international staff would incite a political storm in the country if it became known before an occupation – and after an occupation it would provide an excellent basis for enemy propaganda', the NIS memorandum critically retained.[27]

Despite these Norwegian concerns, over the years the CIA and MI6 had gained a considerable amount of control over the Norwegian secret army. In 1955 Harbitz Rasmussen, a leading member of the ROC, informed NIS chief Evang in a memorandum that copies of the personal files of the secret ROC personnel had been deposited in Washington and in London. In addition, the CIA and MI6 had also been given information that was needed to establish and run the radio communications of the stay-behind networks. Rasmussen lamented the situation and stressed that the information was contained in sealed envelopes. He suggested that Evang should initiate action in order to get these sealed envelopes back and store them under 'exclusive Norwegian control' in London and Washington, meaning at the Norwegian embassies in the two capitals.[28]

Whether Evang was successful in his operation remains unclear due to the lack of documents. But it is clear that Evang's trust in the United States was severely shaken in 1957, leading to an acute crisis between the Norwegian NIS, the CIA and the US-dominated NATO. Evang had received information that an American member of NATO's Headquarters Allied Forces Northern Europe (HQ AFNORTH) at Kolsas in Norway 'was showing a distinct interest in general military intelligence material and had also had translated at AFNORTH data on Norwegian citizens, especially people who had strongly pacifist and negative attitudes to NATO'. The Norwegian authorities arrested the US-American and it was revealed that he had also spied upon high-ranking Norwegian officials and reported to a named officer at SHAPE. Evang was furious and demanded that this matter be the first item on the agenda at the next meeting of the stay-behind control centre CPC in Paris on November 19, 1957.

The atmosphere therefore was tense when the European Directors of the secret services met at Avenue Deloison, Neuilly, in Paris. Colonel Blaer, a British officer, chaired the CPC meeting and introduced the session by indicating that the NIS 'was extremely worried about activities carried out by officers at Kolsas.

This concerned SB [stay-behind], Psywar and Counter Intelligence.' Then Evang himself took the floor and delivered a stern warning to NATO to keep its hands off the Norwegian stay-behind: 'Things were quiet until the past year when we became aware that there were still officers at AFNORTH who worked on Psywar, E&E [Evasion and Escape] and, in this connection, also engaged in the blacklisting of people at high levels', Evang explained. 'When high ranking persons in Norway are being included on such a blacklist, then something must be wrong. My government also views this in a very serious light, and I have standing orders not to take part in international planning if such activities are going on.' NIS chief Evang was seriously concerned and threatened that Norway would leave the CPC if NATO secretly continued to violate the sovereignty of its members. 'As far as Norway is concerned, our interest in CPC planning as such has since 1954 declined steadily because there is no future in it for us. We are of the opinion that we are developing a stay-behind which is to be used at home for the purpose of liberation from an occupation.'[29]

Brigadier Simon, chief of NATO's Special Projects Branch at SHAPE with responsibilities also for CPC, tried to calm the Norwegian representatives. In a classical plausible denial Simon admitted that the questionable American had worked in a section of Special Projects, but denied that he had had instructions to act in the way Evang had recently uncovered. Evang insisted that he was not mistaken and threatened to withdraw Norway from the secret CPC until things had been put into order. NATO and the White House were surprised when Evang made his threat a reality and withdrew Norway from the secret CPC meetings. Several high-level NATO officials wrote to him trying to convince him to return his NIS back into the CPC. On October 14, 1958 Evang met with a US General who was able to convince the Norwegian Director to bring back his secret service and the clandestine army to the CPC. Before returning Evang wanted an official letter of excuse containing the following main points: 'a) The affair had been resolved, b) SHAPE would promise not to continue activity of the sort that has been criticised, c) An appeal to Norway to rejoin.'[30] As the letter was forthcoming, Norway with its ROC rejoined NATO's stay-behind command centre CPC and the row ended.

Does it amount to a serious security risk if a top-secret army exists within the state, run partly by the national military secret service and partly by foreign powers with specific interests within a Cold War framework? Or does, on the contrary, such a secret army protect the state from great risks to its security? Such questions troubled the Norwegian stay-behind commanders during the Cold War as well as observers across Europe after the exposure of the clandestine network in 1990. Obviously trust in the integrity and reliability of the stay-behind sponsors, United States and Great Britain, was crucial. 'We must trust our allies!', Norwegian stay-behind commander Sven Ollestad insisted even after the CPC scandal. Yet given the known covert action operations and manipulations of political systems by CIA and MI6 across the globe in the Cold War and beyond, trust was lacking among certain Norwegian officials. 'There was a tense atmosphere' at the headquarters of the

Norwegian stay-behind in Oslo on the corner of Gronlandsleiret and Platous Gate, Gladio researchers Bye and Sjue relate, when the question was discussed whether the allies should have an entire and independent control of the secret network. But 'the boss, lieutenant colonel Sven Ollestad had made up his mind on the issue and had given the order that the national security code which can release the whole stay-behind network was to be handed over to the MI6'. The Norwegian secret army had thus given away part of the sovereignty of Norway and 'active and intense protests from his closest co-workers' resulted. The protests were ignored.[31]

Norwegian journalists during the politically agitated period of the late 1960s – characterised by flower power, say-no-to-violence movements, student protests and anti-Vietnam demonstrations – decided that the United States should not be trusted and in December 1967 published a top-secret undated NATO document to support their claim. 'In the case of domestic unrest, that might seriously affect the US troops or their mission, such as a military uprising or a large domestic resistance against the government of the host country [the US army] has to do everything in its power to suppress such unrest, using its own resources.' The document made specific reference to Western Europe, in particular, Norway, Greece, Turkey, West Germany, France, Italy, Holland, Belgium, Luxemburg and Denmark. The United States feared, due to the massive anti-Vietnam demonstrations, that governments or populations in Western Europe including Norway might turn against them and threaten the operability of both US Forces and NATO. Signed by US General J. P. Mc. Connell, vice-commander of the US Forces in Europe, the document continued to explain most sensitively that under special circumstances the US shall intervene in a European NATO country even without the consent of the national government in order to suppress domestic unrest: 'If these initiatives do not suffice, or in case the government concerned asks for assistance, or if the Commander of the US forces comes himself to the conclusion that the government is not able to suppress such unrest, then the US troops can carry out those measures deemed necessary by the US Commander on their own initiative or in co-operation with the government concerned.'[32] Whether in the context of such operations secret stay-behind armies under NATO command would have become involved remains unclear.

The attitude of the White House and the Pentagon in Washington towards the sovereignty of other nations did not strengthen the confidence which certain members of the Norwegian stay-behind placed in NATO, CIA and MI6. And hence, similar to the situation within the CPC stay-behind command centre, concerns were raised on the international level also in the ACC stay-behind command centre. ROC together with the European secret armies took part in the meetings of the NATO stay-behind command ACC linked to SHAPE, to which Norwegian documents at times also refer to as the 'Allied Clandestine Co-operation Groups' (ACCG). Norwegian historian Riste relates that in ACC documents it was stated 'positively half a dozen times: "Command and control will at all times be retained by the respective National Clandestine Services"', while Norwegian documents critically noted that 'misgivings are expressed concerning the superior role assumed by ACCG SHAPE' over the sovereignty of Norway.[33]

The Norwegian secret army, as most other Gladio armies in Europe, cooperated closely with the British SAS and US Green Berets Special Forces as Norwegian Gladiators trained in the United States and England. Major Sven Blindheim, a prominent member of the Norwegian secret army, had himself been for many years an instructor at 'the Nursery', the special operations training centre of the British at Fort Monckton in Great Britain where the Italian Gladiators were also trained. And Colonel Sven Ollestad together with instructor Sven Blindheim in 1952 had absolved CIA Gladio training courses in the United States, presumably together with the Green Berets Special Forces at the US headquarters for unorthodox warfare in Fort Bragg.[34]

Judged from Blindheim's minutes, Bye and Sjue relate that 'the essence of the CIA teaching can be summed up in the "10 clandestine commandments"' which explicitly stressed that the secret armies could engage in both military and political warfare. After emphasising the clandestine nature of the operation the CIA stay-behind doctrine highlighted that '1. Clandestine operations are a way to lead political and military warfare. 2. The goal of stay-behind is to secure a continuous and permanent operational ability to conduct sabotage, espionage, guerrilla, evacuation and escape in areas and countries which can come under Soviet and Communist control.' In order to be able to carry out these missions the network had to be watertight: '3. The principle of "need to know" is holy. Every link/person must know absolutely the least possible about the whole, and every link/person must be cut off from the possibility to find out anything about the other part of the organisation and people involved. 4. Parallel units in a stay-behind organisation must be kept apart and only "meet" at the top headquarters', including the ACC and CPC linked to NATO's SHAPE. '5. When the agent candidate is to be considered and analysed with regards to recruiting – use all possible and impossible sources and means of control and check: police, schools, societies, work places, friends, relatives, neighbours, eaves dropping, house searches. There must be a continuous and long lasting surveillance of the candidate before recruitment.'[35]

Whether American and British instructors and Special Forces members also came to Norway to train the secret ROC army as they had done, for instance, in Belgium and neutral Switzerland, remains unclear. According to historian Riste, the Norwegian secret service was 'wary of any suggestion which could lead to British or American interference in the work on Norwegian soil. This concerned, among other things, a proposal of support from the American Special Forces which were stationed in Germany, or the British Special Air Service units, whose tasks included the support of resistance groups in the NATO countries.'[36] It remains equally unclear to what degree Norway's cooperation with CIA, MI6, NATO's CPC and ACC changed after NIS chief Evang, never much liked by Washington for his left-wing past and critical statements in the CPC, was replaced by Colonel Johan Berg in 1966. Allegedly the bonds strengthened.

The most serious threat to total exposure of the Norwegian Gladio came in 1978 when a Norwegian policeman tracking illegally produced alcohol stumbled across a large ROC underground arms cache containing at least 60 weapons including many machine guns, 12,000 rounds of ammunitions, explosives and sophisticated communications equipment. Unaware of the existence of the stay-behind network the policeman reported his finding and the news were leaked to the press. 'If the policeman had been cleared with intelligence, it probably would have been covered up', academic Nil Gleditzch at the International Peace Research Institute in Oslo reasoned in 1990.[37] The owner of the property on which both the illegal alcohol distillery and the stay-behind arms cache was found was identified to be Hans Otto Meyer, a member of the Norwegian secret service. Meyer was arrested but to the surprise of the investigators his claim that the arsenal had been put up by the secret service for use by a resistance cell was eventually confirmed.

As the scandal unfolded, the Norwegian parliament became involved and was stunned to learn from Defence Minister Rolf Hansen that a secret resistance network had been formed after the war. According to his explanations, the network had originated from private groups that however had been placed under the supervision of the Norwegian secret service. Aware of the sensitive situation Hansen claimed that the 'Norwegian network was not answerable to NATO or other countries, dismissing any connections to the CIA. But he would not discuss details, saying the organisation's activities had to be kept secret.'[38] These claims of Hansen in 1978 were at best misleading, at worst they were simply untrue. But within a Cold War context the majority of the Norwegian parliament trusted Hansen and saw no reason to investigate or close down the secret network and the story was quickly buried.

By coincidence the strongest evidence contradicting Hansen's claim that the CIA was not involved in the secret operation surfaced exactly in the same year as Hansen testified in front of parliament when former CIA Director William Colby published his memoirs. In his book, written to enhance the public image of the discredited CIA, Colby proudly related how he had been involved in setting up a secret army in the north of Europe, including in Norway, from 1951 to 1953, when he was a young CIA agent at the US Embassy in Stockholm. 'The situation in each Scandinavian country was different', Colby explained. 'Norway and Denmark were NATO allies, Sweden held to the neutrality that had taken her through two world wars, and Finland was required to defer in its foreign policy to the Soviet power directly on its borders. Thus, in one set of these countries the governments themselves would build their own stay-behind nets, counting on activating them from exile to carry on the struggle', Colby revealed with implicit reference to Norway and Denmark.[39]

'These nets had to be co-ordinated with NATO's plans, their radios had to be hooked to a future exile location, and the specialised equipment had to be secured from CIA and secretly cached in snowy hideouts for later use', Colby continued, and with respect to neutral Sweden and Finland explained: 'In the other set of countries, CIA would have to do the job alone or with, at best, "unofficial" local help, since the politics of those governments barred them from collaborating with NATO, and any exposure would arouse immediate protest from the local Communist press, Soviet diplomats and loyal Scandinavians who hoped that neutrality or nonalignment would allow them to slip through a World War III unharmed.'[40] Given the discovery of the arms cache and the confessions of Colby, the cover of the Norwegian secret army had thus been blown in 1978 and the entire European network was threatened with exposure. 'It was a little surprising that no one in the other NATO countries picked up on it, and raised questions about their own countries', researcher Nil Gleditzch therefore in 1990 commented on the Norwegian 1978 discoveries.[41]

When in November 1990, in the wake of the Italian revelations, the Norwegian ROC secret army was rediscovered Defence Ministry spokesman Erik Senstad answered the Gladio questions of the press with one short sentence: 'What Hansen said then still applies.'[42] While the Norwegian population reacted with surprise and criticism, members of the Norwegian military stressed that also from a democratic point of view it had been correct to keep the army within the state secret. Rear Admiral Jan Ingebristen confirmed to the press in 1990 that the stay-behind army still existed in 1985 when he stepped down as head of the Norwegian Supreme Defence Command intelligence service. Amidst public criticism Ingebristen insisted that it was logical and sensible that stay-behind units are kept top-secret and that the public, media and parliament only learn about them by accident: 'There is nothing suspicious about it. But these are units that would stay-behind in occupied territory and it is therefore necessary that they be kept top-secret.'[43]

Norwegian journalists Ronald Bye and Finn Sjue wanted to know more details about the Norwegian Gladio and in the absence of a parliamentary investigation interviewed numerous former participants and members of the secret services and in 1995 published their account of the Norwegian secret army under the title 'The Secret Army of Norway. History of the Stay-Behind'.[44] The well-informed and critical Norwegian population resented the idea of a secret CIA-linked army within their state uncontrolled by parliament and serious criticisms were raised. In order to prevent a loss of trust the Norwegian Defence Department thereafter took the unprecedented but wise step to commission a research project. Historians Olav Riste and Arnfinn Moland of the respected Oslo Institute for Defence Studies were trusted with the delicate investigation of the history of the Norwegian secret army up to 1970 and were given access to all 'archival material and all oral sources which may be of importance to their work', as the terms of the project stated. Before publication the manuscript was submitted to the Ministry of Defence for declassification and release and minor deletions were made.[45]

15

THE SECRET WAR IN GERMANY

The German parliament (Reichstag) in the capital Berlin started to burn heavily towards nine o'clock in the evening of February 27, 1933. Although firemen succeeded to save large parts of the building, the German parliament as such as well as the German democracy died from the vicious attack. Adolf Hitler from the National Socialist German Workers Party (Nationalsozialistische Deutsche Arbeiterpartei, NSDAP, later referred to as 'Nazi'), who had become German Prime Minister (Reichskanzler) but one month before the mysterious fire, immediately publicly blamed the crime on the German Communist Party (Kommunistische Partei Deutschlands, KPD). Together with NSDAP Interior Minister Wilhelm Frick and NSDAP Minister Hermann Göring, responsible for the police forces, Prime Minister Hitler lost no time and in the early morning hours of the next day arrested 4,000 political opponents and critical journalists, among which many members of the KPD and the German Socialist Party SPD (Sozialdemokratische Partei Deutschland).

After the Communists had been removed and many Socialists had been arrested, the German parliament one month after the mysterious fire with a majority decision against the protests of the remaining Socialists passed a far-reaching new law (Gesetz zur Behebung der Not von Volk und Reich) which effectively abolished parliament and transferred all powers to the executive headed by Hitler. During the same month the first concentration camps were set up in Germany and already in April 1933 they were filled with more than 25,000 political opponents seized by Hitler's Special Forces, the Schutzstaffel (SS), and the German secret service Gestapo. The fire in the Reichstag was blamed on the Dutch Communist Marinus van der Lubbe who had been arrested in the building on the night of the fire, was put on trial, sentenced and killed. Even before the trial against van der Lubbe had started, a British investigation had concluded that the NSDAP itself had orchestrated the mysterious fire-terror in order to gain total control of the state apparatus. Hitler in early 1933 together with his numerous supporters had effectively transformed Germany into a dictatorship run by himself and the Nazi party. Six years later he started the Second World War which lead to hitherto unfold suffering and the death of 60 million people, marking the darkest however in mankind's history. When the Red Army captured the German capital and hissed the flag of the Soviet Union on the Reichstag Hitler gave up and killed himself in Berlin on April 30, 1945.[1]

'The setting up of Stay-Behind organisations of the NATO countries started already shortly after the end of the Second World War', the official German governmental report on the stay-behind confirmed in 1990.[2] After the defeat of Germany in 1945 the chaotic post-war conditions were ideal for the United States to set up a stay-behind. As occupying power the US armies controlled the territory together with the French, British and the Soviet forces in their respective zones. Above all the supply of thoroughly anti-Communist men trained in guerrilla warfare and experienced with arms and explosives was abundant. And thus the United States secretly recruited former Nazis for the German stay-behind network. In the midst of the Gladio revelations in 1990 the private TV channel RTL shocked the German public by revealing in a special Gladio report that former members of Hitler's dreaded SS, who under Hitler had hunted the Communists, had been part of Germany's Gladio network.

The US Army General's Staff Top Secret March 28, 1949 Overall Strategic Concepts highlighted that Germany 'has an excellent potential of trained men for both underground and Secret Army Reserves [stay-behind units]. Effective resistance can and should be organized.'[3] On the orders of the Pentagon in Washington the newly created US Counter Intelligence Corps (CIC) tracked down German Nazis and brought them to the Nurnberg trials, while the CIC also secretly recruited selected right-wing extremists for the anti-Communist army. This practice of the Pentagon was revealed only in 1986 when the US Department of Justice in a large press conference – which had maybe drawn the biggest crowd of journalists in Washington since the Watergate days – admitted that the CIC had recruited a high-ranking Nazi in the post-war years. Specifically a 600-page long study, compiled by Allan Ryan for the US Justice Department, confirmed that SS and Gestapo officer Klaus Barbie had been recruited by the CIC in 1947, had thereafter been hidden from the war crimes investigators and had then been spirited out of Europe to Argentina through a clandestine 'ratline' in 1951.

Barbie was saved not because the United States secret service officers were impressed with his moral record, but because he was most useful in the setting up of the German stay-behind network. 'Among those who were recruited and did some recruiting for the scheme in the first years', the British press reported during the Gladio revelations, 'were an ex-SS Obersturmführer, Hans Otto, and other smaller fish. But the prize catch was Klaus Barbie who functioned as a recruiter for ex-Nazis and members of the fascist Bund Deutscher Jugend (BDJ).'[4] Barbie, during the war known as the 'Butcher of Lyon', had during his stay in the French town from 1943 to 1944 been responsible for the murder of at least 4,000 resistance workers and Jews, as well as the deportation of another 15,000 to concentration death camps. Barbie was condemned to death in absentia by a French court soon after the war for crimes against humanity as witnesses described him as a sadistic torturer, who terrified men, women and children with his whip and Alsatian dog.

The US Justice Department during its 1986 press conference did not reveal the use of Barbie for the stay-behind and wrongly stressed that next to Barbie 'no other case was found where a suspected Nazi war criminal was placed in the ratline, or where the ratline was used to evacuate a person wanted by either the United States government or any of its post-war allies'.[5] This claim was false as the most prominent Nazi recruited by the CIC was not the Butcher of Lyon Klaus Barbie but Hitler's General Reinhard Gehlen. General Gehlen had started his secret service career under Hitler when in April 1942 he became chief of Fremde Heere Ost (FHO, Foreign Armies East) with the task to combat the Soviet Union. 'Gehlen derived much of his information from his role in one of the most terrible atrocities of the war: the torture, interrogation, and murder by starvation of some 4 million Soviet prisoners of war', US historian Christopher Simpson found in his detailed account of the US recruitment of Nazis.[6] Gehlen was well aware of the fact that his war crimes had earned him the merit to appear on the blacklist of the Soviet secret service NKVD. When he realised that Germany was losing the war he therefore made sure that the Russians would not get him by delivering himself to the US CIC on May 20, 1945.

General Gehlen was right in assuming that the data which he had collected during his torture operations on the Soviet Union and its Communists was of great interest to the United States. Together with a small group of senior Nazi officers he had therefore at the end of the war carefully microfilmed the extensive FHO data on the USSR, had packed the films in watertight steel drums and had secretly buried these in meadows in the Austrian Alps. After several weeks of CIC internment Gehlen got into contact with US General Edwin Luther Siber to whom he revealed his secret. The US General was so impressed that he promoted Gehlen's career in the years to come. He introduced Gehlen to senior US intelligence officials, including General Walter Bedell Smith, then the highest US Army intelligence officer in Europe, and later Director of the CIA from 1950 to 1953. Siber also introduced Gehlen to General William Donovan, chief of the US wartime secret service Office of Strategic Services (OSS), and Allen Dulles of the OSS, later chief of the CIA, as well as Frank Wisner of the OSS, later chief of CIA's OPC which set up the European stay-behind network.[7]

With Gehlen's help the US dug up the FHO microfilms in Austria and in August 1945 Siber shipped Gehlen with his data to Washington for debriefing. President Truman was impressed and named Gehlen, together with a large number of Gehlen's Nazi network, chief of the first post-war German secret service, tellingly named Organisation Gehlen (ORG). 'In the end Gehlen', historian Simpson concludes, 'and several hundred other senior German officers succeeded in making deals with Britain or the United States...General Gehlen, however, proved to be the most important of them all.'[8] With US financial and material help ORG headquarters were first erected in Oberursel near Frankfurt, and then moved to the former Waffen SS training facility Pullach near Munich, still today site of the headquarters of the German secret service Bundesnachrichtendienst (BND). Clandestinely CIA and ORG signed cooperation contacts and CIA senior officer

James Critchfield was deployed to Germany. Called 'Herr Marshall' by the Germans, Critchfield monitored Gehlen's service and made sure that at all times the names of Gehlen's top 150 officers were given to him. For each of them the CIA created a file. So that the German secret service was firmly in US hands.

Erhard Dabringhaus who had worked with the US CIC in Germany from 1948 to 1949 recalled in a documentary on Gladio that he himself had taken part in the recruitment of Nazis, an activity which he strongly resented. 'In 1948 I was a special agent with CIC, that's our counterintelligence corps in occupied Germany', retired Dabringhaus explained. 'I was stationed in Augsberg, and since I spoke fluent German I was assigned to handle a network of German informants, among them was Klaus Barbie, and Klaus Barbie was, ehm...later on I discovered that he was wanted for murder by the French', Dabringhaus explained in front of the camera, 'and that I reported to my superiors, and they told me to keep nice and quiet, "He's still valuable, when he's no longer valuable we will turn him over to the French." I thought that I was gonna get a promotion when I told 'em about Barbie, and they told me to keep quiet!'[9]

Former US CIC officer Dabringhaus, who now lives in Florida in the United States, explained how several German Nazis on US orders had set up the stay-behind arms caches in Germany. 'Colonel Gunther Bernau was an agent, an informant working for the military intelligence in Stuttgart. We [of the US CIC] had provided him a home, a safe-house in Ludwisburg, and there I met him three times a week and he brought us information about Communists and whatever we wanted to hear he told us.' The aim of the United States was to fight Communism, no matter the means, Dabringhaus related, although he himself was little impressed with Bernau: 'He was certainly a very strong Nazi. I sat in his office one day and opened his album of pictures from the war, and in the middle of the album it showed a nice picture of Adolf Hitler. Several other high-ranking SS officers came to visit him in his safe house that we provided, and he told me that if for any reason he needs help by one telephone call he could contact 200 former SS leaders from Hamburg to Munich.'

Bernau, according to Dabringhaus, was centrally involved in setting up the German stay-behind army: 'I remember him taking me to one particular spot which we uncovered and dug it out and there were rifles, small arms, grenades, all nicely wrapped in cosmolene and he said "We have thousands of these all over the country." And that sort of made me a little suspicious and I reported this and they said, "Well, we know this. They are all working for us in case the Communists come across the Iron Curtain."' Senior US officials, according to the need-to-know principle, did not explain the details of the secret stay-behind army to CIC officer Dabringhaus, but the latter had learned enough to understand that it was a top-secret project involving a large number of Nazis: 'A former General, SS General, Paul Hauser, was a frequent visitor at Bernau's house, and they worked together hand in gloves about certain programmes which we didn't know anything about, and I wasn't even asked to find out more about it. Somebody above me must have been running this network already at that time.'[10]

When the Gladio scandal erupted in 1990 an unnamed former NATO intelligence official explained that the covert action branch of the CIA under Frank Wisner in order to set up the German secret army had 'incorporated lock, stock and barrel the espionage outfit run by Hitler's spy chief Reinhard Gehlen. This is well known, because Gehlen was the spiritual father of Stay Behind in Germany and his role was known to the West German leader, Konrad Adenauer, from the outset.' According to the unnamed NATO officer, US President Truman and German Chancellor Adenauer had 'signed a secret protocol with the US on West Germany's entry into NATO in May 1955 in which it was agreed that the West German authorities would refrain from active legal pursuit of known right-wing extremists. What is not so well known is that other top German politicians were privy to the existence of secret resistance plans. One of these was the then German State Secretary and former high-ranking Nazi, Hans Globke.'[11]

In Germany one of the Nazi-dominated US networks named 'Bund Deutscher Jugend' (BDJ) and its stay-behind 'Technischer Dienst' (TD) were discovered in 1952. Klaus Barbie had played a leading role in setting up the German stay-behind BDJ-TD.[12] But the secret was not kept for long. The *New York Times* reported on October 10, 1952 under the somewhat misleading headline 'German Saboteurs betray US Trust. Wide Investigation Follows Confirmation of Financing Guerrillas' War Training', that 'Authoritative officials here privately confirmed today that the United States had sponsored and helped finance the secret training of young Germans, including many former soldiers, to become guerrilla fighters in the event of a war with the Soviet Union.' The US newspaper reported that the 'disclosure yesterday in the State Parliament of Hesse and the banner headline publicity today in the German press have caused the United States Department and the Army considerable embarrassment', above all because 'it was discovered that the projected guerrilla group had engaged in political activities. Their leaders...drew up blacklists of persons who were to be "liquidized", if they were deemed unreliable in a war against the Russians.' Therefore 'Several joint German–United States meetings were held' because many acting 'Socialists, including government officials, were on the list, as well as Communists'.

This early discovery of a part of the German stay-behind caused a major scandal on both sides of the Atlantic and *Newsweek* in the United States reported on October 20, 1952 that the CIA had organised a group of 'stay-behinds' in Germany. Interestingly enough the German news magazine *Der Spiegel* on October 29, 1952 correctly reported that stay-behind networks existed next to Germany also in numerous countries of Western Europe: 'The BDJ affair has caused considerable worries in the different headquarters of the American secret service in Europe. Because the "Technischer Dienst" in Germany is but one branch of a partisan network supported by the United States and spreading over the whole of Europe.' Specifically, as the *Spiegel* reported, 'This network is most strongly developed in France, Belgium, the Netherlands, Luxemburg, Italy and the Iberian peninsula. In France this organisation was created already in 1948, with the support of the leader of the Socialists, [Minister of the Interior] Jules Moch.'

What had happened and who had blown the cover? On September 9, 1952 former SS officer Hans Otto had walked after his own personal decision into the headquarters of the criminal police in the city of Frankfurt in the German state of Hesse and according to the German governmental records 'declared to belong to a political resistance group, the task of which was to carry out sabotage activities and blow up bridges in case of a Soviet invasion'. According to Otto, who felt alienated with the terrorist preparations, 'about 100 members of the organisation had been instructed at a specific school in politics, trained to use American, Russian and German arms, and drilled in military tactics. Members of the organisation were mostly former officers of the Air Force, the Army or the Waffen-SS.' The official German transcripts record that 'Although officially neo-fascist tendencies were not required, most members of the organisation featured them. The financial means to run the organisation had been provided by an American citizen with the name of Sterling Garwood.' Next to waiting for the Soviet invasion the German secret army also had domestic subversion tasks: 'As for domestic politics the tactics of the organisation were aimed at the KPD [Communist Party of Germany] and SPD [Socialist Party of Germany].'[13]

The 'organisation' that Otto was talking about was part of the German stay-behind network, but with all probability did not represent the entire German network even at the time. The branch was misleadingly labelled BDJ, short for 'German Youth Federation', although the average age of its members was around 42. Already before Otto's testimony the BDJ had been well known for its extreme anti-Communism. But what remained unknown was that the BDJ had fronted for the so-called Technischer Dienst (TD, Technical Service), which was in the top-secret paramilitary German stay-behind, staffed with former Nazis, paid by the US, and equipped with weapons and explosives. According to the German statistics BDJ membership, which spread across the whole of Western Germany, officially amounted to 17,000 people, whereas according to the German governmental investigation TD membership counted only around 2,000 people.[14]

Otto's testimony in 1952 lead to a large-scale police investigation. Near Waldmichelbach, a small romantic village in the Odenwald forest district of Hesse, the stay-behind training centre was discovered. The Waldmichelbach centre had only become operational in June 1951, and before that date, members of the German stay-behind had been directly trained on the US Army base Grafenwöhr in Germany.[15] Called 'Wamiba' by insiders after its location, the training centre consisted in essence of a house with an underground shooting area and a bunker close by, all located inconspicuously in a side valley, half a kilometre away from the country road. Villagers remembered, 'that the Americans used to carry out shooting exercises or something like that over there'.[16]

Otto testified to the German authorities that the contact of the BDJ-TD with the CIA was to a large degree handled by the mysterious American whom he called Mr Garwood. Garwood, probably of the CIA, regularly instructed the TD members in the Odenwald and repeatedly insisted that the whole stay-behind was a top-secret organisation, and that nobody may say anything to anybody at any time.

This, it seems, was taken very seriously. For when at one time it was suspected that a TD member of another German state, Bavaria, 'had filled out a questionnaire with another resistance organisation', the assassination of that member was seriously contemplated within the TD, as Otto highlighted with a certain disgust.[17] 'I do not have the impression that Mr. Garwood had any objections to such methods', Otto testified to the German authorities. 'He taught us for instance, how to kill a person without leaving a trace, by simply making him unconscious with chloroform, put him in his car, and use a pipe to guide the exhausts of the car into the cabin. He taught us how with certain interrogation techniques, violence could be used without leaving a trace.' Otto was also instructed in torture techniques: 'One has for instance to blindfold the eyes of the person to be interrogated. Then a piece of meat must be grilled close to the scene while a piece of ice is being pressed on selected body parts of the person to be interrogated. The coldness of the ice, combined with the smell of burnt meat, leaves the interrogated in the belief, that he is being treated with burning metal.'[18]

Otto explained that Garwood provided the money and most of the equipment. Some 130 men were trained in the Wamiba centre, almost all former German Nazis, in interrogation techniques, shooting, use of explosives, setting up of traps, wireless communication and assassination methods. Most interestingly TD member Otto also elaborated on that rarely discussed, but very existential and central, stay-behind question concerning the willingness of secret soldiers to indeed stay-behind in case of a Soviet invasion. From a militarily strategic perspective it is clear that the chances of long-term survival of a stay-behind in an occupation context, and especially in a Soviet occupation context, are very slim. The war-experienced Nazi officers of the TD were fully aware of this and Otto made it a point in his testimony that most TD members were not eager to stay-behind and try to survive under Soviet occupation: 'The ideas of the Americans was to have all members overrun by the Soviets, and to use them after that as partisans. This plan of the Americans could however not be realised by [TD chief] Peters, because all men interested in the organisation wanted to escape to the West under all circumstances in case of a Soviet invasion.'[19]

Two days after Otto's testimony the Wamiba stay-behind base was stormed by the German police on September 13, 1952 and closed down. Offices and private apartments of TD members were also stormed and closed for further investigations. The stay-behind members were arrested. Arms, explosives and munitions were confiscated, together with a lot of paperwork. One of the confiscated files was of particular interest. To the surprise of the investigators it contained the names of persons to be eliminated on day X: 'The proscription list contains names of persons, which were to be eliminated. The list was not complete, for it was still being worked on' the German police found, indicating that TD member Hans Breitkopf had compiled the list for the Hesse area.[20] TD member Otto Rietdorf, who had suggested the name 'proscription list' explained: 'I have taken the term "proscription" from my reading of Russian literature, which uses the term to describe certain preparations against the West. According to the Russian use, people on the list are to be secured. And what that means in Russia seems to be clear.' Rietdorf added that the CIA was informed of the procedure: 'Mr. Garwood was fully aware of these things.' Also TD member Hans Otto confirmed that this 'information and personal reports had been handed on to the Americans from the BDJ and the TD'. The Americans who collected the data were allegedly 'Dr. Walter' and again Garwood. The German investigation into this early secret army concluded solemnly and precisely: 'According to this testimony, the use of violence against domestic targets was planned in case of X.'[21] Whether the variable 'X' only referred to invasion day or also to some other specific occasion such as mass protests or a landslide left-wing election victories could not be established.

The Gladio proscription lists contained many known German Communists and also moderate Socialists, of which many were prominent acting politicians and journalists at the time, such as Heinrich Zinnkann, Socialist Interior Minister of Hesse, Socialist Hans Jahn, chairman of the German Railway Union, Emil Carlebach, journalist with the *Frankfurter Rundschau*, and many others. German journalist and Gladio author Leo Müller relates that after the proscription lists were found 'the surprise was so massive, that the first reactions were often characterised by a feeling of disbelief'.[22] 'The leaders of the TD of the BDJ understood it to be one of their primary tasks to liquidate what they considered "leftist" German politicians in case of a Soviet attack', US historian Christopher Simpson found. 'The German Communists ranked of course top on the killer list of the TD. They were followed by the leading exponents of the West German SPD. The TD had planned to assassinate more than 40 top functionaries of the Social Democrats, among them also Erich Ollenhauer, President of the SPD since 1952.' Simpson found that the United States did not trust the German left during the Cold War and therefore trained secret agents of the BDJ who 'infiltrated the SPD and spied upon the leaders of the party, so that they could kill more quickly, once the moment had come'.[23]

Not too surprisingly the state of Hesse found it unbelievable and completely unacceptable that the White House in Washington had secretly trained and equipped neo-Nazis in Germany who possessed killer lists targeting some of the most respected citizens of the country and heated debates ensued in Hesse's capital Frankfurt. The delicate post-war political relationship between Germany and the United States was seriously damaged and nervous high-level meetings between US and German officials followed. German chancellor Konrad Adenauer claimed to have been ignorant about the whole affair while the Americans tried to cover up as much as possible. US ambassador to Germany Donelly explained that the organisation had been created in the context of the Korean War, adding that the network would have been dissolved precisely in these months anyway, regardless of the testimony of Otto, and that indeed payments had been halted already in August 1952. This of course was utter nonsense and TD members testified that they had received their money also in September.

Paul Lüth, senior member of the BDJ-TD and CIA contact man, controlled the money flow which came from the United States, as the subsequent investigation revealed.[24] Lüth regularly met with Americans for reporting, and he always composed four duplicates of all written reports on important issues, which he handed on to the CIA.[25] When the German stay-behind was discovered, Lüth was hidden by the Americans, could not be arrested, and disappeared without a trace. Next to Lüth Erhard Peters too held a senior function in the German secret army. A close school friend of Lüth, Peters became the leader of the TD due to his expert knowledge in radio communications and guerrilla warfare. He was flattered when the network was referred to as 'Organisation Peters' and to underline his status bought a dashing Mercedes 170 V and a BMW Cabriolet. When the cover of his secret army was blown Peters also could not be arrested for 'he had given himself under American protection' as the investigative report recorded. Later Lüth reappeared in front of the German police, after having 'given the Americans his word of honour, not to reveal anything'. According to his own testimony, the White House in Washington had offered him and other compromised TD Nazis the possibility to emigrate to the States, which he had declined.[26] In front of the police Peters admitted to have burned many files containing reports on the TD for the Americans.

For Germany the BDJ-TD scandal was not a federal, but a national affair. Yet if Frankfurt had expected help from the capital Bonn they soon learned otherwise. After lengthy conversations with the United States, senior officials of the CDU party and the Adenauer conservative government covered up and hindered the investigations and on September 30, 1952, causing a juridical outcry in Germany, the Supreme Court in Karlsruhe ordered all arrested Gladio TD members to be released. The police in Frankfurt had neither been informed nor consulted beforehand. And while the two attorneys Schrübbers and Wagner who had issued the critical declaration made a considerable career jump, the Gladiators walked free. Hesse's Prime Minister August Zinn commented angrily: 'The only legal explanation for these releases can be that the people in Karlsruhe [Supreme Court] declared that they acted upon American direction.'[27]

Zinn was so furious that he decided to raise the scandal in front of his federal parliament, regardless of very heavy US pressure to prevent him from doing so. And thus on October 8, 1952 the public at large and the press in Germany and abroad were informed for the first time about the existence of secret US-paid German Nazi stay-behind armies. 'Mr. President, honourable ladies and Gentleman', Zinn addressed his parliament on that day, 'after a meeting which I had with Chancellor Dr. Adenauer on October 3 in Frankfurt, and a discussion which I had this morning in my office with Mr. Reeber of the United States, the representative of the US High Commissioner, I must inform the house of the following: On September 9, 1952', Zinn explained with a serious expression on his face, 'the German criminal police learned of a secret organisation which had been created in 1950/1951 by leaders of the BDJ under the designation TD, "Technischer Dienst"'. Zinn informed his baffled audience that 'the organisation was designed as a political, armed resistance movement, erected with the knowledge and cooperation of BDJ President Paul Lüth. Gerhard Peters was the leader of the organisation.'

It was the first time the politicians learned of a secret stay-behind army and Zinn explained that 'This TD of the BDJ had the task, to create a partisan army, which according to the original plan, would have stayed behind enemy lines in case of a Soviet invasion, to carry out sabotage activities in occupied territory such as the blowing up of bridges and the attacking of camps.'

After these broad outlines of the classical stay-behind pattern Zinn, reported on the US backing and the domestic dimension of the secret army when he declared that 'Domestically the organisation was, according to the testimony of a prime witness and the confiscated material, aimed at the KPD, and above all against the SPD. After the organisation was discovered, immediate arrests and confiscations followed on September 18, 1952', Prime Minister Zinn told his parliament. 'But on October 1, the High National Prosecutor [Oberbundesanwalt] ordered that the suspects be released, as the organisation had been created on the orders of United States agencies', whereupon a roar went through the parliament with many parliamentarians, according to the original transcripts, shouting 'Hear! Hear!', or 'Incredible!' As the parliamentarians calmed down Zinn continued: 'According to the testimony of a senior member of the TD, liquidations were also planned', whereupon an even greater roar went through parliament, with members shouting 'Hear! Hear! That's how far we have come already again!' Zinn continued: 'A training centre was set up in Waldmichelbach in Odenwald' and 'The members of the organisation were mostly former officers of the Air Force, the Army and the SS.' Again the parliament was in agitation, for all present had lived through the Second World War and now shouted: 'Listen to this! Incredible!'

Zinn explained that the agents were between 35 and 50 and 'The organisation received very generous funding, confiscated documents suggest that it received about 50,000 DM a month'. Whereupon a parliamentarian shouted: 'Where did the money come from!?' Zinn related that 'The money came from faked orders of an allegedly US agency to the TD' and went on to explain that 'The same organisation had a domestic task... According to the testimony of a leading member selected "unreliable" people should be eliminated in case X', which sent a new storm of criticism through the parliament with voices shouting 'Killed, that means! Incredible!' Zinn was well aware of the storm he caused and solemnly continued that 'interestingly there were 15 sheets of paper on Communists, but 80 pages on leading Social Democrats... SPD Interior Minister Heinrich Zinnkann of Hesse was suspected of Communist connections', which next to criticism was commented with laughter in parliament. 'According to testimonies, much secret material had been destroyed, some material has been collected by a US official, now therefore also inaccessible. The money and the weapons were provided by an American, who supervised the training' leaving parliamentarians once again shouting 'Hear! Hear!'

Zinn had not yet finished: 'What is very important, is to realise, that such secret organisations outside all German control are the starting base for illegal domestic activities, this is sad experience our people has had to make already three decades ago, and these features were manifest also with this organisation', a fierce criticism which was applauded by parliament with voices shouting 'Correct! That's right!'

'Mr. Reeber of the United States this morning', Zinn continued, 'agreed with me, that such organisations are the starting point for domestic terror... expressed his most sincere regret and condemned the organisation sharply... He promised not only his full support to clarify the entire affair completely and uproot all rests of the organisation, but also to prevent the phenomena from reoccurring.'[28]

Of course the German Gladio was not dissolved, as the discoveries in 1990 showed. Traces were destroyed whenever possible. Former US High Commissioner McCloy in October 1952 insisted that the United States were not rearming the Nazis and that 'during all those years, that I have spent in Germany, our aims and efforts have been directed towards the aim of strengthening all democratic forces in Germany, and to fight both the Communists, as well as Neo- and Pro Nazis'. McCloy emphasised that 'It is therefore unthinkable, that a responsible American would have supported such activities, as they have been reported by Prime Minister Zinn. This fact must be expressed clearly, for the sake of truth and friendship.'[29] Despite these assurances the parliament of Hesse decided to have the phenomena fully investigated by the Interior Minister of Hesse who in a solid democratic performance in 1953 presented an impressive three-volume long report.[30]

Four decades later former CIA officer Thomas Polgar, who retired in 1981 after a 30-year long CIA career, well remembered the German Gladio scandal for he had been stationed in Germany in the early 1950s and in the early 1970s had come back to the country to replace Ray Cline as the Chief of the German CIA station. 'The "Bund Deutscher Jugend" was a right-wing political organisation loosely affiliated with one of the political parties in the state of Hesse in Germany and it was deemed that these people have the motivation and the willingness to service part of the underground should the Soviet army indeed overrun all or part of West Germany', Polgar related in the 1990s. 'When the story broke there was a considerable flap, and it was deemed desirable that [US] General Truscott should personally explain to the people involved what had happened and we explained the situation first to Konrad Adenauer of Germany.' This, as seen above did not solve the problem and Polgar remembers that 'then we explained it to General Matthew Ridgeway, who was then the commander-in-chief of NATO, and finally, and most importantly, we explained it to Prime Minister Georg Zinn of Hesse, who himself was on that list, and Truscott explained to the Hessian Prime Minister that this was an unauthorised activity, to be sure only a paper exercise, but of which he was unaware and it certainly shouldn't be interpreted as in any way casting aspersions on our confidence in Prime Minister Zinn'.[31]

That clandestine German stay-behind cells existed not only in the state of Hesse, but also in other parts of Germany was confirmed by Dieter von Glahn after the Gladio revelations in 1990. 'Our mission and our organisation were identical with what is now known about Gladio', Glahn explained.[32] An ambiguous figure of the militant German anti-Communist scene Glahn had fled from a Soviet prisoner-of-war camp during the Second World War and after the war had joined the stay-behind secret army as a BDJ-TD member in the northern German state of Bremen. 'At the time of the Korean war', Glahn explained in his autobiography in 1994, 'the Americans were very worried, that something similar could also happen in Germany'. Thus 'the Americans decided to recruit and set up a reliable German unit for day X, the invasion of the Red Army. The unit was to be trained with American arms, equipped from arms caches, and designed to go under ground immediately in case of an attack.' Glahn related that 'the BDJ was but the cover, something like the official arm of an anti-Communist organisation. The unofficial arm Technischer Dienst, or "Organisation Peters", as it was also called after its leader, was the real combat core' and existed in numerous parts of Germany. 'The TD thus became an important part of the US-German anti-Soviet defence. The Americans were mainly interested in former members of the German army' including himself. 'As my anti-Communist attitudes were well known, I was recruited. Officially I now was leader of the BDJ in the city of Oldenburg/Ost-friesland. Unofficially I was the leader of the TD for the entire area Oldenburg and Bremen–Ostfriesland [northern Germany].'[33]

Glahn proudly related in his memoirs that the German 'FBI', the Bundesamt für Verfassungsschutz (BfV), knew of the secret stay-behind armies and covered them. 'I worked very closely together... with Neubert of the BfV', Glahn recalled the anti-Communist battle which united them. At 'nights we regularly hung up posters, and covered the posters of the Communists... and exposed some Oldenburger businessmen, who collaborated with the Communists. In this there were often violent clashes.' It was at 'that time I founded many subgroups of the BDJ in my area' with support of the CIA who trained in Waldmichelbach and the US base Grafenwöhr. 'I myself have taken part in such trainings several times. Members received a brownish US combat dress, were only allowed to communicate by first name, came from all over Germany, but were forbidden to tell the others where they lived. Practically we were completely isolated from the world there for four weeks.' Gladiators received 'extensive training for day X. At that time secret American arms caches were erected in all parts of Western Germany. In my area only my deputy and I knew the exact location of the arms cache... our cache was well buried in a little forest.'[34]

Not only the German stay-behind network, but also the German secret service ORG and its staff survived the 1952 discovery of parts of the German Gladio almost without a scratch due to the protection of the powerful CIA. General Reinhard Gehlen remained in charge and in 1956 the 'Organisation Gehlen' changed its label to 'Bundesnachrichtendienst' (BND). When CIA Director Allan Dulles was once asked whether he did not feel ashamed to cooperate with Nazi Gehlen the former replied: 'I don't know if he is a rascal. There are few arch-bishops in espionage... Besides, one needn't ask him to one's club.'[35] When even the German government, under Conservative chancellor Kurt Georg Kiesinger and Socialist vice-chancellor and Foreign Minister Willy Brandt, started to distrust its compromised secret service BND the latter was investigated in detail for the first time in its history.

The ensuing 'Mercker Report' allegedly was 'a horror document for the BND, which is kept under lock and key until today', the German press reported still in 1995. 'Its shattering conclusion on the BND: "A corrupt organisation".'[36] Reinhard Gehlen, sharply attacked by the governmental investigation, was not even allowed to read the report. And the German Socialists who with Willy Brandt, for the first time after the war, had entered the government were so embarrassed by the top Nazi within the executive that upon receiving the Mercker report they sacked Gehlen after a remarkably long career of more than 20 years at the head of the German secret service on worker's day May 1, 1968. In order not to upset the White House Gehlen was replaced by Gerhard Wessel who had served as West Germany's military attaché in Washington after 1945 and ever since cultivated close links with the CIA and the US national security establishment.

It is unknown whether the classified Mercker report also contained data on the stay-behind activities of the ORG and the BND, but evidence which surfaced during the 1990 Gladio investigations suggests that it does. The short report of the German government on the BND and its stay-behind of December 1990, claims that a legal basis for the German stay-behind had been created in December 1968, thus only a few months after the Mercker report had been completed: 'In December 1968 the Chief of the Chancellors Ministry had explicitly stated in article 16 of the "General Directives for the BND" that preparations for a defence situation shall be taken.' Presumably the government at the time had decided to continue to run the stay-behind but wanted to back the operation with a legal basis: 'That directive reads: "The BND carries out the necessary preparations and planning for the defence case, in general questions upon agreement with the chief of Chancellor's Ministry."'[37] German journalist and Gladio author Leo Müller wondered in 1990 'how much anti-democratic secret organisations substance was also contained in the later stay-behinds of the German secret service, which were discovered in October 1990?'[38]

Whether the removal of Gehlen and the introduction of the new law reduced the dominant role of the CIA in the German stay-behind remains doubtful. Former German Gladio member Glahn in his book makes it a point that ultimately the CIA was in charge: 'I intentionally write of "secret services" in the plural, because we were later united with the secret service Organisation Gehlen on the orders of the Americans.' Glahn relates that although Gehlen was the key player in the German stay-behind, overall command rested with the US: 'This organisation had been named after its founder, General Gehlen . . . He set up an excellent secret service centre in Pullach close to Munich', Glahn relates and stressed that 'The Technische Dienst TD was in constant contact with the residents of the Gehlen Organisation. The military task, however, for day X, remained firmly in the hands of the Americans.'[39] When the cover of the German secret army was blown in 1952 Gehlen and others had been offered an exile in the United States in order to protect them from further German investigations. 'I was offered to be flown to the United States, as other members of the TD, which were involved in a criminal trial. I have discussed this with my wife at length . . . but decided that I did not want to be an émigré. My place was here in Germany.'[40]

In May 1955 Germany became a member of NATO. Exactly like the other stay-behind secret armies the German network, through the secret service BND, was integrated into NATO's planning for secret unorthodox warfare. The official stay-behind report of the German government written by Lutz Stavenhagen in 1990 confirmed that in order 'to coordinate their planning with the military leadership of NATO, the intelligence services taking part in the operation established in 1952 the so called Coordinating and Planning Committee (CPC). In order to coordinate the cooperation among themselves they established in 1954 the so called Allied Coordination Committee (ACC).' The German government furthermore confirmed that the 'BND has been a regular member of both CPC and ACC ever since 1959'. In an ill-advised attempt to limit the damage the governmental report however wrongly claimed that both 'coordination committees have never been, and are not now, parts of the NATO structure', while the Belgian parliamentary stay-behind investigation revealed that both ACC and CPC had been set up by NATO's SACEUR, at all times a US General, and were directly linked to NATO's SHAPE. The German governmental report meanwhile attempted to highlight the sovereignty of the German secret army and insisted that 'the fact that the BND has been a member of these units has not changed the fact that the stay-behind is no part of NATO and has remained the own organisation of the BND. There has not been, and there does not exist now, a subordinate relationship of the different intelligence services with respect to ACC and CPC.'[41]

'Cooperation with partner services was carried out bilaterally as well as multilaterally under the coordination of ACC', the German governmental report explained on the international dimension of the secret stay-behind army. 'Partners in this cooperation are besides West Germany: Belgium, Denmark, France, Great Britain, Italy, Luxemburg, Norway and the United States of America.' The report related that this cooperation 'included for instance joint exercises, the acquiring of a standardised radio set [Harpoon transmitters], the exchange of training experience, the standardisation of the intelligence terminology and other things'.[42] Also due to the dominant presence of right-wing extremists, Stavenhagen was reluctant to give detailed figures as to how many Gladiators had operated in Germany during the Cold War: 'At the end of the 1950s, the organisation was made up of about 75 full-time members,' Stavenhagen said. 'The number of intelligence contacts was as high as 500, at times. In 1983, stay-behind personnel were also being trained to carry out acts of sabotage in enemy occupied territory against the occupying power and to organise and lead resistance units.'

The German government according to the report was informed of the existence of the secret army 'in the years following 1974 (in the context of a presentation of the overall strategy of BND defence preparations). One can however assume that oral information on the basics of the Stay-Behind was passed on to the directive level already before.' As for the German legislative a branch of parliament, obliged to keep certain secrets, had been informed about the stay-behind in the 1980s when special funds were needed to buy new Harpoon communication equipment: 'In the context of a purchase of a new radio set the committee of special trust (Vertrauensgremium) has been informed on its employment in the Stay-Behind.'[44] The Harpoon radio transmitters, as further investigations revealed, had been developed and produced on the orders of NATO's stay-behind centre ACC by the German firm AEG Telefunken, daughter concern to the Daimler holding. The German secret service BND had functioned as a go-between and had bought the Harpoon system from AEG Telefunken, as the ACC had to remain unknown and could not itself figure as the purchaser. The BND had ordered a total of 854 Harpoon transmitters for which they paid a total of 130 million German Mark. The BND itself only kept transmitters in the value of 20 million German Mark while selling the rest to other national stay-behind armies across Western Europe. Satisfying the highest technological standards at the time the Harpoon system was able to send and receive encrypted radio messages across 6,000 km and thus connected the different stay-behinds among themselves and across the Atlantic.[45]

As Germany was a divided country during the Cold War the West German secret service BND, strongly dependent on the US CIA, and the East German secret service MfS (Ministerium für Staatssicherheitsdient), short Stasi, strongly dependent on the Soviet KGB, were constantly engaged in secret battles, espionage affairs and the infiltration of spies on the other side of the Berlin Wall. The operations were eased by the fact that both the members of the Stasi and the BND as a rule were Germans, spoke fluent German, and shared a common culture. With a conviction based on experience both the CIA and the MI6 therefore nicknamed the BND the 'leaky intelligence service'.[46] And the leading German news magazine Der Spiegel after the end of the Cold War concluded: 'The KGB and the Stasi in East Berlin could place moles in the highest positions in Pullach [BND headquarters], with access to the complete personal staff ... The BND was but a laugh for the competitors in the field.'[47]

With respect to the stay-behind secrets the question therefore arises naturally how well the Stasi and hence Moscow were informed. The evidence available indicates that at least as of the late 1970s they were well-informed. A documented leak in the BND on stay-behind concerns the tragic biography of secretary Heidrun Hofer who worked in the Department IV of the BND in Munich which directed the German stay-behind. With access to highly classified documents Hofer saw NATO documents with the highest NATO security clearance 'cosmic'. What exactly she revealed to the Stasi and the KGB is still unclear. But it is confirmed that she passed on information on a top-secret German stay-behind command centre designed as an exile base for the government located outside Germany on the Atlantic, which, after having been revealed, had to be built elsewhere anew for 100 million German Mark.

Hofer passed on all her information unknowingly. A daughter of a conservative German officer she was directly targeted by the KGB who had sent a man to Argentina to make contacts with right-wing Germans, to make himself a reputation and then came back to propose to Heidrun. Her father liked 'Hans' for his right-wing background and assented. After the marriage 'Hans' confessed to Heidrun that he was working for a right-wing conservative organisation and stunned her with his knowledge on the BND. Heidrun felt as part of a conspiracy and passed all available information to Hans.

Only slowly the BND counterintelligence became aware of the KGB mole. In December 1976 BND counterintelligence units ambushed their place after Hofer had worked unknowingly for the KGB for six years. Hans escaped through a back door while Heidrun was arrested, accused of high treason and informed that Hans was a KBG spy. The shock was immense for the conservative right-leaning woman. During the BND interrogation on the sixth floor in Munich she allegedly jumped out of the window in an attempt to kill herself. She survived severely handicapped and has lived on social welfare ever since. The case against her was closed in 1987 owing to lapse of time.[48] A second and more highly placed leak in the BND during the Cold War was Joachim Krase, deputy chief of the BND, who died in 1988. Krase had been in Stasi's pay and, as the British press claimed, had 'passed on everything about Gladio and stay-behind. So much for the secret the Russians knew all along.'[49]

When after the fall of the Berlin Wall Germany was reunited the Stasi secret service was closed down while the BND extended its operations. Declassified original Stasi documents from the archives now confirm that the East German secret service had been well-informed about the stay-behind. During a NATO manoeuvre in 1979 the Stasi signals intelligence unit had detected a parallel network which they investigated in detail in the following years by cracking the code of the BND stay-behind agents and identifying more than 50 stay-behind locations in West Germany, spread across the country with a concentration along the border to East Germany and Czechoslovakia.

General Major Horst Männchen, the Director of the Stasi Department III and responsible for signals intelligence, informed the Ministers of the East German government in detail in 1984 on the stay-behind network of the BND. 'On the basis of analysis of secret radio signals of the BND that we were able to decode...we have gathered reliable details on a special category of BND agents.' The report of Männchen, dated August 3, 1984, went on to explain that theses special BND agents, that the Stasi referred to as 'roll over agents' (Ueberrollagenten), are preparing for a military invasion of the Warsaw Pact forces and are trained to carry out subversive operations in the rear of the enemy. These secret agents, Männchen highlighted, 'represent a serious danger for successful operations of the Warsaw Pact forces' and should therefore be identified as soon as possible in order to be immediately neutralised 'in case of military conflict'.[50]

In another report dated November 6, 1984 Männchen correctly pointed out that within the BND 'these special agents are referred to as "stay-behind"', and that their creation seems to go back to NATO planning for a first-strike invasion of Warsaw Pact forces. Männchen related that also women were part of the stay-behind network, and that an entire set of secret radio signals sent from BND headquarters to the stay-behind agents had been decoded by the Stasi. 'These agents are male and female citizens of West Germany, they live on the territory of West Germany, many along the border to East Germany and Czechoslovakia. They know their area of operations well and operate alone or in groups of three to four and carry out assignments within 40 kilometers of their home. From what we know by now 16 to 20 agent units communicate regularly with the BND. The total number of these agents according to sources from within the BND is estimated at 80.' Männchen concluded that these special agents of the BND were 'dangerous' and that the Stasi should try to identify as many as possible.[51]

In a subsequent report the Stasi concluded that the data gathered 'clearly indicated that the BND placed great importance in the training and readiness of these special agents'. Radio signals intercepted by the Stasi also indicated that the German stay-behind was well-connected, and that it communicated with 'NATO secret services' in Sardinia (Italy), in Huy (Belgium) and in Lille and Grenoble (France).[52] By closely monitoring the stay-behind radio signals of the BND the Stasi was also able to detect the installation of the new Harpoon communication system in West Germany and on May 22, 1984 reported that new and faster communication equipment was being used by the special agents.[53] A very detailed 11-page-long Stasi report on the BND stay-behind observed in 1985 with regret that the new and faster equipment, that sent out the radio signals within less than 3 seconds, made it more difficult for the Stasi to locate the BND stay-behind agents.[54]

When the secret German network was discovered in 1990 the press focused on the hardware traces of the secret network and questioned the German government whether there existed secret Gladio arms caches in Germany. 'For the support of resistance units in occupied territory allied secret services had erected secret arms caches in the early phase of the stay-behind organisation. These contained among other things spare parts for communication equipment, medicaments, gold and jewellery for black market transactions, and a few pistols', the German government confirmed the well-known pattern also for Germany but surprisingly thereafter misleadingly went on to claim that 'these arms caches were dissolved by the stay-behind unit of the BND before 1972. The pistols were destroyed. Today's equipment and training of the intelligence connections is strictly limited to the intelligence-gathering mission and the evacuation mission. The equipment includes a special radio set, but no arms, nor explosives.'[55]

German journalists suspected that government spokesman Lutz Stavenhagen had been misleading the press by suggesting that in 1972 all arms caches had been dissolved, for it was well known that still in the early 1980s mysterious arms caches had been discovered in Germany. The most prominent discovery had taken place on October 26, 1981 when forest workers by chance had stumbled across a large arms cache in the soil, filled with guns and other combat equipment, near the German village of Uelzen in the Lüneburger Heide area. Following the sensational discovery forest ranger and right-wing extremist Heinz Lembke was arrested. He later guided the police to a massive connected arsenal of 33 underground arms caches. 'These discovered arms caches were immediately attributed to right wing extremist Lembke', an anonymous but well-informed article on Gladio from the Austrian Defence Ministry commented in 1991. 'Yet this brilliant solution featured one flaw. The arms caches contained next to automatic weapons, chemical combat equipment [Arsen and Zyankali] and about 14,000 shots of munitions, also 50 anti tank guns, 156 kg of explosives, as well as 230 explosive devices and 258 hand grenades. It is remarkable, that a state with extensive security measures against terrorists should not have noted a robbery or deviation of such a large amount of combat equipment.'[56]

US journalist Jonathan Kwitny in his article on 'The CIA's Secret Armies in Europe' elaborated on the Austrian Gladio article and concluded 'that Germany's stay-behind program may have suffered a second scandal, similar to the one in 1952, but one that never became public.' For the arms caches discovered in 1981 had been 'traced to the military training of a youth group run by neo-Nazi Heinz Lembke, who was arrested. At the time Lembke was portrayed as a crazed extremist training troops secretly in the forest.' Yet Kwitny noted that he was not the only one to link the Lembke arsenal to the BND stay-behind, for also the Austrain Gladio publication had discredited the claim that Lembke was only a crazed and isolated extremist. 'The editor of the Austrian Defense Ministry publication, retired General Franz Freistaetter, says he personally oversaw the article suggesting Lembke was using stay-behind caches to train his neo-Nazi troops, and believes it, though its author insisted on anonymity.'[57]

Both the Kwitny article on and the Austrian article on Gladio seem correct to suggest that the Lembke arms caches were part of the German stay-behind. Among the documents secured in 1952, when the BDJ-TD stay-behind was discovered, was also a BDJ-TD directive for day X, invasion day. It specified that the Lünenburger Heide was to be the northern German stay-behind meeting point should the invasion come: 'Area leaders were instructed to find out where trucks in large numbers are stationed. In case of X these trucks must be confiscated immediately, if necessary using violence, by members, who then must drive them to the specified BDJ meeting points in the villages and cities', the BDJ-TD directive read. 'From there the trucks shall transport the members to the northern German meeting point in the Lüneburger Heide.'[58]

The discovery of the Lembke arms caches in October 1981 was a scandal in its own right in Germany. But the affair became even more sensitive when sources suggested that the arsenals had not simply lain dormant for the distant day of a Soviet invasion but that Lembke might have used the arsenal to supply fellow right-wingers who, one year before the discovery of the arms caches, had used the deadly weapons for a terrorist bomb attack in Munich in 1980. This far-reaching claim was raised by German journalist Harbart who believes that Gladio was 'a sword in the hand of right wingers' and relates that 'traces from the Munich October massacre lead to the forest ranger Lembke of Niedersachsen'. Harbart is convinced that the bombs and the strategy of tension were not limited to Italy but reached also into the heart of Germany.[59]

The Munich bomb massacre is the largest terrorist bomb massacre in Germany's post-war history. At twenty past ten in the evening of September 26, 1980 a bomb exploded in the midst of the popular Munich October beer fest. Like every year, thousands of people had gathered for what to many were the nicest three days of the year. The bomb left a bloody trail, killing 13 and wounding 213, many gravely. Germany and the city of Munich were shocked. The police investigation revealed that German right-wing extremists had carried out the atrocity. The bomb trail lead to neo-Nazi groups, among which was the 'Wehrsportgruppe Hoffmann'. Gundolf Köhler, a 21-year-old right-wing member of the Wehrsportgruppe Hoffmann, according to the police investigation, had planted the Munich bomb. Experts explained that the bomb, which consisted of a specially prepared hand grenade placed in a fire extinguisher, had been constructed with remarkable expertise, and doubts were raised whether Köhler could have constructed such a complex bomb himself. Köhler could not be questioned for he was himself torn apart by the bomb and was one of the 13 victims.

Ignaz Platzer, who was at the festival on the fateful day and lost his two children in the Munich massacre, in a 1996 interview told the German daily *Sueddeutsche Zeitung* that the background of the right-wing network responsible for the terror had never been investigated. 'You have been asking for a reopening of the investigations for years now. Do you not believe that Gundolf Köhler was the actor?', the journalist asked Platzer. 'No, too many signs speak against this. Why should somebody who plans such an act a passport, through which he can immediately be identified? At least he was certainly not alone', the father of the victims replied. 'I have fought for a long time to know who really was or were the people behind it. Yet I had to learn that I would never be given an honest answer to this question.' Upon which the journalist enquired: 'You have stopped to ask for clarification?' Whereupon Platzer concluded: 'I have started to learn that you only get into trouble if you insist.'[60]

Some of the troubles might have derived from the fact that the Munich massacre lead police to the Lembke arms caches which led to the German stay-behind army which led to the world's largest military alliance NATO and the world's superpower United States. Even if the US, NATO and the BND had nothing to do with the Munich terror, the discovery of a secret army linked to right-wing extremists would have raised very serious questions. For example, how well were the secret soldiers and their arms arsenals controlled by Germany's democratic institutions?

Already one day after the massacre the German criminal police investigating the crime had received information that Lembke had supplied the right-wing extremists. 'Mister Lembke showed us different sorts of explosives, detonators, slow matches, plastic explosive and military explosive', right-winger Raymund Hörnle, a member of the Wehrsportgruppe Hoffmann, revealed to the police during the interrogation. 'He said that he had many caches full of such material buried in the wood, and that he could provide a lot of them...Mister Lembke told us, that he was instructing people in the use of explosive devices and explosive'[61] Next to training the German Gladiators Lembke, according to the police protocols, thus supported German right-wing terrorists. 'I have heard from Helmuth Meyer that explosives can be gotten from Mister Lembke', right-wing extremist Sibylle Vorderbrügge also testified after the massacre. 'Lembke showed us different explosives... He told us, that he had several arms caches in the wood.'[62]

Despite these testimonies the police did not search and dig up the secret arms caches of Lembke so that another year went by until forest workers stumbled across the secret Gladio arms arsenal by coincidence and their existence could no longer be denied. Yet again the crucial link between the massacre and the stay-behind arms cache was not pursued. This despite the fact that on November 25, 1981 Mrs Dr Däubler-Gmelin of the German Socialist party had raised the right question in the national German parliament, the Bundestag, when she asked the government: 'Could you tell us now whether after the discovery of the arms caches and the arrest of Mister Lembke a new understanding of the... Munich massacre has arisen?' The question was good, but the answer was poor. For the government State Secretary von Schoeler answered: 'There is no connection.'[63]

This governmental explanation covered up the Gladio connection as the existence of the stay-behind army had to remain secret. It also contradicted the testimonies from right-wingers given to the German police. Immediately after the discovery of the secret arms caches on October 26, 1981 the German police stormed Lembke's house and secured an empty G3 gun magazine and a roll of slow matches for a bomb. Yet right-wing extremist Lembke himself seemed untouchable and was not arrested. Born in 1937 in Stralsund in Eastern Germany Lembke had experienced the so-called Socialism of the DDR first-hand and, aged 22, had fled to West Germany where he had joined right-wing circles and gained notoriety. He became the leader of the right-wing 'Bund Vaterländischer Jugend' (BVJ, Alliance of Patriotic Youth), where as chief ideologist he composed fascist slogans such as: 'A fellow, worth to be hanged, is a German who thinks like a Jew.'[64] Similar to the BDJ, which was outlawed in 1952, the BDV right-wing alliance was prohibited in 1962. But Lembke did not abandon the right-wing track. In 1968 he attempted to enter the federal parliament of the German county Niedersachsen as a candidate for the right-wing NPD party. But failed to become a politician and thereafter engaged in violent battles against German anti-Fascist activists. For this he was prosecuted until a higher court mysteriously declared him 'not guilty'.

It was only several weeks after the discovery of the arms caches that Lembke was arrested and jailed. But for a different reason. He was accused of having unlawfully refused to testify in the case against his friend and fellow right-wing leader Manfred Roeder of the terrorist group 'Deutsche Aktionsgruppen'. In prison Lembke suddenly changed his mind and declared that he was going to testify, both on the Roeder case, and the arms caches, and many other things he knew. Lembke insisted that he was willing to speak only to the public prosecutor who without success had interrogated him in the Roeder case. The request was granted and the prosecutor immediately travelled to Lembke's prison cell. There Lembke finally talked, revealing in detail all the 33 arms caches of which until then only some had been found. That evening Lembke said to his interrogator that he might reveal to him the next day who was supposed to use the guns and explosives. The next day, November 1, 1981, Lembke was found hanging on a rope from the ceiling of his prison cell.[65]

The Lembke case thereafter was taken away from the local investigators in Niedersachsen and transferred to the national crime investigators in Bonn. This legally astonishing manoeuvre lead Interior Minister of Niedersachsen Möcklinghoff to speak of a 'criminal trick'.[66] Then, a year later, on December 3, 1982 Bonn closed the Lembke case with no clear findings as to the connection between the secret arsenals and the Munich massacre deciding that Lembke was 'a private case'. The investigators claimed in their final report that 'there are not sufficient indications to suggest that Lembke wanted to disrupt the constitutional order of the German Republic through bomb attacks or assassinations'. The final report went only as far as to admit that Lembke had most probably feared an invasion from the East against which he wanted to conduct 'partisan warfare' and concluded 'that the found combat gear has been collected and buried by him over years in order to be able to carry out resistance operations in the case of an invasion, which he feared'.[67]

In what many regarded as an astonishing conclusion the court found 'that there has not originated from Lembke's activity such a large danger, as has initially been feared. For his efforts had not been directed against the present order of the country.' At the same time the court seems to have understood the stay-behind strategy when it declared that Lembke had lead a 'Werwolf' operation. For this was a reference to the stay-behind networks of the Nazis called 'Werwolf' which the latter had left behind in numerous countries with secret arms caches when retreating at the end of the Second World War. Mythological figure within German literature the Werwolf designates a human being which over night enigmatically turns into a deadly wolf, attacking and killing other people as the new day breaks. The court found that 'More to the point, the forest ranger had undertaken some preparations for the case of a Communist raise to power, so that then a "Werwolf" could become active.'[68] As Lembke himself was dead he could not comment on these findings. A number of right-wing friends of Lembke received modest fines. And of the entire massive arms cache only the origin of three weapons could be clarified. A private firm that produced weapons for the German Army and NATO had provided them.

Due to the confirmed links to right-wing extremists and suspected links to the Munich massacre Germany has had great difficulties when it came to investigating and clarifying its stay-behind history. Green parliamentarian Manfred Such on November 5, 1990 following the discoveries of the secret armies across Europe had issued a formal request to the German government of Helmut Kohl concerning the suspected existence of Gladio structures in Germany. German government spokesman Hans Klein to the amusement and bewilderment of both parliamentarians and journalists thereafter explained that 'the German Gladio was *not*, as has been claimed, a secret commando troop or a guerrilla unit', that however he could not discuss details for reasons of strict secrecy.[69] Klein's statements caused an outcry among opposition Social Democrats and Green politicians. Parliamentarian Hermann Scheer, defence expert of the SPD, criticised that this mysterious right-wing network might well be some sort of a 'Ku-Klux-Klan', designed more for peacetime actions against the democracy than for an unlikely Soviet invasion. In order to find out the facts, Scheer asked for an immediate and thorough juridical inquiry on the highest level into NATO's shadow army by the German public prosecutor 'because the existence of an armed military secret organisation outside all governmental or parliamentary control, is incompatible with the constitutional legality, and therefore must be prosecuted according to the criminal law'.[70] Scheer stressed that the investigation had to be started soon 'in order to avoid that a cover up destroys the traces'.[71]

The call for a full-fledged Gladio investigation suddenly evaporated among the German Socialists when it was revealed that their Ministers while in office had also been part of the conspiracy. As the German Socialists, in view of the upcoming elections, for tactical reasons shied away from further stay-behind investigations only the German Green Party, founded in 1980, continued to ask for a sound investigation and clarification because the Green party was not compromised as it had never held governmental responsibilities. The request of the Green party to discuss the stay-behind affair and its suspected links to terrorism and right-wing extremists openly in parliament was however defeated by the Conservative and Socialists alliance of CDU/CSU, FDP and SPD who feared for a massive scandal and moved the debate to a session held behind closed doors in the secrecy-bound Parliamentary Control Commission (Parlamentarische Kontrollkommission PKK) on November 22, 1990. There Volker Foertsch, the last stay-behind Director of the BND, informed the parliamentarians that the secret unit would be closed down. The Green party had no parliamentarians in this important commission and lamented that the PKK, which oversees the German secret service BND, was well known as a group 'that covers up more often than it clears up'.[72] When journalists attempted to gain more information from Eberhard Blum, Gehlen's personal assistant and Director of the BND from 1983 to 1985, the latter declared: 'Gladio? Something like that has never existed in Germany.'[73]

Unwilling to concede defeat the German Green party on November 29 placed a formal request with the government. 'At the end of October 1990 the now acting Italian Prime Minister Giulio Andreotti confirmed in a report to parliament the existence of a secret NATO service, code-named Gladio', the request began and then specifically asked: 'Has such a NATO-linked supranational secret service organisation also become active in Germany?' Dr Lutz Stavenhagen, Minister in the government of Helmut Kohl with responsibilities for the secret service BND, answered this question with a short and flat lie: 'No.' Furthermore the Green parliamentarians wanted to know: 'What exact agreements with which exact content has the German government signed when it joined NATO, or later, which would allow for the activities of such organisations?' Stavenhagen sticked to his line and claimed: 'The German government has made no such agreements.' The parliamentarians inquired: 'In what exact relationship with NATO stood or stands this secret service, which was active in Germany and/or other NATO countries?' to which Stavenhagen answered: 'Due to the answer to question one, this question is redundant.' Finally the Green Party asked: 'Is the government willing, to inform on its own initiative the questioners in more detail, as soon as for Germany relevant information becomes available in this context. And in case the government is not prepared to do so, why not?' to which Stavenhagen replied: 'This question can only be answered, when such documents become available. For the answer depends on the conditions under which such documents may be accessed.'[74]

The Green parliamentarians were furious but could do nothing. The government of Chancellor Helmut Kohl of the Christian Democratic Union (CDU), in office ever since 1982, had decided to offer a set of lies in order not to endanger its position in the first national elections in united Germany which were held on December 2, 1990 and led to a victory for Kohl. Thereafter, on Monday December 3, 1990 Lutz Stavenhagen hurriedly sent out a fax of four pages on the German stay-behind to the media entitled: 'Report of the Government on the Stay-Behind Organisation of the BND' in which, contrary to his earlier statements, he confirmed that a secret NATO-linked stay-behind had also existed in Germany: 'The units which had been built up by allied secret services on German territory until 1955 for intelligence gathering and evacuation operation were taken over in 1956 by the BND.' The government furthermore confirmed that the secret army was still active: 'At the moment 104 persons work together with the BND in the context of stay-behind', while stressing that on November 22 the parliamentary control commission charged with the oversight of the BND had been informed of the relevant details. The report concluded: 'Following the global changes the BND has looked at dissolving the Stay-Behind organisation already in the Summer of 1990. After agreements with the allied partners the dismantling will have been carried out by April 1991.'[75]

While the BND assured the public that the secret army had been closed down and that there existed no secret arms caches in the country the topic resurfaced on August 17, 1995. On that day Peter Naumann, a 43-year-old neo-Nazi, trained chemist and expert at building bombs, guided the surprised police in front of recording cameras to a total of 13 arms caches which he had, according to his own testimony, erected in Niedersachsen and Hesse during the last 17 years. The arsenals contained arms, munitions and around 200 kg of explosives. Interestingly enough Naumann was a friend of Lembke and confirmed to the police that most of his weapons and explosives had been taken over from Lembke's arms cache.[76]

It is surprising that despite the confirmed presence of right-wing terrorists in its ranks and the suspected links to acts of right-wing terrorism there was no parliamentary investigation of the German secret army, let alone a detailed public report. 'As for democratic transparency, Germany for the moment classified last in Europe', German investigative journalist Leo Müller concluded in a short and early book on Gladio.[77] Other investigative journalists who have reported on the Gladio story in Germany like Ulrich Stoll of the ZDF national television chain in Berlin believe that the affair is far from over. When in late 2002 Stoll received declassified Stasi reports on the stay-behind he concluded 'the Gladio research can go on'.[78]

16

THE SECRET WAR IN GREECE

Under Benito Mussolini's fascist directives Italian troops attacked Greece during the Second World War in 1940, but were defeated by the massive resistance of the Greek population. Hitler, who had observed the failure of Mussolini with disapproval, in 1941 sent his German troops which conquered the country and placed it under the control of the Axis Powers. The Greeks once again organised a massive resistance operation and throughout the war the German army faced great difficulties with keeping the country under control. As in Italy and France, in Greece the strongest resistance organisation to the fascist occupation was dominated by Communists. ELAS, the People's Liberation Army, had been founded on the initiative of the Greek Communist Party (KKE) some months after the German invasion. Its partisans cut across the entire left of the political spectrum and many women, priests and even some archbishops fought in its ranks. EAM, the political wing of the People's Liberation Army, was also dominated by the Greek Communists. Out of a population of seven million up to two million Greeks were members of the EAM party, while 50,000 were actively fighting in the ranks of ELAS army.

ELAS was the thorn in the flesh of the Nazis who essentially wrestled the country back from the German occupiers. In its operations ELAS was supported by the British secret army SOE whose officers advised ELAS on the ground and supplied it with weapons and munitions. Many personal friendships developed between the Greek ELAS resistance fighters and the British SOE liaison officers. Yet the brothers in arms were abruptly separated when Prime Minister Winston Churchill in March 1943 decided to halt all support for ELAS as he feared that Greece after the defeat of the Axis Powers could come under Communist control. Churchill secretly sent his foreign minister Anthony Eden to Stalin in October 1943 to carve up the Balkans. The deal, cemented at Yalta, gave Britain and the United States a free hand in Greece, while Bulgaria and Rumania were to fall under the influence of the Soviet Union.

In order to minimise the power of the Greek Communists and Socialists, London planned to reinstall the Greek conservative king together with a right-wing government after the war. The crucial British Foreign Office directive of March 20, 1943 which signalled the turn around emphasised that 'SOE should always veer in the direction of groups willing to support the King and Government, and furthermore impress on such groups as may be anti-monarchical the fact that the King and Government enjoy the fullest support of His Majesty's Government.'[1] The King was less than popular among many Greeks after having cooperated with the fascist dictator Metaxas. Inspired by Mussolini and Hitler, Metaxas had introduced the fascist salute, the rigid outstretched right arm, as well as a brutal secret police during his rule in the late 1930s. Yet London pursued the conservative policy and in October 1943 the British Foreign Office even contemplated 'a downright policy of attacking and weakening EAM by every means in our power', an approach which was postponed however for it was 'likely to sacrifice all chance of military advantage and to defeat its own ends by strengthening EAM politically'.[2]

The turn around of the British came as a shock to ELAS and its difficulties increased when former Nazi collaborators and right-wing special units, such as the fascist X Bands of Cypriot soldier George Grivas, with British support started to hunt and kill ELAS resistance fighters. Churchill, who observed the battle from a distance, noticed however that the X Bands, for complete lack of popular support, never numbered more than 600 Greeks and hence ELAS remained the strongest guerrilla on the territory. It was in this context that in late 1944 he decided that something more had to be done in order to prevent the Greek Communists from reaching positions of power. Churchill therefore gave orders that a new Greek right-wing secret army had to be set up whereupon, as journalist Peter Murtagh relates, a 'new Greek army unit was established, which came to be known variously as the Greek Mountain Brigade, the Hellenic Raiding Force, or LOK, its Greek acronym (Lochos Oreinon Katadromon)'. As it was aimed against the Communists and the Socialists the unit excluded 'almost all men with views ranging from moderate conservative to left wing. Under British military supervision and at Churchill's express orders, the unit was filled with royalists and anti-republicans.'[3]

Field Marshall Alexander Papagos was made the first commander of the Hellenic Raiding Force and with British support he recruited right-wingers into the network and fought ELAS.[4] As ELAS fought against both the German Nazi occupiers and the British-sponsored Hellenic Raiding Force, Churchill feared a public relations disaster should it be revealed to the British public that London was secretly supporting the fascists against the Communists in Greece. In August 1944 he therefore instructed the BBC to eliminate 'any credit of any kind' to ELAS when reporting on the liberation of Greece.[5] But only weeks later ELAS secured victory over the German occupiers and Hitler was forced to withdraw his soldiers also from Greece. Churchill immediately demanded that the resistance should disarm, an order which ELAS was willing to obey if it was equally applied to their only remaining enemy on the field, the British-sponsored Hellenic Raiding Force.

As Great Britain refused to disarm the secret right-wing army, a large democratic demonstration organised by EAM in Athens against British interference in the post-war government of Greece took place on December 3, 1944, a mere six weeks after the German occupation forces had been pushed out of the country. The organisers of the demonstration had made it clear that they wanted to combat the British with peaceful means, announcing the demonstration as the prelude to a general strike. Shortly after 11 o'clock in the morning of that day a group of Greek protesters, numbering between 200 and 600, walked into Syntagma Square in Athens, the main square in front of the Greek parliament. This small group, among which were women and children in a festive mood, was part of a much larger group of 60,000, delayed by police blocks. As the small group ambled into the square, a line of armed men, a motley collection of police and freelance gunmen, presumably including members of the Hellenic Raiding Force, met them. British troops and police with machine guns were positioned on the rooftops. The atmosphere was tense.

Suddenly, and without warning, the peaceful demonstration was turned into a massacre as the command was given: 'Shoot the bastards'. A hail of bullets came down on the unarmed protesters who scattered in all directions. Allegedly the massacring went on for almost an hour. It left 25 protesters dead, including a six-year-old boy, and 148 wounded. Not long after the killings the main group of protesters arrived. In a display of remarkable restraint, the 60,000 held an entirely peaceful emotional and solemn rally among the corpses of their fellow protesters. Banners dipped in the blood of the slain demanded that the British stay out of Greek affairs. Many carried American and Greek flags. Some the red flag of Socialism. But only very few the Union Jack of Great Britain. In London, Churchill faced an angry House of Commons which demanded an explanation for the barbarity. While admitting that it had been a 'shocking thing', Churchill stressed that it was equally stupid to bring large numbers of unarmed children to a demonstration, while the city was full of armed men. The role of the secret right-wing army in the Syntagma massacre was not investigated.[6]

After this demonstration of force the British reinstalled the king, and ELAS handed over its arms to the British in return for the promised national democratic elections that were held in March 1946. As the Greek Communist Party and the centre left unwisely decided to boycott the polls due to the British occupation of the country, the right emerged victorious from the elections. A succession of weak British puppet governments with conservative and right-wing leanings followed. Convinced that Greece would fall under the control of brutal Soviet dictator Stalin if the Greek left should come to power, the government continued to arrest EAM members, many of whom were tortured on notorious island prison camps.

In 1945 most parts of the world celebrated the end of the Second World War and, in order to prevent such a tragedy from reoccurring, established the United Nations Organisation. Yet Greece remained a battlefield and already one year after the Second World War the Cold War started. As the frustration of the Greek left grew a fraction rearmed and took to the hills and in the fall of 1946 started a civil war against the British and the local right. Britain, exhausted by World War, could no longer control the country and in early 1947 asked the United States for support. CIA expert William Blum relates that 'Washington officials well knew that their new client government was so venal and so abusive of human rights that even confirmed American anti-Communists were appalled.'[7] Yet as Communist Yugoslavia supported the Greek left with arms and the country seemed on the brink of turning red, President Truman with his famous 'Truman Doctrine' in March 1947 was able to convince Congress to openly intervene in Greece. Greece was the first country to be invaded by the United States during the Cold War according to its strategy of combating Communism globally. In the following decades Washington put forward the argument used in Greece to justify its open or covert invasions of Korea, Guatemala, Iran, Cuba, Vietnam, Kambodscha, Nicaragua, Panama and several other countries.

By some ideological alchemy Truman labelled the corrupt right-wing regime in Athens as 'democratic' and dismissed its opponents on the left as 'terrorists', as US forces with heavy military equipment landed in Greece. The left-wing partisan force of some 20,000 men and women, scattered in the Greek mountains, was outnumbered six to one as the US special units linked up with the Hellenic Raiding Force and other units of the Greek right. When Stalin realised that the civil war in Greece could lead to a superpower confrontation, Yugoslavia was excluded from the Soviet Bloc in 1948 where upon the arms supply for the Greek partisans ebbed away. Their situation became desperate as the Hellenic Raiding Force operating under US command was excellently equipped and gained strength. The United States secretly started 'Operation Torch' and used chemical warfare to defeat the Greek partisans by dropping thousands of gallons of Napalm on Greece. In late 1948 the Greek resistance, which on their native soil had defeated both the German Nazis and the British troops, collapsed. 'The end of the civil war meant total victory for the Greek Right and its patron, the United States.'[8]

The secret anti-Communist army Hellenic Raiding Force was not disbanded but remained operational to control the Greek opposition. Greece joined NATO in 1952 and by that time 'had been moulded into a supremely reliable ally-client of the United States. It was staunchly anti-Communist and well integrated into the NATO system.'[9] Secretly the CIA and the Greek army cooperated to jointly run, train and equip the Hellenic Raiding Force under Field Marshall Alexander Papagos. The secret CIA anti-Communist army was a most valuable asset to influence the political situation in the country. The clandestine cooperation between the US secret service, the Greek military and the Greek government was repeatedly confirmed in secret documents, the existence of which the Greek public learned with some surprise during the Gladio discoveries in 1990. They included a document on the Greek secret army dated March 25, 1955 signed by US General Trascott for the CIA, Konstantin Dovas, Chief of Staff of the Greek military, as well as Greek Prime Minister Alexander Papagos.[10] The parties involved reconfirmed the agreement on the Greek secret army on May 3, 1960.[11]

According to Murtagh the running of the Hellenic Raiding Force was a major project of the CIA in Greece. 'In the mid 1950s, the CIA helped supply and equip the Force, and consciously re-modelled it on existing elite units in the US army and Britain–America's Delta Force and Britain's Special Air Service, the SAS.

Under CIA direction, Raiding Force members were issued with green berets, long before the US army's own Green Berets unit came into being.' As was the case in all Western European countries, contact with British and American Special Forces remained cordial. Greek officers took much pride in having been selected for the special unit after receiving special training abroad. Murtagh correctly relates that the Greek secret army through the CIA was also linked to NATO and the stay-behind command centre ACC in Brussels. 'The Raiding Force doubled as the Greek arm of the clandestine pan-European guerrilla network set up in the 1950s by NATO and the CIA which was controlled from NATO headquarters in Brussels by the Allied Coordination Committee.' Next to its domestic control tasks the Hellenic Raiding Force was trained for the classical stay-behind task. 'The idea behind the network was that it would operate as a "stay-behind" force after a Soviet invasion of Europe. It would co-ordinate guerrilla activities between Soviet occupied countries and liaise with governments in exile. Those involved would be members of the conquered nations' secret police and intelligence services, plus civilian volunteers. The Greek branch of the network was also known as Operation Sheepskin.'[12] As the Raiding Force, or LOK, had already been created in 1944 by the British, it arguably remains the oldest of the secret stay-behind armies active in Europe during the Cold War.

The existence of the secret army had been revealed by former CIA agent Philip Agee already in 1987 in his book 'Dirty Work: The CIA in Western Europe', for which he was heavily criticized by the CIA and the Pentagon. Agee, who had been a CIA operative in Latin America in the 1950s, left the agency on moral grounds in 1969 and thereafter publicly criticised the terrorist operations and the human rights violations of the CIA in numerous countries by revealing both operations and names of active CIA agents. Years before the secret Gladio armies were discovered in Italy, Agee revealed that 'paramilitary groups, directed by CIA officers, operated in the Sixties throughout Europe'. He stressed that 'perhaps no activity of the CIA could be as clearly linked to the possibility of internal subversion'.[13]

As far as Greece was concerned the CIA according to Agee had played a decisive role. 'The Greek-American CIA officer recruited several groups of Greek citizens for what the CIA called, "a nucleus for rallying a citizen army against the threat of a leftist coup." Each of the several groups was trained and equipped to act as an autonomous guerrilla unit, capable of mobilising and carrying on guerrilla warfare with minimal or no outside direction.' Control of the secret army rested with the CIA and the Greek officers whom the American secret service trusted. 'The members of each such group were trained by the CIA in military procedures. As far as can be determined, most of the paramilitary groups trained in two camps: one near Volos, and the second on Mount Olympos. After the initial training sessions, these groups would drill in isolated areas in Pindos and the mountains near Florina.' As with all secret armies in Western Europe run by the CIA, the units were equipped with light weapons hidden in arms caches. 'These guerrilla groups were armed with automatic weapons, as well as small mountain mortars. The weapons were stored in several places. Most of the military supplies were cached in the ground and in caves. Each member of these paramilitary groups knew where such cached weaponry was hidden, in order to be able to mobilise himself to a designated spot, without orders.'[14]

Due to the involvement of numerous persons the need-to-know had to be extended to several groups which in turn made it extremely difficult to keep the army and its links to the CIA top-secret. 'Constant problems developed with keeping the project secret. One CIA officer described it as "a nightmare"', Agee related and highlighted: 'The Paramilitary Group, as far as can be determined, was never disbanded. In the eyes of senior CIA officials, the groups under the direction of the paramilitary branch are seen as long term "insurance" for the interests of the United States in Greece, to be used to assist or to direct the possible overthrow of an "unsympathetic" Greek government. "Unsympathetic" of course to American manipulation.'[15] The CIA invested millions into the secret Greek army and built an entire complex of huts and training centres near Mount Olympus in east-central Greece where the members of the Hellenic Raiding Force were tutored by CIA instructors in a varieties of skills including skiing, parachute training and scuba diving.[16] About 800 secret arms caches were erected all over the country while the secret army allegedly counted as many as 1,500 officers, which were in need to recruit immediately another 2,000, to give the Hellenic Raiding Force a nucleus strength of 3,500 elite soldiers.[17]

The Greek-American CIA officer who played a central role in setting up and running the secret Greek army mentioned by Agee was Thomas Karamessines. Like many of his colleagues in the CIA, Karamessines during the Second World War had served in the US secret service Office of Strategic Services (OSS). Due to his strong anti-Communist convictions and Greek roots he was transferred to the US Embassy in Greece in January 1946 under the cover of military attaché. During the civil war he established contacts with the British and Greek security officials and the members of the Hellenic Raiding Force. After the CIA was created in 1947 to replace the OSS, Karamessines set up the CIA headquarters in Greece located in Athens on the fifth floor of the pale monolith Tamion Building just off Syntagma Square. Within a few years the CIA station numbered more than 100 full-time agents, most of whom were Greek-Americans as Karamessines himself. And Athens became the hub of all CIA activity in the Balkans and the Middle East, as far as Iran.

Directly involved with secret warfare and the anti-Communist CIA armies Karamessines in 1958 was transferred to Rome where as CIA chief of station he controlled the Italian Gladio and the battle against the Italian Communists. In 1962 Karamessines was forced to leave Rome amidst rumours that he had been involved in the non-clarified death of Italian industrialist and ENI boss Enrico Mattei. Back in the United States secret, warrior Karamessines became chief of CIA global covert actions when he was promoted to Deputy Director of Plans. Allegedly secret warrior Karamessines had carried the battle also to the United States and after the assassination of President Kennedy in 1963 was accused to have covered up traces and destroyed sensitive documents.

Karamessines saw to it that the CIA not only financed but also controlled the Greek military secret service KYP, despite the fact that the latter repeatedly engaged in torture. 'With coinciding aims and purposes, and of course our money, it was easy to work with them', a former CIA agent stationed in Greece later recalled. 'KYP were good at noodling out Greek Communists and those who flirted with the Soviets.'[18] KYP entertained listening posts targeting Bulgarian and Russian radio traffic, and sent the tapes to the United States in order to be decoded by the NSA. Monitoring the Greek opposition KYP together with the CIA amassed 15 tons of information on 16-and-a-half million individual files on Greeks regarded as a threat to the state. When paper storage started to become a serious problem the CIA provided KYP with a computer system. In what in retrospect amounts almost to an irony of history the first democracy of the modern age, namely the United States, had hence provided the first democracy of Ancient history, namely Greece, with the first computers in order to control the population. The KYP chief was greatly exited over the new machine and invited the press to inspect it. Standing next to the rather large and heavy machine he boasted that 'You in Greece may sleep peacefully because this marvellous accomplishment of American science never sleeps', whereupon in order to demonstrate the quality of the system he pressed an 'enemy of the country' button which to the embarrassment of the KYP produced a file on one of the journalists present at the meeting.[19]

As the CIA together with the local oligarchy through the Hellenic Raiding Force and the KYP controlled the Greek left and the Communists the only danger to the balance of power rested with democratic elections. Laughlin Campbell, CIA station chief from 1959 to 1962, was greatly worried that in the national elections of October 1961 the left was going to secure a victory and therefore a large number of people were either terrorised or paid in cash to vote according to KYP directives. In some villages the CIA and the army's candidates polled more votes than there were people eligible to vote. The CIA was successful and in the end the left-leaning Centre Union got only a little over a third of the vote and a 100 seats in parliament. Its leader, George Papandreou, protested at the election fraud, later had it investigated by an independent commission which confirmed the claim, and announced a relentless struggle against the government.

With strong popular support Papandreou had the courage to pick a fight with the CIA and the KYP and in 1963 forced US-supported Greek Prime Minister Constantine Karamanlis to resign. Tensions heightened as in the following elections in November 1963 the Centre Union secured 42 per cent of the popular vote and 138 of the 300 seats in parliament. Papandreou, who headed the single largest party, was elected Prime Minister in February 1964. For the first time since the occupation of Greece by Hitler the Greek right faced the prospect of having to come to terms with a serious loss of political power. Papandreou was guaranteed four years in government, a development which 'sent shock waves through the right-wing establishment. Many, including several key advisers, believed it signalled that the country was well on the road to a Communist take-over. That was something they were determined to stop.'[20] Prime Minister George Papandreou had to be removed.

Jack Maury, who had replaced CIA Chief of station Campbell in Athens, was given the order to remove Papandreou. Adopting an arrogantly visible profile by wearing loud suits and large rings and driving a large American car – 'bigger than the ambassador's', as he was fond of pointing out – the CIA chief of station demonstrated his power publicly. Secretly he conspired with King Constantine, royalists and right-wing officers of the Greek military and secret service and in July 1965 manoeuvred George Papandreou out of office by royal prerogative.[21] Several short-lived governments followed each other after the silent coup while the secret army, advised by KYP officer Konstantin Plevris, engaged in a clandestine battle to manipulate the political climate. Several bombs exploded in the country. In 1965, the Gorgopotamos bridge was blown to pieces by a bomb, just as the political left and right joined to commemorate their resistance to the Nazi occupation and, in particular, to commemorate their success in sopping the Germans from blowing up the bridge during the occupation. The massacre left five dead and almost 100 wounded, many gravely. 'Well, we were officially trained terrorists', an officer involved in the secret stay-behind operations declared later, highlighting that they had enjoyed powerful support.[22]

The support came from the administration of Lyndon Johnson in Washington who already in the context of the war in Cyprus had made it clear to the Greek government who was in charge. In summer 1964 President Johnson summoned Greek ambassador Alexander Matsas to the White House and told him that the problems in Cyprus had to be solved by dividing the island into a Greek and a Turkish part. When Matsas refused the plan, Johnson thundered: 'Then listen to me, Mr. Ambassador, Fuck your parliament and your constitution. America is an elephant. Cyprus is a flea. Greece is a flea. If those two fleas continue itching the elephant, they may just get whacked by the elephant's trunk, whacked good.' The government of Greece, as Johnson insisted, had to follow the orders of the White House. 'We pay a lot of good American dollars to the Greeks, Mr. Ambassador. If your Prime Minister gives me talk about democracy, parliament and constitution, he, his parliament and his constitution may not last very long.'[23]

When Matsas in consternation uttered 'I must protest your manner', Johnson continued shouting 'Don't forget to tell old Papa – what's his name – what I told you. Mind you tell him, you hear', whereupon Matsas cabled the conversation to Prime Minister George Papandreou. As the US secret service NSA picked up the message the phone of Matsas rang. The President was on the line: 'Are you trying to get yourself into my bad books, Mr. Ambassador? Do you want me to get really angry with you? That was a private conversation me and you had. You had no call putting in all them words I used on you. Watch your step.'[24] Click. The line went dead.

Andreas, the son of George Papandreou, witnessed the manipulations and the secret war in his country with disgust. After having flirted with a Trotskyist group as a student, Andreas had left Greece for America in the 1930s to escape the repression of the Metaxas dictatorship. He became a US citizen, embarked on a flourishing career as an economist and academic, heading the department of economics at the University of California at Berkley. During the Second World War he served in the US Navy and after the war was contacted by the CIA to work in the Mediterranean policy group. When he started to understand the role of the United States in Greece he cut his bonds with the CIA and in the late 1950s returned to Greece to become one of the most prominent and most vitriolic demagogic critics of the United States. In a style reminiscent of Castro, the younger Papandreou in inflammatory speeches attacked the United States' interference in Greek affairs, NATO, the corruption of the king, the Greek conservative parties and the Greek establishment in general.

The Pentagon and the CIA were shocked to see that yet another Papandreou challenged their power in Greece. And Murtagh relates that 'it would be difficult to understate the degree to which the former Prime Minister's son was loathed by the Right and the CIA'.[25] In 1964 Andreas Papandreou assumed ministerial duties and discovered that the KYP routinely bugged ministerial conversations and turned the data over to the CIA. He furiously dismissed two top KYP officers and attempted to replace them with more reliable officers whom he ordered to stop all cooperation with the CIA. Yet, as Papandreou recalled, the new KYP Director 'came back apologetically, to say he couldn't do it. All the equipment was American, controlled by the CIA or Greeks under CIA supervision. There was no kind of distinction between the two services. They duplicated functions in a counterpart relationship. In effect, they were a single agency.'[26]

As Papandreou challenged the KYP, Norbert Anshutz, US Deputy Chief of Mission of the US embassy, came to see him and advised him to rescind his orders to the KYP. Andreas Papandreou refused and ordered the US official to leave his office, whereupon Anshutz angrily warned that 'there would be consequences'.[27] The military coup d'état came on the night of April 20/21, 1967, one month before the scheduled elections for which opinion polls, including those of the CIA, predicted an overwhelming victory of the left-leaning Centre Union of George and Andreas Papandreou. The secret army Hellenic Raiding Force started the coup which was based on the Prometheus plan, a NATO-designed scheme to be put into action in the event of a Communist insurgency. In the event of opposition, Prometheus was unequivocal: 'Smash, without hesitation, any probable enemy resistance.'[28] Around midnight the Hellenic Raiding force took control over the Greek Defence Ministry which in admiration for the United States had been baptised Pentagon. They met little to no resistance and under the command of Lieutenant Colonel Costas Aslanides, a trained paratrooper, the building was secured. After the coup leaders controlled the Pentagon, phase two of the plan started and in the dark of night tanks with flashlights rolled into the capital and under the command of Brigadier General Sylianos Pattakos rounded up the parliament, the royal palace, the radio and the communication centres. Pattakos directed his column along the same route into the city taken by the Germans when they had conquered Athens in April 1941. Occasionally the tanks stopped, the officers looked around for signs of opposition. But there was none. Athens was asleep.

Also 78-year-old George Papandreou was asleep that night in his modest, whitewashed villa in Kastri, just outside the capital. The procedure, as in every military coup, was frightfully simple. Armed men knocked at his door, Papandreou was arrested and driven away in one of two military vehicles that had surrounded the house. At the same time eight men burst into the house of Andreas Papandreou, seven with fixed bayonets, one with a machine gun. A commotion followed, and Andreas escaped to the roof, but a soldier found his 14-year-old son, and, holding a gun to the boy's head, forced the younger Papandreou to give up. In the space of some five hours, over 10,000 people were arrested by military squads according to detailed files and planning, and were taken to 'reception centres'.

Colonel Yannis Ladas, the 47-year-old Director of the Greek military police, a year later in an interview took pride in the precision and speed with which the NATO plan had been implemented. 'Within twenty minutes every politician, every man and anarchist who was listed could be rounded up... it was a very simple, diabolic plan.'[29] The Greek population waking up in the morning found first of all that their phones were not working and soon thereafter that the military had taken over control. At 6 a.m. Colonel George Papadopoulos declared through the media that he had taken over power in order to secure democracy, freedom and happiness. Eleven articles of the constitution were suspended. People could now be arrested on the spot and without warrant, to be brought before military courts. Demonstrations and strikes were outlawed and bank deposits were frozen. The new ruler George Papadopoulos had operated as KYP's liaison officer with the CIA ever since 1952 and within the KYP was known to be the trusted man of CIA chief of station Maury. Yet not all officials of the United States agreed with the brutal procedure of the CIA. US Senator Lee Metcalf, days after the coup, criticised the administration of President Johnson sharply when on Capitol Hill he denounced the Greek junta as 'a military regime of collaborators and Nazi sympathisers... [who are] receiving American aid'.[30] And the US ambassador in Athens, Phillips Talbot, complained to Maury one week after the brutal change of power that the US coup represented 'a rape of democracy'. Maury answered: 'How can you rape a whore?'[31]

Due to the direct involvement of the Hellenic Raiding Force the Greek military coup has been labelled 'a Gladio coup'. Only in one other country, namely in Turkey, the secret anti-Communist armies were equally involved in coup d'états. In Italy the Gladio network carried out a 'silent coup' in June 1964 when CIA's trusted General De Lorenzo in operation 'Piano Solo' entered Rome with tanks, armoured personnel carriers, jeeps and grenade launchers while NATO forces staged a large military manoeuvre in the area which led the Socialists to silently abandon their ministerial posts. US historian Bernard Cook has rightly stressed that 'Plan Solo resembles the subsequent Prometheus Plan utilised by Colonel George Papadopoulos in 1967 to impose a military government on Greece. With its intent to destabilise Italy to prevent the advance of the Left, the plan was no more than "a carbon copy of Gladio".'[32] And military expert Collin agrees that 'What De Lorenzo had in mind was a plan similar in its mechanical aspects to the one successfully executed a few years later by Colonel Papadopoulos of Greece.'[33]

The Greek junta consolidated its power through a regime of imprisonment and torture, the like of which had not been seen in Western Europe since the end of the Second World War. Most of those who had been arrested in the first hours after the coup were later moved to police and army cells. Communists, Socialists, artists, academics, journalists, students, politically active women, priests, including their friends and families, were tortured. Their toe and fingernails were torn out. Their feet were beaten with sticks, until the skin came off and the bones were broken. Sharp objects were shoved into vaginas. Filthy rags, often soaked in urine, and sometimes excrement, were pushed down their throats to throttle them, tubes were inserted into their anus and water driven in under very high pressure, and electro shocks were applied to their head.[34] 'We are all democrats here' Inspector Basil Lambro, the chief of the secret police in Athens, was fond of stressing. 'Everybody who comes here talks. You're not spoiling our record.' The sadist torturer made it clear to his victims: 'We are the government, you are nothing. The government isn't alone. Behind the government are the Americans.' If in the mood Basil also offered his analysis of world politics: 'The whole world is in two parts, the Russians and the Americans. We are the Americans. Be grateful we've only tortured you a little. In Russia, they'd kill you.'[35]

The Italian right and their secret soldiers were impressed with how efficiently the Greeks together with the CIA had defeated the left. In April 1968 the Greek colonels invited some 50 Italian right-wingers including notorious Stefano Delle Chiaie to come over to Greece and look for themselves. Upon their return to Italy the secret soldiers escalated the violence and started to place bombs in public places which killed and maimed hundreds and for which they blamed the Italian Communists. The Greek junta was impressed with how efficiently their Italian friends were pushing the country towards a coup d'état and on May 15, 1969 Papadopoulos sent a telegram to congratulate them: 'His excellence the Prime Minister notes that the efforts that have been undertaken for some time in Italy by the national Greek government start to have some impact.'[36]

The military dictatorship in the end imploded due to a near total lack of internal support, after the colonels had engaged in a foreign imperialistic adventure and in 1974 had sponsored a coup in Cyprus, seeking to replace the legitimate left-leaning government of Archbishop Makarios with a puppet regime and annex Cyprus. The Turkish troops in response to the coup invaded the island and waves of violence ensued, killing thousands, leaving the island divided into a Turkish northern and a Greek southern part. The colonels were arrested and dealt with in front of a court, with Papadopoulos being sentenced to death in 1975 for high treason, a verdict later changed into life imprisonment. In a popular vote the Greek monarchy was abolished, and a new constitution was passed.

Andreas Papandreou after his release from the prison cells of the junta and years of exile spent in Canada and Sweden returned to Greece and re-entered politics upon the fall of the dictatorship. He formed the Pan Hellenic Socialist Movement (PASOK), won the elections of 1981 and as Prime Minister formed the first Socialist government of Greek's post-war history. Greece in the same year became a full member of the European Union, but Papandreou kept his radical style and repeatedly threatened to take Greece out of NATO. This he never did, but six years before his death Andreas Papandreou witnessed the exposure of the Gladio network in Italy and was the first former foreign official to confirm that such a secret army had also existed in Greece. With this the scandal crossed the Italian border and started to embarrass governments across the continent. On October 30, 1990 Andreas Papandreou testified to the Greek newspaper *Ta Nea* that it had been in 1984 when he as acting Prime Minister had discovered a secret NATO army in Greece very similar to the Italian Gladio which he had ordered to dissolve. Former Greek Defence Minister Nikos Kouris confirmed that the Greek secret army had been operative throughout the Cold War. 'Our clandestine structure started in 1955', Kouris claimed, 'with a contract between the chief of the Greek special services and the CIA. When I learned about the existence of this unacceptable pact...I informed Andreas Papandreou...and the order was given, to dismantle Red Sheepskin.'[37]

Passionate calls of the Socialist opposition for a parliamentary investigation of the secret army followed in late 1990 but were defeated by the acting conservative government and the conservative New Democracy Party. Defence Minister Ioannis Varvitsiotis in front of parliament was forced to confirm that the information provided by Papandreou was correct and that the CIA and local commandos indeed had set up a secret network, an operation code-named Sheepskin, which had allegedly been 'dismantled in 1988'.[38] Yet Greek Public Order Minister, Yannis Vassiliadis, stressed that the police was not going to investigate 'fantasies', connecting Operation Sheepskin with domestic terrorism. As many others in Europe the Minister in his answers to journalists highlighted the stay-behind function of the Greek secret army, while categorically denying the domestic control function: 'Sheepskin was one of 50 NATO plans which foresaw that when a country was occupied by an enemy there should be an organised resistance. It foresaw arms caches and officers who would form the nucleus of a guerrilla war. In other words, it was a nationally justifiable act.'[39] As nevertheless calls for an investigation intensified Defence Minister Varvitsiotis urged that there was no need for a parliamentary investigation of the Greek secret army, for he himself was going to take care of the delicate affair in his Defence Department. Varvitsiotis trusted a General with the potentially explosive investigation who had served in NATO and as Greek military attaché in Washington. Even before the report on the Greek stay-behind was finished, Varvitsiotis hence was able to assure his fellow ministers that 'The government must not fear anything.'[40]

17

THE SECRET WAR IN TURKEY

The history of the secret army in Turkey is more violent than that of any other stay-behind in Western Europe. Strongly linked to the nationalist movement of the ethnic Türks the violence has roots which go back to the beginning of the twentieth century. During the First World War the large and proud Ottoman Empire broke apart and in 1923 was replaced with the much smaller Turkish republic. Almost the entire population remained Muslim, but violent clashes erupted along the dividing lines of the ethnic groups of Türks, Kurds and Armenians. Representing 80 per cent of the population as well as the ruling elite in the new capital Ankara, the Turkish ethnic group attempted to create a homogenous state by targeting the two other ethnic groups. While the Kurdish ethnic group of some 12 million, divided by the new national borders, lived in parts of Syria, Iran and Iraq the majority dwelled in south eastern Turkey, making up almost 20 per cent of the population of the new republic. In the years following the First World War the much smaller Armenian ethnic group tragically became the target of a Turkish genocide as out of about 2 million Armenians who had lived in the Ottoman Empire only about 200,000 survived while 1,800,000 were killed. During the same period the Kurds also suffered great losses and paid a high death toll. But the Türks were unable to kill all Kurds and the violent battle between the two groups continues also in the twenty-first century.

The violent birth of the new Turkish state also brutally targeted the Turkish Communist Party. In 1921 the entire leadership of the newly founded Communist Party was assassinated and the party was outlawed throughout the century. Nationalist Türks continued to criticise the fact that due to the fall of the Ottoman Empire many ethnic Türks after the First World War were forced to live as 'captive Turks' outside the borders of the new Turkish state. They based their ideology on the so-called Pan Turkism movement which already in the late nineteenth century had hoped to reunite all Turk peoples in a single nation stretching from western China to parts of Spain. After the fall of the Ottoman Empire many of these 'captive Turks' lived in the new Communist Soviet Union and in Cyprus. The destruction of the Soviet Union and Communism hence became an imperative for those Türks who united in the Pan-Turkism movement and hoped to include the captive Türks in an enlarged Turkish state once the Soviet Union was defeated.

Although Turkey was officially neutral during the Second World War, and in order to side with the winners only in 1945 declared war on Germany, the support for Hitler and Mussolini was strong among the nationalists of the Pan-Turkism movement. Under the influence of racial theories of the fascist movement in Germany Pan-Turkism increasingly emphasised the common racial ties of the Turkish people and preached a doctrine of racial superiority.[1] The German invasion of the Soviet Union in 1941 was openly greeted with enthusiasm by the Pan-Turkism movement. And in 1942, anticipating the fall of Stalingrad, Pan-Turkism organisations concentrated troops on the Caucasian border in order to take advantage of the fall of the Soviet Union.[2] The disappointment was widespread when instead of collapsing the Soviet Union emerged as a victor from the Second World War. But when half-a-century later the Soviet Union collapsed in 1991, Pan-Turkism organisations saw to it that a regime supporting the idea of Pan-Turkism was installed in Azerbaijan on Turkey's eastern boarder.[3]

After the end of the Second World War the main priority of the United States with regard to Turkey was to integrate the country solidly within the Western anti-Communist defence system. Due to its geographic location Turkey was a highly valuable strategic territory. Both during and after the Cold War it functioned as an important balcony for US and NATO operations in the oil countries of the Middle East and the Caucuses region, most prominently during the Second Gulf War in 1991. Furthermore the country represented the most eastern land post of NATO during the Cold War. Nobody else, not even Norway in the north, was closer to Moscow and hence Turkey was equipped with high-tech gear and used as a listening post.

As Turkey furthermore guarded a third of NATO's total borders with Warsaw Pact countries, the Turkish elite became an excellent defence contractor for the United States military industry and recipient of billions of US aid. Armed by the United States during the Cold War, Turkey set up the largest armed forces in Europe, and the second largest in NATO after the United States. In a reckless gamble the United States in 1961 stationed even nuclear missiles in Turkey targeting the Soviet Union. When Soviet leader Nikita Khrushchev a year later copied the reckless strategy and stationed nuclear missiles in Cuba targeting the United States, the Cuban Missile Crisis ensued and pushed the world to the brink of nuclear war. President Kennedy resolved the crisis peacefully by promising to remove the Jupiter missiles from Turkey in return for Khrushchev's promise to remove his nuclear missiles from Cuba.[4]

In order to integrate Turkey firmly within NATO the United States had to exploit the dominant and violent Pan-Turkism movement. In this process, which the Pan-Turkism movement in turn used to its own advantage, right-wing extremist Colonel Alparsan Türks played a central role. During the Second World War Colonel Türks had been the contact person of the German Nazis in Turkey. He first came to national prominence in 1944 when he and 30 others were arrested for having participated in an anti-Communist demonstration. Convinced of the theories of racial superiority in general and the superiority of the Türks in particular, Colonel Türks in many of his speeches during his career quoted from Hitler's book *Mein Kampf*. Following the war he made contacts with the CIA in 1948 and allegedly during this time on the orders of the CIA started to set up a secret anti-Communist stay-behind army in Turkey. As the collaboration with the United States intensified, charismatic leader Colonel Türks travelled extensively between his home country and the United States and established intimate contacts both with the Pentagon and the CIA. From 1955 to 1958 he served in Washington in the Turkish military mission to NATO.[5]

When Turkey joined NATO on April 4, 1952 Colonel Türks had already set up a Turkish secret army. Its headquarters was labelled Tactical Mobilisation Group (Seferberlik Taktik Kurulu, STK) and was located in the building of the CIA organisation, American Yardim Heyeti (American Aid Delegation – JUSMATT), in the Bahcelievler district of the Turkish capital Ankara. The Tactical Mobilisation Group was restructured in 1965 and renamed Special Warfare Department (Ozel Harp Dairesi, OHD), the name under which the command centre of the Turkish secret soldiers became known during the 1990 Gladio revelations. Due to this exposure the Special Warfare Department had to change its name once again and today is called Special Forces Command (Ozel Kuvvetler Komutanligi, OKK).[6]

Under the headline 'The Origins of "Gladio" in Turkey' the Paris-based *Intelligence Newsletter* reported in 1990 that they had obtained 'one of the recently declassified original strategy documents engendering the Western European "stay-behind" or "Gladio" network: US Army General Staff's Top-Secret March 28, 1949 Overall Strategic Concepts.' In an adjoining document, JSPC 891/6, section 'Tab B', a specific reference is made to Turkey highlighting how the Pan-Turkism movement could be exploited strategically by the United States. Turkey, according to the Pentagon document, is an 'extremely favourable territory for the establishment of both guerrilla units and Secret Army Reserves. Politically the Turks are strongly nationalistic and anti-Communistic, and the presence of the Red Army in Turks will cause national feeling to run high.' *Intelligence Newsletter* thereafter correctly related that the Turkish secret army called Counter-Guerrilla was run by the Special Warfare Department and consisted of five branches: 'Training Group, including interrogation and psychological warfare techniques; Special Unit, specialised since 1984 in anti-Kurd operations, Special Section, special operations in Cyprus; Coordination Group, also called the Third Bureau; and Administrative Section.'[7]

Despite the change of names during the entire Cold War, the task and strategies of the CIA-funded Special Warfare Department remained the same and consisted in employing violent secret unorthodox warfare in a number of operations, according to the directives of its leaders. In a classic operation to create tensions, Turkish agents of the stay-behind Special Warfare Department on September 6, 1955 threw a bomb into a house in Thessalloniki in Greece that was used as the

Mustafa Kemal Museum and was thus highly esteemed by all Türks. The Turkish stay-behind agents left hardly any trace and blamed the act on the Greek police. The false-flag operation worked and the Turkish government and the press blamed the Greeks for the attack. Promptly, on September 6 and 7, 1955, Turkish fanatical groups fired up by the Counter-Guerrilla wrecked hundreds of Greek homes and business in Istanbul and Izmir, killing 16 Greeks, wounding 32 and raping 200 Greek women in the process.[8]

Officially the task of the Special Warfare Department and its Counter-Guerrilla was: 'To use guerrilla methods and all possible underground activities in the case of a Communist occupation or of a rebellion in order to bring an end to the occupation.'[9] Yet as the stay-behind function was mixed with domestic control and false-flag operations it became increasingly difficult to distinguish the Counter-Guerrillas from classical terrorists. A military accord between the CIA and the Turkish government of Adnan Menderes in 1959 stressed the domestic task of the secret army by specifying that the secret soldiers were to become operational 'also in the case of an internal rebellion against the regime'.[10]

If indeed the secret CIA army had been designed to prevent a coup d'état it was less than entirely successful. For on May 27, 1960 Turkey suffered from a military coup d'état when 38 officers including CIA liaison officer Colonel Türks overthrew the government and arrested Prime Minister Adnan Menderes. Secret warfare expert Selahattin Celik later claimed that far from being a unit designed to protect the Turkish democracy, the Special Warfare Department ranged itself amongst the largest threats to the Turkish democracy as behind its secretive walls the Turkish military had repeatedly conspired against the elected government. Before being promoted to the top-secret Special Warfare Department Turkish military Generals as a rule officially 'retired' in order to serve with low visibility thereafter in the secret command post.[11] 'The most important actions of the Special Warfare Department', Celik concludes, 'were the three military coups'.[12]

While the exact role of the United States in the 1960 coup remains unclear the evidence available as of now suggests that the White House tolerated the coup because it had been assured beforehand that Turkey's membership in NATO was not endangered. 'Although the United States were informed about the coup d'état and due to special bilateral agreements even would have had the legal possibilities to intervene, they did nothing', Fikret Aslan and Kemal Bozay note in their analysis of the Pan-Turkism movement. 'They knew that most of the putschists were not against the United States and NATO.'[13] The Turkish putschists kept their promise and right after the coup the new ruler of Turkey, General Gürsel, emphasised publicly: 'Turkey remains faithful to its Western Alliance.'[14] Secret warfare expert Selahattin Celik too relates that the United States had been informed long before the coup was carried out. 'An officer named Samet Kuscu contacted in 1957 the US embassy in Istanbul and reported that there was going to be a coup d'état and gave the names of the officers which would make the coup.'[15]

After the coup CIA contact man Colonel Türks became the right hand and personal secretary of General Gürsel. Türks oversaw the process in which the democratic structures were destroyed. Arrested Prime Minister Adnan Menderes was killed together with four political leaders, while 449 senior politicians and magistrates were arrested and condemned to serve heavy prison sentences. Thereafter the 38 officers who had carried out the coup started to disagree on how to proceed. While Colonel Türks was eager to promote his Pan-Turkish vision and together with a dozen officers favoured an authoritarian regime, the majority of the coup officers were convinced that a new constitution had to be passed and elections had to be held to restore law and order in the country. Colonel Türks due to his radical beliefs was effectively removed from the political scene by being sent as military attaché to the Turkish embassy in New Delhi in India. The remaining officers wrote a new constitution which the population accepted by vote in July 1961.

Unable to abandon his support for Pan-Turkism, a vision which inspired him throughout his life, Colonel Türks upon coming back from India in May 1963 together with officer Talat Aydemir once again attempted to overthrow the government. The coup failed and Aydemir was sentenced to death while Colonel Türks was arrested and then released 'due to the lack of evidence'.[16] Taking over the traditional Turkish party of the right, the Republican Peasants' Nation Party (RPNP), Colonel Türks immediately after the failed coup re-entered politics, and in 1965 founded the Turkish extreme-right National Action Party MHP (Millietci Hareket Partisi). The foundation of the MHP provided the basis for Colonel Türks' power in the decades to come. With little respect for democratic procedures and non-violent solutions of conflicts Colonel Türks ran an armed right-wing force as the 'Youth Organisation' of the MHP, the notorious Grey Wolves (Bozkurt). Based explicitly on the Pan-Turkism movement, the Grey Wolves derived their name and flag – the head of a Grey Wolf – from the legend that the grey wolfs led the Turk peoples out of Asia to their homeland in Anatolia. As 80 per cent of the population in Turkey belong to the ethnic group of the Türks, Colonel Türks with his nationalist and right-wing ideology was able to capture the hearts and minds of millions. Those who did not admire the Grey Wolves feared them.

The Grey Wolves, far from being a youth organisation, were a brutal network of trained and armed men ready to use violence to further the cause of Pan-Turkism. 'The creed of the Grey Wolves' an article in *Bozkurt*, the official magazine of the organisation, specified the ideology and the strategy of the movement in the following way: 'Who are we? We are the members of the Grey Wolf (Bozkurtcu). What is our ideology? The Turkism of the Grey Wolf (Bozkurt). What is the creed of the Bozkurtcu? They believe, that the Turkish race and the Turkish nation are superior. What is the source of this superiority? The Turkish blood.' With roots going back to the fall of the Ottoman Empire and the division of the Türks into several countries the article stressed the Pan-Turkish struggle: 'Are the Bozkurtcu PanTurks? Yes! It is the holy aim of the Bozkurt Turks to see that the Turkish state grows to become a nation of 65 millions. What justification do you have for this? The Bozkurtcu have a long time ago declared their principles on this issue: You do not receive right, you get it yourself.' In order to attain its aims the Grey Wolves specifically trained to use violence: 'War? Yes, war, if necessary. War is a great and holy principle of nature. We are the sons of warriors. The Bozkurtcu believe that war, militarism and heroism should receive the highest possible esteem and praise.'[17]

It was this national fascist movement which the CIA exploited and supported while running its secret army in Turkey. After the discovery of NATO's secret stay-behind armies across Western Europe in 1990 it was revealed in Turkey that CIA liaison officer Türks had recruited heavily among the Grey Wolves to staff the secret stay-behind army which in Turkey operated under the name Counter-Guerrilla. Yet due to the broad public support which the Grey Wolves enjoyed, and due to their known brutality even in the 1990s few in Turkey and beyond had the courage to address the issue in frank terms. Among those who spoke out was General Talat Turhan. In 1960 Turhan together with other officers had taken part in the coup d'état, four years later he was dismissed from the Turkish army in the rank of General. After the coup of 1971 the military tried to do away with him and the Counter-Guerrilla tortured him as he kept to be most outspoken about the darkest secrets of the Turkish security system. Already then he declared: 'This is the secret unit of the NATO countries', but within the Cold War context of the 1970s nobody was eager to listen.[18]

Turhan survived the Counter-Guerrilla torture and dedicated his life to the research of the Counter-Guerrilla secret army and covert action in Turkey, publishing three books on the topic.[19] 'When it was discovered in 1990 that Italy had an underground organisation called Gladio, organised by NATO and controlled and financed by the CIA, which was linked to acts of terrorism within the country', Turhan recalled, 'Turkish and foreign journalists approached me and published my explanations as they knew that I have been researching the field for 17 years.'[20] Turhan insisted that especially given the continuing succession of non-clarified assassinations in Turkey, a complete investigation and clarification of the activities of the Counter-Guerrilla and its links to the CIA, the Turkish secret service and the Defence Department was extremely urgent. Yet after three military coup d'états it has become something of a truism to observe that the armed military and paramilitary forces and the secret service occupy an unusually powerful role in Turkish society, and hence no such investigation of the Counter-Guerrilla has ever been carried out. 'In Turkey the special forces in the style of Gladio are called Counter-Guerrilla by the public', Turhan explained and urged for an investigation by the European Union, lamenting that 'despite all my efforts and initiatives of political parties, democratic mass organisations and the media the Counter-Guerrilla has still not been investigated'.[21]

The presence of the Grey Wolves among the Counter-Guerrilla was discovered by Turhan first-hand in the notorious torture chambers of the Ziverbey villa in Istanbul's Erenköy district. As of the 1950s the villa was used to 'interrogate' people from the former Socialist countries, especially Yugoslavia and Bulgaria, and it was in this process that the anti-Communist Counter-Guerrilla received its first training in torture techniques. Also in subsequent years the dark chambers of the villa were used extensively as the Counter-Guerrillas murdered or caused permanent damage to hundreds of people. 'In the torture villa in Erenköy in Istanbul the torture team of retired officer Eyüp Ozalkus, chief of the MIT's interrogation team for the combat of Communism, blindfolded me and tied up my arms and feet', Turhan recalled. 'Then they told me that I was now "in the hands of a Counter-Guerrilla unit operating under the high command of the Army outside the constitution and the laws." They told me that they "considered me as their prisoner of war and that I was sentenced to death".'[22] Describing the traumatic experience was one of the main strategies for Turhan to get to terms with what he had lived through: 'In this villa I was with tied up arms and feet chained to a bed for a month and tortured in a way which a human being has difficulty to imagine', he recorded. 'It was under these circumstances that I first was made familiar with the name Counter-Guerrillas', whereupon he also learned of the direct involvement of the Grey Wolves: 'The torturers, which called themselves Counter-Guerrilla, were largely made up of men of the Turkish secret service MIT and of Grey Wolves. Although these facts have been on the agenda of the parliament they have not been clarified to this day [1997].'[23]

Inspired by the Pan-Turkism movement and the racial superiority of the Türks many members of the Turkish military secret service MIT (Milli Istihbaarat Teskilati – National Intelligence Organisation) served in the Counter-Guerrilla and could hardly be distinguished from their Grey Wolves colleagues. The stay-behind research in Turkey discovered that both the MIT and the Counter-Guerrilla units were institutionally united because both were commanded by the notorious and secretive CIA-sponsored Special Warfare Department in Ankara. The special warfare methods taught and commanded by the Special Warfare Department and carried out by the MIT and the Counter-Guerrilla included 'assassinations, bombings, armed robbery, torture, attacks, kidnap, threats, provocation, militia training, hostage-taking, arson, sabotage, propaganda, disinformation, violence and extortion'.[24]

The MIT in 1965 had replaced the MAH secret service (Milli Amele Hizmet, Organisation for national security affairs). Both were dominated by military personnel and strongly dependent on the CIA. A third of the MIT's functionaries during the Cold War were active members of the armed forces while most of the others were retired military officers. As a legal requirement the Director of MIT, appointed by the General Staff or the Special Warfare Department, had to be a member of the armed forces. Turkish civil servants during the Cold War repeatedly criticised the dominant influence of the CIA on the MIT and other Turkish secret services, as well as their notorious habit to interfere clandestinely in politics.

Field Manuals of the US Pentagon, including the top-secret FM 30–31, explicitly stressed that intense cooperation between the US secret service and the Turkish secret service was an essential component of the American influence on the country. 'The success of internal stabilisation operations, which are promoted in the context of strategies for internal defence by the US military secret service, depends to a large extent on the understanding between the US personnel and the personnel of the host country', the Field Manual written for US secret service agents and Special Forces explained. The manual highlighted how the CIA and other US secret services can keep a low profile in the host country by letting the local secret service carry out the dirty work: 'However high the mutual understanding between US personnel and the personnel of the host country might be, the option to win over agents of the secret service of the host country for actions is a much more reliable basis for the solution of the problems of the US military secret service. The recruitment of senior members of the secret service of the host country as long time agents is thus especially important.'[25]

In accordance with the directives of FM 30–31 contacts between the Turkish and the American military and secret services forces were intensively cultivated and under the Military Assistance Program and the International Military Education and Training Program 19,193 Türks received US training between 1950 and 1979.[26] 'As for the recruitment of long time agents the members of the following categories deserve particular attention', FM 30–31 had explicitly stated: 'Officers, that had the opportunity to familiarise with US military training programs, especially those which had been trained directly in the United States.'[27] The CIA was so effective in penetrating the web of Turkish secret services that even the leading officers of the MIT admitted that they were dependent on the White House. Vice Director of MIT Sabahattin Savasman, upon having been arrested on the charge of having cooperated with the CIA, in 1977 declared that such an accusation was ridiculous and ignorant of the most basic facts of the Turkish security system.

'The CIA has a group of at least 20 persons which work together with the MIT and within the MIT are the highest organ', Savasman explained. 'They assure both the exchange of intelligence as well the cooperation in joint operations both within and outside Turkey.' The cooperation, as he insisted, had not begun under his term in office: 'Our secret service has been working together with the CIA ever since the 1950s... all technical equipment that we use has been made available by the CIA. A large part of our personnel has been trained by the CIA abroad. The MIT headquarters was built by the CIA.' Tellingly the CIA had also provided the Türks with the torture equipment: 'The complete equipment of the interrogation chambers from the simplest to the most complex devices stems from the CIA. This I know for I directly worked with it.' The MIT was entirely dependent on the CIA, above all because the CIA paid the bill as Savasman stressed: 'The costs for operations within and outside Turkey are charged to the CIA budget.'[28]

Highlighting that the 'secret service has penetrated the entire fabric of the Turkish society', secret warfare expert Celik has argued that 'the net of secret services is the most influential power in Turkey... the number of persons they employ was never made public in Turkey. But estimates suggest... a massive body of several hundreds of thousands.'[29] Due to this strong US influence on the Turkish security system investigations into the operations of the CIA and MIT have remained scarce. Duane Clarridge, born in 1932 and maybe the most powerful chief of the CIA station in Istanbul during the Cold War, in his 1997 memoirs 'An Agent for All Seasons' has particularly praised MIT agent Hiram Abas for his services. According to his own testimony, Abas 'was closer to him than his own brother'. Clarridge stressed that 'Hiram was one of a kind. In his time he was the best intelligence gatherer in Turkey. All members of the foreign intelligence community who knew him held this view. By the end he was assistant to the chairman of the Turkish intelligence service; he was the first civilian to hold this position.'

Abas had been trained in the United States in covert action operations and as an MIT agent first gained notoriety in Beirut where from 1968 to 1971 he cooperated with the Israeli secret service Mossad and carried out numerous bloody attacks on Palestinians. Sabahattin Savasman, Vice Director of MIT, on trial confirmed that Hiram Abas 'took part in joint operations with the CIA in Lebanon, winning for himself a considerable salary and financial rewards, targeting left-wing youths in the Palestinian camps and receiving bounty for the results he achieved in actions'.[30] Upon his return to Turkey Abas due to his close links with the CIA was constantly promoted within the MIT hierarchy and continued to engage in sensitive terror operations. His career did not stop even when his mentor CIA chief of station Clarridge was transferred to head the CIA station in Italy. Clarridge stayed in touch with Abas, when he served under President Ronald Reagan and CIA chief Bill Casey in 1981. At that time, he worked on the Latin American desk at CIA headquarters in the United States, where he was involved in US sponsorship of the Contras in Nicaragua, an activity he then lied about to the US Congress during the Iran Contra scandal.

In Turkey one of the secret operations in which Turkish CIA agent Abas played a leading role was the so-called Kizildere massacre of March 30, 1972. Abas carried out the operation together with MIT agent Mehmet Eymür, later promoted to direct the MIT's department for counter-espionage, who recalled the day like that: 'We arrived in Unye in the afternoon, along with Nurettin Ersin, a lieutenant-general in service with the MIT, as well as the head of the Ankara department and six or seven other people from Ankara.' The agents used torture to find out the exact location of left-wing militants. 'The MIT representative on duty at the time conducted the necessary talks and ordered the MIT members to take over questioning, and he ordered the gendarmerie, in connection with the results of the questioning, to take charge of arrests as well as the storming.'

Among those seized was left-winger Cayan. 'Cayan and his friends continued their songs and from time to time annoyed the soldiers', Eymür recalled. 'They recognised us from our civilian clothing. They tried to annoy us with expressions like "Uncle Sam's men" and "Fascist MIT members". We were about 150 to 200 meters from them. We also gave them an answer. They tried to influence the soldiers with statements like that they should not obey the orders of fascist generals.'[31] In the ensuing massacre nine left-wing militants were killed. Convinced that violence had to be applied in order to solve some of Turkey's greatest problems, MIT agent Eymür in his memoirs later proudly related how good he had been at using torture during interrogations together with the Counter-Guerrilla in villa Ziverbey.[32] In revenge the Turkish militant left massacred 'Uncle Sam's man' Abas, whereupon former CIA chief of station Clarridge once again came to Turkey in order to visit Abas' grave.[33]

Turkish Counter-Guerrilla expert Celik stressed that although the United States were behind the creation of the Turkish Counter-Guerrilla, and sponsored both the MIT and the Special Warfare Department, it would be simplistic to assume that the White House completely controlled the secret military forces in Turkey during the Cold War. 'It is oversimplified', Celik emphasised, 'to characterise the Counter-Guerrilla as being only a US product reacting purely to US orders'.[34] Due to the very specific nature of Pan-Turkism which accounts for much of the ideology that instilled the Turkish secret soldiers, the secret NATO stay-behind cannot be readily compared with other stay-behinds in Western Europe. 'The definition of the Turkish Counter-Guerrilla is not identical to the one of other NATO countries', Celik underlined. 'It would be wrong to use the same definition, for like that it would remain far behind the actual dimensions', above all the violence of the unit as well as its institutional embedding in the state could be quickly underestimated, 'because in Turkey the Counter-Guerrilla is a mechanism that has penetrated the entire state'.[35] Approaching the same issue from a different angle Turkish Defence Minister General Hasan Esat Isik highlighted the influence of the White House and harshly criticised the subversion of Turkish sovereignty through the US-sponsored Counter-Guerrilla: 'The idea came from the United States. The financing as well...One cannot understand at all how one can reach the point of allowing a foreign nation to monitor organisations in Turkey, to influence and shape them.'[36]

Training for the Counter-Guerrilla secret army was carried out across Turkey in numerous places and also in countries abroad. Paramilitary training centres included the schools at Ankara, Bolu, Kayseri, Buca near Izmir, Canakkale and after 1974 also Cyprus. In the mountain commando school in Bolu US Special Forces including the Green Berets preparing for the war in Vietnam were trained together with the Counter-Guerrilla. Selected Counter-Guerrilla officers were instructed in the USA in the School of the Americas (SOA). The notorious training centre for Special Forces and terrorists had opened in 1946 in Panama and had moved in 1984 to the US Army Fort Benning some 85 miles southeast of Atlanta in Georgia. The school which next to stay-behind officers turned out some 60,000 Latin American soldiers gained world fame as a breeding ground for violence. US Army Major Joseph Blair who taught at the SOA for three years with some regret recalled: 'Officers were taught they can pick [people] up, throw them on the back of a bus, and shoot them in the back of the head.'[37]

The training for the secret soldiers from Europe at SOA included ideological indoctrination during which the stay-behind members were 'shown films which demonstrate the aggression and subversion of the Communists', secret forces scholar Celik relates. Allegedly the SOA terror training centre in the USA was almost identical to the Al Qaida terror training centers of Osama Bin Laden in Afghanistan as far as the methods taught were concerned, 'They learn how to handle explosives under the supervision of Green Berets in Matamoros near the Mexican border, and they are taught how to kill, stab or strangle somebody silently.'[38] Among the instruction manuals was also the notorious classified Field Manual 30–31 together with its appendices FM 30–31A and FM 30–31B written by US terrorism experts of the Pentagon secret service DIA and translated into numerous languages.[39] On some 140 pages the manual offers in non-euphemistic clear-cut language advice for activities in the fields of sabotage, bombing, killing, torture, terror and fake elections.

As maybe its most sensitive advice FM 30–31 instructs the secret soldiers to carry out acts of violence in times of peace and then blame them on the Communist enemy in order to create a situation of fear and alertness. Alternatively, the secret soldiers are instructed to infiltrate the left-wing movements and urge them to use violence: 'There may be times when Host Country Governments show passivity or indecision in the face of Communist subversion and according to the interpretation of the US secret services do not react with sufficient effectiveness', the manual describes the situation when a so-called false flag operation must be applied. 'US army intelligence must have the means of launching special operations which will convince Host Country Governments and public opinion of the reality of the insurgent danger. To reach this aim US army intelligence should seek to penetrate the insurgency by means of agents on special assignment, with the task of forming special action groups among the most radical elements of the insurgency.' The agents within the movement of the enemy were thereafter to escalate the violence to which in turn the regular forces and the Counter-Guerrilla were to react. 'In case it has not been possible to successfully infiltrate such agents into the leadership of the rebels it can be useful to instrumentalise extreme leftist organisations for one's own ends in order to achieve the above described targets.'[40]

FM 30–31 stressed explicitly as its main point that the involvement of the Pentagon had to remain secret under all circumstances: 'These special operations must remain strictly secret. Only those persons which are acting against the revolutionary uprising shall know of the involvement of the US Army in the internal affairs of an allied country. The fact, that the involvement of forces of the US military goes deeper shall not become known under any circumstances.'[41] In order to limit the need-to-know of FM 30–31 and its appendices copies were, as the book stresses, 'strictly limited to the persons named on the distribution list'. At best no paper trail should be left. 'Whenever possible detailed instructions on the basis of this appendix shall be handed on orally. The extremely sensitive character of this affair must be stressed.'[42]

Yet as secrets can never be kept forever the Turkish newspaper *Baris* in 1973 in the midst of a whole range of mysterious acts of violence and brutality which shocked the Turkish society announced the publication of the FM 30–31.

Thereafter the *Baris* journalist who had come into the possession of the secret manual disappeared and was never heard of again. Despite the apparent danger Talat Turhan two years later published a Turkish translation of the top-secret FM 30–31, whereupon publications of the US terror manual appeared also in Spain and Italy.[43] After the discovery of the secret NATO armies across Europe researchers started to investigate the direct link between FM 30–31 and the stay-behind armies. Allan Francovich in his BBC documentary on Gladio presented a copy of FM 30–31B to senior US officials. Ray Cline, Deputy CIA Director for Intelligence in the 1960s, confirmed: 'This is an authentic document.' William Colby, CIA Director from 1973 to 1976 and closely involved with operation Gladio and the stay-behinds in numerous countries of Western Europe, in front of the camera, was reluctant to face this dark side of his country and claimed: 'I have never heard of it.' Also CIA propaganda expert Michael Ledeen shed away from the sensitive document and claimed it to be a Soviet forgery. While Licio Gelli, the Italian Freemason and leader of the anti-Communist P2 frankly told Francovich: 'The CIA gave it to me.'[44]

Violence erupted in Turkey on a scale unseen since the 1920s after on March 12, 1971 the Turkish military right staged its second coup since the end of the Second World War and once again took over power. The decade following the coup was marked by extremely violent conflicts in which the Counter-Guerrilla, the Grey Wolves and the MIT protected by the military and the political right fought the political left as the country sank into a situation resembling outright civil war. The overall death toll of the terror of the 1970s is estimated at 5,000 with right-wing commandos responsible for the majority of murders. A statistics for the year 1978 recorded 3,319 fascist attacks, in which 831 were killed and 3,121 wounded.[45]

Observers noted that the most reactionary faction[!] of the Turkish military, the Air Force, had sent a representative to Washington before the 1971 coup and before the second coup nine years later. While prior to the 1971 coup Muhsin Batur, the commander of the Turkish Air Force, had visited Washington, Air Force commander Tahsin Sahinkaya also undertook the same journey in 1980.[46] Acting Turkish Foreign Minister Ihsan Caglayangil, in office from 1965 to 1971 and from 1975 to 1978, later recalled the coup like that: 'On March 12 the CIA was present, and moreover present in great strength.' Without blaming the CIA directly for having removed him and other ministers during the coup, Caglayangil reflected upon the intimate ties of the CIA with the MIT and the Counter-Guerrilla secret army: 'How will the CIA go about it? The CIA does it through the organic ties it has. I am speaking of the psychological influence it wields among the intelligence community. The CIA is able to pick and choose in my intelligence service without let or hindrance.'[47]

Colonel Talat Turhan accused the United States for having fuelled the brutality from which Turkey suffered in the 1970s by setting up the Special Warfare Department, the Counter-Guerrilla secret army and the MIT and training them according to FM 30–31. 'The suggestions in this directive, most of which are according to my opinion incompatible with the constitution and the laws, were implemented almost entirely after the military coups of March 12, 1971 and September 12, 1980', Turhan criticised and stressed that 'the directives contradict our constitution and prove clearly the politics of intervention of the American secret service'.[48]

As the Counter-Guerrilla stay-behind began to extend its operations Bulent Ecevit, who became Turkish Prime Minister in 1973, also noticed the presence of the clandestine force. According to his own testimony he was startled when in 1974 he first heard of the existence of a secret so-called Special Warfare Department. His surprise increased when the clandestine department asked him for funds which allegedly were needed for a new headquarters. When Ecevit inquired how long the secretive Special Warfare Department had existed and who had funded it the commander of the Turkish army, General Semih Sancar, informed the Prime Minister that the United States had financed the unit ever since the immediate post-war years, and advised Ecevit not to look too closely at the matter for it was touching on the greatest secrets of the state.[49]

Ecevit did not follow the advice of General Sancar and investigated the state budget. Yet there he found no organisation called Special Warfare Department. Upon his insistence he thereafter received a military stay-behind debriefing: 'There are a certain number of volunteer patriots whose names are kept secret and are engaged for life in this special department. They have hidden arms caches in various parts of the country.' Ecevit perceived the danger well and worried that these so-called patriots might follow a right-wing agenda and use their weapons against domestic targets. Yet as he had to acknowledge the realities of Turkey, i.e. the predominance of the military apparatus over the civilian apparatus, he grudgingly consented to the secret operation, released the funds and never discussed the matter with the United States.[50]

The concerns of Ecevit, however, had been well-founded. For the Counter-Guerrilla indeed engaged in domestic terrorism. A prominent massacre took place in 1977. Throughout the terror years of the 1970s the major trade unions of Turkey had organised a protest rally on Istanbul's main Taskim Square on the traditional labour day, the first of May. In 1976, in the face of the continuing and increasing domestic terror, 100,000 had taken part in a peaceful demonstration. And in 1977 at least 500,000 gathered on the square. The horror started as the sun was setting and snipers on surrounding buildings started firing at the speaker's platform. The crowd panicked. Thirty-eight were killed, hundreds were injured. The shooting had lasted for 20 minutes, yet several thousand police at the scene did not intervene.

Turkish CIA agent Hiram Abas, who 'was closer than his own brother' to CIA chief of station Clarridge was personally present on the May Day massacre.[51] The Hotel International, from which the shots were fired belonged to the ITT company which had already been involved in financing the coup against President Allende in Chile in 1973 and was on good terms with the CIA. Three days before May Day the hotel had been emptied of guests and no reservations were accepted. On May 1 a group of foreigners entered the hotel. After the massacre the hotel had been taken over by another company and its name was changed to 'Marmara Hotel'. During the investigation which followed crucial video and audio material suddenly disappeared.[52]

When Bulent Ecevit heard of the massacre he went to President Fahri Koruturk and told him that he thought the Counter-Guerrilla was involved in the terror. 'Koruturk relayed my fears to the then Prime Minister Süleyman Demirel' who had succeeded Ecevit in office and upon hearing the news 'reacted in a very agitated manner' but was unable to challenge the Special Warfare Department.[53] Ecevit stayed alert with regard to the Counter-Guerrilla. Once, at a dinner party with a high-ranking Turkish military officer in eastern Turkey, Ecevit learned that the General had worked in the Special Warfare Department. Ecevit seized the occasion and told the General, 'I have deep suspicions about the civilian extension of that department.' The General assured him, 'The civilians work very honestly, very faithfully. There is nothing to be afraid of.' Ecevit insisted, 'Simply as a hypothesis, it's quite possible, General, that one of those lifetime patriots might at a certain later date become the party chief of the National Action Party MHP which is involved in right-wing terrorism in this very town.' 'Yes, this is the case', the General replied. Adding 'But he's a very nice man.'[54]

Encouraged by Ecevit, Ankara's Deputy State Attorney Dogan Oez followed the lead and investigated the links between Colonel Türks' right-wing party MHP, the Counter-Guerrilla, the Special Warfare Department and the terror that Turkey suffered in the 1970s. In his final report he found that 'Military and civilian security services are behind all this work. The Contra-Guerrilla are subordinate to the Special Warfare Department (Oezel Harp Dairesi).' Furthermore also the MIT was directly involved in the massacres while 'all these activities are guided by MHP members and cadres'.[55] The Attorney had discovered the secret and described it correctly and was thereafter killed on March 24, 1978. His assassin, Grey Wolves member Ibrahim Ciftci, confessed to the crime but mocked the judiciary by claiming that he was untouchable and indeed each time the civilian courts condemned him the highest military court overruled the sentence. The civilian courts were left to note for the record: 'The murder of the state attorney Dogan Oez is an established fact. But we cannot appeal against the decision of the military court. The accused is released.'[56]

Even more than Ciftci, Grey Wolves member Abdullah Catli ranged among the most notorious Counter-Guerrillas during the 1970s. Graduating from street gang violence Catli became a brutal enforcer for the Grey Wolves as a member of the Counter-Guerrilla operating under the direction of the Special Warfare Department. After the military coup in 1971 Catli rose quickly within their ranks, emerging second in command in 1978. It was in that year that he had to go underground because the police had linked him to the murder of seven left-wing activists. Supported by other right-wing terrorists Catli linked up with notorious Italian right-wing terrorist Stefano Delle Chiaie and together they travelled to

Latin America and the United States.[57] Closely linked to terror operations in Turkey and abroad Catli cultivated excellent contacts with the Turkish elite. He died near Susurluk on November 3, 1996 in a car crash together with high officials of the Turkish state. [58]

Another feared Grey Wolf was Haluk Kirci, nicknamed 'Idi Amin' by his colleagues after the dictator of Uganda, who in the 1970s had slaughtered thousands. Aged 20 and a student at Ankara University, Kirci was a fervent follower of Alparsan Türks' anti-Communist Pan-Turkish ideology. On October 8, 1978 he carried out the Bahcelievler massacre executing seven students of the leftist, non-militant Turkish Worker's Party (TIP). Kirici, internationally wanted for mass murder, later recalled the massacre in his memoirs: 'I went and took the two out of the car and put them face down on the floor. Then I fired three bullets each through their heads. Then we went back to that apartment. There the other five were lying without conscience on the floor... First I had tried to strangle one of them with a wire, but this did not work. Then I choked him with a towel.'[59] When Grey Wolves leader Catli died in the Susurluk accident in 1996 Kirci and a group of bodyguards were in the car behind Catli's Mercedes. Seeing Catli smashed inside the Mercedes Kirici in total panic phoned a set of numbers of leading Grey Wolves figures, asking for help and shouting 'The Chief is gravely wounded. He is dying.' In vain. Catli died and Kirici took over the leadership of the Grey Wolves.[60]

Next to Catli the most famous Grey Wolf and Counter-Guerrilla member was his friend Ali Agca, who became world famous when on May 13, 1981 he shot John Paul II in St Peter's Square in Rome. The Pope was gravely wounded, but survived. During his student years in the late 1970s Agca had been a well-known fascist militant, who allegedly in one of his less-violent operations had shot two students in their legs during an attack on a leftist hostel. His notoriety in terrorist circles was such that leftists tried to kill him on a number of occasions. Together with Catli, Agca participated in the killing of Turkey's most prominent newspaper editor, Abdi Ipekci on February 1, 1979. Ipekci had been deeply concerned about the domestic terror of the Turkish right and the support it enjoyed from the CIA and allegedly had urged CIA chief of station Paul Henze to stop the violence. Ipekci belonged to those Turkish journalists who risked their lives when revealing the darkest secrets of the state and the source of most of the violence. Ugur Mumcu was also among them. During his torture he was informed: 'We are the Counter-Guerrilla. Even the President of the republic cannot touch us.' Mumcu continued to expose the Counter-Guerrilla by writing in the daily *Cumhuriyet*, whereupon he was killed by a car bomb in 1993.[61]

After the assassination of editor Ipecki, Agca was arrested and he quickly confessed to the crime. Yet when he threatened in court to name 'the truly responsible parties' the signal was clear enough and the next day a group of Grey Wolves smuggled Agca through eight checkpoints out of a high security prison. After his attack on the Pope he was once again arrested. Testifying in Rome in September 1985 Catli disclosed that he had supplied Agca with fake IDs and had given him the pistol that wounded the pontiff. Had the Grey Wolves been seriously investigated in the wake of their assassination attempt on the Pope, the Turkish stay-behind Counter-Guerrilla most certainly would have been exposed. Yet this did not happen as the CIA in order to divert attention blamed the KGB to have recruited the Grey Wolves for the operation.[62]

When Ecevit, who had long been worried about the brutal operations of the Turkish stay-behind Counter-Guerrilla, became Prime Minister in 1977 he complained towards Army Chief of Staff General Kenan Evren: 'During the Kizildere incidents the Special Warfare Department is said to have been used. I am worried about this civilian organisation. There is no means of knowing or controlling what a young recruit may get up to after twenty years in such an organisation.' To which Evren allegedly replied: 'There is nothing to worry about. We will deal with it.' Thereafter Ecevit declared publicly that 'We must all be respectful towards the Turkish Armed Forces and help them in the realisation of their desire to remain out of politics.'[63]

General Evren kept his promise. The military coup came on September 12, 1980 when Evren seized power while NATO's Allied Mobile Force in Turkey carried out its manoeuvre Anviel Express.[64] A right-wing extremist on trial later plausibly argued that the massacres and terrors of the 1970s had been a strategy to bring Evren and the military right to power: 'The massacres were a provocation by the MIT. With the provocations by the MIT and the CIA the ground was prepared for the September 12 coup.'[65] Later it was found that General Evren at the time of the coup had presided the Special Warfare Department and commanded the Counter-Guerrilla secret army. As General Evren changed the battle dress for suit and tie and made himself President of Turkey all terrorist attacks miraculously came to a halt all of a sudden.[66]

US President Carter was at the opera when the coup in Turkey took place. When he heard about it he called Paul Henze, former Chief of the CIA station in Turkey who had left Ankara shortly before the coup to become a security adviser to President Carter in Washington on the Turkey desk of the CIA. On the phone Carter told Henze what the latter already knew: 'Your people have just made a coup!'[67] The President was right. Paul Henze, the day after the coup, had triumphantly declared to his CIA colleagues in Washington: 'Our boys have done it!'[68] Henze, according to Counter-Guerrilla expert Celik, 'was the chief architect of the September 12, 1980 coup'.[69] Years later Carter commented that 'before the September 12 movement [sic], Turkey was in a critical situation with regard to its defences. After the intervention in Afghanistan and the overthrow of the Iranian monarchy, the movement for stabilisation in Turkey came as a relief to us.'[70]

Carter's National Security Adviser Zbigniew Brzezinski supported the position of Henze. During a discussion in the National Security Council of the situation in Iran where in 1979 Khomeiny had seized power Brzezinski expressed his view that 'for Turkey as for Brazil a military government would be the best solution'.[71] The international press reported the day after the coup that a spokesperson of the

Foreign Ministry in Washington 'has confirmed that the United States had been informed before the coup d'état by the military that they were going to take over power'. Turkish military officers declared that the Turkish military would not intervene unless they had previous consent from Washington.[72]

At the time of the military coup d'état there were some 1,700 Grey Wolves organisations in Turkey with about 200,000 registered members and a million sympathisers.[73] They had been a formidable asset for the strategy of tension operations in the 1970s which paved the way for the coup. Now they represented a security risk and General Evren in an attempt to consolidate his power outlawed the right-wing MHP party and arrested Colonel Türks and other members of the MHP as well as numerous Grey Wolves. In its indictment of the MHP in May 1981 the Turkish military government charged 220 members of the MHP party and its affiliates with the responsibility for 694 murders.[74]

Despite his arrest the popularity of Colonel Türks remained high, and when on April 4, 1997 he died from a heart failure in a Turkish hospital half a million gathered at his funeral while Grey Wolves organised flights from all over the world. Islamic Prime Minister Necmettin Erbakan explained that Türks had greatly shaped the recent history of Turkey and 'that until his death he had marked the political life in Turkey greatly and with his loyal services always deserved the highest praise'. Foreign Minister Tansu Ciller added to the praise when she declared that 'Türks was a historical personality. He deserves a special place in our democratic history. I was always in excellent contact with him.' While former police chief Kemal Yazicioglu stressed: 'My Chief Wolf! I have learned everything from you!'[75]

After numerous arrests the Turkish prisons filled with Grey Wolves terrorists, whereupon agents of the MIT came to visit their former brothers in arms and made them an attractive offer: the release from prison plus assured income if they agreed to fight the Kurdish minority in the south east of Turkey.[76] Many accepted and started to combat the left-wing Kurdish militant movement PKK which in 1984 had taken up arms after thousands had been tortured in the previous years. As hatred and radical violence increased on both sides the conflict dragged on. Allegedly also the Turkish stay-behind Counter-Guerrilla was involved in the conflict in which 25,000 died on both sides while millions of Kurds were displaced as Ankara was supported with guns, helicopters and jet fighters from the United States. The families of the victims were not amused when US President Bill Clinton called Turkey a 'shining example to the world of the virtues of cultural diversity'.[77]

Until today the involvement of NATO's stay-behind in the massacres against the Kurds ranges among the greatest secrets in Turkey and in Washington. Major Cem Ersever, a former commander of Turkish paramilitary units that had operated against the PKK later quite openly described in his book how the Counter-Guerrilla and other paramilitary units employed secret warfare and terror against the PKK. Ersever also revealed how his terror units became rich by raising private taxes along the 'Heroin Highway' as the drugs coming from

Afghanistan on their way to the west had to pass through Turkey. Among the operations of the Counter-Guerrilla which Ersever revealed were the false flag operations in which the Counter-Guerrilla, dressed up as PKK fighters, attacked villages, raped and executed people randomly. This, if the disguise was effective, weakened the support for the PKK in the area and turned the people against the PKK. Ersever confirmed that many former Grey Wolves and other right-wing extremists had been recruited directly from prisons into the stay-behind death squads, which also included captured PKK deserters and Islamists. Ersever had described the situation correctly and after the publication of his book in November 1993 was executed following the classical Counter-Guerrilla method: Tortured and shot through the head Ersever's body was found with his hands bound behind his back.[78]

The Turkish secret army Counter-Guerrilla remained operative also after the discovery of the secret stay-behind armies of NATO across Western Europe. Like a cancer the paramilitaries had become so deeply embedded in the Turkish system that they could no longer be simply closed down. After the revelations of Italian Prime Minister Giulio Andreotti on the secret NATO army the military government in Turkey also had to take a stand. On December 3, 1990 General Dogan Beyazit, President of the Operations Department (Harekat Dairesi) of the Turkish military, and General Kemal Yilmaz, Chief of the Turkish Special Forces (Ozel Kuvvetler), reacted to public pressure and issued a press statement. In it they admitted the existence of secret NATO troops in Turkey explaining that the secret unit was directed by the Special Warfare Department (Ozel Harp Dairesi), with the task 'to organise resistance in the case of a Communist occupation'.[79]

The Generals stressed that the members of the Turkish Gladio were all good 'patriots'. This officially confirmed the report of journalist Mehmet Ali Birand, who already on November 13 1990 had reported in the Turkish independent daily *Milliyet*, that Turkey, too, had a secret Gladio army. Birand quoted former Prime Minister Bulent Ecevit as saying that the secret unit had first been funded by the United States, and that 'patriotic volunteers were members of the group. They were trained specially to launch a counter guerrilla operation in the event that the country was occupied.'[80] Next to Ecevit also Jaques Santer, Prime Minister of Luxemburg, had on November 13 revealed: 'The name of the secret organisation in Turkey is Counter-Guerrilla.'[81] Also former CIA Director William Colby confirmed: 'As Turkey is a NATO member, the existence of such an organisation is very probable.'[82] As always Colby had insisted that the aim had been to fight Communism, despite the fact that the Turkish Communist Party had been outlawed throughout the Cold War: 'In order to prevent Turkey from falling into the hands of the Communists, anti-Communist organisations are being supported.'[83]

In Switzerland the *Neue Zürcher Zeitung* headlined: 'Doubts on the credibility of the State. Unmasking of a Secret Army in Turkey', and reported that the Counter-Guerrilla had their headquarters in the building of the US military secret service DIA in Turkey.[84] The German news magazine *Der Spiegel* with a long report on Gladio highlighted the parallels between the Greek and the Turkish Gladio reporting that in both countries the secret stay-behind forces had been involved in the military coup d'états. The German magazine highlighted that the Special Warfare Department's Counter-Guerrilla squads had been directly involved in the 1980 military coup d'état, similar to the Gladio network in Greece in 1967.

But while the international press pondered on the question of how directly NATO and the US Pentagon had sponsored the massacres in Turkey, the ruling military in Turkey in 1990 blocked all further investigations. There was no parliamentary commission to investigate either the Counter-Guerrilla stay-behind or the Special Warfare Department. The ruling military also refused to answer questions from both parliament and Ministers and Turkish Defence Minister Giray, deposed a month before the Gladio scandal, insisted that 'Ecevit had better keep his fucking mouth shut! [sic].'[85]

In 1992 the commander of the Special Warfare Department, General Kemal Yilmaz assured journalists that, 'The department is still active in security operations against armed members of the PKK in Turkey's south-eastern provinces.'[86] As the Counter-Guerrilla continued its operations even the US State Department in its 1995 human rights report noticed that in Turkey 'Prominent credible human rights organisations, Kurdish leaders, and local Kurd asserted that the government acquiesces in, or even carries out, the murder of civilians.' The report of the State Department noted that 'Human rights groups reported the widespread and credible belief that a Counter-Guerrilla group associated with the security forces had carried out at least some "mystery killings".'[87] New York journalist Lucy Komisar in 1990 had tried to gain more information from the democratic institutions of her country: 'As for Washington's role, Pentagon would not tell me whether it was still providing funds or other aid to the Special Warfare Department; in fact, it wouldn't answer any questions about it', Komisar reported. 'I was told by officials variously that they knew nothing about it, that it happened too long ago for there to be any records available, or that what I described was a CIA operation for which they could provide no information. One Pentagon historian said, "Oh, you mean the stay-behind organisation. That's classified".'[88]

If the Pentagon had hoped that the sensitive affair of the secret armies in Western Europe, in general, and in Turkey, in particular, would go away, it was mistaken. The case resurfaced in the form of an unusual accident. On November 3, 1996 a speeding black Mercedes hit a tractor and overturned on a remote highway near the Turkish village of Susurluk, some 100 miles south of Istanbul. Three of its four passengers were killed: A high-ranking police officer who commanded Turkish counter-insurgency units named Husseyin Kocadag, a convicted fugitive wanted for murder and drug trafficking who directed the Grey Wolves named Abdulla Catli, and Catli's girlfriend Gonca Us, a former Turkish beauty queen turned Mafia hit-woman. The only survivor was Sedat Bucak, a right-wing member of the Turkish parliament and warlord whose militia had been armed and financed by the Turkish government to fight the Kurds. A policeman, a parliamentarian, a druglord and a hit-woman were a somewhat unusual combination of passengers as the press immediately noticed and former Prime Minister Bulent

Ecevit rightly commented to parliament that 'The accident unveiled the dark liaisons within the state.'[89]

Following the accident Turkey witnessed maybe its strongest movement against the Counter-Guerrilla and corrupt governmental officials when every night at 9 p.m. angry crowds called for 'cleansing the country from the gangs'. For weeks on end the press and the TV channels were dominated by the scandal and the newest revelations of the corrupt 'Susurluk state'. Nearly 100,000 workers marched in protest in the Turkish capital demanding the truth about the stay-behind soldiers while people on the streets in opinion polls expressed their belief that the Turkish judicial system was not working properly and that the government was corrupt, declaring that they were sick and tired of all the violence and secret operations. Millions followed the country-wide protest action 'One minute of darkness for complete Clarification' and in protest switched off all lights each evening at 9 p.m. for over a month and thus darkened whole cities.[90]

The *Washington Post* picked up the Susurluk story and its relations to the Counter-Guerrilla and reported that 'there are people here who have personal nightmares, stories of killings, torture, kidnappings and other crimes against them or their families' and in a somewhat less well-researched paragraph added that the United States 'has been critical of human rights abuses committed by the government'.[91] Meanwhile *The New York Times* commented: 'Now, with new information emerging almost daily and the press and the public talking of little else, evidence suggests that officially sanctioned criminality may have reached levels few had imagined.'[92]

Turkish President Suleyman Demirel in front of the press confirmed the obvious when he declared that 'claims are of a highly serious nature' according to which there exists within the Turkish state 'a special operations section at the General Directorate of Security. Some staff members of that section have been engaged in narcotics trading, gambling schemes, extortion and murder...These are murderers working under orders from the state.'[93] While Prime Minister Erbakan stressed: 'You cannot have a gang within the state. Nobody can be allowed to do anything illegal, with no exceptions. Nothing, including fighting the PKK, can be an excuse for crime. If such things happen, those gangs, whatever their makeup, must be disbanded.'[94] The press sharply attacked the secret service and declared that the 'MIT does not just engage in repression and terror against the people. It is involved in every kind of dirty business, such as the drugs trade, extortion and prostitution...the MIT bears responsibility for the disappeared, for massacres and torture.'[95]

Together with the MIT also the CIA came into the line of fire when the press highlighted the intimate relationship between the two secret services. Amongst growing criticism MIT Under-secretary Sonmez Koksal declared: 'Why should the MIT apologise? The MIT would do no such things on its own without securing permission from a political authority. The MIT is a state organ.'[96] In Parliament Fikri Saglar of the Republican People's Party (CHP) stressed that 'The links between the illegal right-wing organisations and the Turkish security should be traced back to Gladio...Unless the operations of Gladio, the NATO-linked international counterinsurgency organisation within the Turkish security system, is investigated, the real source of the security corruption will not be effectively discovered. It is necessary to investigate the Special Forces Command, previously known as the Special Warfare Department of the Chief of Staff.'[97]

The suggestion was wise, but it was not followed as parliament decided to investigate the Susurluk scandal only. In January 1998 new Prime Minister Mesut Ylmaz had the pleasure to inform millions of television viewers in Turkey on the results of the seven-month-long parliamentary investigation into the Susurluk scandal. 'It is the anatomy of a disgraceful mess', he declared and confirmed that 'An execution squad was firmed within the state.' He concluded by admitting that 'All parts of the state were aware of what was going on.'[98] As the government remained vague the Turkish Human Rights Association (IHD) concluded that 'Through the facts that have emerged in the wake of the Susurluk accident there are around 3,500 crimes of the Counter-Guerrilla, which have been committed with the support of the state and which are covered up until today by the state', whereupon IHD President Akin Birdal was shot at in May 1998 but survived gravely wounded.[99] Researcher Martin Lee with a focus on fascist movements found that 'US sponsored stay-behind operatives in Turkey and several European countries used their skills to attack domestic opponents and forment violent disorders. Some of those attacks were intended to spark right-wing military coups.' Witnessing the inability of the Türks to eradicate the terror without the help of the White House and the Pentagon, Lee concluded: 'Across the Atlantic in Washington, the US government has yet to acknowledge any responsibility for the Turkish Frankenstein that US Cold War strategy helped to create. When asked about the Susurluk affair, a State Department spokesperson said it was "an internal Turkish matter". He declined further comment.'[100]

CONCLUSION

'Prudent Precaution or source of Terror?' the international press pointedly asked when the secret stay-behind armies of NATO were discovered across Western Europe following the Gladio revelations in Italy in late 1990.[1] After more than ten years of research and investigation the answer is now clear: Both.

The secret stay-behind armies of NATO were a prudent precaution, as the available documents and testimonies amply demonstrate. Based on the experiences of the Second World War and the rapid and traumatic occupation of most European countries by the German and Italian forces, military experts feared the Soviet Union and became convinced that a stay-behind army could be of strategic value when it came to the liberation of the occupied territory. Behind enemy lines the secret army could have strengthened the resistance spirit of the population, helped in the running of an organised and armed national resistance, sabotaged and harassed the occupying forces, exfiltrated shot down pilots, and gathered intelligence for the government in exile.

Based on the fear of a potential invasion after the Second World War highly placed officials in the national European governments, in the European military secret services, in NATO as well as in the CIA and the MI6 therefore decided that a secret resistance network had to be set up already during peacetime. On a lower level in the hierarchy citizens and military officers in numerous countries of Western Europe shared this assessment, joined the conspiracy and secretly trained for the emergency. These preparations were not limited to the 16 NATO member countries, but included also the four neutral countries in Western Europe, namely Austria, Finland, Sweden and Switzerland, on which the author is preparing a second publication. In retrospect it has become obvious that the fear was without reason and the training had been futile for the invasion of the Red Army never came. Yet such a certainty was not available at the time. And it is telling that the cover of the network, despite repeated exposures in many countries during the entire Cold War, was only blown completely at exactly the same moment when the Cold War ended and the Soviet Union collapsed.

The secret stay-behind armies of NATO, however, were also a source of terror, as the evidence available now shows. It has been this second feature of the secret war that has attracted a lot of attention and criticism in the last decade, and which in the future will need more investigation and research. As of now the evidence indicates that the governments of the United States and Great Britain after the end of the Second World War feared not only a Soviet invasion, but also the Communist Parties, and to a lesser degree the Socialist Parties. The White House and Downing Street feared that in several countries of Western Europe, and above all in Italy, France, Belgium, Finland and Greece, the Communists might reach positions of influence in the executive and destroy the military alliance NATO from within by betraying military secrets to the Soviet Union. It was in this sense that the Pentagon in Washington together with the CIA, MI6 and NATO in a secret war set up and operated the stay-behind armies as an instrument to manipulate and control the democracies of Western Europe from within, unknown to both European populations and parliaments. This strategy lead to terror and fear, as well as to 'humiliation and maltreatment of democratic institutions', as the European press correctly criticised.[2]

Experts of the Cold War will note that Operation Gladio and NATO's stay-behind armies cast a new light on the question of sovereignty in Western Europe. It is now clear that as the Cold War divided Europe, brutality and terror was employed to control populations on both sides of the Iron Curtain. As far as Eastern Europe is concerned, this fact has long been recognised, long before it had been openly declared. After the Red Army had in 1968 mercilessly crushed the social reforms in Prag, Soviet leader Leonid Breschnew in Moscow with his infamous 'Breschnew doctrine' had openly declared that the countries of Eastern Europe were only allowed to enjoy 'limited sovereignty'. As far as Western Europe is concerned the conviction of being sovereign and independent was shattered more recently. The data from Operation Gladio and NATO's stay-behind armies indicates a more subtle and hidden strategy to manipulate and limit the sovereignty, with great differences from country to country. Yet a limitation of sovereignty it was. And in each case where the stay-behind network in the absence of a Soviet invasion functioned as a straightjacket for the democracies of Western Europe, Operation Gladio was the Breschnew doctrine of Washington.

The strategic rationale to protect NATO from within cannot be brushed aside lightly. But the manipulation of the democracies of Western Europe by Washington and London on a level which many in the European Union still today find difficult to believe clearly violated the rule of law and will require further debate and investigation. In some operations the secret stay-behind soldiers together with the secret military services monitored and filed left-wing politicians and spread anti-Communist propaganda. In more violent operations the secret war led to bloodshed. Tragically the secret warriors linked up with right-wing terrorists, a combination that led – in some countries including at least Belgium, Italy, France, Portugal, Spain, Greece and Turkey – to massacres, torture, coup d'états and other violent acts. Most of these state-sponsored terrorist operations, as the subsequent cover-ups and fake trials suggest, enjoyed the encouragement and protection of selected highly placed governmental and military officials in Europe and in the United States. Members of the security apparatus and the government on both sides of the Atlantic who themselves despise being linked up with right-wing terrorism must in the future bring more clarity and understanding into these tragic dimensions of the secret Cold War in Western Europe.

If Cold War experts will derive new data from NATO's stay-behind network for their discourse on limited sovereignty during the Cold War, then international legal experts and analysts of dysfunctions of democracies will find data on the breakdown of checks and balances within each nation. The Gladio data indicates that the legislative was unable to control the more hidden branches of the executive, and that parliamentary control of secret services is often non-existing or dysfunctional in democracies on both sides of the Atlantic. Totalitarian states have long been known to have operated a great variety of largely uncontrolled and unaccountable secret services and secret armies. Yet to discover such serious dysfunctions also in numerous democracies comes as a great surprise, to say the least.

Within this debate of checks and balances military officials have been correct to point out after the discovery of Operation Gladio and NATO's stay-behind network that there can never be such a thing as a 'transparent stay-behind army', for such a network would be exposed immediately in case of invasion and its members would be killed by the invasion force. Parliamentarians and constitutional lawyers meanwhile have been equally correct to emphasise that both the armed forces and the secret services of a democracy must at all times be transparent, accountable, controlled and supervised closely by civilian representatives of the people as they represent the most powerful instruments of the state.

This clash between mandatory secrecy and mandatory transparency, which lies at the heart of the Gladio phenomenon, directly points to the more general question of how much secrecy should be granted to the executive branch of a democracy. Judged from the Gladio evidence, where a lack of transparency and accountability has lead to corruption, abuse and terror, the answer is clear: The executive should be granted no secrecy and should at all times be controlled by the legislative. For a secret government, as it manifested itself in the United States and parts of Western Europe, can lead to abuse and even state terrorism. 'The growth of Intelligence abuses reflects a more general failure of our basic institutions', US Senator Frank Church had wisely noted after a detailed investigation of CIA covert operations already in the 1970s. Gladio repeats this warning with a vengance.

It can hardly be overemphasised that running a secret army and funding an unaccountable intelligence service entails grave risks every democracy should seek to avoid. For the risks do not only include uncontrolled violence against groups of citizens, but mass manipulation of entire countries or continents. Among the most far-reaching findings on the secret war, as seen in the analysis, ranges the fact that the stay-behind network had served as a tool to spread fear amongst the population also in the absence of an invasion. The secret armies in some cases functioned as an almost perfect manipulation system that transported the fears of high-ranking military officers in the Pentagon and NATO to the populations in Western Europe. European citizens, as the strategists in the Pentagon saw it, due to their limited vision were unable to perceive the real and present danger of

CONCLUSION

Communism, and therefore they had to be manipulated. By killing innocent citizens on market squares or in supermarkets and blaming the crime on the Communists the secret armies together with convinced right-wing terrorists effectively translated the fears of Pentagon strategists into very real fears of European citizens.

The destructive spiral of manipulation, fear and violence did not end with the fall of the Soviet Union and the discovery of the secret armies in 1990, but on the contrary gained momentum. Ever since the vicious terrorist attacks on the population of the United States on September 11, 2001 and the beginning of the 'War on Terrorism' fear and violence dominate not only the headlines across the globe but also the consciousness of millions. In the West the 'evil Communist' of the Cold War era has swiftly been replaced with the 'evil Islamist' of the war on terrorism era. With almost 3,000 civilians killed on September 11, and several thousands killed in the US-led war on terrorism so far with no end in sight, a new level of brutality has been reached.

Such an environment of fear, as the Gladio evidence shows, is ideally suited to manipulate the masses on both sides into more radical positions. Osama Bin Laden and his Al Qaida terror network manipulated millions of Muslims, above all young male adults, to take up a radical position and believe in violence. On the other side also the White House and the administration of George Bush junior has fuelled the spiral of violence and fear and lead millions of Christians and seculars in the United States and in Europe to believe in the necessity and justice of killing other human beings in order to enhance their own security. Yet human security is not being advanced, but on the contrary decays, as the atmosphere is drenched with manipulation, violence and fear. Where the manipulation and the violence originate from and where they lead to, is at times very difficult to dissect. Hitler and the Nazis had profited greatly from manipulation and the fear in the wake of the mysterious Reichstagsbrand in Berlin in 1933, whereupon the Third Reich and Second World War followed. In 2001 the war on terrorism began, and once again radical critics have argued that the White House had manipulated 9/11, the largest terrorist attack in history, for geostrategic purposes.[3]

As people across the globe share a vague sensation 'that it cannot go on like that' many search for an exit strategy from the spiral of violence, fear and manipulation. In Europe a consensus is building that terrorism cannot be defeated by war, as the latter feeds the spiral of violence, and hence the war on terrorism is not part of the solution but part of the problem. Furthermore also more high-tech – from retina scanning to smart containers – seems unable to really protect potential targets from terror attacks. More technology might even increase the challenges ahead when exploited for terrorist purposes and asymmetric warfare, a development observable ever since the invention of dynamite in the nineteenth century. Arguably more technology and more violence will therefore not solve the challenges ahead.

A potential exit strategy from the spiral of fear, manipulation and violence might have to focus on the individual human being itself and a change of consciousness. Given its free will the individual can decide to focus on non-violent solutions of given problems and promote a dialogue of understanding and forgiveness in order to reduce extremist positions. The individual can break free from fear and manipulation by consciously concentrating on his or her very own feelings, thoughts, words and actions, and by focusing all of them on peaceful solutions. As more secrecy and more bloodshed are unlikely to solve the problems ahead the new millennium seems a particularly adequate time to begin with such a shift in consciousness which can have positive effects both for the world and for oneself.

CHRONOLOGY

1940

In England, Prime Minister Winston Churchill creates the secret stay-behind army Special Operations Executive (SOE) to set Europe ablaze by assisting resistance movements and carrying out subversive operations in enemy-held territory. After the end of the Second World War the stay-behind armies are created on the experiences and strategies of SOE with the involvement of former SOE officers.

1944

London and Washington agree on the importance of keeping Western Europe free from Communism. In Greece the first secret stay-behind army is being set up under the label LOK. As large Communist demonstration taking place in Athens against British interference in the post-war government is dissolved by gunfire of secret soldiers leaving 25 protesters dead and 148 wounded.

1945

In Finland, Communist Interior Minister Leino exposes a secret stay-behind which is closed down.

1947

In the United States, President Harry Truman creates the NSC and the CIA. The covert action branch of the CIA, the OPC under Frank Wisner sets up stay-behind armies in Western Europe.

1947

In France, Interior Minister Edouard Depreux reveals the existence of a secret stay-behind army in France code-named 'Plan Bleu'.

1947

In Austria, a secret stay-behind is exposed which had been set up by right-wing extremists Soucek and Rössner. Chancellor Körner pardons the accused under mysterious circumstances.

1948

In France, the 'Western Union Clandestine Committee' (WUCC) is created to coordinate secret anti-Communist unorthodox warfare. After the creation of NATO a year later the WUCC is integrated into the military alliance under the name 'Clandestine Planning Committee' (CPC).

1949

NATO is founded and the European headquarters is established in France.

1951

In Sweden, CIA agent William Colby based at the CIA station in Stockholm supports the training of stay-behind armies in neutral Sweden and Finland and in the NATO member countries Norway and Denmark.

1952

In Germany, former SS officer Hans Otto reveals to the criminal police in the city of Frankfurt in Hessen the existence of the fascist German stay-behind army BDJ-TD. The arrested right-wing extremists are found not guilty under mysterious circumstances.

1953

In Sweden, the police arrests right-winger Otto Hallberg and discovers the Swedish stay-behind army. Hallberg is set free and charges against him are mysteriously dropped.

1957

In Norway, the Director of the secret service NIS, Vilhelm Evang, protests strongly against the domestic subversion of his country through the United States and NATO and temporarily withdraws the Norwegian stay-behind army from the CPC meetings.

1958

In France, NATO founds the ACC to coordinate secret warfare and the stay-behind armies. When NATO in 1966 is expelled from France and establishes its new European headquarters in Brussels, the ACC under the code name SDRA11 is hidden within the Belgian military secret service SGR with its headquarters next to NATO.

1960

In Turkey, the military supported by secret armies stages a coup d'état and kills Prime Minister Adnan Menderes.

1961

In Algeria, members of the French stay-behind and officers from the French War in Vietnam found the illegal OAS and with CIA support stage a coup in Algiers against the French government of de Gaulle which fails.

1964

In Italy, the secret stay-behind army Gladio is involved in a silent coup d'état when General Giovanni de Lorenzo in Operation Solo forces a group of Socialist Ministers to leave the government.

1965

In Austria, police forces discover a stay-behind arms cache in an old mine close to Windisch-Bleiberg and force the British authorities to hand over a list with the location of 33 other MI6 arms caches in Austria.

1966

In Portugal, the CIA sets up Aginter Press which under the direction of Captain Yves Guerin Serac runs a secret stay-behind army and trains its members in covert action techniques including hands-on bomb terrorism, silent assassination, subversion techniques, clandestine communication and infiltration and colonial warfare.

1966

In France, President Charles de Gaulle forces NATO to leave french soil. As the military alliance moves to Brussels secret NATO protocols are revealed that allegedly protect right-wingers in anti-Communist stay-behind armies.

1967

In Greece, the stay-behind army Hellenic Raiding Force takes control over the Greek Defence Ministry and starts a military coup d'état installing a right-wing dictatorship.

1968

In Sweden, a British MI6 agent closely involved with the stay-behind army betrays the secret network to the Soviet secret service KGB.

1969

In Mocambique, the Portuguese stay-behind army Aginter Press assassinates Eduardo Mondlane, President of the Mocambique liberation party and leader of the FRELIMO movement.

1969

In Italy, the Piazza Fontana massacre in Milan kills 16 and injures and maims 80 and is blamed on the left. Thirty years later during a trial of right-wing extremists General Giandelio Maletti, former head of Italian counterintelligence, alleges that the massacre had been carried out by the Italian stay-behind army and right-wing terrorists on the orders of the US secret service CIA in order to discredit the Italian Communists.

1970

In Spain, right-wing terrorists including Stefano delle Chiaie of the Gladio stay-behind army are hired by Franco's secret police. They had fled Italy following an aborted coup during which right-wing extremist Valerio Borghese had ordered the secret army to occupy the Interior Ministry in Rome.

1971

In Turkey, the military stages a coup d'état and takes over power. The stay-behind army Counter-Guerrilla engages in domestic terror and kills hundreds.

1972

In Italy, a bomb explodes in a car near the village Peteano killing three Carabinieri. The terror, first blamed on the left, is later traced back to right-wing terrorist Vincenzo Vinciguerra and tends to the exposure of the Italian stay-behind code-named Gladio.

1974

In Italy, a massacre during an anti-Fascist demonstration in Brescia kills eight and injures and maims 102, while a bomb in the Rome to Munich train 'Italicus Express', kills 12 and injures and maims 48.

1974

In Denmark, the secret stay-behind army Absalon tries in vain to prevent a group of leftist academics from becoming members of the directing body of the Danish Odense University, whereupon the secret army is exposed.

1974

In Italy, General Vito Miceli, chief of the military secret service, is arrested on charges of subversive conspiracy against the state and reveals the NATO stay-behind secret army during trial.

1976

In Germany, the secret service BND secretary Heidrun Hofer is arrested after having revealed the secrets of the German stay-behind army to her husband who was a spy of the Soviet secret service KGB.

1977

In Turkey, the stay-behind army Counter-Guerrilla attacks a demonstration of 500,000 in Istanbul by opening fire at the speaker's platform leaving 38 killed and hundreds injured.

1977

In Spain, the secret stay-behind army with support of Italian right-wing terrorists carries out the Atocha massacre in Madrid and in an attack on a lawyer's office, closely linked to the Spanish Communist Party, kills five people.

1978

In Norway, the police discovers a stay-behind arms cache and arrests Hans Otto Meyer who reveals the Norwegian secret army.

1978

In Italy, former Prime Minister and leader of the DCI, Aldo Moro, is taken hostage in Rome by an armed secret unit and killed 55 days later. He was about to form a coalition government that includes the Italian Communist Party.

1980

In Italy, a bomb explodes in the waiting room of the second class at the Bologna railway station, killing 85 and seriously injuring and maiming a further 200. Investigators trace the crime back to right-wing terrorists.

1980

In Turkey, the commander of the stay-behind army Counter-Guerrilla, General Kenan Evren, stages a military coup and seizes power.

1981

In Germany, a large stay-behind arsenal is discovered near the German village of Uelzen in the Lüneburger Heide. Right-wing extremists are alleged to have used the arsenal in the previous year to carry out a massacre during the Munich October fest killing 13 and wounding 213.

1983

In the Netherlands strollers in the forest discover a large arms cache near the Dutch village Velp and force the government to confirm that the arms were related to NATO planning for unorthodox warfare.

1984

In Turkey, the stay-behind army Counter-Guerrilla fights against the Kurds and kills and tortures thousands in the following years.

1984

In Italy, right-wing terrorist Vincenzo Vinciguerra in court reveals Operation Gladio and the involvement of NATO's stay-behind army in acts of terrorism in Italy designed to discredit the Communists. He is sentenced to life and imprisoned.

1985

In Belgium, a secret army attacks and shoots shoppers in supermarkets randomly in the Brabant county killing 28 and leaving many wounded. Investigations link the terror to a conspiracy among the Belgian stay-behind SDRA8, the Belgian Gendarmerie SDRA6, the Belgian right-wing group WNP and the Pentagon secret service DIA.

1990

In Italy, Judge Felice Casson discovers documents on Operation Gladio in the archives of the Italian military secret service in Rome and forces Prime Minister Giulio Andreotti to confirm the existence of a secret army within the state to parliament. As Andreotti insists that Italy had not been the only country involved in the conspiracy, the secret anti-Communist stay-behind armies are discovered across Western Europe.

1990

In Switzerland, Colonel Herbert Alboth, a former commander of the Swiss secret stay-behind army P26, in a confidential letter to the Defence Department declares that he is willing to reveal 'the whole truth'. Thereafter he is found in his house stabbed with his own military bayonet. The detailed parliamentary report on the Swiss secret army is presented to the public on November 17.

1990

In Belgium, the NATO-linked stay-behind headquarters ACC meets on October 23 and 24 under the presidency of Belgian General Van Calster, Director of the Belgian military secret service SGR.

1990

In Belgium, on November 5, NATO categorically denies the allegations of Prime Minister Andreotti concerning NATO's involvement in Operation Gladio and secret unorthodox warfare in Western Europe. The next day NATO explains that the denial of the previous day had been false while refusing to answer any further questions.

1990

In Belgium, the parliament of the European Union (EU) sharply condemns NATO and the United States in a resolution for having manipulated European politics with the stay-behind armies.

1991

In Sweden, the media reveals that a secret stay-behind army existed in neutral Finland with an exile base in Stockholm. Finnish Defence Minister Elisabeth Rehn calls the revelations 'a fairy tale', adding cautiously 'or at least an incredible story, of which I know nothing'.

1991

In the United States, the National Security Archive at the George Washington University in Washington files a Freedom of Information (FOIA) request concerning the secret stay-behind armies with the CIA in the interest of public information and scientific research. The CIA rejects the request with the standard reply: 'The CIA can neither confirm nor deny the existence or non-existence of records responsive to your request.'

1995

In England, the London-based Imperial War Museum in the permanent exhibition 'Secret Wars' reveals next to a big box full of explosives that the MI6 and SAS had set up stay-behind armies across Western Europe.

1995

In Italy, the Senate commission headed by Senator Giovanni Pellegrino researching Operation Gladio and the assassination of former Prime Minister Aldo Moro files a FOIA request with the CIA. The CIA rejects the request and replies: 'The CIA can neither confirm nor deny the existence or non-existence of records responsive to your request.'

1996

In Austria, stay-behind arms caches set up by the CIA are discovered. For the Austrian government Oliver Rathkolb of Vienna University files a FOIA request concerning the secret stay-behind armies with the CIA. The CIA rejects the request and replies: 'The CIA can neither confirm nor deny the existence or non-existence of records responsive to your request.'

2001

The author asks NATO for documents on the stay-behind secret armies and specifically transcripts of the ACC and CPC meetings. Lee McClenny, head of NATO press and media service, denies that NATO had been involved with Operation Gladio and claims that neither ACC nor the CPC transcripts exist.

2001

The author files a FOIA request with the CIA which is rejected with the comment: 'The CIA can neither confirm nor deny the existence or non-existence of records responsive to your request.' The author appeals against the decision and argues that it would be unwise to 'deprive the CIA from its voice and the possibility to take a stand in a Gladio disclosure discourse, which will take place regardless of whether the CIA decides to participate or not'. The CIA accepts the appeal and informs the author that the Agency Release Panel, dealing with appeals 'on a first-received, first-out basis', with a present 'workload of approximately 315 appeals' will reply in due course.

NOTES

INTRODUCTION

1 British daily *The Times*, November 19, 1990.
2 British daily *The Observer*, November 18, 1990.

1 A TERRORIST ATTACK IN ITALY

1 British daily *The Observer*, November 18, 1990.
2 Hugh O' Shaughnessy, *Gladio: Europe's best kept secret.* They were the agents who were to 'stay behind' if the Red Army overran Western Europe. But the network that was set up with the best intentions degenerated in some countries into a front for terrorism and far-right political agitation. In: British daily *The Observer*, June 7, 1992.
3 Secret service researchers Fabrizio Calvi and Frederic Laurent produced probably the best documentary on the Piazza Fontana terror: *Piazza Fontana: Storia di un Complotto* broadcasted on December 11, 1997 at 8:50 p.m. on the Italian state television Rai Due. And shown again in its French version *L' Orchestre Noir: La Strategie de la tension* in two blocks on Tuesday, January 13, 1998, and Wednesday, January 14, 1998, at 20:45 on French Channel Arte. In their documentary they question a large number of witnesses including the judges that for years investigated the massacres, Guido Salvini and Gerardo D'Ambrosio, as well as right-wing extremists Stefano Delle Chiaies, Amos Spiazzi, Guido Giannettini, Vincenzo Vinciguerra, and Captain Labruna, former Prime Minister Giulio Andreotti as well as Victor Marchetti and Marc Wyatt of the CIA.
4 Quoted in Giovanni Fasanella e Claudio Sestieri con Giovanni Pellegrino, *Segreto di Stato. La verità da Gladio al caso Moro* (Torino: Einaudi Editore, 2000), introduction.
5 Allan Francovich, *Gladio: The Puppeteers.* Second of total three Francovich Gladio documentaries, broadcasted on BBC2 on June 17, 1992.
6 Philip Willan, *Terrorists 'helped by CIA' to stop rise of left in Italy.* In: British daily *The Guardian*, March 26, 2001. Willan is an expert on US covert action in Italy. He published the very valuable book *Puppetmasters. The Political Use of Terrorism in Italy* (London: Constable, 1991).
7 *Senato della Repubblica Italiana. Commissione parlamentare d'inchiesta sul terrorismo in Italia e sulle cause della mancata individuazione dei responsabili delle stragi: Il terrorismo, le stragi ed il contesto storico-politico.* The final report of the commission was published under this title in 1995.
8 British daily television news program *Newsnight* on BBC1 on April 4, 1991.
9 British daily *The Observer*, June 7, 1992.

NOTES

10 Ed. Vulliamy, *Secret agents, freemasons, fascists ... and a top-level campaign of political 'destabilisation': 'Strategy of tension' that brought carnage and cover-up.* In: British daily *The Guardian*, December 5, 1990.
11 British political magazine *Statewatch*, January 1991.
12 Jean-Francois Brozzu-Gentile, *L' affaire Gladio* (Paris: Editions Albin Michel, 1994), p. 105.
13 Italian political magazine *Europeo*, November 16, 1990.
14 Ed. Vulliamy, *Secret agents, freemasons, fascists...and a top-level campaign of political 'destabilisation': 'Strategy of tension' that brought carnage and cover-up.* In: British daily *The Guardian*, December 5, 1990.
15 No author specified, *Spinne unterm Schafsfell. In Südeuropa war die Guerillatruppe besonders aktiv – auch bei den Militärputschen in Griechenland und der Türkei?* In: German news magazine *Der Spiegel*, Nr. 48, November 26, 1990.
16 Mario Coglitore (ed.), *La Notte dei Gladiatori. Omissioni e silenzi della Repubblica* (Padova: Calcusca Edizioni, 1992), p. 131.
17 Quoted in Coglitore, *Gladiatori*, p. 132.
18 For an excellent biography of Andreotti, see Regine Igel, *Andreotti. Politik zwischen Geheimdienst und Mafia* (München: Herbig Verlag, 1997).
19 British daily *The Guardian*, December 5, 1990.
20 Leo Müller, *Gladio – das Erbe des Kalten Krieges. Der Nato-Geheimbund und sein deutscher Vorläufer* (Hamburg: Rowohlt, 1991), p. 26.
21 For a detailed description of the sequence of events see the Italian newspapers *La Repubblica, Corriere della Sera* and *La Stampa* of October 24, 1990.
22 No author specified, *50,000 seek truth about secret team.* In: Canadian daily *The Toronto Star*, November 18, 1990.
23 Franco Ferraresi, *A secret structure codenamed Gladio.* In: *Italian Politics. A Review*, 1992, p. 30. Ferraresi quotes directly from the document Andreotti had handed over to the parliamentary commission. The Italian daily *L'Unita* published both the first and the second version of Andreotti's document in a special edition on November 14, 1990. Also Jean Francois Brozzu Gentile gives the full text of Andreotti 'Il SID parallelo – Operazione Gladio' (in French translation). See Gentile, *Gladio*, Appendix.
24 Ferraresi, *Gladio*, p. 30, quoting directly from the Andreotti document.
25 Padre Giuciano testifying in front of his church in Allan Francovich, *Gladio: The Puppeteers.* Second of the total three Francovich Gladio documentaries, broadcasted on BBC2 on June 17, 1992.
26 Ferraresi, *Gladio*, p. 31, quoting directly from the Andreotti document.
27 Ibid.
28 As quoted in Ferraresi, *Gladio*, p. 31.
29 Norberto Bobbio as quoted in Ferraresi, *Gladio*, p. 32.
30 Müller, *Gladio*, p. 27.
31 British daily *The Observer*, November 18, 1990.
32 International news service *Reuters*, November 12, 1990.
33 Ferraresi, *Gladio*, p. 32.
34 British periodical *The Economist*, March 30, 1991.
35 *Senato della Repubblica. Commissione parlamentare d'inchiesta sul terrorismo in Italia e sulle cause della mancata individuazione dei responsabiliy delle stragi: Stragi e terrorismo in Italia dal dopoguerra al 1974.* Relazione del Gruppo Democratici di Sinistra l'Ulivo. Roma June 2000. As quoted in Philip Willan, *US 'supported anti-left terror in Italy'. Report claims Washington used a strategy of tension in the cold war to stabilise the centre-right.* In: British daily *The Guardian*, June 24, 2000.

2 A SCANDAL SHOCKS WESTERN EUROPE

1 The coalition included Kuwait, the United States, Saudi Arabia, Great Britain, France, the Netherlands, Egypt, Syria, Oman, Qatar, Bahrain, United Arab Emirates, Israel, Afghanistan, Bangladesh, Canada, Belgium, Czechoslovakia, Germany, Honduras, Italy, Niger, Romania and South Korea. On November 29, 1990 the UN Security Council issued with resolution 678 an ultimatum and authorised the forces cooperating with Kuwait to use 'all necessary means... to restore world peace and international security in the area', if Iraq should not withdraw from Kuwait until January 15, 1991. As Saddam Hussein did not respect the UN ultimatum Operation Desert Storm under US command began with a massive air attack on January 17, 1991 followed on February 24 by the invasion of allied land forces. The Iraqi forces were quickly defeated and on February 27, Kuwait City was liberated. The following day all coalition fighting ended. As many as 100,000 Iraqi troops are estimated to have died while deaths of coalition troops totaled about 370. On March 3, 1991 Iraq accepted the ceasefire and Saddam Hussein remained in power.

2 Leo Müller, *Gladio. Das Erbe des Kalten Krieges. Der NATO Geheimbund und sein deutscher Vorläufer* (Hamurg: Rowohlt, 1991), p. 27.

3 No author specified, *Spinne unterm Schafsfell. In Südeuropa war die Guerillatruppe besonders aktiv – auch bei den Militärputschen in Griechenland und der Türkei?* In: German news magazine *Der Spiegel*, Nr. 48, November 26, 1990.

4 Presse- und Informationsamt der Bundesregierung. Pressemitteilung Nr. 455/90, durch Hans Klein, November 14, 1990. See also Müller, *Gladio*, p. 30.

5 No author specified, *Das blutige Schwert der CIA. Nachrichten aus dem Kalten Krieg: In ganz Europa gibt es geheime NATO Kommandos, die dem Feind aus dem Osten widerstehen sollen. Kanzler, Verteidigungsminister und Bundeswehrgenerale wussten angeblich von nichts. Die Spuren führen nach Pullach, zur 'stay-behind organisation' des Bundesnachrichtendienstes.* In: German weekly news magazine *Der Spiegel*, November 19, 1990.

6 Quoted in Müller, *Gladio*, p. 14.

7 Ibid., p. 75.

8 No author specified, *Das blutige Schwert der CIA. Nachrichten aus dem Kalten Krieg: In ganz Europa gibt es geheime NATO Kommandos, die dem Feind aus dem Osten widerstehen sollen. Kanzler, Verteidigungsminister und Bundeswehrgenerale wussten angeblich von nichts. Die Spuren führen nach Pullach, zur 'stay-behind organisation' des Bundesnachrichtendienstes.* In: German weekly news magazine *Der Spiegel*, November 19, 1990.

9 Quoted in Jan devWillems, *Gladio* (Brussels: Editions EPO, 1991), p. 13.

10 Willems, *Gladio*, p. 13.

11 Senate de Belgique: Enquête parlementaire sur l'existence en Belgique d'un résau de renseignements clandestin international. Rapport fait au nom de la commission d'enquête par MM. Erdman et Hasqeuin. Brussels. October 1, 1991.

12 Willems, *Gladio*, p. 14.

13 International news agency *Associated Press*, November 11, 1990.

14 Müller, *Gladio*, p. 30.

15 French daily *Le Monde*, November 13, 1990. See also Swiss weekly *Wochenzeitung*, December 14, 1990.

16 Jean-Francois Brozzu-Gentile, *L' affaire Gladio* (Paris: Editions Albain Michel, 1994), p. 140.

17 French daily *Le Monde*, November 14, 1990. International news agency *Reuters*, November 12, 1990. British daily *The Guardian*, November 14, 1990.

18 Compare Gentile, *Gladio*, p. 141.

19 British daily *The Guardian*, November 14, 1990.

20 Richard Norton Taylor, *Secret Italian unit 'trained in Britain'*. In: British daily *The Guardian*, November 17, 1990.

21 Hugh O' Shaughnessy, *Gladio: Europe's best kept secret*. They were the agents who were to 'stay behind' if the Red Army overran western Europe. But the network that was set up with the best intentions degenerated in some countries into a front for terrorism and far-right political agitation. In: British daily *The Observer*, June 7, 1992.

22 International news service *Associated Press*, November 14, 1990. The entire text of Lubber's letter to parliament is reprinted in Dutch in the Dutch daily *NRC Handelsblatt* in the edition of November 14 1990: *'Brief premier Lubbers "geheime organisatie"'*. It is also contained as Kamerstuk Nr. 21895 among the official papers of the Dutch parliament.

23 International news agency *Associated Press*, November 14, 1990.

24 Quoted in full in the Luxemburg daily, *Luxemburger Wort*, November 15, 1990.

25 British daily *The Guardian*, November 10, 1990.

26 Portuguese daily *Diario De Noticias*, November 17, 1990.

27 Joao Paulo Guerra, *'Gladio' actuou em Portugal*. In: Portuguese daily *O Jornal*, November 16, 1990.

28 *Calvo Sotelo asegura que Espana no fue informada, cuando entro en la OTAN, de la existencia de Gladio. Moran sostiene que no oyo hablar de la red clandestina mientras fue ministro de Exteriores*. In: Spanish daily *El Pais*, November 21, 1990.

29 Danish daily *Berlingske Tidende*, November 25, 1990.

30 International news service *Associated Press*, November 14, 1990.

31 Serdar Celik, *Turkey's Killing Machine: The Contra Guerrilla Force*. Online: (http://www.ozgurluk.org/mhp/0061.html) His source: Interview with the President of the Turkish General Staff Dogan Gures. In: Turkish daily *Milliyet*, September 5, 1992.

32 Lucy Komisar, *Turkey's terrorists: A CIA legacy lives on*. In: *The Progressive*, April 1997.

33 Ibid.

34 Hugh Pope, *Turkey Promoted Death Squads and Drug Trafficking. Prime Minister's Probe of 1996 Car Crash Scandal Excoriates Rival Mrs Ciller*. In: US periodical *Wall Street Journal*, January 26, 1998.

35 The members of the EU in November 1990 were: France, Germany, Italy, Belgium, the Netherlands, Luxemburg, Denmark, Ireland, Great Britain, Greece, Spain and Portugal.

36 Debates of the European Parliament, November 22, 1990. Official transcripts.

37 Ibid.

38 Ibid.

39 Ibid.

40 Ibid.

41 Resolution of the European Parliament on the Gladio Affair, November 22, 1990.

3 THE SILENCE OF NATO, CIA AND MI6

1 British daily *The European*, November 9, 1990.

2 Ibid. It seems that the NATO official who issued the correction was Robert Stratford. Compare: Regine Igel, *Andreotti. Politik zwischen Geheimdienst und Mafia* (München: Herbig Verlag, 1997), p. 343.

3 British daily *The Observer*, November 18,1990.

4 British daily *The Guardian*, November 10, 1990.

5 Ibid., January 30, 1992.

6 Ibid., January 16, 1991.

7 International news service *Reuters*, November 15, 1990.

8 No author specified, *Gladio. Un misterio de la guerra fria. La trama secreta coordinada por mandos de la Alianza Atlantica comienza a salir a la luz tras cuatro decadas de actividad.* In: Spanish daily *El Pais*, November 26, 1990.

9 No author specified, *El servicio espanol de inteligencia mantiene estrechas relaciones con la OTAN. Serra ordena indagar sobre la red Gladio en Espana.* In: Spanish daily *El Pais*, November 16, 1990.

10 Erich Schmidt Eenboom, *Schnüffler ohne Nase. Der BND. Die unheimliche Macht im Staate* (Düsseldorf: Econ Verlag, 1993), p. 365.

11 Portuguese daily *Expresso*, November 24, 1990.

12 Ibid.

13 International news service *Reuters*, November 13, 1990. British daily *The Independent*, November 16, 1990.

14 International news service *Associated Press*, November 14, 1990. International news service *Reuters*, November 12, 1990. International news service *Reuters*, November 15, 1990.

15 British weekly *The Independent on Sunday*, June 21, 1998. Review of a book on Nixon (Nixon in Winter) by Nixon's former research assistant Monica Crowley.

16 These were: 1951–1952 Gen. *Dwight D Eisenhower, US Army*; 1952–1953 Gen. *Matthew B Ridgway, US Army*; 1953–1956 Gen. *Alfred M Gruenther, US Army*; 1956–1962 Gen. *Lauris Norstad, US Air Force*; 1963–1969 Gen. *Lyman L Lemnitzer, US Army*; 1969–1974 Gen. *Andrew J Goodpaster, US Army*; 1974–1979 Gen. *Alexander M Haig Jr, US Army*; 1979–1987 Gen. *Bernard W Rogers, US Army*; 1987–1992 Gen. *John R Galvin, US Army*; 1992–1993 Gen. *John M Shalikashvili, US Army*; 1993–1997 Gen. *George A Joulwan, US Army*; 1997–2000 Gen. *Wesley K. Clark, US Army*.

17 Jonathan Kwitny, *The CIA's Secret Armies in Europe.* In: *The Nation*, April 6, 1992, p. 445.

18 German daily *Der Spiegel*, Nr. 47, p. 20, November 19, 1990.

19 Pietro Cedomi, *Services Secrets, Guerre Froide et 'stay-behind' Part III. Repetoire des resaux S/B.* In: Belgian periodical *Fire! Le Magazin de l'Homme d'Action*, November/December 1991, p. 82.

20 Belgian Parliamentary Commission of Enquiry into Gladio, as summarised in British periodical *Statewatch*, January/February 1992.

21 Philip Willan, *Puppetmasters: The Political Use of Terrorism in Italy* (London: Constable, 1991), p. 27.

22 Arthur Rowse, *Gladio: The Secret US War to subvert Italian Democracy.* In: *Covert Action Quarterly*, Nr. 49, Summer 1994, p. 3.

23 Quoted in Willan, *Puppetmasters*, p. 27.

24 Mario Coglitore (ed.), *La Notte dei Gladiatori. Omissioni e silenze della Repubblica* (Padova: Calusca Edizioni, 1992), p. 34. 'It remains an established fact that for sure secret NATO protocols exist, because De Gaulle denounced them explicitly on March 7, 1966 and the Parliament of West Germany has recently admitted that they exist' (ibid.).

25 British periodical *Searchlight*, January 1991.

26 Inzerilli, Paolo, *Gladio. La Verità negata* (Bologna: Edizioni Analisi, 1995), p. 61.

27 Inzerilli, *Gladio*, p. 62.

28 Gerardo Serravalle, *Gladio* (Roma: Edizione Associate, 1991), p. 78.

29 Ibid., p. 79.

30 Ibid., p. 78.

31 Belgian Parliamentary Commission of Enquiry into Gladio, as summarised in Belgium periodical *Statewatch*, January/February 1992.

32 Inzerilli, *Gladio*, p. 63.

33 Ibid.
34 Michel Van Ussel: *Georges 923. Un agent du Gladio belge parle. Témoignage* (Brussels: Editions La Longue Vue, 1991), p. 139.
35 Inzerilli, *Gladio*, p. 64.
36 Email of Anne-Marie Smith at NATO's Archives Section to the author, August 18, 2000.
37 Letter of the Chief of the Swiss mission to NATO, ambassador Anton Thalmann, to the author, dated May 4, 2001.
38 Letter of Lee McClenny, NATO head of press and media, to the author, dated May 2, 2001.
39 Ibid.
40 *Presidential Directive, National Security Decision Memorandum 40, Responsibility for the Conduct, Supervision and Coordination of Covert Action Operations, Washington February 17 1970. Signed: Richard Nixon.*
41 For probably the best global overview of CIA covert actions since the Second World War see William Blum: *Killing Hope. US Military and CIA interventions since World War II* (Maine: Common Courage Press, 1995).
42 As given on the homepage www.terrorism.com.
43 The three commissions were the Committee of the Senate directed by Frank Church, the Committee of the House of Representatives directed by Ottis Pike, and the Murphy Commission of President Ford.

  1 *Report of the House Select Committee on Intelligence [Pike Committee], Ninety-fourth Congress,* Published by Village Voice, New York City, February 1976.

  2 *Report of the Commission on the Organization of the Government for the Conduct of Foreign Policy [Murphy Commission], US Government Printing Office, Washington DC, June 1975.*

  3 *Final Report, of the United States Senate Select Committe to Study Governmental Operations with Respect to Intelligence Activities [Church Committee], US Government Printing Office, Washington DC, April 1976.*

Arguably the best of the three reports, the 'Final Report of the US Senate Select Committee to study Governmental Operations with respect to Intelligence activities', is made up of six books. Book one focuses on 'Foreign and Military Intelligence', CIA, covert action operations and the democratic problem to control secret services. In book two, entitled '*Intelligence Activities and the Rights of the Americans*', the Church report reveals how the NSA and the FBI have violated the privacy of US citizens. Book three, entitled '*Supplementary detailed staff reports on the intelligence activities and the rights of the Americans*', extends the analysis of book two and suggests that 'Counter-Intelligence' is a misnomer for 'domestic covert action'. Book four is entitled '*Supplementary Detailed Staff Reports on Foreign and Military*' and presents a history of the CIA from 1946 to 1975. Book five, entitled '*The Assassination of President John F. Kennedy and the performance of the Intelligence Agencies*' investigates whether the US secret services have conspired to keep the JFK assassination a mystery. Book six, entitled '*Supplementary Reports on Intelligence Activities*', deals with the historical evolution and organisation of the federal intelligence function from 1776 to 1976.

44 Kathryn Olmsted, *Challenging the Secret Government: The Post-Watergate Investigations of the CIA and FBI* (Chapelhill: University of North Carolina Press, 1996), p. 9.
45 British daily *The Independent*, December 1, 1990.
46 Kwitny, Jonathan, *The CIA's Secret Armies in Europe.* In: *The Nation*, April 6, 1992, p. 445.
47 Arthur Rowse, *Gladio. The Secret US War to Subvert Italian Democracy.* In: *Covert Action Quarterly*, No. 49, Summer 1994.

48 FOIA request: CIA's 'Operation Gladio', handed in by Malcolm Byrne on April 15, 1991. FOIA request number 910113.
49 Italian daily *Corriere della Sera*, May 29, 1995.
50 Austrian political magazine *Zoom*, Nr. 4/5, 1996: *Es muss nicht immer Gladio sein. Attentate, Waffenlager, Erinnerungslücken*, p. 6.
51 Bericht betreff US Waffenlager. Oesterreichisches Bundesministerium für Inneres. Generaldirektor für die öffentliche Sicherheit. Mag. Michael Sika. November 28, 1997. Wien, p. 10.
52 Letter dated December 28, 2000 of the CIA to the author concerning Gladio FOIA request number F-2000-02528.
53 Letter dated January 23, 2001 of the author to Mrs Dyer at the CIA.
54 Letter dated February 7, 2001 from the CIA's Information and Privacy Coordinator Kathryn I. Dyer to the author.
55 International news service *Associated Press*, November 14, 1990.
56 British television. BBC Newsnight, April 4, 1991, 10:30 p.m. Gladio report by journalist Peter Marshall.
57 Ibid.
58 Imperial War Museum, London. Secret Wars exhibition. Visited by the author on May 20, 1999. On June 4, 1999, the author met Mark Siemens, of the museum's research division, responsible for the Secret Wars exhibition, who stressed that the British secret army SOE during the Second World War was a direct predecessor to the Gladio stay-behinds, but otherwise saw no possibilities to gain more data from the MI6 on the phenomenon.
59 Michael Smith, *New Cloak, Old Dagger: How Britain's Spies Came in from the Cold* (London: Gollancz, 1996), p. 117. Based on interviews with Simon Preston on October 11, 1995, and with Michael Giles on October 25, 1995.
60 Smith, *Dagger*, p. 117.
61 Ibid., p. 118.

4 THE SECRET WAR IN GREAT BRITAIN

1 Denna Frank Fleming, *The Cold War and its Origins 1917–1960* (New York, 1961), p. 4.
2 Compare Fleming: *Cold War*.
3 Figures taken from Andrew Wilson, *Das Abrüstungshandbuch: Analysen, Zusammenhänge, Hintergründe* (Hamburg: Hoffmann und Campe, 1984), p. 38. Compare the US losses: 300,000 soldiers killed, 600,000 injured. No civilian victims. Total human beings killed in the Second World War: 60 million (ibid.).
4 Compare. Valentin Falin, *Die Zweite Front* (München: Börner Knaur, 1995).
5 Mackenzie, W. J. M., *History of the Special Operations Executive: Britain and the resistance in Europe* (London: British Cabinet Office, 1948), pp. 1153 and 1155. Unpublished original of the Public Records Office London, publication with Frank Cass forthcoming.
6 Mackenzie, *Special Operations Executive*, p. 2.
7 An early functionary of SOE, Lt. Col. Holland, 'an officer with personal experience in irregular warfare in Ireland and India ... and a lively appreciation of its technique and possibilities'. Quoted in Mackenzie, *Special Operations Executive*, p. 9.
8 Next to MI6's Section D two other British organisations in the subversive field had been established in 1938. One was a section of the General Staff at the War Office, known as GS(R) and later as MI(R), which concentrated on studying techniques of irregular warfare. The other, labelled EH after its London headquarters Electra House, specialised in 'black' (unattributable) propaganda to Europe. Compare David Stafford, *Britain and European Resistance 1940–1945: A survey of the Special Operations Executive* (Oxford: St Antony's College, 1980), pp. 19–21.

9 Tony Bunyan, *The History and Practice of the Political Police in Britain* (London: Quartet Books, 1983), p. 265.

10 Peter Wilkinson, *Foreign Fields: The Story of an SOE Operative* (London: Tauris Publishers, 1997), p. 100.

11 Imperial War Museum London, visited by the author in May 1999.

12 Wilkinson, *Fields*, p. 101.

13 Stafford, *Resistance*, p. 20.

14 Letter by Minister Hugh Dalton to Foreign Minister Halifax on July 2, 1940. Quoted in M. R. D. Foot, *An outline history of the Special Operations Executive 1940–1946* (London: British Broadcasting Cooperation, 1984), p. 19.

15 *Statewatch Background Document File No. 0391: GLADIO.* January 1991. Also online: http://users.patra.hol.gr/~cgian/gladio.html. Compare on the role of Gubbins also the Belgium periodical *Fire! Le Magazin de l'Homme d'Action*, September/October 1991, p. 77.

16 E. H. Cookridge, *Inside SOE. The Story of Special Operations in Western Europe 1940–45* (London: Arthur Barker Limited, 1966), p. 13.

17 Mackenzie, *Special Operations Executive*, p. 1152.

18 Ibid., pp. 1153 and 1155.

19 Stafford, *Resistance*, in his epilogue, p. 203.

20 Frans Kluiters, *De Nederlandse inlichtingen en veiligheidsdiensten* (1993), p. 309.

21 Stafford, *Resistance*, in his conclusion, p. 211.

22 Roger Faligot and Rémi Kauffer, *Les maîtres espions. Histoire mondiale du renseignement. Volume two. De la guerre froide à nos jours* (Paris: Editions Laffont, 1994), p. 53.

23 Michael Smith, *New Cloak, Old Dagger: How Britain's Spies Came in from the Cold* (London: Gollancz, 1996), p. 117. Based on interviews with Simon Preston on October 11 1995, and with Michael Giles on October 25, 1995.

24 Allan Francovich, *Gladio: The Ringmasters*. First of the total three Francovich Gladio documentaries, broadcasted on BBC2 on June 10, 1992.

25 Michael de la Billiere, *Looking for Trouble* (London: HarperCollins, 1994), p. 150. The work is an autobiography of Billiere and his time in the SAS.

26 International news service *Associated Press*, November 14, 1990.

27 *The Unleashing of Evil*, produced by Richard Norton Taylor, who for the Guardian also reported extensively on the Gladio revelations in 1990. Broadcast on BBC on June 29, 1988. Announced in British daily *The Guardian* of the same day: '*British soldiers used torture*'.

28 SAS officer to distinguished investigative journalist John Pilger. British daily *The Guardian*, October 16, 1990. The Reagan Administration was furious when in 1986 the correspondence of congressional lawyer Jonathan Winer exposed that the US had been funding Pol Pot with 85 million dollars between 1980 and 1986 according the logic 'the enemy of my enemy is my partner' (John Pilger in the British daily *The Guardian*, October 6, 1990). The British side was not less embarrassed. In 1990 British Prime Minister Thatcher according to plausible denial logics denied British involvement in the training of Khmer Rouge units despite the testimonies of SAS officers. Finally in a libel case in 1991 involving John Pilger the British department of defence admitted that Britain had helped train Khmer Rouge allies (The British daily *The Guardian*, April 20, 1993).

29 Joseph Paul de Boucherville Taillon, *International Cooperation in the Use of elite military forces to counter terrorism: The British and American Experience, with special reference to their respective experiences in the evolution of low intensity operations* (1992), p. 200 (PhD thesis London School of Economics and Political Science, unpublished). Letter from Carver to Boucherville Taillon, dated December 24, 1985.

30 British periodical *Lobster*, December 1995.
31 British monthly *Searchlight*, January 1991.
32 Richard Norton-Taylor, *UK trained secret Swiss force*. In: British daily *The Guardian*, September 20, 1991.
33 Urs Frieden, *Die England Connection. PUK EMD: P26 Geheimarmist Hürlimann im Manöver*. In: Swiss weekly *Wochenzeitung*, November 30, 1990.
34 *Schweizer Bundesrat: Schlussbericht in der Administrativuntersuchung zur Abklärung der Natur von allfälligen Beziehungen zwischen der Organisation P26 und analogen Organisationen im Ausland. Kurzfassung für die Oeffentlichkeit.* September 19, 1991, pp. 4–5.
35 Ibid., p. 2.
36 British periodical *Searchlight*, January 1991.
37 The Broccoli letter of October 1, 1951, entitled 'Organizzazione informativa operativa nel territorio nazionale suscettibile di occupazione nemica' is an important Gladio document. The Italian parliamentary commission quotes from it. A good summary can be found in Mario Coglitore, *La notte dei Gladiatori. Omissioni e silenzi della Repubblica* (Padova: Calusca Edizioni, 1992), pp. 132–133. Also the Italian political magazine *Espresso*, in possession of the original Broccoli document, quotes extensively from the letter in their edition of January 18, 1991.
38 Coglitore, *Gladiatori*, p. 133.
39 Pietro Cedomi, *Service secrets, guerre froide et 'stay-behind. Part II': La mise en place des resaux*. In: Belgian periodical *Fire! Le Magazin de l'Homme d'Action*, September/October 1991, p. 80.
40 Allan Francovich, *Gladio: The Ringmasters*. First of the total three Francovich Gladio documentaries, broadcasted on BBC2 on June 10, 1992.
41 *Enquête parlementaire sur l'existence en Belgique d'un réseau de renseignements clandestin international, rapport fait au nom de la commission d'enquête par MM. Erdman et Hasquin.* Document Senat, session de 1990–1991. Brussels, pp. 212–213.
42 Ibid., p. 213. Also quoted in British daily *The Observer*, June 7, 1992.
43 Quoted in Olav Riste, *The Norwegian Intelligence Service 1945–1970* (London: Frank Cass, 1999), p. 16.
44 Thomas Kanger and Oscar Hedin, *Erlanders hemliga gerilla. I ett ockuperat Sverige skulle det nationella motstandet ledas fran Äppelbo skola i Dalarna*. In: Swedish daily *Dagens Nyheter*, October 4, 1998.
45 British daily *The Guardian*, November 14, 1990.
46 Hugh O' Shaughnessy, *Gladio: Europe's best kept secret*. They were the agents who were to 'stay behind' if the Red Army overran western Europe. But the network that was set up with the best intentions degenerated in some countries into a front for terrorism and far-right political agitation. In: British daily *The Observer*, June 7, 1992.
47 British television. BBC Newsnight, April 4, 1991, 10:30 p.m. Gladio report by journalist Peter Marshall.
48 Ibid.
49 Obituary in British daily *The Independent*, April 28, 1997.
50 Allan Francovich, *Gladio: The Ringmasters*. First of the total three Francovich Gladio documentaries, broadcasted on BBC2 on June 10, 1992; *Gladio: The Puppeteers*. Second of the total three Francovich Gladio documentaries, broadcasted on BBC2 on June 17, 1992; and *Gladio: The Foot Soldiers*. Third of the total three Francovich Gladio documentaries, broadcasted on BBC2 on June 24, 1992.
51 Allan Francovich, Gladio: *The Ringmasters*. First of the total three Francovich Gladio documentaries, broadcasted on BBC2 on June 10, 1992.
52 British daily *The Times*, June 28, 1992.

5 THE SECRET WAR IN THE UNITED STATES

1 William Colby, *Honorable Men: My life in the CIA* (New York: Simon & Schuster, 1978), p. 100.

2 Walter Trohan in US daily *The Chicago Tribune*, February 9, 1945.

3 Related in Christopher Andrew, *For the President's Eyes Only: Secret Intelligence and the American Presidency from Washington to Bush* (New York: HarperCollins, 1995), p. 164.

4 Christopher Shoemaker, *The NSC staff: counselling the council* (1991), p. 1.

5 John Prados, *Keepers of the Keys: A history of the National Security Council from Truman to Bush* (New York: William Morow, 1991), p. 567. Previously John Prados published the valuable book, *Presidents' Secret Wars: CIA and Pentagon Covert Operations since World War II* (New York: William Morrow, 1986). By that time the secret armies in Western Europe had not yet been discovered and the book contains no reference to Gladio.

6 Thomas Etzold and John Gaddis, *Containment: Documents on American Policy and Strategy 1945–1950* (New York: Coumbia University Press, 1978), p. 12.

7 Philip Willan, *Puppetmasters: The Political Use of Terrorism in Italy* (London: Constable, 1991), p. 20.

8 Quoted in Andrew, *Eyes Only*, p. 171.

9 Andrew, *Eyes Only*, p. 171.

10 Arthur Darling, *The Central Intelligence Agency: An Instrument of Government. To 1950* (University Park: Pennsylvania State University Press, 1990), p. 245.

11 Darling, *Agency*, p. 246.

12 *NSC 10/2: National Security Council Directive on Office of Special Projects*, June 18, 1948. Formerly Top Secret. Contained in full in Etzold and Gaddis, *Containment*, p. 125. The fundamental importance of NSC 10/2 for the secret anti-Communist armies in Western Europe has been realised by almost all Gladio scholars. Compare Jan de Willems (ed.), *Gladio* (Brussels: Editions EPO, 1991), p. 145; Jens Mecklenburg (ed.), *Gladio: Die geheime Terror organisation der Nato* (Berlin: Elefanten Press 1997), pp. 17 and 51; Leo Müller, *Gladio – das Erbe des Kalten Krieges. Der Nato-Geheimbund und sein deutscher Vorläufer* (Hamburg: Rowohlt, 1991), p. 63.

13 Quoted in Andrew, *Eyes Only*, p. 171. Allen Dulles, Director of CIA from 1953 to 1961, privately reminded Truman that he could not escape responsibility in the Greek, Turkish, Italian or Philippine US covert action operations. To the CIA legal counsel Dulles wrote on the subject that 'At no time did Mr. Truman express other than complete agreement with the viewpoint I expressed' (ibid.).

14 Andrew, *Eyes Only*, p. 198.

15 *Moscow Embassy Telegram Nr. 511: 'The Long Telegram'*, February 22, 1946. In: Etzold and Gaddis, *Containment*, p. 63.

16 George Kennan as quoted in Etzold and Gaddis, *Containment*, p. 125.

17 *United States Senate. Final Report of the Select Committee to Study Governmental Operations with respect to Intelligence activities. Book IV: Supplementary detailed staff reports on foreign and military intelligence*, p. 36.

18 Harris Smith, *OSS. The Secret History of America's First Central Intelligence Agency* (Berkley: University of California Press, 1972), p. 240.

19 Thomas Powers, *The Man Who Kept the Secrets: Richard Helms and the CIA* (London: Weidenfeld and Nicolson, 1980), p. 37. There does not seem to exist a biography of Frank Wisner. The best-published source on him thus remains the biography on Richard Helms by Powers. Helms first served under Wisner in the covert action department and in 1958 replaced Wisner when he was promoted to become the chief of CIA covert actions.

20 Powers, *Helms*, p. 32.

21 Darling, *Agency*, p. 279.
22 Pietro Cedomi, *Service secrets, guerre froide et 'stay-behind. Part II': La mise en place des resaux*. In: Belgian periodical *Fire! Le Magazin de l'Homme d'Action* September/October 1991, p. 78.
23 Powers, *Helms*, p. 48. Same figures by Andrew: *Eyes Only*, p. 193.
24 Ludwell Montague, *General Walter Bedell Smith as Director of Central Intelligence* (University Park: Pennsylvania University Press, 1992), p. 209. This would most probably be a good book were it not so heavily censored by the CIA. Every second paragraph features '[one line deleted], [three paragraphs deleted], [seven lines deleted]' etc. It is in this context that brilliant American writer Mark Twain observed a century ago in his *Following the Equator* (1897) 'It is by the goodness of God in our country that we have those three unspeakably precious things: freedom of speech, freedom of conscience, and the prudence never to practise either of them.'
25 Montague, *Smith*, p. 213.
26 Colby, *Honorable Men*, p. 83.
27 Ibid., pp. 81 and 82.
28 Ibid., p. 83.
29 This document, found by the author, has not previously been discussed in the context of the Gladio discoveries, but clearly is of direct importance for investigations into the Gladio command centre CPC. Memorandum by Lieutenant General Leon W. Johnson, US Representative to the NATO Military Committee Standing Group, of January 3, 1957, to the US Joint Chiefs of Staff on Clandestine Intelligence. Formerly Top Secret. Declassified in 1978. Found through computer-based *Declassified Documents Reference System* at LSE in London.
30 As counter-insurgency became a fashionable word in the Kennedy administration all branches of the US military rushed to create 'special operations units' with the Navy forming for instance the SEAL (sea, air, land) teams trained to parachute into the sea, wearing scuba gear, equipped to blow up ships, and trained to fight on land once they emerged from the water.
31 Colonel Aaron Bank, *From OSS to Green Berets: The Birth of Special Forces* (Novato: Presidio Press, 1986), pp. 175–176.
32 Bank, *Special Forces*, pp. 168–169.
33 Belgium periodical *Fire! Le Magazin de l'Homme d'Action*, p. 84. Also Austrian political magazine *Zoom*, Nr. 4 /5, 1996: *Es muss nicht immer Gladio sein. Attentate, Waffenlager, Erinnerungslücken*, p. 61.
34 Mecklenburg, *Gladio*, p. 50.
35 Gerardo Serravalle, *Gladio* (Roma: Edizioni Associate, 1991), p. 90.
36 Powers, *Helms*, p. 89.
37 British monthly *Searchlight*, January 1991.
38 Pietro Cedomi, *Service secrets, guerre froide et 'stay-behind. Part II': La mise en place des resaux*. In: Belgian periodical *Fire! Le Magazin de l'Homme d'Action* September/October 1991, p. 77.
39 Powers, *Helms*, p. 77.
40 Christopher Simpson, *Blowback. America's Recruitment of Nazis and its Effects on the Cold War* (London: Weidenfeld and Nicolson, 1988), p. 289. Powers, *Helms*, p. 77.
41 Address of Richard Helms, Director of CIA, at the funeral of Frank Gardiner Wisner, 1909–1965. Found through computer-based *Declassified Documents Reference System*.
42 Jonathan Kwitny, *An International Story. The CIA's Secret Armies in Europe*. In: US periodical *The Nation*, April 6, 1992, pp. 444–448, p. 445.
43 British daily *The Times*, May 7, 1996.
44 Ramsey Clark, *The Fire this Time: US War Crimes in the Gulf* (New York: Thunder's Mouth Press, 1992), p. 31.

45 Clark, *Fire*, p. 32.
46 Resolution of the European Parliament on the Gladio Affair, November 22, 1990.
47 US daily *The Washington Post*, November 14, 1990. The only other article by the *Washington Post* which features the keyword 'Gladio' appeared on August 8, 1993, again solely on Italy. In Europe reporting on Gladio was much more widespread. The two articles of the Washington Post compare to 39 articles on Gladio in numerous countries in the same time period in the British daily newspaper *The Guardian*.
48 British daily *The Independent*, December 1, 1990.

6 THE SECRET WAR IN ITALY

1 While it has been confirmed that the PCI received strong financial support from Moscow the historical debate as to the precise relationship between the PCI and the Soviet Communist Party during the Cold War is still going on. Sergio Romano, Italian ambassador to the Soviet Union from 1985 to 1989, related that until the late 1970s the majority of the financial assets of the Italian Communist Party were provided by the Soviet Communist Party. Research on the links between PCI and Moscow available in English include: Joan Barth Urban, *Moscow and the Italian Communist Party: From Togliatti to Berlinguer* (Ithaca: Cornell University Press, 1986). Gianni Cervetti, *L'Oro di Mosca: La Verita sui Finanziamenti Sovietici al PCI Raccontata dal Diretto Protagonista* (Milano Baldini & Castoldi 1993, second edition 1999); and Valerio Rima, *Oro da Mosca. I Finanziamenti Sovietici al PCI dalla Rivoluzione d'Ottobre al Crollo dell' URSS* (Milano: Mondadori, 1999).
2 *Senato della Repubblica. Commissione parlamentare d'inchiesta sul terrorismo in Italia e sulle cause della mancata individuazione dei responsabiliy delle stragi: Il terrorismo, le stragi ed il contesto storico politico*. Redatta dal presidente della Commissione, Senatore Giovanni Pellegrino. Roma 1995, p. 20. This report of the Italian Senate ranges certainly among the most authoritative documents on Gladio and US covert action in Italy in general. It investigates Gladio, terrorism and long unclarified massacres. In order to avoid confusion with the equally valuable Senate report on Gladio presented in 2000, it will be quoted hereafter as 'Italian 1995 Senate report on Gladio and the massacres'.
3 Italian magazine *Panorama*, February 10, 1976. Quoted in Italian 1995 Senate report on Gladio and the massacres, p. 13.
4 Roberto Faenza, *Gli americani in Italia* (Milano: Editore Feltrinelli, 1976), pp. 10–13. The connection between the United States and the Mafia had already been revealed in 1951 by the US Senate investigation under Senator Kefauver. Compare *US Senate Special Committee, Hearings on Organised Crime and Interstate Commerce*, part 7, p. 1181 (1951). Italian historian Roberto Faenza was one of the first analysts to realise the enormous impact that US covert action had on Italy. His first book on the topic, published together with Marco Fini, came out in 1976 and focused on the immediate post-war years, entitled simply: *Gli Americani in Italia*. The foreword to the book read: 'For many people all around the world, including the average citizen of the United States, it has really been very hard and painful to realise slowly but surely the fact that the United States of America are the most conservative and the most counter-revolutionary force that there is in this world. But this is exactly how the situation is as this book demonstrates brilliantly showing the secret interventions of the American government into the internal affairs of the Italian population...the picture is the same as it has already been revealed by other studies for Greece, Iran, Guatemala, the Dominican Republic and many other countries...It is difficult to convince oneself of these dire facts.'
5 British daily *The Observer*, January 10, 1993. Referring to the January 1993 BBC2 television documentary: *Allied to the Mafia*.

6 Mackenzie, W. J. M., *History of the Special Operations Executive: Britain and the resistance in Europe* (London: British Cabinet Office, 1948), pp. 842 and 853. Unpublished original of the Public Records Office London, publication with Frank Cass forthcoming. In the Pacific theatre and specifically in the Philippines the same strategy of supplying and then weakening left-wing guerrillas during the Second World War was employed by the United States. Japan had invaded the Philippines in January 1942. The United States supported and trained partisans of various political orientations against the Japanese occupation in the Philippines including the left-wing strong Huk partisan movement which presented a strong force for social revolution. But as in Italy and Greece, the brothers in arms were betrayed. Once the Japanese were defeated the United States disarmed the guerrillas and the Huks were massacred in the presence of US officers till at least 1945. US historian Gabriel Kolko comments: The 'Huk leadership naively expected the Americans to tolerate them.' Compare Gabriel Kolko, *Century of War Politics, Conflict, and Society since 1914* (New York: The New Press, 1994), p. 363.

7 Geoffrey Harris, *The Dark Side of Europe: The Extreme Right Today* (Edinburgh: Edinburgh University Press, 1994), pp. 3 and 15.

8 Allan Francovich, *Gladio: The Ringmasters*. First of the total three Francovich Gladio documentaries, broadcasted on BBC2 on June 10, 1992.

9 William Blum, *Killing Hope: US Military and CIA Interventions since World War II* (Maine: Common Courage Press, 1995), p. 28.

10 Martin Lee, *The Beast Reawakens* (Boston: Little Brown and Company, 1997), p. 100.

11 Jonathan Dunnage, *Inhibiting Democracy in Post-War Italy: The Police Forces, 1943–48*. In: Italian Studies, 51, 1996, p. 180.

12 Stuart Christie, *Stefano delle Chiaie* (London: Anarchy Publications, 1984), p. 6.

13 Ibid., p. 4.

14 Tom Mangold, *Cold Warrior: James Jesus Angleton; The CIA's Master Spy Hunter* (London: Simon & Schuster, 1991), p. 20. It is unfortunate that Angleton's biographer Mangold does not give any details of Angleton's work with Fascists in the years after 1945 and does not mention how Angleton saved Borghese.

15 William Corson, *The Armies of Ignorance: The Rise of the American Intelligence Empire* (New York: The Dial Press, 1977), pp. 298 and 299. As the operation was secret the money was dirty and had to be laundered first. Corson explains that this was done by first withdrawing 10 million dollars in cash from the Economic Stabilization Fund, laundering it through individual bank accounts and from there 'donate' it to a variety of CIA front organisations.

16 Christie, *delle Chiaie*, p. 175.

17 Denna Frank Fleming, *The Cold War and Its Origins 1917–1960* (New York: Doubleday, 1961), p. 322.

18 Thomas Powers, *The Man Who Kept the Secrets: Richard Helms and the CIA* (London: Weidenfeld and Nicolson, 1980), p. 30.

19 British daily *The Guardian*, January 15, 1992.

20 During Italy's First Republic the military secret service due to repeated scandals was repeatedly forced to change its name. From its creation in 1949 until the first major scandal in 1965 the Italian military secret service was called SIFAR, while from 1965 to 1977 it operated with almost the same personnel under the name of SID. After yet another scandal, SID as of 1978 was split into two new branches which still operate today. The civilian branch was placed under the Interior Ministry and labelled SISDE (Servizio Informazioni Sicurezza Democratica), while the military branch remained under the Defence Ministry and operated under the label SISMI. The Directors of the Italian military secret services during the First Republic were: General Giovanni Carlo (1949–1951, SIFAR), General Umberto Broccoli (1951–1953, SIFAR), General Ettore

Musco (1953–1955, SIFAR), General Giovanni De Lorenzo (1956–1962, SIFAR), General Egidio Viggiani (1962–1965, SIFAR), General Giovanni Allavena (1965–1966, SID), General Eugenio Henke (1966–1970, SID), General Vito Miceli (1970–1974, SID), General Mario Casardi (1974–1978, SID), General Giuseppe Santovito (1978–1981, SISMI), General Nino Lugaresi (1981–1984, SISMI), Admiral Fulvio Martini (1984–1991, SISMI), Sergio Luccarini (1991, SISMI), General Luigi Ramponi (1991–1992, SISMI), General Cesare Pucci (1992–1993, SISMI).

21 Philip Willan, *Puppetmasters: The Political Use of Terrorism in Italy* (London: Constable, 1991), p. 34.

22 Mario Coglitore (ed.), *La Notte dei Gladiatori. Omissioni e silenze della Repubblica* (Padova: Calusca Edizioni, 1992), p. 34.

23 British daily *The Observer*, November 18, 1990

24 Italian 1995 Senate report on Gladio and the massacres, p. 49.

25 Coglitore, *Gladiatori*, p. 133.

26 Pietro Cedomi, *Service secrets, guerre froide et 'stay-behind. Part II': La mise en place des resaux*. In: Belgian periodical *Fire! Le Magazin de l'Homme d'Action*, September/October 1991, p. 80.

27 British daily *The Observer*, June 7, 1992.

28 The document was declassified in 1994 and caused widespread criticism in Italy. Compare Italian daily *La Stampa*, November 27, 1994.

29 William Colby, *Honourable Men: My Life in the CIA* (New York: Simon & Schuster, 1978), p. 110.

30 Roberto Faenza, *Il malaffare. Dall' America di Kennedy all'Italia, a Cuba, al Vietnam* (Milano: Editore Arnoldo Mondadori, 1978), p. 312.

31 The existence of the document was revealed during the Gladio revelations in 1990. Italian 1995 Senate report on Gladio and the massacres, p. 25.

32 Italian periodical *Europeo*, January 18 1991. The Italian parliamentary commission knew of the existence of the 1956 document on Gladio only because it had come into the possession of a June 1, 1959 document on Gladio which referred back to the other document in precise terms, saying that it is dated November 26, 1956 and in its Italian version entitled 'Accordo fra il Servizio Informazioni Italiano ed il Servizio Informazioni USA relativo alla organizzazione ed all'attivita della rete clandestina post-occupazione (stay-behind) italo-statunitense.' [Agreement between SIFAR and the CIA concerning the organisation and activity of the secret Italian–US post-occupation network (stay-behind).] The original 1959 document is contained in Coglitore, *Gladiatori*, pp. 118–130.

33 Belgian periodical *Fire*, January 1992, p. 59.

34 Ibid., p. 62.

35 Allan Francovich, *Gladio: The Puppeteers*. Second of the total three Francovich Gladio documentaries, broadcasted on BBC2 on June 17, 1992.

36 Colby, *Honourable Men*, p. 128.

37 Ibid., pp. 109–120.

38 The document is quoted in Faenza, *Malaffare*, p. 313. Italian historian Roberto Faenza in the 1970s researched in the US archives and by using the FOIA got hold of the Demagnetize document revealing for the first time 'this heavy deviation of the Italian Secret Service'.

39 *Stato Maggiore della Difesa. Servizio Informazioni delle Forze Armate. Ufficio R – Sezione SAD: Le forze speciali del SIFAR e l'operazione GLADIO. Roma, 1 Giugno 1959.* This document was found by judge Felice Casson in the archives of SIFAR in Rome in 1990 and started the Gladio revelations in Italy and beyond. The document is contained in Coglitore, *Gladiatori*, pp. 118–130.

40 Cobly, *Honourable Men*, p. 136.

41 Telegram sent by the Secretary of State to the US embassy in Rome on October 18, 1961. Quoted in Faenza, *Malaffare*, p. 311. Faenza offers a very good analysis on

Kennedy's plan to open Italy to the left. Compare Faenza, *Malaffare*, pp. 307–373 ('L' apertura a sinistra).
42 Quoted in Regine Igel, *Andreotti. Politik zwischen Geheimdienst und Mafia* (München: Herbig Verlag, 1997), p. 49. Her undated reference is the US magazine *New Statesman*.
43 Faenza, *Malaffare*, p. 310.
44 Igel, *Andreotti*, p. 50.
45 Faenza, *Malaffar*, p. 356.
46 Jens Mecklenburg (ed.), *Gladio: Die geheime Terrororganisation der Nato* (Berlin: Elefanten Press, 1997), p. 30. And Coglitore, *Gladiatori*, p. 185. It was a former General of the SID who revealed that these attackers were Gladiators during interrogations in the 1980s in the context of the Propaganda Due (in short P2) scandal.
47 Jean Francois Brozzu-Gentile: *L' affaire Gladio* (Paris: Editions Albin Michel, 1994), p. 77. And Faenza, *Malaffare*, p. 315. See also Willan, *Puppetmasters*, p. 84.
48 Italian 1995 Senate report on Gladio and the massacres, p. 85.
49 Ibid.
50 *Stato Maggiore della Difesa. Servizio Informazioni delle Forze Armate. Ufficio R – Sezione SAD: Le forze speciali del SIFAR e l'operazione GLADIO. Roma, 1 Giugno 1959.* The document is contained in Coglitore, *Gladiatori*, pp. 118–130. Investigations into Piano Solo suggested that 731 persons were to be deported, while the Senate commission investigating Operation Gladio found that it is much more likely that between 1100 and 1200 influential people were to be imprisoned in the Gladio headquarters CAG on Sardinia. Scandalously the military secret service refused to make the Gladio proscription lists available to the parliamentary commission. 'This is a very grave situation, for one can assume that the list contains the names of parliamentarians and political functionaries. and the publication of it would withdraw any basis from the claim that the events of 1964 had been cautious operations in order to prevent public disturbances', the Senators concluded. See Italian 1995 Senate report on Gladio and the massacres, p. 89.
51 A good description of the coup is contained in Richard Collin, *The De Lorenzo Gambit: The Italian Coup Manque of 1964* (Beverly Hills: Sage, 1976). Collin, who graduated from Harvard, lectured in Maryland, specialised in military affairs and served as an officer of staff of the US Secretary of the Army, later as the adviser to the Defense attache at the US Embassy in Rome and later as a consultant to the Saudi Defence Forces, offers a remarkably good early narrative of Piano Solo in his 60-pages booklet. Unfortunately he excludes almost completely the role that the United States played behind the scenes.
52 Collin, *Coup*, p. 60.
53 Ibid. His source is the Italian political magazine *Avanti!*, July 26, 1964.
54 Coglitore, *Gladiatori*, p. 186. See also Willan, *Puppetmasters*, p. 85.
55 Italian 1995 Senate report on Gladio and the massacres, p. 87. Bernard Cook, *The Mobilisation of the Internal Cold War in Italy*. In: History of European Ideas. Vol. 19, 1994, p. 116.
56 Franco Ferraresi, *A Secret Structure Codenamed Gladio*. In: Italian Politics. A Review, 1992, p. 41. The silent Gladio coup would never have been exposed without the work of investigative journalists. Starting in Spring 1967 journalist Raffaele Jannuzzi (who later entered parliament to represent the Socialists) in the political magazine *Espresso* informed a startled Italian public that they had only narrowly escaped a coup d'état (Complotto al Quirinale, Espresso, May 14, 1967). De Lorenzo's attempt to make journalist Jannuzzi shut up with a defamation suit led to counter-productive results as in the process such a large quantity of evidence surfaced that the government was ultimately forced to concede to a full parliamentary investigation into 'the events of 1964'

(Italian Senate. Commissione parlamentare d'inchiesta sugli eventi del giungo-luglio 1964. Findings published in two volumes (Majority and Minority Report) in Rome in 1971).

57 *Relazione della Commissione parlamentare d'inchiesta sugli eventi del giungno-luglio 1964, Roma 1971*, p. 67. Quoted in Igel, *Andreotti*, p. 51. And Willan, *Puppetmasters*, p. 38.

58 *Commissione parlamentare d'inchiesta sugli eventi del giugno-luglio 1964, Relazione di minoranza, Roma 1971*, p. 307. Compare Igel, *Andreotti*, p. 53.

59 Quoted in Igel, *Andreotti*, p. 52.

60 Italian judge Carlo Palermo, upon having discovered links of Licio Gelli to right-wing terrorists, had ordered the anti-terror office of SISMI to help him in his investigation. The anti-terror office of the SISMI on April 16, 1983, presented details on the US secret hand in Italy. It was maybe the first time that the unit had carried out its duty and tellingly the anti-terror office of the SISMI was thereafter closed down immediately. The promising career of Emilio Santillos, Director of the SISMI anti-terror office, ended abruptly soon after the report while also the biographies of his fellow investigators took a tragic twist. SISMI Colonel Florio died in a mysterious car accident, SISMI Colonel Serrentiono left the service 'for reasons of ill health', Major Rossi committed suicide and only Major Antonio de Salvo left the anti-terror office in good health and joined the Freemasons. Quoted in Igel, *Andreotti*, p. 232.

61 British daily *The Observer*, February 21, 1988.

62 *Senato della Repubblica Italiana. Relazione della Commissione Parlamentare d'Inchiesta Sulla Loggia P2, Roma 1984*.

63 In an interview with Willan. Quoted in Willan, *Puppetmasters*, p. 55.

64 Igel, *Andreotti*, p. 229.

65 Quoted in the British periodical *The New Statesman*, September 21, 1984.

66 Hugh O'Shaughnessy: *Gladio. Europe's best kept secret*. They were the agents who were to 'stay behind' if the Red Army overran Western Europe. But the network that was set up with the best intentions degenerated in some countries into a front for terrorism and far-right political agitation. In British daily *The Observer*, June 7, 1992.

67 Gentile, *Gladio*, p. 28.

68 Ibid.

69 British daily television news program *Newsnight* on BBC1 on April 4, 1991.

70 Willan, *Puppetmasters*, p. 41.

71 Italian 1995 Senate report on Gladio and the massacres, p. 97.

72 Ibid., p. 164.

73 Willan, *Puppetmasters*, p. 97. Buscetta testified to Falcone in December 1984. Later courageous Falcone was killed by the Mafia.

74 Liggio to the Reggio Calabria assize court in 1986. Quoted in Willan, *Puppetmasters*, p. 97.

75 Willan, *Puppetmasters*, p. 94.

76 Colby, *Honourable Men*, p. 395.

77 Compare for instance McNamara, Robert, *In Retrospect: The Tragedy and Lessons of Vietnam* (New York: Random House, 1995).

78 Willian, *Puppetmasters*, p. 93.

79 British political magazine *Statewatch*, January 1991.

80 Gentile, *Gladio*, p. 105.

81 British political magazine *Statewatch*, January 1991. And Gentile, *Gladio*, p. 19.

82 Italian political magazine *Europeo*, November 16, 1990.

83 Allan Francovich, *Gladio: The Puppeteers*. Second of the total three Francovich Gladio documentaries, broadcasted on BBC2 on June 17, 1992.

84 Ibid.

85 The results in the subsequent years in the elections for the Italian parliament were these for the three dominating parties DCI, PCI and PSI:

	DCI (%)	PCI (%)	PSI (%)	PCI + PSI (%)
1968	39.1	26.9	14.5	41.4
1972	38.7	27.1	9.6	36.7
1976	38.7	34.4	9.6	44.0
1979	38.3	30.4	9.8	40.2
1983	32.9	29.9	11.4	41.3
1987	34.3	26.6	14.3	40.9
1992	29.7	23.6	13.6	37.2
1994	dissolved	28.3	2.2	30.5

Source: http://www.aitec.it/paradisi/costitutz/c_app3.htm.

86 Pike Report: Report of the House Select Committee on Intelligence [Pike Committee], Ninety-fourth Congress (New York: Village Voice, 1976), pp. 193 and 195.
87 Joe Garner, We Interrupt this broadcast. The Events that stopped our lives. From the Hindenburg Explosion to the Death of John F. Kennedy Jr (Naperville: Sourcebooks, 2000), p. 87.
88 Quoted in Willan, Puppetmasters, p. 220.
89 Willan, Puppetmasters, p. 325.
90 Quoted in Willan, Puppetmasters, p. 219.
91 Italian 1995 Senate report on Gladio and the massacres, pp. 294 and 295.
92 Ibid., p. 294
93 British daily The Guardian, January 16, 1991.
94 International news service Associated Press, November 20, 1990.
95 BBC reporter Peter Marshall interviewing Serravalle for the Newsnight special report on Gladio of April 4, 1991.
96 Allan Francovich, Gladio: The Puppeteers. Second of the total three Francovich Gladio documentaries, broadcasted on BBC2 on June 17, 1992.
97 Italian 1995 Senate report on Gladio and the massacres, pp. 242 and 364.
98 Senato della Repubblica. Commissione parlamentare d'inchiesta sul terrorismo in Italia e sulle cause della mancata individuazione dei responsabili delle stragi: Stragi e terrorismo in Italia dal dopoguerra al 1974. Relazione del Gruppo Democratici di Sinistra l'Ulivo. Roma June 2000. Hereafter quoted as 2000 Senate report on Gladio and the massacres. The 8 members were: On. Valter Bielli, On. Antonio Attili, On. Michele Cappella, On. Piero Ruzzante, Sen. Alessandro Pardini, Sen. Raffaele Bertoni, Sen. Graziano Cioni, Sen. Angelo Staniscia. As quoted in Philip Willan, US 'supported anti-left terror in Italy'. Report claims Washington used a strategy of tension in the cold war to stabilise the centre-right. In: British daily The Guardian, June 24, 2000.
99 Italian 2000 Senate report on Gladio and the massacres, p. 41.
100 Ibid.
101 Ibid., p. 42.
102 Philip Willan, US 'supported anti-left terror in Italy'. Report claims Washington used a strategy of tension in the cold war to stabilise the centre-right. In: British daily The Guardian, June 24, 2000.
103 Philip Willan, US 'supported anti-left terror in Italy'. Report claims Washington used a strategy of tension in the cold war to stabilise the centre-right. In: British daily The Guardian, June 24, 2000.

7 THE SECRET WAR IN FRANCE

1 The First French Republic followed the French Revolution of 1789 and lasted from 1792 to 1799. The Second French Republic followed the European revolutions and lasted from 1848 to 1852. The Third French Republic began in 1886 and ended with the defeat during the Second World War in 1940.
2 Edward Rice-Maximin, *Accommodation and Resistance: The French Left, Indochina and the Cold War 1944–1954* (New York: Greenwood Press, 1986), p. 12.
3 Philip Agee and Louis Wolf Louis, *Dirty Work: The CIA in Western Europe* (Secaucus: Lyle Stuart Inc., 1978), p. 182.
4 Quoted in Rice-Maximin, *Resistance*, p. 95. The speech was held on January 28, 1950.
5 Hoyt S. Vandenberg, Memorandum for the President Harry S. Truman. Central Intelligence Group, Washington, November 26, 1946. First classified as top-secret, now in the Harry Truman library.
6 Roger Faligot and Pascal Krop, *La Piscine. Les Services Secrets Francais 1944–1984* (Paris: Editions du Seuil, 1985), p. 84.
7 Roger Faligot and Rémi Kaufer, *Les Maitres Espions. Histoire Mondiale du Renseignement. Tome 2. De la Guerre Froide à nos jours* (Paris: Editions Laffont, 1994), p. 56.
8 Faligot and Krop, *Piscine*, p. 85.
9 Rice-Maximin, *Resistance*, p. 53.
10 Faligot and Krop, *Piscine*, p. 85.
11 Ibid., p. 86.
12 Faligot and Kaufer, *Espions*, p. 56.
13 Faligot and Krop, *Piscine*, p. 86.
14 Hoyt S. Vandenberg, Memorandum for the President Harry S. Truman. Central Intelligence Group, Washington, November 26, 1946. First classified as top-secret, now in the Harry Truman library.
15 Trevor Barnes, *The Secret Cold War: The CIA and American Foreign Policy in Europe, 1946–1956.* In: *The Historical Journal*, Vol. 24, No. 2, 1981, p. 413.
16 Quoted in Jan de Willems, *Gladio* (Brussels: Editions EPO, 1991), p. 35.
17 Jean-Francois Brozzu-Gentile, *L' affaire Gladio* (Paris: Editions Albin Michel, 1994), p. 190.
18 Christopher Simpson, *Blowback: America's Recruitment of Nazis and its Effects on the Cold War* (London: Weidenfeld and Nicolson, 1988), p. 127.
19 *Senato della Repubblica. Commissione parlamentare d'inchiesta sul terrorismo in Italia e sulle cause della mancata individuazione dei responsabiliy delle stragi: Il terrorismo, le stragi ed il contesto storico politico.* Redatta dal presidente della Commissione, Senatore Giovanni Pellegrino. Roma 1995, p. 36.
20 Irwin Wall, *The United States and the Making of Postwar France, 1945–1954* (Cambridge: Cambridge University Press, 1991), p. 150.
21 Faligot and Krop, *Piscine*, p. 88. And Jacques Baud: *Encyclopédie du renseignement et des services secrets* (Paris: Lavauzelle, 1997), p. 546.
22 No author specified, *Spotlight: Western Europe: Stay-Behind.* In: French periodical *Intelligence Newsletter. Le Monde du Renseignement*, December 5, 1990.
23 Faligot and Krop, *Piscine*, p. 90.
24 Ibid., their interview with Louis Mouchon. Ibid., *Piscine*, p. 89.
25 Faligot and Kaufer, *Espions*, p. 57.
26 British weekly *The Economist*, April 16, 1994.
27 Jonathan Kwitny, *The CIA's Secret Armies in Europe: An International Story.* In: *The Nation*, April 6, 1992, pp. 446 and 447.
28 Ibid.
29 Ibid.
30 Italian periodical *Europeo*, January 18, 1991.

31 The Italian daily *L'Unita* published the document in Italian in a special edition on November 14, 1990.
32 The document is quoted in Roberto Faenza, *Il malaffare. Dall' America di Kennedy all'Italia, a Cuba, al Vietnam* (Milano: Editore Arnoldo Mondadori, 1978), p. 313.
33 Faenza, *Malaffare*, p. 313.
34 Gentile, *Gladio*, p. 144.
35 French daily *Le Monde*, November 16, 1990. And Pietro Cedomi: *Service secrets, guerre froide est 'stay-behind. Part II': La mise en place des resaux*. In: Belgian periodical *Fire! Le Magazin de l'Homme d'Action*, September/October 1991, pp. 74–80.
36 Faligot and Krop: *Piscine*, p. 165.
37 French daily *Le Monde*, January 12, 1998.
38 Douglas Porch: *The French Secret Services: From the Dreyfus Affair to the Gulf War* (New York: Farrar, Straus and Giroux, 1995), p. 395.
39 Porch, *Secret Services*, p. 395.
40 This description of Operation Ressurection is from Ph. Bernert who offers it in his book: *Roger Wybot et la bataille pur la DST*. Quoted in Gentile, *Gladio*, p. 286.
41 Porch, *Secret Service*, p. 396.
42 Ibid.
43 Ibid., p. 408.
44 Jonathan Kwitny, *The CIA's Secret Armies in Europe: An International Story*. In: *The Nation*, April 6, 1992, pp. 446 and 447.
45 William Blum, *Killing Hope: US Military and CIA interventions since World War II* (Maine: Common Courage Press, 1995), p. 149.
46 Ibid.
47 Ibid.
48 Porch, *Secret Services*, p. 398.
49 As revealed for instance by former 11th Demi Brigade Du Choc commander officer Erwan Bergot in his memoirs: *Le Dossier Rouge. Services Secrets Contre FLN* (Paris: Grasset Publishers, 1976)
50 Erich Schmidt Eenboom in the 1990s wrote on Gladio and the secret French terror operations in his unpublished nine-pages essay *Die 'Graue' und die 'Rote' Hand. Geheimdienste in Altenstadt*. Both quotes Ibid., pp. 3 and 7. French terrorist operations against the FLN in Germany included: Assassination, by machine gun, of FLN General Secretary Ait Acéne in Bonn on November 5, 1958. Assassination, by a single short-range shot of FLN member Abd el Solvalar in the railway station of Saarbrücken on January 19, 1959. Assassination of Lorenzen, friend of Hamburger arms producer Otto Schlüter, by a bomb explosion in Schlüters warehouse on September 28, 1956. On June 3, 1957 Schlüter himself survived an assassination attack, but his mother was killed in the event (ibid.).
51 British daily *Sunday Times*, October 12, 1997. And French daily *Le Monde*, October 17, 1996.
52 Jean-Luc Einaudi, *La Bataille de Paris* (Paris: Seuil, 1991).
53 Swiss weekly *Wochenzeitung*, December 14, 1990.
54 British daily *Sunday Times*, October 12, 1997. And French daily *Le Monde*, October 17, 1996.
55 Ibid.
56 Jeffrey M. Bale, *Right wing Terrorists and the Extraparliamentary Left in Post World War 2 Europe: Collusion or Manipulation?* In: *Lobster Magazine* (UK), Nr. 2, October 1989, p. 6.
57 Jonathan Kwitny, *The CIA's Secret Armies in Europe: An International Story*. In: *The Nation*, April 6, 1992, pp. 446 and 447.
58 Porch, *Secret Services*, p. 409.
59 Ibid., p. 419.

60 *Stato Maggiore della Difesa. Servizio Informazioni delle Forze Armate. Ufficio R – Sezione SAD: Le forze speciali del SIFAR e l'operazione GLADIO. Roma, 1 Giugno 1959.* The document is contained in Mario Coglitore (ed.), *La Notte dei Gladiatori. Omissioni e silenze della Repubblica* (Padova: Calusca Edizioni, 1992), pp. 118–130.

61 Belgian Parliamentary Commission of Enquiry into Gladio, as summarised in British periodical *Statewatch*, January/February 1992.

62 Jan de Willems, *Gladio* (Brussels: Editions EPO, 1991), p. 24.

63 Willems, *Gladio*, p. 81.

64 Quoted in Willan, op. cit., p. 27.

65 Arthur Rowse, Gladio. *The Secret US War to subvert Italian Democracy.* In: *Covert Action Quarterly*, No. 49, Summer 1994, p. 3.

66 Baud, *Encyclopedie*, p. 546.

67 Porch, *Secret Services*, p. 439.

68 Ibid., p. 438.

69 Ibid., p. 395.

70 Ibid., p. 439.

71 Ibid., p. 437.

72 Ibid., p. 438, referring to Foccart's biographer Pierre Péan.

73 Ibid., p. 439.

74 Baud, *Encyclopedie*, p. 546 and French daily *Le Monde*, November 16, 1990.

75 Porch, *Secret Services*, p. 446. The report of the French parliamentarian commission into SAC is called: 'Rapport de la commission d'enquête sur les activités du Service d'Action Civique', Assemblée Nationale. Seconde session ordinaire de 1981–1982, No. 955, Alain Moreau, Paris 1982.

76 *Intelligence Newsletter*, November 21, 1990.

77 Porch, *Secret Service*, p. 590.

78 Ibid., p. 446.

79 Ibid., p. 404.

80 Jonathan Kwitny, *The CIA's Secret Armies in Europe: An International Story.* In: *The Nation*, April 6, 1992, pp. 446 and 447.

81 French daily *Le Monde*, November 14, 1990. International news agency *Reuters*, November 12, 1990. British daily *The Guardian*, November 14, 1990.

82 Quoted in Gentile, *Gladio*, p. 141. Also quoted by international news service *Associated Press*, November 13, 1990.

8 THE SECRET WAR IN SPAIN

1 In his introduction to Ian Mac Dougall, *Voices from the Spanish Civil War. Personal Recollections of Scottish Volunteers in Republican Spain, 1936–1939* (Edinburgh: Polygon, 1986).

2 Paul Vallely, *Romancing the past: Sixty years ago, thousands of men and women went to fight in the Spanish Civil War. Are there any ideals for which we would take up arms today?* In: British daily *The Independent*, July 22, 1996.

3 Brian Catchcart, *They kept the red flag flying: It is 60 years since General Franco launched his assault on the Spanish Republic and thousands of young Britons joined the International Brigades to defend it. What drove them to leave homes, jobs and families, risking their lives? And what did they find when they returned?* In: British weekly *The Independent on Sunday*, July 21, 1996.

4 US daily *The New York Times*, October 16, 1936.

5 James Hopkins, *Into the Heart of Fire. The British in the Spanish Civil War* (Stanford: Stanford University Press, 1998), p. 294.

NOTES

6 Example taken from the British daily *The New Statesman*, April 26, 1958.
7 *Calvo Sotelo asegura que Espana no fue informada, cuando entro en la OTAN, de la existencia de Gladio. Moran sostiene que no oyo hablar de la red clandestina mientras fue ministro de Exteriores.* In: Spanish daily *El Pais*, November 21, 1990.
8 Roger Faligot and Remi Kaufer, *Le Maitres Espions. Histoire mondiale du renseignement. De la Guerre Froide a nos jours* (Paris: Editions Robert Laffont, 1994), p. 282.
9 Faligot and Kaufer, *Espions*, p. 284.
10 For a good biography on Franco compare Paul Preston, *The folly of appeasement: Franco: A Biography* (London: HarperCollins, 1993).
11 Faligot and Kaufer, *Espions*, pp. 281–285.
12 *Calvo Sotelo asegura que Espana no fue informada, cuando entro en la OTAN, de la existencia de Gladio. Moran sostiene que no oyo hablar de la red clandestina mientras fue ministro de Exteriores.* In: Spanish daily *El Pais*, November 21, 1990.
13 Faligot and Kaufer, *Espions*, p. 55.
14 Angel Luis de la Calle, *Gladio: Ligacoes obscuras em Espanha.* In: Portuguese daily *Expresso*, December 8, 1990.
15 Josef Manola, *Spaniens Geheimdienste vor der Durchleuchtung. Naehe zu Rechtsradikalen.* In: German daily *Der Standard*, November 17, 1990.
16 The Swiss Gladio investigator judge Cornu later simply claimed that Moyen was an untrustworthy source.
17 *Calvo Sotelo asegura que Espana no fue informada, cuando entro en la OTAN, de la existencia de Gladio. Moran sostiene que no oyo hablar de la red clandestina mientras fue ministro de Exteriores.* In: Spanish daily *El Pais*, November 21, 1990.
18 Faligot and Kaufer, *Espions*, p. 285.
19 Pietro Cedomi, *Services Secrets, Guerre Froide et 'stay-behind' Part III. Repetoire des resaux S/B.* In: Belgian periodical *Fire! Le Magazin de l'Homme d'Action*, November/December 1991, p. 83.
20 Stuart Christie, Martin Lee and Kevin Coogan, *Protected by the West's Secret Services, Hired by South American's Drug Barons, the Man they called 'Shorty' Terrorised Two Continents.* In: British periodical *News on Sunday Extra*, May 31, 1987. Christie is a leading expert on Delle Chiaie. Compare his book Stuart Christie, *Stefano Delle Chiaie* (London: Anarchy Publications, 1984).
21 Miguel Gonzalez, *Un informe oficial italiano implica en el crimen de Atocha al 'ultra' Cicuttini, relacionado con Gladio. El fascista fue condenado en el proceso que ha sacado a la luz la estructura secreta de la OTAN.* In: Spanish daily *El Pais*, December 2, 1990.
22 *Senato della Repubblica. Commissione parlamentare d'inchiesta sul terrorismo in Italia e sulle cause della mancata individuazione dei responsabiliy delle stragi: Il terrorismo, le stragi ed il contesto storico politico.* Redatta dal presidente della Commissione, Senatore Giovanni Pellegrino. Roma 1995, p. 203.
23 Angel Luis de la Calle, *Gladio: ligacoes obscuras em Espanha.* In: Portuguese daily *Expresso*, December 8, 1990. And Miguel Gonzalez, *Un informe oficial italiano implica en el crimen de Atocha al 'ultra' Cicuttini, relacionado con Gladio. El fascista fue condenado en el proceso que ha sacado a la luz la estructura secreta de la OTAN.* In: Spanish daily *El Pais*, December 2, 1990.
24 International news agency *Agence France Press*, April 17, 1998.
25 Gerardo Serravalle, *Gladio* (Roma: Edizione Associate, 1991). Another Italian General who commanded the Gladio army from 1974 to 1986, Paolo Inzerilli, also wrote a somewhat apologetic book on the secret army, Paolo Inzerilli, *Gladio. La Verità negata* (Bologna: Edizioni Analisi, 1995).
26 Serravalle, *Gladio*, p. 81.
27 Ibid, p. 82.

28 Ibid, p. 82.
29 Pietro Cedomi, *Services Secrets, Guerre Froide et 'stay-behind' Part III. Repetoire des resaux S/B.* In: Belgian periodical *Fire! Le Magazin de l'Homme d'Action*, November/ December 1991, p. 83.
30 Josef Manola, *Spaniens Geheimdienste vor der Durchleuchtung. Naehe zu Rechtsradikalen.* In: German daily *Der Standard*, November 17, 1990.
31 *Spain says it never joined Gladio. TV says agents trained there. Reuters*, international news service, November 23, 1990. Compare also Leo Müller, *Gladio. Das Erbe des Kalten Krieges. Der NATO Geheimbund und sein deutscher Vorläufer* (Hamurg: Rowohlt, 1991), p. 53.
32 *Calvo Sotelo asegura que Espana no fue informada, cuando entro en la OTAN, de la existencia de Gladio. Moran sostiene que no oyo hablar de la red clandestina mientras fue ministro de Exteriores.* In: Spanish daily *El Pais*, November 21, 1990.
33 *Calvo Sotelo asegura que Espana no fue informada, cuando entro en la OTAN, de la existencia de Gladio. Moran sostiene que no oyo hablar de la red clandestina mientras fue ministro de Exteriores.* In: Spanish daily *El Pais*, November 21, 1990.
34 *Germany to dissolve Gladio resistance network. Reuters* international news service, November 16, 1990.
35 *IU recabara en Bruselas informacion sobre la red Gladio en Espana.* In: Spanish daily *El Pais*, November 20, 1990.
36 *El servicio espanol de inteligencia mantiene estrechas relaciones con la OTAN. Serra ordena indagar sobre la red Gladio en Espana.* In: Spanish daily *El Pais*, November 16, 1990
37 Spain says it never joined Gladio. TV says agents trained there. *Reuters* international news service, November 23, 1990.
38 *IU recabara en Bruselas informacion sobre la red Gladio en Espana.* In: Spanish daily *El Pais*, November 20, 1990.
39 *Calvo Sotelo asegura que Espana no fue informada, cuando entro en la OTAN, de la existencia de Gladio. Moran sostiene que no oyo hablar de la red clandestina mientras fue ministro de Exteriores.* In: Spanish daily *El Pais*, November 21, 1990.

9 THE SECRET WAR IN PORTUGAL

1 John Palmer, *Undercover NATO Group 'may have had terror links'.* In: British daily *The Guardian*, November 10, 1990.
2 Michael Parenti, *Against Empire* (San Francisco: City Light Books, 1995), p. 143.
3 Joao Paulo Guerra, *'Gladio' actuou em Portugal.* In: Portuguese daily *O Jornal*, November 16, 1990.
4 *Senato della Repubblica. Commissione parlamentare d'inchiesta sul terrorismo in Italia e sulle cause della mancata individuazione dei responsabiliy delle stragi: Il terrorismo, le stragi ed il contesto storico politico.* Redatta dal presidente della Commissione, Senatore Giovanni Pellegrino. Roma 1995, pp. 204 and 241.
5 Commissione parlamentare d'inchiesta sul terrorismo in Italia e sulle cause della mancata individuazione dei responsabili delle stragi. 12th session, March 20, 1997. URL: www.parlamento.it/parlam/bicam/terror/stenografici/steno12.htm.
6 Commissione parlamentare d'inchiesta sul terrorismo in Italia e sulle cause della mancata individuazione dei responsabili delle stragi. 9th session, February 12, 1997. URL: www.parlamento.it/parlam/bicam/terror/stenografici/steno9.htm.
7 Jeffrey M. Bale, *Right wing Terrorists and the Extraparliamentary Left in Post World War 2 Europe: Collusion or Manipulation?* In: British periodical *Lobster Magazine*, Nr. 2, October 1989, p. 6.
8 French periodical *Paris Match*, November 1974. Quoted in Stuart Christie, *Stefano delle Chiaie* (London: Anarchy Publications, 1984), p. 27.

9 Egmont Koch and Oliver Schröm, *Deckname Aginter. Die Geschichte einer faschistischen Terror Organisation*, p. 4. (Unpublished essay of 17 pages. Undated, ca. 1998).
10 See Christie, *delle Chiaie*, passim.
11 Ibid., p. 29.
12 This document was allegedly found in the former office of Guerain-Serac after the Portuguese revolution of 1974. It is contained in the Belgian dictionary on terrorism in Belgium by Manuel Abramowicz. See entry 'Guerin Serac' in: Le dictionnaire des années de plomb belges. On the Internet: www.users.skynet.be/avancees/idees.htm.
13 Quoted in Christie, *delle Chiaie*, p. 32. Also in Lobster, October 1989, p. 18.
14 Ibid., p. 30.
15 Joao Paulo Guerra, *'Gladio' actuou em Portugal*. In: Portuguese daily *O Jornal*, November 16, 1990.
16 Ibid. And Christie, *delle Chiaie*, p. 30.
17 *Senato della Repubblica. Commissione parlamentare d'inchiesta sul terrorismo in Italia e sulle cause della mancata individuazione dei responsabiliy delle stragi: Il terrorismo, le stragi ed il contesto storico politico.* Redatta dal presidente della Commissione, Senatore Giovanni Pellegrino. Roma 1995, p. 157.
18 Fabrizio Calvi and Frederic Laurent produced a remarkable documentary on the massacre entitled *Piazza Fontana: Storia di un Complotto* broadcasted on December 11, 1997 at 8:50 p.m. on the Italian state television Rai Due. And was shown again in its French version, *L' Orchestre Noir: La Strategie de la tension*, in two blocks on January 13, 1998 and January 14, 1998 at 20:45 on French Channel Arte. Relying strongly on oral history they questioned a large number of witnesses including the judges that for years investigated the massacres, Guido Salvini and Gerardo D'Ambrosio, as well as right-wing extremists Stefano Delle Chiaies, Amos Spiazzi, Guido Giannettini, Vincenzo Vinciguerra, and officials including Captain Labruna and Prime Minister Gulio Andreotti of the DCI. Moreover they interviewed Victor Marchetti and Marc Wyatt of the CIA.
19 Commissione parlamentare d'inchiesta sul terrorismo in Italia e sulle cause della mancata individuazione dei responsabili delle stragi. 9th session, February 12, 1997. URL: www.parlamento.it/parlam/bicam/terror/stenografici/steno9.htm.
20 Philip Willan, *Terrorists 'helped by CIA' to Stop Rise of Left in Italy*. In: British daily *The Guardian*, March 26, 2001. Willan is an expert on US covert action in Italy. He published the very valuable book *Puppetmasters. The Political Use of Terrorism in Italy* (London: Constable, 1991).
21 Italian daily *La Stampa*, June 22, 1996.
22 Peter Dale Scott, *Transnational Repression: Parafascism and the US*. In: British periodical *Lobster Magazine*, Nr. 12, 1986, p. 16.
23 Joao Paulo Guerra, *'Gladio' actuou em Portugal*. In: Portuguese daily *O Jornal*, November 16, 1990.
24 Koch and Schröm, *Aginter*, p. 8.
25 Quoted in Christie, *delle Chiaie*, p. 28.
26 Commissione parlamentare d'inchiesta sul terrorismo in Italia e sulle cause della mancata individuazione dei responsabili delle stragi. 9th session, February 12, 1997. URL: www.parlamento.it/parlam/bicam/terror/stenografici/steno9.htm.
27 Koch and Schröm, *Aginter*, pp. 11–12.
28 Portuguese daily *Expresso*, November 17, 1990.
29 Portuguese daily *Diario De Noticias*, November 17, 1990.
30 No author specified, *Ministro nega conhecimento da rede Gladio. Franco Nogueira disse ao DN que nem Salazar saberia da organizacao*. In: Portuguese daily *Diario De Noticias*, November 17, 1990.
31 Ibid.

32 No author specified, *Manfred Woerner explica Gladio. Investigadas ligacoes a extrema-direita.* In: Portuguese daily *Expresso*, November 24, 1990.

33 Joao Paulo Guerra, *'Gladio' actuou em Portugal.* In: Portuguese daily *O Jornal*, November 16, 1990.

10 THE SECRET WAR IN BELGIUM

1 *Enquête parlementaire sur l'existence en Belgique d'un réseau de renseignements clandestin international, rapport fait au nom de la commission d'enquête par MM. Erdman et Hasquin.* Document Senat, session de 1990–1991. Brussels, p. 24. Hereafter quoted as *Belgian Senate 1991 Gladio Report.* Upon the discovery of the secret stay-behind armies in Western Europe in late 1990, Belgian socialist parliamentarian Dirk van der Maelen had introduced a request in the Belgian parliament which suggested the creation of a parliamentary commission to investigate the secret network. The Senate adopted the law with 143 votes in favour, 1 vote against and 5 abstentions. With 19 Senators and presided by Senator Roger Lallemand, the Belgian Gladio investigation held 57 sessions and heard and recorded the testimony of 37 persons. These included three ministers, the chief of staff of the army, the chief of the police, the chief of the secret service SGR, several former chiefs of the SGR, several instructors of the SGR, and specifically personnel of the SGR Gladio sections SDRA8 and STC/Mob. Also witnesses who wanted to remain anonymous were heard. 'Certain auditions lasted five or six hours. They took place under conditions of total calmness.' On October 1, 1991, the Belgian Gladio Senate Commission presented its 250-pages strong final report and concluded its work. Together with the Report on Gladio of the Italian Senate and the report on P26 of the Swiss parliament the Belgium report represents a solid democratic performance and ranges among the best investigations into the stay-behind network.

2 *Belgian Senate 1991 Gladio Report*, p. 33.

3 Ibid., pp. 148 and 149.

4 Ibid., p. 29.

5 Ibid.

6 Ibid., pp. 24 and 25.

7 Mackenzie, W. J. M., *History of the Special Operations Executive: Britain and the Resistance in Europe* (London: British Cabinet Office, 1948), p. 976, Unpublished original of the Public Records Office London, publication with Frank Cass forthcoming.

8 Mackenzie, *Special Operations Executive*, p. 981.

9 Allan Francovich, *Gladio: The Ringmasters.* First of the total three Francovich Gladio documentaries, broadcasted on BBC2 on June 10, 1992.

10 Ibid.

11 For more details on Lahaut's assassination, see the research by Etienne Verhoyen and Rudi Van Doorslaer, *L'assassinat de Julien Lahaut. Une histoire de l'anticommunisme en Belgique* (Anvers: EPO Press, 1987).

12 The letter is given in full in the *Belgian Senate 1991 Gladio Report*, pp. 212–213.

13 *Belgian Senate 1991 Gladio Report*, p. 213. Also quoted in British daily *The Observer*, June 7, 1992.

14 Ibid., p. 18.

15 Frans Kluiters, *De Nederlandse inlichtingen en veiligheidsdiensten* (1993), p. 311.

16 Jan de Willems, *Gladio* (Brussels: Editions EPO, 1991), p. 147.

17 Kluiters, *Nederlandse*, p. 311. Willems, *Gladio*, p. 147.

18 *Belgian Senate 1991 Gladio Report*, op. cit., p. 18.

19 Quoted in Willems, *Gladio*, p. 147.

20 Ibid., p. 148.

21 Ibid., p. 149.
22 *Belgian Senate 1991 Gladio Report*, p. 22.
23 Ibid., pp. 20 and 21.
24 Michel Van Ussel, *Georges 923. Un agent du Gladio belge parle. Témoignage* (Brussels: Editions la Longue Vue, 1991), p. 150.
25 British periodical *Statewatch*, January 1992.
26 *Belgian Senate 1991 Gladio Report*, p. 22.
27 British periodical *Statewatch*, July/August 1992.
28 *Belgian Senate 1991 Gladio Report*, pp. 6, 29, 30. And Van Ussel, *Georges 923*, pp. 19–27.
29 Ibid., p. 38.
30 Ibid., p. 58.
31 Ibid., p. 55.
32 Ibid.
33 Quoted in *Belgian Senate 1991 Gladio Report*, p. 25.
34 Ibid.
35 Ibid., p. 137.
36 Ibid., p. 62.
37 Van Ussel, *Georges 923*, p. 141.
38 *Belgian Senate 1991 Gladio Report*, p. 57.
39 Van Ussel, *Georges 923*, p. 81.
40 *Belgian Senate 1991 Gladio Report*, p. 61.
41 Allan Francovich, *Gladio: The Ringmasters*. First of the total three Francovich Gladio documentaries, broadcasted on BBC2 on June 10, 1992.
42 Van Ussel, *Georges 923*, p. 79.
43 Ibid., p. 59.
44 Ibid., p. 86.
45 Ibid., pp. 51 and 107.
46 *Belgian Senate 1991 Gladio Report*, p. 28.
47 Ibid., p. 33.
48 Ibid., p. 37.
49 Ibid., p. 45.
50 Ibid., p. 59.
51 Ibid., p. 47.
52 Ibid., p. 45.
53 Ibid., p. 66.
54 Ibid., p. 44.
55 Ibid., p. 47.
56 Van Ussel, *Georges 923*, p. 43.
57 Ibid., p. 57.
58 *Belgian Senate 1991 Gladio Report*, p. 78.
59 Hugh O'Shaughnessy, *Gladio. Europe's best kept secret*. They were the agents who were to 'stay behind' if the Red Army overran Western Europe. But the network that was set up with the best intentions degenerated in some countries into a front for terrorism and far-right political agitation. In: British daily *The Observer*, June 7, 1992.
60 *Belgian Senate 1991 Gladio Report*, pp. 47–48.
61 Allan Francovich, *Gladio: The Foot Soldiers*. Third of the total three Francovich Gladio documentaries, broadcasted on BBC2 on June 24, 1992.
62 Ibid.
63 Ibid.
64 Ibid.
65 Ibid.

66 Hugh O'Shaughnessy, *Gladio. Europe's best kept secret*. They were the agents who were to 'stay behind' if the Red Army overran Western Europe. But the network that was set up with the best intentions degenerated in some countries into a front for terrorism and far-right political agitation. In: British daily *The Observer*, June 7, 1992.

67 Manuel Abramowicz, *Le dictionnaire des 'annés de plomb' belges*. Online: www.users. skynet.be/avancees/idees.html. For more details on CCC, see also Jos Vander Velpen, *Les CCC – L'Etat et le terrorisme* (Anvers: EPO Dossier, 1988).

68 Allan Francovich, *Gladio: The Foot Soldiers*. Third of the total three Francovich Gladio documentaries, broadcasted on BBC2 on June 24, 1992.

69 Quoted in Willems, *Gladio*, p. 13.

70 Chronology of the crimes attributed to the Killers of Brabant:

Date	Place	Victims	Target
14.8.1982	Maubeuge, Brabant	1 wounded	attack on food shop
30.9.1982	Wavre, Brabant	1 killed, 3 wounded	attack on arms shop
30.9.1982	Hoeilaart, Brabant	2 wounded	firing on BSR members
23.12.1982	Bruxelles, Brabant	1 killed	attack on hotel Chevaliers
9.1.1983	Mons, Brabant	1 killed	assassination of a taxi driver
25.2.1983	Uccle, Brabant	1 wounded	attack on Delhaize supermarket
3.3.1983	Hal, Brabant	1 killed, 1 wounded	attack on Colruyt food shop
10.9.1983	Temse, Brabant	1 killed, 1 wounded	attack on textile shop
17.9.1983	Nijvel, Brabant	3 killed, 1 wounded	attack on Colruyt food shop
17.9.1983	Braine-l'Alleud, Brabant	1 wounded	firefight with police
2.10.1983	Ohain, Brabant	1 killed	attack on restaurant
7.10.1983	Beersel, Brabant	1 killed, 3 wounded	attack on Delhaize supermarket
1.12.1983	Anderlues, Brabant	2 killed	attack on jeweller's store
27.9.1985	Braine-l'Alleud, Brabant	3 killed, 1 wounded	attack on Delhaize supermarket
27.9.1985	Overijse, Brabant	5 killed, 1 wounded	attack on Delhaize supermarket
9.11.1985	Aalst, Brabant	8 killed, 9 wounded	attack on Delhaize supermarket

Quoted after *Chambre des Représentants de Belgique: Enquête parlementaire sur les adaptions nécessaires en matiière d'organisation et de fonctionnement de l'appareil policier et judiciaire, en fonction des difficultées surgies lors de l'enquête sur 'les tuerurs du Brabant'. Rapport fait au now de la comission d'enquête par MM. Renaat Landuyt et Jean-Jacques Viseur*. Brussels, October 14, 1997, pp. 21–22.

71 Allan Francovich, *Gladio: The Foot Soldiers*. Third of the total three Francovich Gladio documentaries, broadcasted on BBC2 on June 24, 1992.

72 Marcus Warren, *The Slaughter that still Haunts Belgium*. In: British weekly *Sunday Telegraph*, November 26, 1995.

73 *Belgian Senate 1991 Gladio Report*, p. 100.

74 Ibid., p. 153.

75 Ibid., p. 141.

76 Ibid., p. 53.

77 Ibid., p. 54. Compare also Boris Johnson, *Secret war over identities of Gladio agents.* In: British daily *The Daily Telegraph*, March 29, 1991.

78 *Belgian Senate 1991 Gladio Report*, p. 54.

79 Ibid., p. 51.

80 British periodical *Statewatch*, May/June 1996.

81 *Chambre des Représentants de Belgique: Enquête parlementaire sur les adaptions nécessaires en matiière d'organisation et de fonctionnement de l'appareil policier et judiciaire, en fonction des difficultées surgies lors de l'enquête sur 'les tuerurs du Brabant'. Rapport fait au now de la comission d'enquête par MM. Renaat Landuyt et Jean-Jacques Viseur.* Brussels, October 14, 1997.

82 John Palmer, *Trial Fuels Claims of Right-Wing Belgian Terrorist Conspiracy.* In: British daily *The Guardian*, January 28, 1988.

83 Allan Francovich, *Gladio: The Foot Soldiers.* Third of the total three Francovich Gladio documentaries, broadcasted on BBC2 on June 24, 1992.

84 Ibid.

85 Ibid.

86 Ibid.

87 Phil Davison, *A Very Right-Wing Coup Plot Surfaces in Belgium.* In: British weekly *The Independent on Sunday*, January 24, 1990.

88 Ed. Vulliamy, *Secret agents, freemasons, fascists... and a top-level campaign of political 'destabilisation': 'Strategy of tension' that brought carnage and cover-up.* In: British daily *The Guardian*, December 5, 1990.

89 Willems, *Gladio*, p. 151.

90 *Reuters* international news service, October 1, 1990 and January 25, 1988.

91 Allan Francovich, *Gladio: The Foot Soldiers.* Third of the total three Francovich Gladio documentaries, broadcasted on BBC2 on June 24, 1992.

92 Ibid.

93 Phil Davison, *A Very Right-Wing Coup Plot Surfaces in Belgium.* In: British weekly *The Independent on Sunday*, January 24, 1990.

94 Manuel Abramowicz, *Le dictionnaire des 'annés de plomb' belges.* Online: www.users.skynet.be/avancees/idees.html.

95 Allan Francovich, *Gladio: The Foot Soldiers.* Third of the total three Francovich Gladio documentaries, broadcasted on BBC2 on June 24, 1992.

96 Manuel Abramowicz, *Le dictionnaire des 'annés de plomb' belges.* Online: www.users.skynet.be/avancees/idees.html.

97 Allan Francovich: *Gladio: The Foot Soldiers.* Third of the total three Francovich Gladio documentaries, broadcasted on BBC2 on June 24, 1992.

98 Ibid.

99 Ibid.

100 Ibid.

101 Ibid.

102 Ibid.

103 Ibid.

104 Hugh O'Shaughnessy, *Gladio. Europe's best kept secret.* They were the agents who were to 'stay behind' if the Red Army overran Western Europe. But the network that was set up with the best intentions degenerated in some countries into a front for terrorism and far-right political agitation. In: British daily *The Observer*, June 7, 1992.

105 Allan Francovich, *Gladio: The Foot Soldiers.* Third of the total three Francovich Gladio documentaries, broadcasted on BBC2 on June 24, 1992.

106 Ibid.

107 Manuel Abramowicz, *Le dictionnaire des 'annés de plomb' belges.* Online: www. users.skynet.be/avancees/idees.html.

11 THE SECRET WAR IN THE NETHERLANDS

1 Paul Koedijk, *De Geheimste Dienst. Gladio in Nederland. De geschiedenis van een halve eeuw komplot tegen de vijand*. In: *Vrij Nederland*, January 25, 1992, p. 9. Information on the Dutch stay-behind as of now stems almost exclusively from two articles of Paul Koedijk of the Amsterdam-based Netherlands Institute for War Documentation. With the help of interviews with former Dutch stay-behind members and archive work Koedijk has succeeded in bringing some light into the history of the Dutch secret army I&O, while arguably more research is needed above all on the secretive O branch of the network.

2 Koedijk, *Geheimste Dienst*, p. 9.

3 Frans Kluiters, *De Nederlandse inlichtingen en veiligheidsdiensten* (Gravenhage: Sdu, 1993), p. 304.

4 Koedijk, *Geheimste Dienst*, p. 9.

5 Officially the BVD was created by royal decree in August 1949. During the four immediate post-war years there was some reshuffling of the Dutch domestic secret service structures, with first the creation of the BNV (Bureau Nationale Veiligheid) in 1945 which basically had the task to unmask German agents left behind in the Netherlands after Allied victory. Then the BNV was restructured in spring 1946, working for a brief period under the label CVD (Central Veiligheidsdienst) until finally in August 1949 the BVD succeeded both BNV and CVD and became the domestic Dutch secret service.

6 During most of its history the IDB worked in the dark, and only rarely draws upon itself public, parliamentarian, academic or media attention. This situation changed abruptly in the 1960s after a botched espionage affair which led to the arrest and imprisonment in the Soviet Union of the Dutch 'tourists' Evert Reydon and Louw de Jager. Several years later a number of scandals including domestic operations led to such strong criticism of the IDB that Prime Minister Lubbers eventually closed the service down. For more details on the IDB, see Cees Wiebes and Bob de Graaf, *Villa Maarheeze. The Netherlands Foreign Intelligence Service* (The Hague: Dutch Government Printing Office, 1992). Wiebes and Graaf have faced many difficulties when researching for their book. Former and active intelligence officials were explicitly warned not to speak with the authors. The authors had to go to court several times, using the Dutch Freedom of Information Act to overcome the resistance of the Dutch Cabinet, to gain documents and to get the book itself released. More than 150 of the record interviews with intelligence officials were made, and what resulted is arguably the best history available on the IDB. Wiebes and Graaf also came across documents on the early roots of the Dutch Gladio and published in Dutch on the topic. Compare Bob de Graaff and Cees Wiebes, *Gladio der vrije jongens: een particuliere geheime dienst in Koude Oorlogstijd* (Gravenhage: Sdu, 1992).

7 Koedijk, *Geheimste Dienst*, p. 10.

8 Paul Koedijk, *Dossier Gladio. Nederland was voorbereid op een nieuwe oorlog*. In: *Vrij Nederland*, July 11, 1992, p. 34.

9 Kluiters, *Nederlandse*, p. 306.

10 Koedijk, *Geheimste Dienst*, p. 13.

11 Kluiters, *Nederlandse*, p. 310.

12 Koedijk, *Dossier Gladio*, p. 36.

13 Ibid.

14 Ibid.

15 Ibid.

16 Kluiters, *Nederlandse*, p. 314.

17 Koedijk, *Geheimste Dienst*, p. 10.

18 Ibid., p. 11.

19 Koedijk, *Dossier Gladio*, p. 34.

20 Kluiters, *Nederlandse*, p. 306.
21 Ibid.
22 Koedijk, *Geheimste Dienst*, p. 12.
23 Kluiters, *Nederlandse*, p. 308.
24 Koedijk, *Dossier Gladio*, p. 35.
25 Ibid.
26 Koedijk, *Geheimste Dienst*, p. 11.
27 Ibid., p. 12.
28 Kluiters, *Nederlandse*, p. 311.
29 Koedijk, *Geheimste Dienst*, p. 12.
30 Kluiters, *Nederlandse*, p. 311.
31 Koedijk, *Geheimste Dienst*, p. 12.
32 Ibid., p. 11
33 Ibid.
34 Ibid., p. 12
35 Ibid., p. 13
36 Kluiters, *Nederlandse*, p. 308.
37 Koedijk, *Dossier Gladio*, p. 34.
38 Ibid., p. 35.
39 Koedijk, *Geheimste Dienst*, p. 12.
40 Ibid.
41 Ibid.
42 Ibid.
43 Koedijk, *Dossier Gladio*, p. 37.
44 Koedijk, *Geheimste Dienst*, p. 13.
45 Both quotes Koedijk, *Dossier Gladio*, p. 36.
46 Ibid.
47 Koedijk, *Geheimste Dienst*, p. 8.
48 International news service *Associated Press*, November 14, 1990. The entire text of Lubber's letter was reprinted in the Dutch daily *NRC Handelsblatt*, November 14 1990: '*Brief premier Lubbers "geheime organisatie"*'. It is also contained as Kamerstuk Nr. 21895 among the official papers of the Dutch parliament.
49 International news agency *Associated Press*, November 14, 1990.
50 Ibid.
51 Ibid., November 21, 1990.
52 British daily *The Guardian*, December 5, 1990.
53 British political magazine *Statewatch* September/October 1993 quoting Dutch daily *Dagblad* of September 7, 1993.
54 International news service *Reuters*, December 14, 1993, quoting Dutch daily *NCR Handelsblad*.

12 THE SECRET WAR IN LUXEMBURG

1 All data from the declarations of Luxemburg Prime Minister Jacques Santer to parliament on November 14, 1990. Quoted in full in the Luxemburg daily *Luxemburger Wort*, November 15, 1990.

13 THE SECRET WAR IN DENMARK

1 Iver Hoj, *Ogsa Danmark havde hemmelig haer efter anden verdenskrig*. Danish daily *Berlingske Tidende*, November 25, 1990. Journalist Iver Hoj offered with this article

what as of now still remains most probably the best information on the Danish stay-behind army.

2 Iver Hoj, *Ogsa Danmark havde hemmelig haer efter anden verdenskrig*. Danish daily *Berlingske Tidende*, November 25, 1990.
3 Ibid.
4 Ibid.
5 William Colby, *Honorable Men: My life in the CIA* (New York: Simon & Schuster, 1978), pp. 82 and 83.
6 Iver Hoj, *Ogsa Danmark havde hemmelig haer efter anden verdenskrig*. Danish daily *Berlingske Tidende*, November 25, 1990.
7 Ibid.
8 Ibid.
9 Ibid.
10 Quoted in Jacob Andersen, *Mere mystik om dansk Gladio*. Danish daily *Information*, November 26, 1990.
11 Iver Hoj, *Ogsa Danmark havde hemmelig haer efter anden verdenskrig*. Danish daily *Berlingske Tidende*, November 25, 1990.
12 Jacob Andersen, *Mere mystik om dansk Gladio*. Danish daily *Information*, November 26, 1990.
13 Iver Hoj, *Ogsa Danmark havde hemmelig haer efter anden verdenskrig*. Danish daily *Berlingske Tidende*, November 25, 1990.
14 Ibid.
15 Jacob Andersen, *Mere mystik om dansk Gladio*. Danish daily *Information*, November 26, 1990.
16 Iver Hoj, *Ogsa Danmark havde hemmelig haer efter anden verdenskrig*. Danish daily *Berlingske Tidende*, November 25, 1990.
17 Ibid.
18 Henrik Thomsen, *CIA sendte vaben til Danmark*. Danish daily *Jyllands Posten*, April 22, 1991.
19 Danish daily *Extra Bladet* quoted in Jacob Andersen, *Mere mystik om dansk Gladio*. Danish daily *Information*, November 26, 1990.
20 Iver Hoj, *Ogsa Danmark havde hemmelig haer efter anden verdenskrig*. Danish daily *Berlingske Tidende*, November 25, 1990.
21 Ibid.
22 Ibid.
23 Ibid.
24 Jacob Andersen, *Mere mystik om dansk Gladio*. Danish daily *Information*, November 26, 1990.
25 Henrik Thomsen, *CIA sendte vaben til Danmark*. Danish daily *Jyllands Posten*, April 22, 1991.
26 Jacob Andersen, *Mere mystik om dansk Gladio*. Danish daily *Information*, November 26, 1990.
27 Ibid.
28 Ibid.
29 Ibid.
30 Iver Hoj, *Ogsa Danmark havde hemmelig haer efter anden verdenskrig*. Danish daily *Berlingske Tidende*, November 25, 1990.
31 International news service *Associated Press*, November 14, 1990.
32 Iver Hoj, *Ogsa Danmark havde hemmelig haer efter anden verdenskrig*. Danish daily *Berlingske Tidende*, November 25, 1990.
33 Ibid.
34 Ibid.

35 Ibid.
36 Ibid.

14 THE SECRET WAR IN NORWAY

1 Ronald Bye and Finn Sjue, *Norges Hemmelige Haer – Historien om Stay Behind* (Oslo: Tiden Norsk Verlag, 1995), p. 39.
2 Mrs Lygren, working as secretary at the Norwegian embassy in Moscow, was arrested by the Norwegian Security Police directed by Asbjorn Bryhn on the suspicion of having worked for the Soviets on September 14, 1965. The arrest came after former KGB agent Anatolyi Golitsyn had defected to the Americans in 1961 and spoken of an unnamed female double agent at the Norwegian embassy in Moscow to CIA's master spy hunter James Jesus Angleton. Bryhn and NIS chief Evang had never been on good working terms and the chief of the Security Police Bryhn had not informed the chief of the Secret Service Evang until after the operation had been carried out at about the time when the affair was leaked to the newspapers. This made Evang furious, who was convinced of Lygren's innocence, and rightly saw a communication problem between the police and the intelligence staff. As it turned out the accusations against Lygren seemed without ground and she was released from prison on December 15, 1965. Probably Golitsyn's information which had been fed to the Norwegians by the Americans was a case of mistaken identity. A different woman, Gunvor Galtung Haavik, who had formerly worked at the Norwegian embassy in Moscow was thereafter put under surveillance. In 1977 she was arrested in Oslo while handing documents to a KGB officer. But for Evang this was history. The Lygren confusion discredited Bryhn who together with Evang in 1966 had to leave office.
3 Quoted in Olav Riste, *The Norwegian Intelligence Service 1945–1970* (London: Frank Cass, 1999), p. 16.
4 Riste: *Norwegian Intelligence Service*, p. 226.
5 Ibid., p. 17.
6 According to former Norwegian Intelligence officer and author Christian Christensen, quoted by the international news agency *Reuters*, November 4, 1988. In 1997 it was revealed and confirmed that CIA agent Alf Martens Meyer had also recruited Norwegian ship captains for covert missions in North Vietnam in the years before the United States had openly started the war. Jorgen Kosmo, Norwegian Defence Minister in 1997, said that if Meyer's men had helped South Vietnamese troops and US-trained commandos to carry out raids in North Vietnam in 1963 and 1964 the missions were in clear violation of Norwegian law (British daily *The Guardian*, May 1, 1997).
7 Bye and Sjue, *Hemmelige Haer*, p. 67.
8 Riste, *Norwegian Intelligence Service*, p. 16.
9 Bye and Sjue, *Hemmelige Haer*, p. 56.
10 Riste, *Norwegian Intelligence Service*, p. 28.
11 Ibid., p. 16.
12 Ibid., p. 19.
13 Ibid., p. 34.
14 Ibid., p. 19.
15 Ibid., p. 20.
16 Ibid.
17 Ibid., p. 40.
18 As Riste summarises, Ibid., p. 37.
19 Ibid., pp. 37 and 53.
20 Ibid., p. 35.
21 Ibid., p. 36.

NOTES

22 Ibid.
23 Ibid., p. 43.
24 Ibid.
25 Quoted in Riste. Ibid., p. 43.
26 Ibid., p. 44.
27 Ibid.
28 Ibid., p. 46.
29 Ibid., p. 47.
30 Ibid., p. 48.
31 Bye and Sjue, *Hemmelige Haer*, p. 145.
32 Leo Müller, *Gladio. Das Erbe des Kalten Krieges. Der NATO Geheimbund und sein deutscher Vorläufer* (Hamburg: Rowohlt, 1991), p. 46. And Jean-Francois Brozzu-Gentile, *L' affaire Gladio* (Paris: Editions Albin Michel, 1994), p. 199. The title of the secret NATO document is: 'Supplement Nr. 3 to the documents of the Civil Affairs Oplan Nr. 100–1'. No date available, but by implication before 1968.
33 Riste, *Norwegian Intelligence Service*, p. 45.
34 Roger Faligot and Rémi Kaufer, *Les Maitres Espions. Histoire Mondiale du Renseignement. Tome 2. De la Guerre Froide à nos jours* (Paris: Editions Laffont, 1994), p. 62.
35 Bye and Sjue, *Hemmelige Haer*, p. 62. Their source is the autobiography of Sven Blindheim: *Offiser i krig og fred* (Officer in war and peace).
36 Riste, *Norwegian Intelligence Service*, p. 33.
37 International news service *Associated Press*, November 14, 1990. Several texts in newspapers, journals and books on the Gladio (re)discoveries in the 1990 related the 1978 Norway revelations. Compare: British daily *The Guardian*, November 15, 1990. *Searchlight* No. 187, January 1991, p. 4. Müller, *Gladio*, p. 59.
38 International news service *Associated Press*, November 14 1990.
39 William Colby, *Honorable Men: My life in the CIA* (New York: Simon & Schuster, 1978), pp. 82 and 83.
40 Colby, *Honorable Men*, pp. 82 and 83.
41 International news service *Associated Press*, November 14, 1990.
42 Ibid.
43 Ibid.
44 Ronald Bye and Finn Sjue, *Norges Hemmelige Haer – Historien om Stay Behind*. Tiden Norsk Verlag. Oslo 1995.
45 Olav Riste and Arnfinn Moland published their book 'Strengt Hemmelig: Norsk etterretningsteneste 1945–1970' in 1997, covering the history of the Norwegian Gladio up to 1970, a date after which relevant research data would probably have compromised still active officials. In 1999 the English translation was published by Olav Riste with Frank Cass in London under the title '*The Norwegian Intelligence Service 1945–1970*', presenting arguably still the most authoritative information on the Norwegian stay-behind now available.

15 THE SECRET WAR IN GERMANY

1 On the debate concerning the actors behind the fire in the Reichstag in 1933 compare Alexander Bahar and Wilfried Kugel, *Der Reichstagsbrand. Wie Geschichte gemacht wird* (Berlin: Quintessenz Verlag, 2000).
2 *Bericht der Bundesregierung über die Stay-Behind Organisation des Bundesnachrichtendienstes*. Four pages written by Lutz Stavenhagen, Bonn. December 3, 1990. Hereafter quoted as '*German 1990 stay-behind report*'.
3 French periodical *Intelligence Newsletter*, December 19, 1990.
4 British periodical *Searchlight*, January 1991.

5 Christopher Simpson, *Blowback: America's Recruitment of Nazis and Its Effects on the Cold War* (London: Weidenfeld and Nicolson, 1988), Prologue. It is noteworthy that the US press followed the Justice Department cover-up strategy and reported the phenomena as an exception. *United Press International* headlined for example the next day: 'BARBIE THE EXCEPTION, NOT RULE.' And ABC TV's Nightline programme featured Ryan that evening explaining that the United States had 'innocently recruited Barbie, unaware of his role in France... [and that] the Barbie case was not typical'. Ryan under questioning expanded on the theme by saying that it was 'very likely there were no other Nazi officials who were relied upon as Klaus Barbie was... [and] this closes the record' (ibid.).

6 Simpson, *Blowback*, p. 44.

7 Ibid., p. 42.

8 Ibid., p. 40.

9 Allan Francovich, *Gladio: The Ringmasters*. First of the total three Francovich Gladio documentaries, broadcasted on BBC2 on June 10, 1992.

10 Ibid.

11 British periodical *Searchlight*, January 1991.

12 Ibid.

13 Leo Müller, *Gladio. Das Erbe des Kalten Krieges. Der NATO Geheimbund und sein deutscher Vorläufer* (Hamburg: Rowohlt, 1991), p. 72. German journalist Leo Müller has certainly offered the best description of the 1952 events in Germany in his early book on NATO's Gladio network. The quote of the testimony of Hans Otto is contained in the so-called BDJ TD report, which the government of Hesse made available to the public in the aftermath of the scandal.

14 Dieter von Glahn, *Patriot und Partisan für Freiheit und Einheit* (Tübingen: Grabert, 1994), p. 58.

15 Other army camps such as the training centre of the German parachute units near Altenstadt in Bavaria also cooperated closely with the German stay-behind units. Compare Erich Schmidt Eenboom, *Die 'Graue' und die 'Rote' Hand. Geheimdienste in Altenstadt*, 1990s. Unpublished.

16 Müller: *Gladio*, p. 123.

17 Ibid., p. 124, quoting the BDJ-TD report.

18 Ibid., quoting the BDJ-TD report.

19 Ibid., p. 130, quoting the BDJ-TD report.

20 Ibid., p. 128, quoting the BDJ-TD report.

21 Ibid., pp. 129 and 130, quoting the BDJ-TD report.

22 Ibid., p. 133.

23 Simpson, *Blowback*, p. 181. And Jens Mecklenburg (ed.), *Gladio: Die geheime Terrororganisation der Nato* (Berlin: Elefanten Press, 1997), p. 74. Mecklenburg ranged among the few who in the second half of the 1990s realised the far-reaching implications of the Gladio phenomenon and published a set of essays on the stay-behind armies in several countries in Western Europe.

24 Müller: *Gladio*, p. 94, quoting the BDJ-TD report.

25 Ibid., p. 107, quoting the BDJ-TD report.

26 Ibid., pp. 136 and 143.

27 William Blum, *Killing Hope. US Military and CIA interventions since World War II* (Maine: Common Courage Press, 1995), p. 64. Blum in his detailed research on the CIA noted correctly that 'this operation in Germany... was part of a much wider network – called "Operation Gladio" – created by the CIA and other European intelligence services, with similar secret armies all over Western Europe'.

28 Speech of Zinn in front of the Landtag in Hesse on October 8, 1952. Reprinted in Müller, *Gladio*, pp. 146–152.

29 Quoted in Glahn, *Patriot*, p. 67. TD member Glahn notes that this US declaration was 'highly unsatisfactory with respect to the TD'.

30 Entitled 'Der Technische Dienst des Bundes Deutscher Jugend' (The TD of the BDJ), the investigative report presented by the Interior Minister of Hesse in 1953 was three-volume long. It consisted of an extensive report of 121 pages (volume one), with two appendices, one of 200 pages containing documents and personalia, another of 300 pages containing copies of letters, lists, reports and decisions (volumes two and three). Without wanting to slight the Belgium, Italian and Swiss stay-behind investigative reports of the 1990s, it can be said that this BDJ-TD report is maybe the only adequate investigation that followed the discovery of a Gladio stay-behind network ever.

31 Allan Francovich, *Gladio: The Ringmasters*. First of the total three Francovich Gladio documentaries, broadcasted on BBC2 on June 10, 1992.

32 Austrian political magazine *Zoom*, Nr. 4/5, 1996: *Es muss nicht immer Gladio sein. Attentate, Waffenlager, Erinnerungslücken*, p. 97. Also Klaus Harbart: *Gladio – ein Schwert in rechter Hand*, In: Der Rechte Rand, Nr. 10, January 1991, p. 4.

33 Glahn: *Patriot*, pp. 41–42.

34 Ibid., pp. 43–47.

35 Simpson, *Blowback*, p. 260.

36 No author specified, *Schnüffler ohne Nase. Die Pannen und Pleiten des Bundesnachrichtendienstes in Pullach*. In: German weekly news magazine *Der Spiegel*, Nr. 17, 1995.

37 *German 1990 stay-behind report*.

38 Müller, *Gladio*, p. 109.

39 Glahn, *Patriot*, p. 48.

40 Ibid., p. 74.

41 *German 1990 stay-behind report*.

42 Ibid.

43 Ibid.

44 Ibid.

45 Mecklenbrug, *Gladio*, p. 64.

46 British periodical *The Economist*, October 27, 1990.

47 No author specified, *Schnüffler ohne Nase. Die Pannen und Pleiten des Bundesnachrichtendienstes in Pullach*. In: German weekly newsmagazine *Der Spiegel*, Nr. 17, 1995.

48 Müller, *Gladio*, p. 20. And Erich Schmidt Eenboom, *Schnüffler ohne Nase. Der BND. Die unheimliche Macht im Staate* (Düsseldorf: Econ Verlag, 1993), p. 376.

49 British daily *The Observer*, December 16, 1990.

50 MfS Hauptabteilung III. Report of General Major Männchen to Genosse Generalleutnant Neiber, Berlin, August 3, 1984. Declassified.

51 MfS Hauptabteilung III. Report of General Major Männchen to Genosse Generalleutnant Neiber, Berlin, November 6, 1984. Declassified.

52 MfS Streng Vertraulich. Information G/02069/13/02/84. Relevante Funkverbindungen von Sonderagenten und der Partnerdienste des BND sowie der NATO Geheimdienste. Declassified.

53 MfS Hauptabteilung III. Schnellautomatische Funksendungen im Funknetz der Ueberrollagenten des BND mit einer neuen Uebertragungsapparatur. Berlin. May 22, 1984. Declassified.

54 MfS Hauptabteilung III. Gegenwärtiger Stand bei der Bearbeitung des Funkverbindungssystems des BND zu Ueberrollagenten. Berlin. July 5, 1985. Declassified.

55 *German 1990 stay-behind report*.

56 Anonymous. Austrian periodical *Oesterreichische Militärische Zeitschrift*, Heft 2, 1991, p. 123.

57 Jonathan Kwitny, *The CIA's Secret Armies in Europe*. In: *The Nation*, April 6, 1992, p. 446.

58 Mecklenburg, *Gladio*, p. 78.

59 Klaus Harbart, *Gladio – ein Schwert in rechter Hand.* In: Der Rechte Rand, Nr. 10, January 1991, p. 5.
60 German daily *Sueddeutsche Zeitung*, September 27, 1996.
61 Mecklenburg, *Gladio*, p 82.
62 Ibid.
63 Transcripts of the German parliament. Deutscher Bundestag. 66. Sitzung, Bonn. November 25, 1981.
64 Quoted in Mecklenburg: *Gladio*, p. 79.
65 Klaus Harbart, *Gladio – ein Schwert in rechter Hand.* In: Der Rechte Rand, Nr. 10, January 1991, p. 5.
66 Ibid.
67 Ibid., p. 6.
68 Mecklenburg, *Gladio*, p. 83.
69 Presse- und Informationsamt der Bundesregierung. Pressemitteilung Nr. 455/90, durch Hans Klein, November 14, 1990. See also Müller, *Gladio*, p. 30.
70 Quoted in Müller, *Gladio*, p. 14.
71 No author specified, *Das blutige Schwert der CIA. Nachrichten aus dem Kalten Krieg: In ganz Europa gibt es geheime NATO Kommandos, die dem Feind aus dem Osten widerstehen sollen. Kanzler, Verteidigungsminister und Bundeswehrgenerale wussten angeblich von nichts. Die Spuren führen nach Pullach, zur 'stay-behind organisation' des Bundesnachrichtendienstes.* In: German weekly news magazine *Der Spiegel*, November 19, 1990.
72 No author specified, *Das blutige Schwert der CIA. Nachrichten aus dem Kalten Krieg: In ganz Europa gibt es geheime NATO Kommandos, die dem Feind aus dem Osten widerstehen sollen. Kanzler, Verteidigungsminister und Bundeswehrgenerale wussten angeblich von nichts. Die Spuren führen nach Pullach, zur 'stay-behind organisation' des Bundesnachrichtendienstes.* In: German weekly news magazine *Der Spiegel*, November 19, 1990.
73 Mecklenburg, *Gladio*, p. 48.
74 Kleine Anfrage der Abgeordneten Such, Frau Birthler, Hoss, Frau Dr Vollmer und der Fraktion DIE GRUENEN. *Tätigkeit eines NATO-Geheimdienstes auch in der Bundesrepublik Deutschland?* Drucksache 11/8452. Inklusive Antworten von Dr Lutz G. Stavenhagen, MdB, Staatsminister beim Bundeskanzler, Beauftragter für die Nachrichtendienste. Bonn, November 30, 1990.
75 *German 1990 stay-behind report.*
76 Austrian political magazine *Zoom*, Nr. 4/5, 1996: *Es muss nicht immer Gladio sein. Attentate, Waffenlager, Erinnerungslücken*, p. 110. And *Reuters*, August 17, 1995.
77 Müller, *Gladio*, p. 19.
78 Ulrich Stoll, *Gladio: Späte Spuren einer NATO-Geheimarmee.* In: Thomas Leif (ed.), *Mehr Leidenschaft Recherche. Skandal-geschictehn und Enthüllungsberichte. Ein Handbuch zur Recherche und Informationsbeschaffung* (Wiesbaden: Westdeutscher Verlag, 2003), p. 184.

16 THE SECRET WAR IN GREECE

1 Mackenzie, W. J. M., *History of the Special Operations Executive. Britain and the resistance in Europe* (London: British Cabinet Office, 1948), p. 703. Unpublished original of the Public Records Office London, publication with Frank Cass forthcoming.
2 Mackenzie, *Special Operations Executive*, pp. 722–723.
3 British *Guardian* journalist Peter Murtagh has written a passionate account of the Anglo-Saxon betrayal of the Greek resistance and the crippling of the Greek democracy during the Cold War. Based on newly released documents and interviews with several

US and British diplomats and CIA employees his book – nomen est omen – is entitled: *The Rape of Greece. The King, the Colonels, and the Resistance* (London: Simon & Schuster, 1994), p. 29.

4 No author specified, *Spinne unterm Schafsfell. In Südeuropa war die Guerillatruppe besonders aktiv – auch bei den Militärputschen in Griechenland und der Türkei?* In: German news magazine *Der Spiegel*, Nr. 48, November 26, 1990. And Leo Müller, *Gladio. Das Erbe des Kalten Krieges. Der NATO Geheimbund und sein deutscher Vorläufer* (Hamburg: Rowohlt, 1991), p. 55.

5 Murtagh, *Rape*, p. 30.

6 Ibid., p. 24. Compare also the 'Concise History of Greece' (Cambridge University Press, 1992), written by Professor Richard Clogg, which claims that 'Ill disciplined police fired on the demonstration in Constitution Square in the centre of the city, leaving some fifteen dead', p. 137.

7 William Blum, *Killing Hope: US Military and CIA interventions since World War II* (Maine: Common Courage Press, 1995), p. 36.

8 Murtagh, *Rape*, p. 39.

9 Blum, *Killing Hope*, p. 38.

10 Müller, *Gladio*, p. 55. And Jens Mecklenburg (ed.), *Gladio: Die geheime Terrororganisation der Nato* (Berlin: Elefanten Press, 1997), p. 19.

11 Jacques Baud, *Encyclopédie du renseignement et des services secrets* (Paris: Lavauzelle, 1997), p. 546.

12 Murtagh, *Rape*, p. 41.

13 Philip Agee and Louis Wolf, *Dirty Work: The CIA in Western Europe* (Secaucus: Lyle Stuart Inc., 1978), p. 154.

14 Agee, *Dirty Work*, pp. 155 and 156.

15 Ibid.

16 Murtagh, *Rape*, p. 42.

17 Austrian political magazine *Zoom*, Nr. 4/5, 1996, *Es muss nicht immer Gladio sein. Attentate, Waffenlager, Erinnerungslücken*, p. 73.

18 Murtagh, *Rape*, p. 43.

19 Ibid., p. 44.

20 Ibid., p. 71.

21 Blum, *Killing Hope*, p. 216.

22 No author specified, *Spinne unterm Schafsfell. In Südeuropa war die Guerillatruppe besonders aktiv – auch bei den Militärputschen in Griechenland und der Türkei?* In: German news magazine *Der Spiegel*, Nr. 48, November 26, 1990.

23 Murtagh, *Rape*, p. 90.

24 Ibid.

25 Ibid., p. 102.

26 Quoted in Blum, *Killing Hope*, p. 217.

27 Ibid., p. 218.

28 Murtagh, *Rape*, p. 114.

29 Ibid., p. 118

30 Christopher Simpson, *Blowback: America's Recruitment of Nazis and its Effects on the Cold War* (London: Weidenfeld and Nicolson, 1988), p. 81.

31 Agee, *Dirty Work*, p. 154.

32 Bernard Cook, *The Mobilisation of the Internal Cold War in Italy*. In: *History of European Ideas*. Vol. 19, 1994, p. 116. Cook puts 'a carbon copy of Gladio' in quotation marks because he quotes Paul Grinsborg, *A History of Contemporary Italy: Society and Politics, 1943–1988* (New York: Penguin, 1990), p. 277.

33 Richard Collin, *The De Lorenzo Gambit: The Italian Coup Manque of 1964* (Beverly Hills: Sage, 1976), p. 40.

34 See Amnesty International, Torture in Greece: The First Toturer's Trial in 1975. London 1977. Passim. Also Blum, *Killing Hope*, pp. 218–220 and Murtagh, *Rape*, pp. 1–9.
35 Murtagh, *Rape*, p. 6.
36 Jean-Francois Brozzu-Gentile, *L' affaire Gladio* (Paris: Editions Albin Michel, 1994), pp. 41, 42 and 90. Allegedly the British daily *The Observer* printed the May 15, 1969 cable of the Greek colonels to their Italian friends in one of their editions at the time. Yet Gentile does not specify in which one. The journey of Italian fascists with Gladio links to the Greek colonels is also related in the Italian Parliamentary Report on Gladio and the Massacres: *Senato della Repubblica. Commissione parlamentare d'inchiesta sul terrorismo in Italia e sulle cause della mancata individuazione dei responsabiliy delle stragi: Il terrorismo, le stragi ed il contesto storico politico.* Redatta dal presidente della Commissione, Senatore Giovanni Pellegrino. Roma 1995, p. 206.
37 Gentile, *Gladio*, p. 137.
38 John Palmer, *Undercover NATO Group 'may have had terror links'.* In: British daily *The Guardian*, November 10, 1990.
39 International news service *Associated Press*, November 14, 1990.
40 No author specified, *Spinne unterm Schafsfell. In Südeuropa war die Guerillatruppe besonders aktiv – auch bei den Militärputschen in Griechenland und der Türkei?* In: German news magazine *Der Spiegel*, Nr. 48, November 26, 1990.

17 THE SECRET WAR IN TURKEY

1 Edward Herman and Frank Brodhead, *The Rise and Fall of the Bulgarian Connection* (New York: Sheridan Square Publications, 1986), p. 45. In their excellent study of the CIA's propaganda success to wrongly blame the 1981 Papal shooting on the KGB Herman and Brodhead offer a very valuable analysis of the Grey Wolves and their ideological background.
2 Ibid., *Bulgarian Connection*, p. 45.
3 In 1992 Alparsan Türks visited his long lost Turkish brothers in Azerbaijan, Turkey's neighbour state to the East which had become newly independent after the fall of the dreaded Soviet Empire. Türks received a hero's welcome in Baku. He endorsed the candidacy of Grey Wolf sympathiser Abulfex Elcibey, who was subsequently elected president of Azerbaijan, and appointed a close Grey Wolf ally as his Interior Minister.
4 The Jupiter missiles in Turkey had become technically obsolete and were replaced with mobile Polaris submarines carrying nuclear missiles. Compare Daniele Ganser, *Reckless Gamble. The Sabotage of the United Nations in the Cuban conflict and the missile crisis of 1962* (New Orleans: University Press of the South, 2000), p. 138.
5 Fikret Aslan and Kemal Bozay, *Graue Wölfe heulen wieder. Türkische Faschisten und ihre Vernetzung in der BRD* (Münster: Unrast Verlag, 1997), p. 69. Due to the fact that Germany is host of the largest exile community of Türks and Kurds, valuable literature on the secret war in Turkey has been published in German. Aslan and Bozay with their book offer most probably one of the finest recent books in a foreign language on the Grey Wolves and Turkish Fascism. The book also contains an essay by Serdar Celik and one by Talat Turhan.
6 Selahattin Celik, *Türkische Konterguerilla. Die Todesmaschinerie* (Köln: Mesopotamien Verlag, 1999), p. 44. Celik is the leading Turkish scholar on the Turkish Gladio Counter-Guerrilla next to officer Talat Turhan. His original work appeared in 1995 in Turkish under the title: *Olüm Makinasi Türk Kontrgerillasi.* Celik, who is a Kurd, studied at Ankara University and worked as a journalist and author. His sister and his brother and three of his cousins were killed by the Counter-Guerrilla and he himself is in danger. Although scrupulous on the facts he admits that the massacres in his family have led to a certain bias and a critical approach towards the Turkish stay-behind: 'I have not written this work as an independent neutral person. I am biased. I have written this book as a

son of the Kurdish people, which fights for its survival against the war machinery of the Turkish regime and fights for its right to live in peace...how can we grasp and communicate the crime of the systematic destruction of the Kurdish intellectuals? A crime which to this degree next to Kurdistan has only taken place in Chile' (*Türkische Konterguerilla*, p. 354). Under his pen name Serdar Celik he also published a ten-page summary of his book in English on the Internet entitled: *Turkey's Killing Machine: The Contra Guerrilla Force* (http://www.ozgurluk.org/mhp/0061.html). I will quote hereafter both from his book (*Türkische Konterguerilla*) and his Internet article (*Turkey's Killing Machine*).

7 No author specified, *The Origins of 'Gladio' in Turkey*. In: *French periodical Intelligence Newsletter*. *Le Monde du Renseignement*, December 19, 1990.
8 Celik, *Die Todesmaschinerie*, p. 50.
9 Turkish newspaper *Cumhuriyet*, November 17, 1990.
10 Celik, *Türkische Konterguerilla*, p. 44. The same information is also found in the Austrian political magazine *Zoom*, Nr. 4/5, 1996: *Es muss nicht immer Gladio sein. Attentate, Waffenlager, Erinnerungslücken*, pp. 74–75. Compare also the valuable contribution by Olaf Goebel, *Gladio in der Türkei*. In: Jens Mecklenburg, *Gladio. Die geheime Terrororganisation der NATO*, (1997), pp. 122–130. Goebel was the first researcher to include a chapter on Turkey in a book on Gladio. Compare also: No author specified, *Spinne unterm Schafsfell. In Südeuropa war die Guerillatruppe besonders aktiv – auch bei den Militärputschen in Griechenland und der Türkei?* In: German news magazine *Der Spiegel*, Nr. 48, November 26, 1990.
11 Celik, *Türkische Konterguerilla*, p. 45.
12 Ibid., *Turkey's Killing Machine*.
13 Aslan and Bozay, *Graue Wölfe*, p. 55.
14 Ibid.
15 Celik, *Türkische Konterguerilla*, p. 51.
16 Aslan and Bozay, *Graue Wölfe*, p. 59.
17 Ibid., p. 50.
18 Leo Müller, *Gladio. Das Erbe des Kalten Krieges. Der NATO Geheimbund und sein deutscher Vorläufer* (1991), p. 57; also Olaf Goebel in Jens Mecklenburg, *Gladio*, p. 128. Also Celik, *Türkische Konterguerilla*, p. 151.
19 All three books are in Turkish and no translations seem available as of now. (1) Talat Turhan, *Doruk Operasyonu*. Publisher: Cagloglu, Istanbul 1989. In this book Turhan deals on 170 pages with the Turkish secret service MIT. (2) Talat Turhan, *Ozel Savas, Teror ve Kontrgerilla*. Publisher: Kadkoy, Istanbul 1992. In this book Turhan deals specifically with the Counter-Guerrilla, the Special Warfare Department (Ozel Harp Dairesi), the CIA, the MIT and terrorism. (3) Talat Turhan, *Kontrgerilla cumhuriyeti: acklamalar, belgeler, gercekler*. Publisher: Tumzamanlaryaynclk, Istanbul 1993. In this book Turhan deals again with the Counter-Guerrilla. Another valuable book in Turkish on the Counter-Guerrilla is the one written by journalist Semih Hicyilmaz, *Susurluk ve Kontrgerilla gercegi*, published by Evrensel Basim Yayin, Istanbul 1997.
20 A German essay by Talat Turhan entitled *Die Konterguerilla Republik* is contained in Aslan and Bozay, *Graue Wölfe*, pp. 101–111.
21 Aslan and Bozay, *Graue Wölfe*, p. 106.
22 Quoted in Celik, *Türkische Konterguerilla*, p. 151.
23 Essay of Talat Turhan, *Die Konterguerilla Republik*. In: Aslan and Bozay, *Graue Wölfe*, pp. 102 and 103.
24 Celik, *Turkey's Killing Machine*. Celik is quoting from *Directive ST 31/15 for Operations Against Irregular Forces*.
25 Regine Igel, *Andreotti. Politik zwischen Geheimdienst und Mafia* (München: Herbig Verlag 1997), p. 354.

26 Herman Brodhead, *Bulgarian Connection*, p. 61.
27 Igel, *Andreotti*, p. 354.
28 Quoted in Celik, *Türkische Konterguerilla*, p. 147.
29 Ibid., p. 145.
30 The quotes are from the Turkish left-wing political magazine *Kurtulus*, Nr. 99, September 19, 1998. *Kurtulus* (Liberation) was first published in 1971 after the military coup and has continued to provide critical information on the secret war in Turkey. It was banned. Its journalists have been subject to threat, arrests and torture. Its premises had been subject to bombings and the press that prints *Kurtulus* had been under pressure to stop doing business with *Kurtulus*. Issues of *Kurtulus* have also appeared on the Internet.
31 Turkish magazine *Kurtulus*, quoting Mehmet Eymür, *Analiz*, pp. 90–96.
32 Turkish magazine *Kurtulus* Nr. 99, September 19, 1998.
33 Lucy Komisar, *Turkey's Terrorists: A CIA Legacy Lives On*. In: *The Progressive*, April 1997.
34 Celik, *Türkische Konterguerilla*, p. 46.
35 Ibid., p. 45.
36 Quoted by Talat Turhan in Aslan and Bozay, *Graue Wölfe*, p. 110.
37 *The Guardian*, November 25, 1998. SOA graduates include former Panamanian strongman Manuel Noriega, former Argentine dictator Leopoldo Galtieri, Haitian coup leader Raoul Cedras, the late Salvadoran death squad organizer Robert D'Aubuisson and Gen. Hector Gramajo, reputed architect of the genocidal 'scorched earth' policy in Guatemala. One of every seven members of the command staff Pinochet's dreaded Chilean torture and intelligence agency DINA was a SOA graduate. Following strong public protests in the 1990s the name of SOA was changed to 'Western Hemisphere Institute for Security Cooperation'.
38 Celik, *Turkey's Killing Machine*.
39 The number 30 indicates that the document is classified as a document of the US military secret service DIA. DIA is subject to the command of the US Joint Chiefs of Staff with headquarters in the Pentagon in Washington. DIA operates in close coordination with the CIA and with a yearly budget of around $4,500,000,000 ranges among the biggest US secret services. Compare Baud, Jacques, *Encyclopédie du renseignement et des services secrets* (Paris: Lavauzelle, 1997), p. 174.
40 Igel, *Andreotti*, pp. 356–357.
41 Ibid., p. 346.
42 Ibid., p. 347.
43 Upon the fall of the dictatorship in 1976 the Spanish newspaper *Triunfo* published excerpts despite heavy pressures to prevent the publication, whereupon on October 27, 1978 excerpts of FM 30–31 also appeared in the Italian political magazine *L'Europeo*. When the Italian monthly *Controinformazione* printed the US terror manual the issues were confiscated. After, in 1981, the cover of the secret anti-Communist P2 Freemason lodge of Licio Gelli was discovered FM 30–31 surfaced once again and the Italian parliamentary investigation into P2 courageously published it in its parliamentary report in 1987 but three years before the discovery of the secret Gladio armies. Regine Igel offers in her German translation the full text of FM 30–31B in her book on Gulio Andreotti and the US subversion of Italy (Igel, *Andreotti*, Appendix, pp. 345–358). Igel's source is the original English version of the FM 30–31B as contained in the collected documents of the Italian Parliamentary Commission of Inquiry into the US-linked P2: Commissione parlamentare d'inchiesta sulla loggia massonica P2. Allegati alla Relazione Doc. XXIII, n. 2-quater/7/1 Serie II, Vol. VII, Tomo I, Roma 1987, pp. 287–298. The document FM 30–31B is dated March 18, 1970, Headquarters of the US Army, Washington DC, and signed by General of the US Army W. C. Westmoreland.

NOTES

44 Allan Francovich, *Gladio: The Foot Soldiers*. Third of the total three Francovich Gladio documentaries, broadcasted on BBC2 on June 24, 1992.
45 British political magazine *Searchlight*, No. 47, May 1979, p. 6. Quoted in Herman and Brodhead, *Bulgarian Connection*, p. 50.
46 Celik, *Türkische Konterguerilla*, pp. 51 and 53. After his retirement in 1974 Muhsin Batur became a member of parliament granting him immunity from prosecution.
47 Turkish daily *Milliyet*, March 23, 1976. Quoted in *Kurtulus*, September 19, 1998.
48 Turhan in Aslan and Bozay, *Graue Wölfe*, p. 109.
49 Komisar, *A CIA Legacy*.
50 Ibid.
51 Turkish magazine *Kurtulus* Nr. 99, September 19, 1998.
52 Turkish left-wing newspaper *Devrimci Sol* (Revolutionary Left), May 1998.
53 Celik, *Türkische Konterguerilla*, p. 41 and Komisar, *A CIA Legacy*.
54 Komisar, *A CIA Legacy*.
55 Turkish extreme left-wing magazine, *Devrimci Sol* (Revolutionary Left), May 1998.
56 Ibid.
57 Celik in his essay in Aslan and Bozay, *Graue Wölfe*, explains: 'Now the public has come to know that Catli was a top senior official of the Turkish Gladio section and that probably he was also connected to the international Gladio network. In 1992 he could pass customs unhindered in Miami together with Delle Chiaie and enter the United States' (ibid., p. 134). Celik most probably got the date wrong, not 1992 but 1982.
58 Prominent among the books on the Turkish Gladio is the biography on terrorist Catli by the academic Dogan Yurdakul and the journalist Soner Yalcin. The nickname of Catli was 'Reis', Turkish for Chief: *Reis. Gladio nun Türk Tetikcisi* (Ankara: Oteki Yay Nevi, 1997). After Catli's death even his daughter, Gokcen Catli, announced that she was going to write a biography about her father, Gladio, Catli's work with the CIA, and 'the important events taking place behind the scenes'.
59 Quoted in the Berlin weekly *Jungle World*, January 20, 1999. Kirici was again arrested on January 10, 1999 in Istanbul. His memoirs appeared in May 1998.
60 Turkish daily *Yeniyuzyil*, December 18, 1996.
61 Komisar, *A CIA Legacy*.
62 The best study in this context is certainly the book of Herman and Brodhead, *Bulgarian Connection*. Catli in his 1985 testimony in Rome revealed that he had been approached by the West German secret service BND who had promised him a large sum of money if he implicated the Bulgarian secret service and the KGB as the sponsor's of the Grey Wolves' attack on the Pope. In 1990, ex-CIA analyst Melvin Goodman admitted to the US Senate Intelligence Committee that 'The CIA had no evidence linking the KGB to the plot', and that only pressure from CIA higher-ups had made them skew their reports to lend credence to the theory that the Soviets were behind the plot to kill the Pope. Herman and Brodhead in their investigation discovered the Turkish Gladio when they noted: 'The most likely avenue linking the CIA to the Turkish Right runs through Turkey's "Counter-Guerrilla", a branch of the Turkish General Staff's Department of Special Warfare ... it was headquartered in the same Ankara building that housed the US military mission, and ... the training of officers assigned to this unit "begins in the US and then continues inside Turkey under the direction of CIA officers and military advisers"' (ibid., p. 61). Their source for this early understanding of the Turkish Gladio is the very good book by Jürgen Roth and Kamil Taylan, *Die Türkei – Republik unter Wölfen* (Bornheim: Lamur Verlag, 1981). See also Martin Lee, *On the Trail of Turkey's Grey Wolves*. Six-page essay available on the Internet: http://www.ozgurluk.org/mhp/story33.html.
63 Komisar, *A CIA Legacy*. In the late 1990s Bülent Ecevit under President Süleyman Demirel again became Prime Minister, already for the third time.

64 Jens Mecklenburg (ed.), *Gladio: Die geheime Terrororganisation der Nato* (Berlin: Elefanten Press, 1997), p. 128.
65 Turkish magazine *Kurtulus* Nr. 99, September 19, 1998. Quoting Günes, September 3, 1987.
66 German news magazine *Der Spiegel: Spinne unterm Schafsfell: In Südeuropa war die Guerrilla truppe besonders aktiv – auch bei den Militärputschen in Griechenland und der Türkei?*, November 26, 1990, pp. 173–177.
67 Celik, *Turkey's Killing Machine*, quoting Cuneyit Arcayurek, *Coups and the Secret Services*, p. 190.
68 Kurkcu Ertugrul, *Turkey: Trapped in a web of covert killers*. In: *Covert Action Quarterly* Nr. 61, Summer 1997. Also online on the Internet: http://caq.com/CAQ/caq61/CAQ61turkey. html. The source of Ertugrul is Mehmet Ali Birand, *12 Eylul Saat 04:00 [September 12, 1980, 12:04]* (Istanbul: Milliyet Publishers, 1985), p. 1.
69 Celik, *Türkische Konterguerilla*, p. 58.
70 Turkish magazine *Kurtulus* Nr. 99, September 19, 1998, quoting Turkish daily *Cumhuriyet*, July 21, 1988.
71 Celik, *Türkische Konterguerilla*, p. 53.
72 German Newspaper *Zeitung am Sonntag*, September 14, 1980. Quoted in Aslan and Bozay, *Graue Wölfe*, p. 78.
73 Herman and Brodhead, *Bulgarian Connection*, p. 50.
74 Ibid.
75 Aslan and Bozay, *Graue Wölfe*, pp. 74 and 75.
76 Ibrahim Ciftci in an interview with the Turkish daily *Milliyet*, October 13, 1996.
77 Quoted by Vera Beaudin Saeedpour, editor of *Kurdish Life* and *International Journal of Kurdish Studies*. URL: http://www.lbbs.org/Kurdish.htm.
78 Mecklenburg, *Gladio*, p. 125.
79 Celik, *Turkey's Killing Machine*. His source is an interview with the President of the Turkish General Staff Dogan Gures in Turkish daily *Milliyet* 5/6 September 1992.
80 Turkish daily *Milliyet*, November 13, 1990.
81 Celik, *Türkische Konterguerilla*, p. 40.
82 Ibid.
83 Aslan and Bozay, *Graue Wölfe*, p. 15.
84 Swiss daily *Neue Zürcher Zeitung*, December 5, 1990.
85 Komisar, *A CIA Legacy*.
86 Ibid.
87 Ibid.
88 Ibid.
89 Ibid.
90 Aslan and Bozay, *Graue Wölfe*, p. 139.
91 Kelly Couturier, *Security Forces Allegedly Involved in Turkish Criminal Gang*. US daily *Washington Post*, November 27, 1996.
92 Stephen Kinzer, *Scandal links Turkish Aides to deaths, drugs and terror*. US daily *New York Times*, December 10, 1996.
93 Turkish daily *Sabah*, December 12, 1996.
94 US daily *New York Times*, December 10, 1996.
95 Turkish magazine *Kurtulus*, September 19, 1998.
96 Turkish daily *Radikal*, January 10, 1997.
97 Kurkcu Ertugrul, *Turkey: Trapped in a web of covert killers*. In: *Covert Action Quarterly* Nr. 61, Summer 1997.
98 Hugh Pope, *Turkey Promoted Death Squads and Drug Trafficking. Prime Minister's Probe of 1996 Car Crash Scandal Excoriates Rival Mrs. Ciller*. In: US periodical *Wall*

Street Journal, January 26, 1998. The article fails to address both the US role in Turkey's Death Squads and the Gladio scandal.

99 Swiss daily *Neue Zürcher Zeitung*, May 13, 1998. And *Eine Aktion der Koterguerilla. Der stellvertretende IHD Vorsitzende Rechtsanwalt Osman Baydemir zum Anschlag auf Akin Birdal.* URL: www.nadir.org/nadir/periodika/kurdistan_report/9891/07.html.

100 Martin Lee, *On the Trail of Turkey's Grey Wolves.* Six-page essay available on the Internet: http://www.ozgurluk.org/mhp/story33.html. US researcher Lee researched extensively on Neofascism and published a book on the topic: *The Beast Reawakens* (Boston: Little Brown, 1997).

CONCLUSION

1 International news service *Reuters Western Europe*, November 15, 1990.

2 Juan Arias, *El laberinto Italiano. Commocion por el descubrimiento de un 'ejercito paralelo' de anticomunistas pagado por la CIA.* In: Spanish daily *El Pais*, November 11, 1990.

3 After the attacks of September 11 2001 US lawyer Stanley Hilton had risen the far-reaching claim that the administration of President George Bush had deliberately allowed Al Qaida terrorists to attack the United States in order to strike fear to the bones of the entire population of the United States, limit civil liberties, and convince the country of the very real danger of Islamic terrorism and the world community of the necessity of 'preventive wars'. This so-called LIHOP thesis (let it happen on purpose) has ever since challenged the dominant 'SURPRISE' thesis and even led to legal action. In June 2002 San Francisco-based lawyer Hilton in the name of families of the victims of 9/11 filed a seven billion dollar suit and declared that only legal instruments and the rule of law will be able to penetrate the secret warfare operations of the state. Compare Nafeez M. Ahmed, *Geheimsache 9/11. Hintergründe über den 11. September und die Logik amerikanischer Machtpolitik* (München: Riemann Verlag, 2002), p. 229. Translation of the English Original: *The War on Freedom* (Joshua Tree: Tree of Life Publications, 2002). Ahmed, with his detailed research, puts forward the thesis that the Bush administration deliberately allowed the 9/11 attacks to take place in order to unite the country for preemptive wars abroad.

SELECT BIBLIOGRAPHY

Note: All sources used in this book are indicated in the endnotes. This selected bibliography lists only books that deal with Operation Gladio or other stay-behind armies.

Agee, Philip and Wolf Louis, *Dirty Work: The CIA in Western Europe* (Secaucus: Lyle Stuart Inc., 1978)

Bale, Jeffrey McKenzie, *The 'Black' Terrorist International: Neo-Fascist Paramilitary Networks and the 'Strategy of Tension' in Italy, 1968–1974*. UMI Dissertation Services. UMI Number 9529217 (Michigan: Ann Arbor, 1996)

Barbacetto, Gianni, *Il Grande vecchio. Dodici giudici raccontano le loro inchieste sui grandi misteri d'Italia da piazza Fontana a Gladio* (Milano: Baldini & Castoldi, 1993)

Baud, Jacques, *Encyclopédie du renseignement et des services secrets* (Paris: Lavauzelle, 1997)

Bellu, Giovanni Maria, *I giorni di Gladio* (Milano: Sperling & Kupfer Editori, 1991)

Bettini, Emanuele, *Gladio. La republica parallela* (Milano: Ediesse, 1996)

Blum, William, *Killing Hope: US Military and CIA interventions since World War II* (Maine: Common Courage Press, 1995)

Brozzu-Gentile, Jean-Francois, *L' affaire Gladio* (Paris: Editions Albin Michel, 1994)

Bye, Ronald and Finn Sjue, *Norges Hemmelige Haer – Historien om Stay Behind* (Oslo: Tiden Norsk Verlag, 1995)

Celik, Selahattin, *Die Todesmaschinerie. Türkische Konterguerilla* (Köln: Mesopotamien Verlag, 1999)

Colby, William, *Honorable Men: My life in the CIA* (New York: Simon & Schuster, 1978)

Collin, Richard, *The De Lorenzo Gambit: The Italian Coup Manqué of 1964* (Beverly Hills: Sage, 1976)

De Lutiis, Giuseppe, *Il lato oscuro del potere. Associazioni politiche e strutture paramilitari segrete dal 1946 a oggi* (Roma: Editori Riuniti, 1996)

Fasanella, Giovanni e Sestieri and Giovanni Claudio con Pellegrino, *Segreto di Stato. La verità da Gladio al caso Moro* (Torino: Einaudi Editore, 2000)

Gijsels, Hugo, *Network Gladio* (Leuven: Utgeverij Kritak, 1991)

Graaff, Bob de and Cees Wiebes, *Gladio der vrije jongens: een particuliere geheime dienst in Koude Oorlogstijd* (Gravenhage: Sdu, 1992)

Igel, Regine, *Andreotti. Politik zwischen Geheimdienst und Mafia* (München: Herbig Verlag, 1997)

Inzerilli, Paolo, *Gladio. La Verità negata* (Bologna: Edizioni Analisi, 1995)

Laurent, Frédéric, *L' Orchestre noir* (Paris: Editions Stock, 1978)

Mecklenburg, Jens (ed.), *Gladio: Die geheime Terrororganisation der Nato* (Berlin: Elefanten Press, 1997)

Moroni, Primo, Mario Coglitore and Sandro Scarso (eds), *La notte dei Gladiatori. Omissioni e silenzi della Repubblica* (Padova: Calusca Edizioni, 1992)

Müller, Leo, *Gladio – das Erbe des Kalten Krieges. Der Nato-Geheimbund und sein deutscher Vorläufer* (Hamburg: Rowohlt, 1991)

Pansa, Giampaolo, *Il Gladio e l'alloro: l'Esercito di Salo* (Milano: Mondadori, 1991)

Peterlini, Hans Karl, *Bomben aus zweiter Hand. Zwischen Gladio und Stasi – Suedtirols missbrauchter Terrorismus* (Bozen: Edition Raetia, 1992)

Prados, John, *President's Secret Wars: CIA and Pentagon Covert Operations since World War II* (New York: William Morrow Inc., York, 1986)

Rowse, Arthur, Gladio: *The Secret US War to Subvert Italian Democracy*. In: *Covert Action Quarterly*, Nr. 49, Summer 1994, p. 3.

Serravalle, Gerardo, *Gladio* (Roma: Edizioni Associate, 1991)

Van Ussel, Michel, *Georges 923: Un agent de Gladio Belge parle. Temoignage* (Brussels: Edideurs La Longue Vue, 1991)

Vinciguerra, Vincenzo, *Ergastolo per la libertà: Verso la verità sulla strategia della tensione* (Firenze: Arnaud, 1989)

Willan, Philip, *Puppetmasters: The Political Use of Terrorism in Italy* (London: Constable, 1991)

Willems, Jan de (ed.), *Gladio* (Brussels: Editions EPO, 1991)

Yalc, Soner and Doagan Yurdakaul, *Reis. Gladio nun Turk tetikcisi* (Ankara: Oteki Yay Nevi, 1997)

INDEX

303

For Product Safety Concerns and Information please contact our EU
representative GPSR@taylorandfrancis.com
Taylor & Francis Verlag GmbH, Kaufingerstraße 24, 80331 München, Germany

www.ingramcontent.com/pod-product-compliance
Lightning Source LLC
Chambersburg PA
CBHW060143280326
41932CB00012B/1622